A Map of Australian Verse

A
MAP
OF
AUSTRALIAN
VERSE

THE TWENTIETH CENTURY

JAMES McAULEY

Melbourne

OXFORD UNIVERSITY PRESS

OXFORD WELLINGTON NEW YORK

Oxford University Press

OXFORD LONDON GLASGOW

NEW YORK TORONTO MELBOURNE WELLINGTON

IBADAN NAIROBI DAR ES SALAAM LUSAKA CAPE TOWN

KUALA LUMPUR SINGAPORE JAKARTA HONG KONG TOKYO

DELHI BOMBAY CALCUTTA MADRAS KARACHI

© *Oxford University Press 1975*

First published 1975
Reprinted 1977

NATIONAL LIBRARY OF AUSTRALIA CATALOGUING IN PUBLICATION DATA

McAuley, James Phillip, 1917-1976

A map of Australian verse/ [by] *James McAuley. — Melbourne: Oxford University Press, 1975.*
ISBN 0 19 550472 0.
ISBN 0 19 550474 7 *Paperback.*

1. Australian Poetry. I. Title.

A821.009

PRINTED IN HONG KONG
PUBLISHED BY OXFORD UNIVERSITY PRESS, 7 BOWEN CRESCENT, MELBOURNE

Contents

Foreword

This volume is similar in scheme to John Press's *A Map of Modern English Verse* (1969). It dips back into the last years of the nineteenth century and moves forward to the 1970s. The selection of poems in the last section, however, is restricted to a few writers who had achieved recognition by 1965. Though I have mentioned many other recent poets and briefly discussed current trends, any attempt at an accounting would be premature.

When invited to undertake the compiling of this literary map, I approached the task with trepidation and misgivings. There were difficult choices to be made in excluding and including, highlighting and proportioning. I have earnestly striven for as much objectivity as the nature of literary judgement allows, but the choices made have inevitably been mine and different from what another editor would arrive at. The personal element is, however, offset in some degree by the fact that the plan of the book allows for important differences in critical estimation to be signalized by quotations or references. In writing the introductions to each section I have tried not to obtrude my personal opinions and attitudes excessively, while avoiding the opposite fault of pretending to a faceless impersonality. A further difficulty I encountered was that I had already published general essays on several of the main poets — C. J. Brennan, Shaw Neilson, Kenneth Slessor, Judith Wright, A. D. Hope, Douglas Stewart, Rosemary Dobson — so that I had to write something different which would nevertheless provide a sound general introduction. And of course the most challenging difficulty of all was that my own work had to be treated. In facing these various difficulties, I have had recourse to the generous advice and criticism of several colleagues and friends, to whom I am most grateful, though the responsibility for what is here presented remains entirely mine.

It will be seen that in writing the various introductions I have not tried to follow a single pattern but in each case have adopted whatever seemed to be the most useful approach. The poets are not introduced in a strictly chronological order, but in an arrangement that seemed suitable, having regard to various considerations. The poems in the selections are, however, generally in chronological order so far as this is ascertainable, and having regard to considerations of layout.

In the presentation of the critical extracts, paragraphing has been observed where this occurs in a continuous text. But where the text has been cut and the parts put together, paragraphing has not been observed. In minor matters of printing style, the texts quoted, in prose or verse, have been brought into conformity with the style of this book.

For the student who may use this book I should like to add some particular comments. The critical extracts are varied. The quotation of a critical opinion does not mean that it is being endorsed. Disagreements will be noticed between opinions expressed or quoted in the introductions, and opinions expressed in the critical extracts, and opinions that can be found in articles cited in the select bibliographies. The purpose of the map is to help the reader to explore and observe and judge for himself. Apart from the poems themselves, and some bare facts, nothing is final or unquestionable — not even comments made by poets on their own work, as the footnote on Slessor's retrospective inter-pretations (p. 122) illustrates.

It should especially be noted that a critical comment may apply only to one period of a poet's work or to one aspect of it: the date and the particular bearing must be taken into account. Students often cripple their understanding by lifting a critical remark out of context and trying to force every part of an author's work into conformity with it.

Four of the fourteen sections into which this book is divided deal with time-spans: the earlier twentieth century, the forties, the fifties, the sixties and after. But to see these time-spans in their fullness one must restore to them the work done in those years by poets who are treated in separate sections.

In the selection of poems the chief aim has been to give examples of the poet's best writing so far as space would allow. Variety has been only a subordinate consideration. If the chief aim had been to illustrate the different kinds of work the poet has attempted, the selection would have been very different; and in some cases poetic quality would have had to be sacrificed to the providing of specimens. It should therefore be borne in mind that the critical comments may sometimes refer to aspects of the poet's work which are not exemplified adequately or at all in the selection. The map is constituted by the whole book, not by the parts taken separately.

General Introduction

Writing in the Sydney University magazine *Hermes* in 1902, Christopher Brennan looked back on the state of Australian culture in the late nineteenth century:

> For all purposes of art and culture Australia was a suburb of that provincial town, London . . . An absolute dependence like this was in itself bad, even given a general high standard of taste in London. But when London had degenerated as it did in the eighties and nineties, Australia was bound to touch shuddering depths of vulgarity.

In literature what Brennan scornfully saw in retrospect was, on one side, a small school which 'maintained, in our ruder land, the glorious traditions of Bohemianism, and proclaimed the sovereignty of the Poet', and a few other 'solemn cultivators of the Muse'; on the other side an aggressive nationalist school:

> It was supposed that you could improvise yourself Australian and a man of letters by simply following your native genius. The writers who devoted themselves to this worthy object could certainly not be charged with dependence on the degenerate culture of London, just as they carefully guarded themselves against all chance of an accusation of going after strange gods — I might explain that this means any 'effete' literary traditions. As Nature had not been good enough to hurry up and fashion a race pervaded with the spirit of the soil, the Australianity of this literature, which largely dealt with and was mainly addressed to mythical individuals called Bill and Jim, was painted on, not too laboriously, from the outside. What ruined the school was that it forgot its main (and only) object after all and took to celebrating imported fauna such as the horse and jackeroo.[1]

Rather rapturously, Brennan saw the newly federated nation in 1902 as suddenly transformed by a new spirit not just for local reasons but as part of a world-wide human revolution: 'We have got rid of the so-called nineteenth century' — 'so-called' because it was only the later part that was meant as the term was generally

1

used. Clearly the 'legend of the nineties' was not working for Brennan.[2]

Norman Lindsay's retrospective view of the state of Australian culture before the turn of the century was no less bleak:

> If ever there was a moribund limbo in all cultural values, it was this country in that era. It was given over to the skullduggery of politicians, to bucolics plucking the wool off sheep, to a press with an intellectual status little above that of the *Bogwallah Banner*, edited mainly by parsons, and to the domination of all moral, social, aesthetic, and intellectual values by a virulent mob of wowsers, extracted from English Nonconformists, Scotch Presbyterians and Irish Catholics — all this plus a lingering flavour of the convict system . . . For the rest, poetry remained at the (for me) unreadable pedestrian ponderosities of Bernard O'Dowd, the pleasing enough verses of Victor Daley and early *Bulletin* bards . . .[3]

In literary history we inevitably think in periods, to which we attribute general characteristics, even though we have to acknowledge that the periods are neither clean-cut segments nor homogeneous, and have to beware of imposing on them our prejudice, resentment, or nostalgia.

Australian poetry seems to divide roughly into three periods: the nineteenth century, marked by the somewhat unsuccessful effort of Harpur and Kendall to create an indigenous 'literary' poetry alongside the popular tradition of balladry; the earlier part of the twentieth century, with some extension back into the nineties and ending at the start of the Second World War; the period from 1940 to the present. It is the second and third of these periods that this book tries to cover.

A treatment of the earlier twentieth-century period must go back into the nineties at some points. John Shaw Neilson's first poems were published singly in the nineties; but it was nearly another decade before he began to find himself as a poet, and his first collection, *Heart of Spring*, did not appear till 1919. Brennan's *XXI Poems* appeared in 1897, and the greater part of his brief decade of intense production lies within the nineties, though its main impact was felt later, with the publication of *Poems [1913]* — the actual date of publication was in 1914 amid the clamour of the outbreak of war. The importance of going back to the nineties for the more popular kind of verse-making is greater. Lawson's first volume of verse, *In the Days When the World was Wide*, was published in 1896, and Paterson's first collection, *The Man from Snowy River*, in 1895. These were the high points of the reign of popular verse.

The earlier twentieth-century period ends with the publication by Slessor of *Five Bells* in 1939, after which he was virtually silent. In Slessor was absorbed whatever of early twentieth-century English modernism Australian poetry found usable. The first edition of *Five Bells* was decorated by Norman Lindsay, who long before had illustrated poems of Victor Daley, Brennan, Neilson, and others. A case could be made for calling the whole period the Lindsay Period, so permeated is it, for good or ill, by this talented family, especially by Norman with his multifarious activity and close contact with poets.

Slessor's work was the summation of its period and a bridge to what was to follow. New vehicles for Australian poetry appeared in quick succession as if in readiness for the new production. *Southerly* began publication under the editorship of R. G. Howarth in 1939. Max Harris began to publish *Angry Penguins* in 1940, and in December of that year C. B. Christesen published the first issue of *Meanjin Papers*. In 1941 Douglas Stewart was appointed literary editor of the *Bulletin,* and the publishing firm Angus and Robertson began their annual anthology, *Australian Poetry*.

Whether the post-1940 period should be regarded as concluded or still continuing is a point on which there can be disagreement. In the late sixties a number of younger poets began to show impatience with the prevailing kinds of poetry and attempted a radical new departure. This is the spirit of editorial comment in two anthologies: *New Impulses in Australian Poetry* (ed. Rodney Hall and Thomas Shapcott, 1968), and *Twelve Poets* (ed. Alexander Craig, 1971). The editors of *New Impulses* wrote:

> . . . we believe this collection amply demonstrates that the younger poets are not mere foothills to the Established Peaks . . . but form a new and distinctive range of their own, some of the peaks of which will come to be recognised as important landmarks (p. 1).

In *Twelve Poets*, Alexander Craig made the note of complaint against the established poets much sharper, and the demand for radical change more explicit:

> My belief is that there's been a general conservatism or lack of experiment in Australian poetry, persisting into the 1960s and accompanied by a discursive, over-explanatory dullness in many poems. It's the second fault which is really the more serious and which has tended to make ours the poor relation of other English-language poetry. However the first drawback's bad enough . . . Fortunately, whether they've read his statement or not, more and more Australian poets — and most of those here — would agree with Ezra Pound, when he says: 'Willingness to experiment is not enough,

but unwillingness to experiment is mere death . . . Experiment is ONE of the elements necessary to its — poetry's, literature's — life' (p. 1).

In surveying the course of Australian poetry in this century a few general observations can be made. In the first place, poetry in the earlier part of the twentieth century takes second rank to prose in strength of achievement. Henry Lawson's short stories and Henry Handel Richardson's and Joseph Furphy's novels bulk as major works of the period, against which we can set the frustrated brooding of Brennan, a handful of fine Neilson lyrics, even fewer plain-language pieces of Gilmore, and the small number of poems in which Slessor showed his full powers. In the post-1940 period poetry shows greater strength of achievement, and may be said to hold its own, even against the maturing of Martin Boyd's talent from *Lucinda Brayford* (1946) on, and the increasing stature of Patrick White after *The Aunt's Story* (1948).

In the second place, the question of nationalism, of what Brennan called 'Australianity', was repeatedly posed in the earlier period, but solved in the later period. Norman Lindsay has written of 'the national ego-mania fostered by the *Bulletin*' under J. F. Archibald.[4] But the problem was not confined to the *Bulletin*'s strident populist nationalism which is reflected in parts of the work of Lawson and continued by others. The problem was with Australian poetry from the beginning, when Harpur's muse in 'The Dream by the Fountain' enjoined him:

Be then the Bard of thy country!

It is visible in Harpur's and Kendall's efforts to assimilate distinctively Australian things and to find an idiom capable of dealing with the full range of their experience in this country. Another form the problem took was with poets like Daley and Brennan, who were disinclined to be literary nationalists and were also not deeply involved imaginatively in the Australian scene: with the result that their language and themes seem too derivative and separated from reality. In spite of Slessor's example of a solution, the problem was still very much with us, in all three forms — populist nationalism, a more refined literary nationalism, and rejection of Australianity — in the early 1940s. It has now been solved, in the only way it could ever be solved — by ceasing to exist: no recent Australian poet seems bothered with it, or needs to be. But it took a hundred years to work itself out.

That is not to say that the Australian poet is not aware of his situation in another way. It remains inescapably true that Australia does not provide a *metropolitan* centre of literary culture, in the sense that the United States, England and Europe provide such centres, drawing talent into themselves and diffusing its products over the world as influences. Whatever vitality and achievement Australian arts and letters may have must occur, for the present, within a situation limited in this way: we are neither metropolitan nor strictly speaking provincial.

It is hard to talk of a tradition in Australian poetry because there has been little downward transmission except for some influence of older writers on younger contemporaries. The sense of making a new start recurs. Harpur and Kendall saw themselves as pioneers. Brennan made a separate start. McCrae's work was heralded by a few as a real beginning at last. Slessor and FitzGerald were at least able to attach themselves for a time to McCrae and Brennan respectively — with results not entirely felicitous. With the new poets of the 1940s there is again the sense of a new start. Although there was some influence from FitzGerald, such as Rosemary Dobson and Francis Webb have acknowledged,[5] for most of the poets emerging at that time there was little sense, so far as I know, that their predecessors were vitally important influences to be absorbed, wrestled with, or rejected.[6] From the 1950s until recently a more substantial influence of older contemporaries on younger poets was evident, and the sense of continuity was therefore greater. But even so, external influences have remained dominant — later Yeats for many poets of the forties and fifties, Lowell for some poets in the sixties.

One feature which has remained fairly constant in both periods and has been frequently remarked on, as in Alexander Craig's comment already quoted, is the conservatism of Australian poetry. This applies to verse form, style, and organization of theme. It is mainly through dissatisfaction with this endemic conservatism that some younger poets want to make a fresh start. Whether poetic conservatism is felt to be sound policy or a deplorable fault depends on one's scheme of values, but the evidence for a predominating conservatism appears everywhere in these pages. Indeed, the story until recently might be seen as an *increasing* conservatism. Brennan is arguably the most avant-garde poet Australia has had. He did not accept the free forms of Whitman and Rimbaud, nor did he accept Rimbaud's break with rationality; but he absorbed and understood and corresponded with Mallarmé when the symbolists were the most advanced and esoteric poetic school: he did not have to wait for Arthur Symons's *The Symbolist Movement in Literature* (1899) which slowly began to initiate English and American poets into the arcanum. He also made use of such innovations in verse as the Patmorean ode, and the mixed form of late nineteenth century prosody which he used in 'The Wanderer', and he adopted the idea of a *livre composé* from French sources as well as from Rossetti. Compared with Brennan, Slessor in his time was a cautious semi-modernist affected in a small degree by modernism's weaker strains, by the Imagists and the Sitwells, and very little by Eliot and Pound. Yet Slessor still seems more of a modernist than poets whose work developed in the 1940s, such as Judith Wright, A. D. Hope, Douglas Stewart, Rosemary Dobson, David Campbell. The Rimbaud-derived prose poems Patrick White gives to his poet Le Mesurier in Chapter 10 of *Voss* (1957) are more avant-garde than anything else in Australian writing of that period.

Part of the conservatism of Australian poetry is the importance in it of 'nature poetry' and more generally poetry with rural themes and settings. This tendency entered Australian poetry from the beginning, under the influence of Thomson's *The Seasons* and other eighteenth-century descriptive pieces, an influence gradually reinforced by that of Wordsworth and later Romantic sources. Its importance has fluctuated, as Vivian Smith has remarked (p. 229). Clearly it is not very important for Brennan and Hope, for instance — and quite a few others. On the other hand nature poetry, of some kind, is a very important element in the work of some of our best poets. That is not to say, however, that it is the same thing in all of them. The different poetic uses to which 'nature' is put by Australian poets is a subject worth further exploration, though Brian Elliott has made a survey of it in his *The Landscape of Australian Poetry* (1967).

COMMENTARY

Scarce any can hear with impartiality a comparison between the writers of his own and another country; and though it cannot, I think, be charged equally on all nations, that they are blinded with this literary patriotism, yet there are none that do not look upon their authors with the fondness of affinity and esteem them as well for the place of their birth, as for their knowledge or their wit.

Samuel Johnson, *The Rambler*, no. 93

Mais, Cher, l'Art n'est plus, maintenant,
—C'est la vérité—de permettre
A l'Eucalyptus étonnant
Des constrictors d'un hexamètre.

Rimbaud, 'Ce qu'on dit au poète à
propos des fleurs'

When a poetic tradition can no longer make a living in
England, it emigrates to the Dominions.

A. A. Phillips, in *Southerly,* vol. 18,
no. 3, 1957, p. 171

It was about that period [1899], by the way, that A. G. Stephens
asked for a four-line description of Australian literature, and I
wrote for his *Bookfellow:*

Whalers, damper, swag and nose-bag, Johnny cakes and billy tea,
Murrumburrah, Meremendicoowoke, Youlgarbudgeree,
Cattle-duffers, bold bushrangers, diggers, drovers, bush racecourses,
And on all the other pages horses, horses, horses, horses.

R. H. Croll, *I Recall,* 1939, p. 58

People who shrilly insist on the uniqueness of their own
identity are likely to be insecure about it.

Robert Alter, in *Commentary* (U.S.A.),
vol. 50, no. 4, 1970, p. 86

Voyage within you, on the fabled ocean,
And you will find that Southern Continent,
Quiros' vision — his hidalgo heart
And mythical Australia, where reside
All things in their imagined counterpart.

It is your land of similes: the wattle
Scatters its pollen on the doubting heart;
The flowers are wide-awake; the air gives ease.
There you come home; the magpies call you Jack
And whistle like larrikins at you from the trees.

James McAuley, 'Terra Australis'

B

Without songs, architecture, history:
The emotions and superstitions of younger lands,
Her rivers of water drown among inland sands,
The river of her immense stupidity

Floods her monotonous tribes from Cairns to Perth.

*   *   *

And her five cities, like five teeming sores,
Each drains her: a vast parasite robber-state
Where second-hand Europeans pullulate
Timidly on the edge of alien shores.

*   *   *

Yet there are some like me turn gladly home
From the lush jungle of modern thought, to find
The Arabian desert of the human mind,
Hoping if still from the deserts the prophets come,

Such savage and scarlet as no green hills dare
Springs in that waste, some spirit which escapes
The learned doubt, the chatter of cultured apes
Which is called civilization over there.

A. D. Hope, 'Australia'

The more I studied the views advanced in this book [*The Writer in Australia,* ed. John Barnes, 1969], the more I was persuaded that the whole debate about nationalism and cultural independence has been conducted with scant respect for the facts upon which it is allegedly based, and with no suspicion that literary tastes and preferences might be the real point at issue. (I suspect that if one had asked the main writers of the nineteenth century if they were struggling to establish an independent tradition, they might well have replied that they were more interested in the struggle to write.) The main line of this particular argument runs from Stephens to Palmer, Stephensen, Ingamells, Buckley and Phillips. But both teams in the debate, those for an assertively national literature and those against it, are accepting the same basic terms of the argument. Even those critics who, like Judith Wright and Buckley, think of maturity as unselfconscious acceptance of nationality, are still employing the logic of the nationalistic debate. They have not broken away from the assumptions (largely untested) about the relationship between environment and creative achievement.

Leonie Kramer, in *Australian Literary Studies,*
vol. 4, no. 2, 1969, p. 187

One of the problems that has faced criticism in Australia is the tendency — common enough at any time in any literature — first to overrate and then to underrate writers; and some of the uncertainty that has dogged Australian criticism in the past has come from the failure to place writers in an accurate historical perspective. I believe, for instance, that it is more fruitful, and that we get a clearer and less partial view, if we compare Hugh McCrae with J. C. Squire and some of the Georgians, or if we compare R. D. FitzGerald with John Masefield rather than with, say, Donne.

> Vivian Smith, in *Southerly*, vol. 27,
> no. 3, 1967, p. 219

Although there is a sizable body of Australian writing, the Australian writer of today does not have a usable literary past, if I may put it that way. One feels the pressure of all those names enshrined in the literary histories, but what is there in our literary past that is meaningful to the present? The attitude towards the past has been conservative: it should be critical. What is needed, I suggest, is a sifting and a re-valuation of the past. This means that there is a need for new approaches, for seminal discussions of the kind which are still quite scarce in Australia. Dr Heseltine's essay, 'The Literary Heritage', *(Meanjin Quarterly* 1/1962), is an example of the sort of discussion that is needed. It happens that I don't agree with his method or his interpretation, but I find his essay refreshing and stimulating, in opening up new lines of thought. Again, Vincent Buckley's 'Utopianism and Vitalism'* challenges the reader to look for the leading ideas in Australian literature.

> John Barnes, 'A. G. Stephens and the Critic's
> Tasks', *Meanjin Quarterly*, vol. 27, no. 4, 1968, p. 470

---

* *Quadrant*, vol. 3, no. 2, 1959; reprinted in *Australian Literary Criticism*, ed. Grahame Johnston, 1962. John Docker's *Australian Cultural Elites* (1974) is an interesting recent contribution to this kind of discussion.

SELECT GENERAL BIBLIOGRAPHY

BIBLIOGRAPHICAL AND RESEARCH AIDS

Annals of Australian Literature, ed. Grahame Johnston, Oxford University Press, Melbourne, 1970. (Covers 1789-1969, giving principal publications and associated data year by year and an index of authors with their works.)

Australian Dictionary of Biography, ed. Douglas Pike, Melbourne University Press, Melbourne, 1966- . (Successive volumes gradually appearing.)

Australian Book Review, 1961- , ed. Geoffrey Dutton 1961-4, Max Harris 1961- , Rosemary Wighton 1962- . (Provides fairly complete coverage of Australian literary publications in book form.)

Australian Literary Studies, 1963- , ed. L. T. Hergenhan 1963-70, L. T. Hergenhan and E. Stokes 1971-   (Nos. 1 and 3 in each two-yearly volume contain an Annual Bibliography of Studies in Australian Literature; no. 2 in each volume contains a check-list of Research in Progress in Australian Literature.)

Australian National Bibliography, 1961- , published by the National Library of Australia. (Books are listed.)

Australian Public Affairs Information Service: A Subject Guide to Literature, 1945- , published by the National Library of Australia. (Periodical articles are listed.)

Index to Australian Book Reviews, 1965- , published by the Libraries Board of South Australia.

The Journal of Commonwealth Literature, 1965- , ed. Arthur Ravenscroft. (Provides an Annual Bibliography of Commonwealth Literature, the Australian section of which is compiled by L. T. Hergenhan.)

Miller, E. Morris and Macartney, Frederick T., *Australian Literature,* Angus & Robertson, Sydney, 1956. (Provides a bibliography to 1939 by Miller, extended to 1950, with an Historical Outline and Descriptive Commentaries, by Macartney.)

GENERAL ANTHOLOGIES

Australian Poetry, Angus & Robertson, Sydney, 1941- , (annual volumes edited by various hands).

A Book of Australian Verse, ed. Judith Wright, Oxford University Press, Melbourne, 1956.

The Penguin Book of Australian Verse, ed. R. G. Howarth, John Thompson, Kenneth Slessor, Melbourne, 1958.

The Penguin Book of Australian Verse, ed. H. P. Heseltine, Melbourne, 1972.

Poetry in Australia (vol. 1: *From the Ballads to Brennan,* ed. T. Inglis Moore; vol. 2: *Modern Australian Verse,* ed. Douglas Stewart), Angus & Robertson, Sydney, 1964.

PERIODICALS PUBLISHING POETRY

(a) *Makar, Meanjin Quarterly, New Poetry, Overland, Poetry Australia,*

Quadrant, Southerly, Twentieth Century, Westerly are literary magazines which regularly publish poetry and criticism or reviews. A number of small, often ephemeral, periodical publications have also been current in recent years.

(b) Some newspapers publish an important part of the work of well-known poets in their Saturday literary pages: the *Age, Australian, Canberra Times, Sydney Morning Herald*.

GENERAL SURVEYS BY SINGLE AUTHORS

Buckley, Vincent, *Essays in Poetry, Mainly Australian,* Melbourne University Press, Melbourne, 1957.
Docker, John, *Australian Cultural Elites: Intellectuals in Sydney and Melbourne,* Angus & Robertson, Sydney, 1974.
Elliott, Brian, *The Landscape of Australian Poetry,* Cheshire, Melbourne, 1967.
Green, H. M., *A History of Australian Literature,* 2 vols, Angus & Robertson, Sydney, 1961.
Hadgraft, Cecil, *Australian Literature: a Critical Account to 1955,* 1960.
Moore, T. Inglis, *Social Patterns in Australian Literature,* 1971.
Serle, Geoffrey, *From Deserts the Prophets Come: the Creative Spirit in Australia 1788-1972,* Heinemann, Melbourne, 1973.
Wilkes, G. A., *Australian Literature: A Conspectus,* Angus & Robertson, Sydney 1969.
Wright, Judith, *Preoccupations in Australian Poetry,* Oxford University Press, Melbourne, 1965.

COLLECTIONS OF CRITICISM

Australian Literary Criticism, ed. Grahame Johnston, Oxford University Press, Melbourne, 1962.
Australian Writers and their Work series, ed. Geoffrey Dutton for Lansdowne Press 1963-7; ed. Grahame Johnston for Oxford University Press 1968-
The Literature of Australia, ed. Geoffrey Dutton, Penguin Books, Melbourne, 1964. (A revised edition is in preparation.)
Twentieth Century Australian Literary Criticism, ed. Clement Semmler, Oxford University Press, Melbourne, 1967.
The Writer in Australia 1856-1964, ed. John Barnes, Oxford University Press, Melbourne, 1969.

NOTES

[1] *The Prose of Christopher Brennan,* ed. A. R. Chisholm and J. J. Quinn, 1962, pp. 222-3.
[2] Vance Palmer in *The Legend of the Nineties* (1954) stresses the utopianism current in the nineties, and points out that the next decade was richer in creative work, and that this coincided with a decline in utopian enthusiasm.
[3] Norman Lindsay, *Bohemians of the Bulletin,* 1965, pp. 120-2.
[4] *op. cit.,* p. 5.

[5] 'Though I now estimate his poetry very highly and acknowledge, with Francis Webb, a grateful indebtedness I did not, I think, fully grasp it during the forties.' (Rosemary Dobson, 'A World of Difference', Blaiklock Memorial Lecture 1973, reprinted in *Southerly*, vol. 33, no. 4, 1973, p. 380.)

[6] In his interesting study *Australian Cultural Elites* (1974), John Docker presents Brennan, Norman Lindsay, Slessor, Hope, and Patrick White as writers reproducing essentially the same pattern of 'a provincial romanticism', but, except for Lindsay's influence on Slessor, arriving at this pattern quite independently of one another.

I

Popular Verse

INTRODUCTION

There have been two kinds of popular verse in Australia. They have in common that they lend themselves easily to oral performance, and that they deal with familiar aspects of life and appeal to commonly held sentiments. The two kinds are: sung ballads, and written verses, for reading and recitation.

Sung Ballads

These have been variously called 'colonial ballads' and 'old bush songs', but the names are inadequate. They are an extension into Australia, not only of British rural song and of street ballad of the broadside type but also of songs in vogue in the English music halls and American minstrel shows.[1] Although most of these sung ballads are anonymous, in some cases attributions have been made with varying degrees of probability, as in the case of 'The Sandy Maranoa' (p. 23).

Some of these sung ballads are narrative in type. Bushranger songs such as 'Bold Jack Donahoe' and 'The Wild Colonial Boy' tend naturally to vivid incident. A large number of ballads, however, subordinate narration to what one may call 'celebration': some aspect of life is described and commented on: the convict's lot, the experience of a whaling crew, or of the bullock-driver, or gold-digger, or shearer, or stockman. The songs answer to a need to rehearse typical features of common experience, with praise, or lament, or comic effect.

Most of the sung ballads belong to the nineteenth century. It was a sign that the day of Australian folksong was drawing to a close when Paterson in 1905 published his collection, *The Old Bush Songs*. It is mainly in this terminal form as collected and recorded material that the sung ballads enter our period — in spite of protestations to the contrary. Paterson commented:

Most of these songs, even in the few years that they have been extant, have developed three or four different readings, and not only have the ballads been altered, but many of them have been forgotten altogether . . . Thirty or forty years ago every station and every shearing shed had its singer, who knew some of the bush songs. Nowadays they are never sung, and even in districts where they took their rise they have pretty well died out (pp. xi-xv).

Paterson was the Sir Walter Scott of our balladry, and like Scott he collected only words, not tunes. Many of the songs were set to well-known tunes; in other cases a new tune may have arisen by the modification of a traditional melody, or by a new combination of stock melodic possibilities. Though Paterson was right in signalizing the decline of folksong, the final fading-out has been gradual. Interest in Australian folksong was at a low ebb in the early decades of this century. The recrudescence of interest in the fifties was in fact proof that it was all over, leaving collectors to gather surviving material, and revivalists to give it an afterlife of a different kind.

Dr Percy Jones pioneered the renewal of interest by his work in the forties in collecting tunes and words. 'Click Go the Shears' (p. 22) was collected by him. The folksong movement of the fifties came with a rush, as Douglas Stewart and Nancy Keesing noted in their *Old Bush Songs* (1957), an enlarged and re-edited edition of Paterson's collection:

> . . . today an astonishing number of people have entered the field: writers, historians, musicians with tape-recorders, American Fulbright scholars.[2] The Australian Folklore Society, founded some three years ago, is flourishing, and, under its sponsorship, a Bush Music Club has been established in Sydney together with the Bushwhacker's Band and the Wattle Recording Company, so that song-sheets and gramophone records are now available (p. vii).

The Australian sung ballads have virtually no poetic quality, as we ordinarily use the term, and no effluxion of time will bestow it on them. Their merit and interest must be found in what they crudely are, not in any pretence that they are otherwise: and the words should be thought of as normally united to a tune. They are different in kind from the written ballads we are about to discuss, as both are from literary or 'hallmarked' poetry.[3] It may be that in the rare cases where folksong or ballad in other national traditions offer poetical satisfactions — as in some of the Border ballads — there is an influence of a more developed artistic tradition. Certainly there was no such artistic influence affecting Australian popular song. An influence from the literary tradition is, however, visible in some of the written work by popular rhymesters which we are now to consider.

Written Verses for Reading or Recitation

The fact that popular written verses are distinguishable in kind from Australian folksong on the one hand and from literary poetry on the other does not mean that there is no contact. The 'Bulletin bards' were aware of the 'old bush songs', and there is a borderland on that side — just as there is on the other side, where literary poetry adjoins. The recognition of kind does not mean that the borders are sharply defined. And literary poetry itself has at times sought to draw upon both the sung and the recited kinds of popular balladry.

The *Bulletin* in its first quarter of a century became the main vehicle of the most popular written poetry Australia has known, work which has probably been very influential in fixing certain abiding notions of Australianness. The deep public impression made by the *Bulletin* poets is attested by a recollection of Norman Lindsay's:

> All over Australia there were liars claiming to be one or another of its [the *Bulletin*'s] notabilities, and strapping up free beer and local distinction on the fraudulent impersonation. There were even arrogant impostors who swaggered in outback pubs under the names of Henry Lawson, Victor Daley, or 'Banjo' Paterson.[4]

It was Adam Lindsay Gordon's *Bush Ballads and Galloping Rhymes* (published 1870, on the same morning he shot himself) that showed the way. Gordon was followed by Barcroft Boake, who hanged himself with his stockwhip in 1892; his 'Where the Dead Men Lie' remains in anthologies. But it would be a mistake to represent the work of A. B. Paterson and Henry Lawson and lesser figures as appearing merely in lineal descent from Gordon. Edgar Waters has put their achievement in the right context and perspective, in saying that their work was 'merely the local sub-species of a kind of verse that flourished throughout the English-speaking world'.[5] Waters points to the deeper background: the fashion of ballad-writing dating from Percy's *Reliques* and Wordsworth's *Lyrical Ballads;* the popular side of the verse of Scott, Shelley, Hood, W. S. Gilbert, and the Browning of 'How They Brought the Good News'. He then draws attention to the 'remarkable suddenness' with which a new kind of balladry appeared with huge success in the work of such men as Bret Harte and John Hay and G. E. Sims in the United States in the 1870s. Paterson and Lawson appeared subsequently, along with Kipling.[6]

In Canada Robert Service began his rise to popularity as late as the first decade of the twentieth century. All these writers received a greater or less degree of international notice — the Australians much less than the others; the influence of overseas examples on Australian production is considerable but there is no sign of a reverse influence. There are doubtless social and cultural reasons why such ballad poems met a massive response at that time. In a world rapidly becoming more and more complex and confusing, they delineated attitudes based on simple virtues, loyalties and prejudices.

In the wake of Lawson and Paterson came Edward Dyson, E. J. Brady, and Will Ogilvie, each writing out of varied rural and urban experience. A special place must be given to the Reverend P. J. Hartigan ('John O'Brien'), whose *Around the Boree Log* (1921) contains some of the most agreeable and amusing verse in the tradition, centred on the life of Irish settlers in rural New South Wales.

The leaders of the *Bulletin* school, Paterson and Lawson, were opposites in character. Paterson's vigorous ballad-writing was more popular than Lawson's. The general verdict has always been that Lawson's powers were more fully shown in the short story.[7] Lindsay has left a vivid sketch of Paterson as a natural aristocrat, with whom he unfavourably compares his rival: 'Lawson's self-image, sodden with self-pity, is that of the underdog'.[8] Lawson and Paterson in 1892 staged a public debate, in verse, about the Bush, Lawson characteristically emphasizing its grimmer aspects against Paterson's zest.[9] Paterson's vision of Clancy and Lawson's of Sweeney may be compared in two of the poems in this section. In selecting another example from Paterson's work, it seemed best to go back to his early masterpiece 'The Man from Snowy River'. This has been the subject of an interesting comment by Judith Driscoll, which may at first seem over-sophisticated, but possibly provides a key to the abiding popularity of the poem, by drawing attention to archetypal elements in it.[10]

The main line of this balladry, the part that lends itself best to recitation, is narrative in kind. But popular versifying cannot be confined in any one formula as regards form or subject or treatment. It was tempting, in working over the material for this section, to distinguish a third kind of popular verse, to be called 'miscellaneous recitation pieces'. Well into the first half of the twentieth century, recitation of verse was one of the features of public and private entertainment — whether as an 'item' by a practised amateur performer at a 'social' or concert, or as a command performance at home by a daughter taking 'elocution' lessons. *The Bulletin Reciter,* edited by A. G. Stephens (1901, second series 1933) catered for this need. The repertoire of suitable pieces contained much Australian material, including narrative ballads but extending beyond. A popular example is 'The Women of the West' written by George Essex Evans in the nineties:

> They left the vine-wreathed cottage and the mansion on the hill,
> The houses in the busy street where life is never still,
> The pleasures of the city, and the friends they cherished best:
> For love they faced the wilderness — the Women of the West.

Russel Ward rightly says of this that it is 'conventionally meditative or descriptive'.[11] Yet this does not make it clearly different in kind from some of Paterson's more meditative verses and many of Lawson's varied productions.[12] Rather than set up a distinction that does not work very well, it seemed best to bring under one head the wide variety of verses of popular appeal that dominated the poetic scene from the nineties for over a quarter of a century. John Shaw Neilson has his place in this tradition with many poems that are moving in their pathos, such as 'The Soldier is Home' and 'The Ballad of Remembrance' — indeed the characteristic techniques of recitation verse, such as reiteration of a phrase or refrain for cumulative effect, and a certain rhetorical cast, are everywhere in Neilson's work; they appear in a sublimated form in his most delicate lyrics. Mary Gilmore's work needs also to be seen as growing within the tradition of popular recitation.

Just as the popular tradition of written ballad seemed to be subsiding, it had a remarkable flare-up in the distinctive work of C. J. Dennis. His popularity was established by *The Songs of a Sentimental Bloke* (published 1915, with a foreword by Henry Lawson), which received more overseas notice than any other book of Australian verse. It is a series of comic poems written in a somewhat unauthentic vernacular idiom,[13] and tells of the love of the larrikin, Bill, for the nice girl, Doreen. Bill's mate, Ginger Mick, is the main figure in a second successful book, *The Moods of Ginger Mick* (1916), in which he is a soldier who meets his death at Gallipoli. The immense success of these books was not durable.[14] A word should, however, be inserted about Dennis's contribution to popular song. In 1915 he wrote *'The Australaise'* as a marching song dedicated to the A.E.F. As A. H. Chisholm recalls, it 'became in some degree a National Anthem with the Diggers of the war of 1914-18, who (adding adjectives to taste) sang it to the tune of "Onward Christian Soldiers" '.[15] The chorus runs:

> Get a ---- move on.
> Have some ---- sense.
> Learn the ---- art of
> Self de----fence![16]

Recitation poetry as a widely popular art belongs to the past. Yet one must not overlook the rise in the sixties of public poetry readings, which appeal to a restricted audience but give scope for entertainment pieces, grave or gay, that perform well. Bruce Dawe's poems are notably well suited. Among examples not in this book is Nancy Keesing's 'Reverie of a Mum' in *Showground Sketchbook* (1968).

COMMENTARY

Sung Ballads

The proper study of folksong is the folk; that is, the great corpus of material that the intellectually unsophisticated of every country produces should be studied first as sociological documents. Until recently America's thousands of folksongs were the province of professors of English literature, who examined them with the yardstick of literary criteria, and found them remarkably inferior to the work of even minor poetasters. Other educated people compare the music of folksong to the classics, and find the inferiority more remarkable still. That is wrong; that is like comparing apples to aeroplanes, and condemning the one because it will not fly and the other because it is not good to eat . . . Australian folksong is not American, nor is it British, though most of its tunes and many of its lyrics can be traced to British origins. Neither Britons nor Americans sing of shearing and bullock-driving, nor do they weep over dying jockeys. They have no Dad and Dave, no 'blackfellows vicious', no strong spirit of mateship, no ill-behaved dogs who sit on tucker-boxes. These are some of the multifarious things that combine to make the unique national Australian character, which is seen nowhere so clearly as in Australian folksong.

John Greenway, 'Anything like Waltzing Matilda:
Observations on Folksong in Australia', *Quadrant*,
vol. 1, no. 2, 1957, pp. 47 and 51

So much for the historical element; now as to the songs themselves. As metrical compositions they cannot be expected to rank
high. In all her history England has produced only a few good
ballads, and ballads do not get justice from cold print. An old
Scotchman, to whom Sir Walter Scott read some of his collected
ballads, expressed the opinion that the ballads were spoilt by
printing. And these bush songs, to be heard at their best, should
be heard to an accompaniment of clashing shears when the voice
of a shearer rises through the din caused by the rush and bustle
of a shearing shed, the scrambling of the sheep in their pens, and
the hurry of the pickers-up; or when, on the roads, the cattle are
restless on their camp at night and the man on watch, riding
round them, strikes up 'Bold Jack Donahoo' to steady their nerves
a little. Drovers know that they must not sneak quietly about
restless cattle — it is better to sing to them and let them know
that someone is stirring and watching; and many a mob of wild,
pike-horned Queensland cattle, half inclined to stampede, has
listened contentedly to the 'Wild Colonial Boy' droned out in true
bush fashion till the daylight began to break and the mob was
safe for another day. Heard under such circumstances as these
the songs have quite a character of their own. A great deal
depends, too, on the way in which they are sung. The true bush-
man never hurries his songs. They are designed expressly to pass
the time on long journeys or slow, wearisome rides after sheep or
tired cattle; so the songs are sung conscientiously through —
chorus and all — and the last three words of the song are always
spoken, never sung.

A. B. Paterson, Introduction to
The Old Bush Songs, 1905, p. xiv

Written Verses for Reading or Recitation
On A. B. Paterson

The best of Paterson's verse deals, not with descriptive matter
(of which his work is full by way of padding mostly) but with the
simple social emotions. There is no depth sounded; psychology is
never strained; generally speaking it is taken for granted that
what lies underneath the surface is the same as what you see.

Brian Elliott, *Singing to the Cattle and Other
Australian Essays*, 1947, p. 144

On Henry Lawson

When, after separate consideration of Lawson's verse and prose,
we place them side by side, we find at the outset that in matter

and motive they approach each other in many respects. But while in his poetry Lawson's personality stands strongly in the fore-ground, in the prose it retreats entirely into the background. Of the poet's socio-political convictions, of his yearning for freedom and his restless spirit, which now looks back wistfully to the past, now with yearning vision peers into a better future and finally gives itself up after a hard and varied struggle to its fate — of all these thoughts and feelings, which struggle for expression in his verses, there is hardly a feeble echo in his prose. It is true that he often endows his heroes with autobiographical features; but in the prose there is never a word of the cynicism and bitter-ness against the world, which ring discordantly through his poems. If his unhappy experiences to a certain extent justify the posture of the embittered cynic that he readily assumes, the character which he thereby gives to a great part of his poetry gains for him only a restricted circle of friends. Moreover, in many respects he embodies in his poems the humours and sentiments of the popular mind, conditioned as they have been by the circumstances of the times and subject as they are to the idea of speedy change; while his prose reflects more the stable and permanent side of the national character and lets the brightest light fall on its truly human element. So it happens that the shackled idiom of the poetry loses much of the natural strength of expression which endows his prose with charm and originality.

> Adele Fuchs, *Henry Lawson: ein australischer Dichter,* Vienna, 1914, tr. Colin Roderick in *Henry Lawson Criticism,* 1972, p. 162

Nevertheless, there are signs that our critics are beginning to realize that Lawson the artist's Australia was never the Australia in which the man ate his bread in pain and sorrow.

Dr Stephen Murray-Smith, in his deft little book on Lawson, published in 1962, has touched what I believe to be the truth. He says: '[Lawson] was, in fact, writing of a world peopled by his characters: a world completely consistent and coherent in itself. He was not writing a series of disconnected stories; in one sense he spent his whole life writing one book'.

I would have said not 'in one sense', but 'in every sense'. Dr Murray-Smith has, in my view, come nearest of all critics to the truth. Lawson's world existed in his imagination, and almost everything of a creative nature that he wrote, in both prose and verse, fits into that world in one way or another: I part company with Dr Murray-Smith on two counts, first when he suggests that

Lawson did not design it that way, and secondly, when he accepts the conventional view that 'Lawson's output . . . falls into two subdivisions which each demand to be treated as a whole — his short stories on the one hand and his verse on the other'.

My view is that no such dichotomy exists. It did not exist in Lawson's mind; it does not exist in the world that grew out of his mind. The earliest poems, whatever we may think of them as isolated fragments, fall into place in the mosaic of that world. His juvenile poems of revolt were the result of an artistic compulsion; they express the need Lawson was under to remove the actual world from his mind and to substitute his imaginative world for it. They are not to be taken literally, as the nineteenth century took them literally . . .

Colin Roderick, Introduction to *Henry Lawson*
Criticism, 1972, p. xxi

On P. J. Hartigan ('John O'Brien')

Every figure in the writings of the genial parish priest of Narrandera ['John O'Brien'] live in his lines . . . They are types and creations at once true and vital, for they are based on great art — often concealed though that art be by the simplicity of the lines and the almost commonplace order of the metrics and measures 'John O'Brien' employs . . .

Bard in Bondage, Essays of P. I. O'Leary,
ed. Joseph O'Dwyer, 1954, pp. 51-2

SUNG BALLADS

Bullocky Bill

As I came down Talbingo Hill
I heard a maiden cry,
'There's goes old Bill the Bullocky —
He's bound for Gundagai.'

A better poor old beggar
Never cracked an honest crust,
A tougher poor old beggar
Never drug a whip through dust.

His team got bogged on the Five-mile Creek,
Bill lashed and swore and cried,
'If Nobbie don't get me out of this
I'll tattoo his bloody hide.'

But Nobbie strained and broke the yoke
And poked out the leader's eye,
Then the dog sat on the tucker-box
Five miles from Gundagai.

Click go the Shears, Boys

Out on the board the old shearer stands,
Grasping his shears in his long, bony hands,
Fixed is his gaze on a bare-bellied 'joe',
Glory if he gets her, won't he make the ringer go.

Chorus   Click go the shears boys, click, click, click,
          Wide is his blow and his hands move quick,
          The ringer looks around and is beaten by a blow,
          And curses the old snagger with the blue-bellied 'joe'.

In the middle of the floor in his cane-bottomed chair
Is the boss of the board, with eyes everywhere;
Notes well each fleece as it comes to the screen,
Paying strict attention if it's taken off clean.

The colonial-experience man, he is there, of course,
With his shiny leggin's, just got off his horse,
Casting round his eye like a real connoisseur,
Whistling the old tune, 'I'm the Perfect Lure'.

Now Mister Newchum for to begin,
In number seven paddock bring all the sheep in;
Don't leave none behind, whatever you may do,
And then you'll be fit for a jackeroo.

The tar-boy is there, awaiting in demand,
With his blackened tar-pot, and his tarry hand;
Sees one old sheep with a cut upon its back,
Hears what he's waiting for, 'Tar here, Jack!'

Shearing is all over and we've all got our cheques,
Roll up your swag for we're off on the tracks;
The first pub we come to, it's there we'll have a spree,
And everyone that comes along it's 'Come and drink with me!'

Down by the bar the old shearer stands,
Grasping his glass in his thin bony hands;
Fixed is his gaze on a green-painted keg,
Glory, he'll get down on it, ere he stirs a peg.

There we leave him standing, shouting for all hands,
Whilst all around him every 'shouter' stands;
His eyes are on the cask, which is now lowering fast,
He works hard, he drinks hard, and goes to hell at last!

The Sandy Maranoa

attributed to A. W. DAVIS*

The night is dark and stormy, and the sky is clouded o'er;
Our horses we will mount and ride away,
To watch the squatters' cattle through the darkness of the night,
And we'll keep them on the camp till break of day.

* In his *A History of Australian Literature* (vol. 1, 1961, p. 193), H. M. Green refers to a letter from Dr H. O. Lethbridge saying that a stockman named Bill Davis employed on Forest Vale station in western Queensland composed this ballad while en route with bullocks to Gunnedah. Green takes this known authorship as removing it from the true ballad class, but every ballad must have been composed by someone, even if modified in transmission.

C

Chorus   For we're going, going, going to Gunnedah so far,
          And we'll soon be into sunny New South Wales;
          We shall bid farewell to Queensland, with its swampy
               coolibah —
          Happy drovers from the sandy Maranoa.

When the fires are burning bright through the darkness of the
     night,
And the cattle camping quiet, well, I'm sure
That I wish for two o'clock when I call the other watch —
This is droving from the sandy Maranoa.

Our beds made on the ground, we are sleeping all so sound
When we're wakened by the distant thunder's roar,
And the lightning's vivid flash, followed by an awful crash —
It's rough on drovers from the sandy Maranoa.

We are up at break of day, and we're all soon on the way,
For we always have to go ten miles or more;
It don't do to loaf about, or the squatter will come out —
He's strict on drovers from the sandy Maranoa.

We shall soon be on the Moonie, and we'll cross the Barwon, too;
Then we'll be out upon the rolling plains once more;
We'll shout 'Hurrah! for old Queensland, with its swampy
     coolibah,
And the cattle that come off the Maranoa.'

WRITTEN VERSES

A. B. PATERSON

The Man from Snowy River

There was movement at the station, for the word had passed
     around
     That the colt from old Regret had got away,
And had joined the wild bush horses — he was worth a thousand
     pound,
     So all the cracks had gathered to the fray.
All the tried and noted riders from the stations near and far
     Had mustered at the homestead overnight,
For the bushmen love hard riding where the wild bush horses are,
     And the stock-horse snuffs the battle with delight.

There was Harrison, who made his pile when Pardon won the cup,
    The old man with his hair as white as snow;
But few could ride beside him when his blood was fairly up —
    He would go wherever horse and man could go.
And Clancy of the Overflow came down to lend a hand,
    No better horseman ever held the reins;
For never horse could throw him while the saddle-girths would
      stand,
    He learnt to ride while droving on the plains.

And one was there, a stripling on a small and weedy beast,
    He was something like a racehorse undersized,
With a touch of Timor pony — three parts thoroughbred at
      least —
    And such as are by mountain horsemen prized.
He was hard and tough and wiry — just the sort that won't say
      die —
    There was courage in his quick impatient tread;
And he bore the badge of gameness in his bright and fiery eye,
    And the proud and lofty carriage of his head.

But still so slight and weedy, one would doubt his power to stay,
    And the old man said, 'That horse will never do
For a long and tiring gallop — lad, you'd better stop away,
    'Those hills are far too rough for such as you.'
So he waited sad and wistful — only Clancy stood his friend —
    'I think we ought to let him come,' he said;
'I warrant he'll be with us when he's wanted at the end,
    'For both his horse and he are mountain bred.

'He hails from Snowy River, up by Kosciusko's side,
    'Where the hills are twice as steep and twice as rough,
'Where a horse's hoofs strike firelight from the flint stones every
      stride,
    'The man that holds his own is good enough.
'And the Snowy River riders on the mountains make their home,
    'Where the river runs those giant hills between;
'I have seen full many horsemen since I first commenced to roam,
    'But nowhere yet such horsemen have I seen.'

So he went — they found the horses by the big mimosa clump —
    They raced away towards the mountain's brow,
And the old man gave his orders, 'Boys, go at them from the jump,
    'No use to try for fancy riding now.

'And, Clancy, you must wheel them, try and wheel them to the
    right.
  'Ride boldly, lad, and never fear the spills,
'For never yet was rider that could keep the mob in sight,
    'If once they gain the shelter of those hills.'

So Clancy rode to wheel them — he was racing on the wing
    Where the best and boldest riders take their place,
And he raced his stock-horse past them, and he made the ranges
    ring
    With the stockwhip, as he met them face to face.
Then they halted for a moment, while he swung the dreaded lash,
    But they saw their well-loved mountain full in view,
And they charged beneath the stockwhip with a sharp and sudden
    dash,
    And off into the mountain scrub they flew.

Then fast the horsemen followed, where the gorges deep and black
    Resounded to the thunder of their tread,
And the stockwhips woke the echoes, and they fiercely answered
    back
    From cliffs and crags that beetled overhead.
And upward, ever upward, the wild horses held their way,
    Where mountain ash and kurrajong grew wide;
And the old man muttered fiercely, 'We may bid the mob good
    day,
    '*No* man can hold them down the other side.'

When they reached the mountain's summit, even Clancy took a
    pull,
    It well might make the boldest hold their breath,
The wild hop scrub grew thickly, and the hidden ground was full
    Of wombat holes, and any slip was death.
But the man from Snowy River let the pony have his head,
    And he swung his stockwhip round and gave a cheer,
And he raced him down the mountain like a torrent down its bed,
    While the others stood and watched in very fear.

He sent the flint stones flying, but the pony kept his feet,
    He cleared the fallen timber in his stride,
And the man from Snowy River never shifted in his seat —
    It was grand to see that mountain horseman ride.
Through the stringy barks and saplings, on the rough and broken
    ground,

Down the hillside at a racing pace he went;
And he never drew the bridle till he landed safe and sound,
    At the bottom of that terrible descent.

He was right among the horses as they climbed the further hill,
    And the watchers on the mountain standing mute,
Saw him ply the stockwhip fiercely, he was right among them still,
    As he raced across the clearing in pursuit.
Then they lost him for a moment, where two mountain gullies
        met
    In the ranges, but a final glimpse reveals
On a dim and distant hillside the wild horses racing yet,
    With the man from Snowy River at their heels.

And he ran them single-handed till their sides were white with
        foam.
    He followed like a bloodhound on their track,
Till they halted cowed and beaten, then he turned their heads for
        home,
    And alone and unassisted brought them back.
But his hardy mountain pony he could scarely raise a trot,
    He was blood from hip to shoulder from the spur;
But his pluck was still undaunted, and his courage fiery hot,
    For never yet was mountain horse a cur.

And down by Kosciusko, where the pine-clad ridges raise
    Their torn and rugged battlements on high,
Where the air is clear as crystal, and the white stars fairly blaze
    At midnight in the cold and frosty sky,
And where around the Overflow the reedbeds sweep and sway
    To the breezes, and the rolling plains are wide,
The man from Snowy River is a household word to-day,
    And the stockmen tell the story of his ride.

Clancy of the Overflow

I had written him a letter which I had, for want of better
    Knowledge, sent to where I met him down the Lachlan, years
        ago,
He was shearing when I knew him, so I sent the letter to him,
    Just 'on spec' addressed as follows, 'Clancy, of The Overflow'.

And an answer came directed in a writing unexpected,
  (And I think the same was written with a thumb-nail dipped
    in tar)
'Twas his shearing mate who wrote it, and *verbatim* I will quote
    it:
  'Clancy's gone to Queensland droving, and we don't know
    where he are.'

In my wild erratic fancy visions come to me of Clancy
  Gone a-droving 'down the Cooper' where the Western drovers
    go;
As the stock are slowly stringing, Clancy rides behind them
    singing,
  For the drover's life has pleasures that the townsfolk never
    know.

And the bush hath friends to meet him, and their kindly voices
    greet him
  In the murmur of the breezes and the river on its bars,
And he sees the vision splendid of the sunlit plains extended,
  And at night the wond'rous glory of the everlasting stars.

I am sitting in my dingy little office, where a stingy
  Ray of sunlight struggles feebly down between the houses tall,
And the foetid air and gritty of the dusty, dirty city
  Through the open window floating spreads its foulness over all.

And in place of lowing cattle, I can hear the fiendish rattle
  Of the tramways and the 'buses making hurry down the street,
And the language uninviting of the gutter children fighting,
  Comes fitfully and faintly through the ceaseless tramp of feet.

And the hurrying people daunt me, and their pallid faces haunt
    me
  As they shoulder one another in their rush and nervous haste,
With their eager eyes and greedy, and their stunted forms and
    weedy,
  For townsfolk have no time to grow, they have no time to
    waste.

And I somehow rather fancy that I'd like to change with Clancy,
  Like to take a turn at droving where the seasons come and go,
While he faced the round eternal of the cash-book and the
    journal —
  But I doubt he'd suit the office, Clancy of 'The Overflow'.

HENRY LAWSON

Middleton's Rouseabout

Tall and freckled and sandy,
  Face of a country lout;
This was the picture of Andy,
  Middleton's Rouseabout.

Type of a coming nation,
  In the land of cattle and sheep,
Worked on Middleton's station,
  'Pound a week and his keep.'

On Middleton's wide dominions
  Plied the stockwhip and shears;
Hadn't any opinions,
  Hadn't any 'idears'.

Swiftly the years went over,
  Liquor and drought prevailed;
Middleton went as a drover,
  After his station had failed.

Type of a careless nation,
  Men who are soon played out,
Middleton was:—and his station
  Was bought by the Rouseabout.

Flourishing beard and sandy,
  Tall and robust and stout;
This is the picture of Andy,
  Middleton's Rouseabout.

Now on his own dominions
  Works with his overseers;
Hasn't any opinions,
  Hasn't any 'idears'.

Sweeney

It was somewhere in September, and the sun was going down,
When I came, in search of 'copy', to a Darling- River town;
'Come-and-have-a-drink' we'll call it — 'tis a fitting name, I
    think —
And 'twas raining, for a wonder, up at Come-and-have-a-drink.

'Neath the public-house verandah I was resting on a bunk
When a stranger rose before me, and he said that he was drunk;
He apologised for speaking; there was no offence, he swore;
But he somehow seemed to fancy that he'd seen my face before.

'No erfence,' he said. I told him that he needn't mention it,
For I might have met him somewhere; I had travelled round a bit,
And I knew a lot of fellows in the bush and in the streets —
But a fellow can't remember all the fellows that he meets.

Very old and thin and dirty were the garments that he wore,
Just a shirt and pair of trousers, and a boot, and nothing more;
He was wringing-wet, and really in a sad and sinful plight,
And his hat was in his left hand, and a bottle in his right.

His brow was broad and roomy, but its lines were somewhat harsh,
And a sensual mouth was hidden by a drooping, fair moustache;
(His hairy chest was open to what poets call the 'wined',
And I would have bet a thousand that his pants were gone
    behind).

He agreed: 'Yer can't remember all the chaps yer chance to meet,'
And he said his name was Sweeney — people lived in Sussex-street.
He was campin' in a stable, but he swore that he was right,
'Only for the blanky horses walkin' over him all night.'

He'd apparently been fighting, for his face was black-and-blue,
And he looked as though the horses had been treading on him,
    too;
But an honest, genial twinkle in the eye that wasn't hurt
Seemed to hint of something better, spite of drink and rags and
    dirt.

It appeared that he mistook me for a long-lost mate of his —
One of whom I was the image, both in figure and in phiz —
(He'd have had a letter from him if the chap were living still,
For they'd carried swags together from the Gulf to Broken Hill.)

Sweeney yarned awhile and hinted that his folks were doing well,
And he told me that his father kept the Southern Cross Hotel;

And I wondered if his absence was regarded as a loss
When he left the elder Sweeney — landlord of the Southern Cross.

He was born in Parramatta, and he said, with humour grim,
That he'd like to see the city ere the liquor finished him,
But he couldn't raise the money. He was damned if he could think
What the Government was doing. Here he offered me a drink.

I declined — 'twas self-denial — and I lectured him on booze,
Using all the hackneyed arguments that preachers mostly use;
Things I'd heard in temperance lectures (I was young and rather
    green),
And I ended by referring to the man he might have been.

Then a wise expression struggled with the bruises on his face,
Though his argument had scarcely any bearing on the case:
'What's the good o' keepin' sober? Fellers rise and fellers fall;
What I might have been and wasn't doesn't trouble me at all.'

But he couldn't stay to argue, for his beer was nearly gone.
He was glad, he said, to meet me, and he'd see me later on;
He guessed he'd have to go and get his bottle filled again,
And he gave a lurch and vanished in the darkness and the rain.

And of afternoons in cities, when the rain is on the land,
Visions come to me of Sweeney with his bottle in his hand,
With the stormy night behind him, and the pub verandah-post —
And I wonder why he haunts me more than any other ghost.

Still I see the shearers drinking at the township in the scrub,
And the army praying nightly at the door of every pub,
And the girls who flirt and giggle with the bushmen from the
    west —
But the memory of Sweeney overshadows all the rest.

Well, perhaps, it isn't funny; there were links between us two —
He had memories of cities, he had been a jackeroo;
And, perhaps, his face forewarned me of a face that I might see
From a bitter cup reflected in the wretched days to be.

I suppose he's tramping somewhere where the bushmen carry
    swags,
Cadging round the wretched stations with his empty tucker-bags:
And I fancy that of evenings, when the track is growing dim,
What he 'might have been and wasn't' comes along and troubles
    him.

P. J. HARTIGAN

('JOHN O'BRIEN')

Said Hanrahan

'We'll all be rooned,' said Hanrahan
  In accents most forlorn
Outside the church ere Mass began
  One frosty Sunday morn.

The congregation stood about,
  Coat-collars to the ears,
And talked of stock and crops and drought
  As it had done for years.

'It's lookin' crook,' said Daniel Croke;
  Bedad, it's cruke, me lad,
For never since the banks went broke
  Has seasons been so bad.'

'It's dry, all right,' said young O'Neil,
  With which astute remark
He squatted down upon his heel
  And chewed a piece of bark.

And so around the chorus ran,
  'It's keepin' dry, no doubt.'
'We'll all be rooned,' said Hanrahan,
  'Before the year is out.

'The crops are done; ye'll have your work
  To save one bag of grain;
From here way out to Back-o'-Bourke
  They're singin' out for rain.

'They're singin' out for rain,' he said,
  'And all the tanks are dry.'
The congregation scratched its head
  And gazed around the sky.

'There won't be grass, in any case,
  Enough to feed an ass;
There's not a blade on Casey's place
  As I came down to Mass.'

'If rain don't come this month,' said Dan,
    And cleared his throat to speak —
'We'll all be rooned,' said Hanrahan,
    'If rain don't come this week.'

A heavy silence seemed to steal
    On all at this remark;
And each man squatted on his heel,
    And chewed a piece of bark.

'We want an inch of rain, we do,'
    O'Neil observed at last;
But Croke 'maintained' we wanted two
    To put the danger past.

'If we don't get three inches, man,
    Or four to break this drought,
We'll all be rooned,' said Hanrahan,
    'Before the year is out.'

In God's good time down came the rain;
    And all the afternoon
On iron roof and window-pane
    It drummed a homely tune.

And through the night it pattered still,
    And lightsome, gladsome elves
On dripping spout and window-sill
    Kept talking to themselves.

It pelted, pelted all day long,
    A-singing at its work,
Till every heart took up the song
    Way out to Back-o'-Bourke.

And every creek a banker ran,
    And dams filled overtop;
'We'll all be rooned,' said Hanrahan,
    'If this rain doesn't stop.'

And stop it did, in God's good time:
    And spring came in to fold
A mantle o'er the hills sublime
    Of green and pink and gold.

And days went by on dancing feet,
    With harvest-hopes immense,
And laughing eyes beheld the wheat
    Nid-nodding o'er the fence.

And, oh, the smiles on every face,
    As happy lad and lass
Through grass knee-deep on Casey's place
    Went riding down to Mass.

While round the church in clothes genteel
    Discoursed the men of mark,
And each man squatted on his heel,
    And chewed his piece of bark.

'There'll be bush-fires for sure, me man,
    There will, without a doubt;
We'll all be rooned,' said Hanrahan,
    'Before the year is out.'

SELECT BIBLIOGRAPHY

Sung Ballads

    The Old Bush Songs: Composed and Sung in the Bushranging, Digging, and Overlanding Days, ed. A. B. Paterson, Angus & Robertson, Sydney, 1905.
    Old Bush Songs and Rhymes of Colonial Times: Enlarged and Revised from the Collection by A. B. Paterson, ed. Douglas Stewart and Nancy Keesing, Angus & Robertson, Sydney, 1957.
    The Penguin Australian Song Book (with melodies), ed. J. S. Manifold, Melbourne, 1964.
    The Penguin Book of Australian Ballads, ed. Russel Ward, Melbourne, 1964.

    Greenway John, 'Folksong — a Protest', *Australian Literary Studies,* vol. 2, no. 3, 1966.
    ——— 'Anything Like Waltzing Matilda', *Quadrant,* vol. 1, no. 2, 1957.
    Hope, A. D., 'A Note on the Ballads', in *An Introduction to Australian Literature,* ed. C. D. Narasimhaiah, 1965 (this is the Australian edition of a special issue of *The Literary Criterion* (Mysore), vol. 6, no. 3, 1964; reprinted in *Readings in Commonwealth Literature,* ed. William Walsh, 1973).
    Manifold, J. S., *Who Wrote the Ballads? Notes on Australian Folksong,* 1964.

Waters, Edgar, 'Collecting our Folksongs', *Overland,* no. 6, February 1956.
———'Ballads and Popular Verse' in *The Literature of Australia,* ed. Geoffrey Dutton, Penguin Books, Melbourne, 1964.

Written Verses for Reading or Recitation

A. B. PATERSON

The Man From Snowy River, Angus & Robertson, Sydney, 1895.
Rio Grande's Last Race, Angus & Robertson, Sydney, 1902.
Collected Verse, Angus & Robertson, Sydney, 1921.
(ed.) *The Old Bush Songs,* Angus & Robertson, Sydney, 1905.

Heseltine, H. P., ' "Banjo" Paterson: a Poet Nearly Anonymous', *Meanjin Quarterly,* vol. 23, no. 4, 1964.
Semmler, Clement, *The Banjo of the Bush,* 1966.
——— *A. B. Paterson* (Great Australians Series), Oxford University Press, Melbourne, 1967.

HENRY LAWSON

Short Stories in Prose and Verse, L. Lawson, Sydney, 1894.
In the Days When the World was Wide, Angus & Robertson, Sydney, 1896.
Verses, Popular and Humorous, Angus & Robertson, Sydney, 1900.
When I Was King, Angus & Robertson, Sydney, 1905.
Poetical Works, 3 vols., Angus & Robertson, Sydney, 1925.
Collected Verse, ed. Colin Roderick, 3 vols, Angus & Robertson, Sydney, 1967-69.

Autobiographical and Other Writings (1887-1922), ed. Colin Roderick, Angus & Robertson, Sydney, 1972.

Henry Lawson Criticism (1894-1971), ed. Colin Roderick, Angus & Robertson, Sydney, 1972.

P. J. HARTIGAN ('JOHN O'BRIEN')

Around the Boree Log, Angus & Robertson, Sydney, 1921.
The Parish of St. Mel's, 1954.

NOTES

1 Edgar Waters in his chapter on 'Ballads and Popular Verse' in *The Literature of Australia* (ed. Geoffrey Dutton, 1964) associates the influence of stage songs with the change in popular entertainment when the crowded goldfields imported many entertainers.

2 One of the American 'Fulbright Scholars' referred to, John Greenway, revisited Australia in 1965 and commented on the deficiencies of Australian academic response to the study of popular material generally, and also on an element of politically motivated falsification in the folksong revival: 'Some of these songs are factitious and forged for political ends. The question for the

scientific folklorist is how much contamination can be tolerated? I say none; therefore, the work is to be done again, from the beginning. And quickly, before the last of the bush singers settle down finally in front of the television set.' ('Folksong — a Protest', *Australian Literary Studies*, vol. 2, no. 3, 1966, p. 192).

3 The term is used by V. de Sola Pinto and A. E. Rodway in their Introduction to *The Common Muse*, (1965), p. 13.

4 *Bohemians of the Bulletin*, 1965, p. 5.

5 Edgar Waters, 'Ballads and Popular Verse', in *The Literature of Australia*, ed. Geoffrey Dutton, 1964, p. 266.

6 *Barrack Room Ballads* (1892). Paterson's *The Man From Snowy River* was published in 1895, Lawson's *In the Days when the World was Wide* in 1896. Service's *Songs of a Sourdough* appeared in 1907.

7 Lawson's latest editor, Colin Roderick, makes much stronger claims for Lawson's poetry than most critics have been willing to allow. See the Introduction to his *Henry Lawson Criticism*, 1972.

8 *op. cit.*, p. 82.

9 See X. Pons, 'La polémique Lawson-Paterson', *Etudes anglaises*, vol. 25, no. 2, 1972, pp. 220-8.

10 'A Thaw on Snowy River', *Australian Literary Studies*, vol. 5, no. 2, 1971, pp. 190-5.

11 *The Penguin Book of Australian Ballads*, 1964, p. 105.

12 Lawson's later verse, from about 1902, often goes well away from the extroverted impersonal norm of the ballad. It carries the impress of his unhappy personal experiences: it is in its own way 'confessional' poetry.

13 W. S. Ramson, 'Distinctive Features of Australian English' in *Good Australian English* ed. G. W. Turner, 1972, p. 38: 'But literary representatives of speech are notoriously unreliable . . . And sometimes the literary representation of actual speech is so widely astray as to become quite artificial . . . C. J. Dennis's portrayal of Melbourne speech in *The Sentimental Bloke*, delightful as it is, is only misleading if used as linguistic evidence.'

14 Critical opinions of Dennis's work are reviewed by Alexander Porteous, '*The Sentimental Bloke* and his Critics', *Australian Literary Studies*, vol. 1, no. 4, 1964.

15 Alec H. Chisholm, *The Making of a Sentimental Bloke*, 1946, p. 2.

16 The placing of the expletive may have been suggested by the poem 'The Great Australian Adjective' written by W. T. Goodge in the nineties:

> The sunburnt ---- stockman stood
> And, in a dismal ---- mood,
> Apostrophized his ---- cuddy;
> 'The ---- nag's no ---- good,
> He couldn't earn his ---- food,
> A regular ---- brumby,
>   ---- !'

2

Christopher Brennan

INTRODUCTION

Neilson and Brennan are the main figures in the poetry of their generation, and they stand in interesting opposition. One without book learning; the other book-learned to an unusual degree in the literature of the main European languages ancient and modern. One a naive lyric poet practising an Australian 'symbolism without doctrines' and expressing an inexplicit metaphysic intuitively and tentatively arrived at; the other a sophisticated rhetorical poet consciously making his own amalgam from the various poetics of nineteenth-century England and Europe, charged moreover with the heavy load of occultist metaphysics which underlies a large part of European Romanticism and Symbolism. One unassertive and non-controversial in political questions, though not lacking in indignation, pity and scepticism; the other given to bursts of literary *saeva indignatio* in public — first against the Boer War and its supporters, later in favour of Australian participation in the First World War and against its objectors. One playing an unobtrusive part in ordinary society; the other creating a legend — the religious apostasy, the unconventional appearance, the brilliant talk, the drinking, the dismissal from his academic post following scandal raised by his divorce, the final years of penury aided by friends and admirers, the return to Catholic faith and practice before death by cancer — everything is so much in order that it tends to hide the real person; the person whom, for the most part, the poetry also hides, though not completely.

Writing about Verlaine in the *Bulletin* in 1925, Brennan made a general comment:

> It is a pet theory of mine — more than that, it is a fact — that every poet worth his salt not only reveals his own secret, but somewhere

infallibly gives us the formula of his own poetic quiddity and utterance.[1]

The nineteenth-century analogy between poetry and alchemy
lurks behind the words; not everyone would agree that the
making of poetry can usefully be thought of in terms of a secret
or formula. But since Brennan spoke of it in this way, and
doubtless regarded himself as a 'poet worth his salt', he must
have considered where in his work his own arcanum was revealed.
Implicitly we are invited to find it.

In the extracts from Brennan's prose writings that follow
something of his central thought and attitude can be found.
A fuller understanding of his poetic theory — and of some
features of his practice — can be reached by reading his collected
prose. But what we find there is a fairly standard kind of
Romantic-Symbolist theory, modified by the notion that poetry
is related to an evolving Absolute coming-to-be rather than a
stationary Absolute already there. No great originality or peculiar
poetic quiddity in that. Moreover, from the point of view of
1925, his prose consisted largely of unpublished lecture notes
and fugitive pieces of literary journalism which Brennan could
not foresee would, thirty-five years later, be solidified into the
dignity of a collected prose volume. The way he expresses himself in the above quotation implies that it is in his poetry that
every poet somewhere reveals his secret; if he applied this thought
to his own work it must be somewhere in the poetry that Brennan
believed that he too had revealed his secret.

It is evident that nowhere do the elements of Brennan's
laboured art fuse and perfect themselves in even one passage
that could be set beside the best work of his European contemporaries. An instructive parallel may be considered in the case
of the German poet Stefan George, born in 1868, two years
before Brennan. George, like Brennan, had a gift for languages,
and he encompassed the literature of the Western tradition even
more widely than Brennan. He absorbed, like Brennan, all the
currents of nineteenth-century thought and dream, and tried to
create a new esoteric religion with the poet central to it. Whatever
one thinks of it, Stefan George's enterprise was successful to a
considerable extent: he unified his diverse literary influences
into a poetic language of some power, and he not only influenced
German poetry but also affected the spiritual life of Germany —
so much so that the Nazis tried to exploit his influence in a way
he rejected. By the time Brennan had completed his main work
in 1902, George had published seven volumes of verse containing
poems of unusual artistic perfection. Brennan's similar range of

aspiration — as magian artist, as winner and communicator of the saving hermetic word, as prophet to the folk — is visible on the surface of his poetry; but the enterprise was defeated on all points. One can, very reasonably, point out that a Stefan George in the context of Germany and Europe is a case very different from a Brennan isolated in the Australia of his time; but one has to consider also whether the relative failure of Brennan does not mainly lie in himself. What matters most, the strictly poetic failure — in the sense that the ambition of his work would, if realized, have placed him with his European contemporaries, with George, Valéry, Rilke, Blok, Yeats — cannot be dismissed merely as a result of an unfavourable environment. Inescapably one feels, as many of his contemporaries already felt, that one needful thing was lacking: there was not enough poetic genius to combine the elements of his art into a new substance of surpassing quality. Any search, therefore, for a passage revealing Brennan's 'secret' must allow for the defect in achievement.

The fact that Brennan failed, relatively to the high standard which he manifestly invokes, does not mean that there is no poetical result which can be sought out and appreciated. Opinions of his work will continue to vary between readers and as times change. We are at present in a phase of literary fashion opposite to his: the predominating preference recently has been for an ordinary-language poetry, with very reduced pretensions to be doctrinal or prophetic, and tending to retreat into the private and subjective. Brennan, in contrast, used a heavy conglomerate of poetic diction (including a contorted syntax),[2] essayed both doctrine and prophecy, and covered the molten burning fluid of intimate personal experience with a dense congealed lava of myth and symbolism. But whatever our judgement, Brennan looms large at the entrance to twentieth-century Australian poetry. And there is a legitimate interest in interpreting his difficult work (which is by no means yet fully deciphered, in spite of the scholarly illuminations provided by Wilkes and Chisholm), because it is the chief representative in Australia of an ambitious Symbolist — or perhaps more accurately, post-Symbolist — kind of poetry. It is post-Symbolist as are Yeats and Rilke and Blok, with the willingness to retreat from the Mallarméan limit of non-statement and reinstate an overt theme, and the tendency towards system in the use of symbols or reliance on an organizing myth.

Brennan aspired to mastery of the hermetic word which has power to transform reality:

D

> What do I seek? I seek the word
> that shall become the deed of might
> whereby the sullen gulfs are stirr'd
> and stars begotten on their night.
>   (42)[3]

He claimed intermittently to have found it:

> soul, let us go, the saving word is won,
> down from the tower of our hermetic thought.
>   (12)

More frequently he acknowledges that the search is in vain, or rewarded only with 'sibyl-hints of song' (68, xi).

The hermetic word is the gnosis, the efficacious higher knowledge, by which man fallen into disunity and degradation can regain the Eden state. In our fallen state we still possess a 'paradisal instinct' (10), by which we seek 'our long lost innocence' (11). Most men seek Eden blindly; they expend themselves on deceptive substitutes — pleasure, wealth, power, religion, the works of our civilization. But the enlightened few know what they seek. Eden is frequently imaged as a bride, and the return to Eden is expressed in nuptial terms, as a marriage, or at least a betrothal with the promise of fulfilment:

> Yes, Eden was my own, my bride;
> whatever malices denied,
> faithful and found again, nor long
> absent from aura of wooing song:
> but promis'd only, while the sun
> must travel yet thro' times undone . . .
>   (105)

Eden is also seen as a mother, to whose womb all individual lives will return as to a primal unity, so that 'we are orb'd in her' (105).

On the basis of this symbolism, Brennan erected a myth in that part of *Poems* which is The Book of Lilith.[4] The mother-bride who is the embodiment of Eden is now Lilith, the Lady of Night who in Jewish legend was Adam's first mate. The essential fall of man, of Adam, is from that primordial union. To fallen man Lilith has a dual aspect: attractive as the real object of man's need and blind desire; but also a source of fear, felt as a temptation to evil (that is, of transgression beyond the all-too-human good and evil which rule this limited daylight world that ignores the cosmic mystery).

The attempt to systematize one's symbols can create problems. When Adam has fallen from the primordial state of union with Lilith, as the ultimate perfection of love and beauty, he is 'born into dividual life' and takes Eve for his spouse. This, however, reduces Eden to a different status: it is now merely the scene of the first encounter of man with the consequences of his fall into multiplicity, the first of his fruitless attempts at gratification by substitutes. Lilith is now, from the point of view of this lower level of existence, a dangerous lure,

> exciting higher
> the arrowy impulse to dim descried
> o'erhuman bliss
> (68, i)

> Nightly thy tempting comes,
> (68, ix)

while Eve is a temptation the other way, to easy acceptance of herself as an earthly inferior surrogate for Lilith ('shaped featly in thy similitude', 68, ix). Adam in this reduced Eden state already plans to step out into history, and begin the futile ages of civilization, whose works, including religion and its man-made gods, are all substitutes for the real but elusive thing which is symbolized by Lilith. Adam says:

> — And shall I not take heart? if no divine
> revealment star me with the diadem
> hermetic, magian, alchemic gem,
> shall I not feel the earth with firmer tread
> if abdicating to the viewless dead
> the invaluable round of nothingness?
> Kingdom awaits me, homage, swords, liesse
> battle, broad fame in fable, song: shall I
> confide all hope to scanty shapes that fly
> in dreams, whom even if they be all I know
> not, or forerunners of the One? I go,
> shaking them from my spirit, to rule and mould
> in my own shape the gods that shall be old.
> (68, ix)

Lilith's reply to this apostasy is to say of herself that she will be

> Terrible, if he will not have me else,

and the rest of this part of the poem traces the ambiguous horror of man's earthly historical existence. Yet Lilith, the

ultimate mystery and beauty man blindly and disastrously seeks
by substitutes in his brutal daylight world, is still there, as bride
and mother for those who can know her however fitfully. Such
fitful knowledge, at the end of the suffering ages, has been, the
poem says, preserved for us in our time by the elect among
European poets — above all Mallarmé. And it is perhaps in this
concluding passage, occurring before the final hymn to Lilith
(p. 52) that Brennan's 'secret' or 'formula' may be found, at
least as he saw it:

> Lilith, a name of dread: yet was her pain
> and loving to her chosen ones not vain
> hinted, who know what weight of gelid tears
> afflicts the widow'd uplands of the spheres,
> and whence the enrapturing breaths are sent that bring
> a perfume of the secular flowering
> of the far-bleeding rose of Paradise,
> that mortal heats in censer-fume arise
> unto the heart that were an ardent peace,
> and whence the sybil-hints of song, that cease
> in pale and thrilling silence, lest they wrong
> her beauty, whose love bade live their fleeting throng,
> even hers, who is the silence of our thought,
> as he that sleeps in hush'd Valvins hath taught.

(Mallarmé, buried at Valvins, died in 1898 as this poem was
being created.)

Brennan's system shares the monism and dualism which co-
exist in all gnostic metaphysics. The monism affirms that there
is an ultimate unity subsuming all apparent multiplicity, so that
the world is in principle good since it is a manifestation of the
One. The dualism affirms that the world is in principle evil,
because it holds the spirit trapped in bondage to matter, pre-
venting it from realizing the primordial unity. The poet's
problem is that he has to use the materials this world offers him,
in order to create a verbal image of the ultimate perfection of
which this world is a deprivation. So in Brennan certain features
of the world are exempted from the general condemnation
because they suggest the paradisal state: dawn, spring, rose, ocean,
starry sky, virginal innocence, and so on. It is the man-made
city that is especially infernal.

Finally we must consider how Brennan saw the relation
between the poet and the folk. In the poem '1908' he sees the
folk as sharing the quest for Eden, but unconsciously: so that
the poet who has become illuminated must try to give them

more understanding of what their need really is. In *The Wanderer* sequence which forms the third part of *Poems,* the poet is the Wanderer whose homelessness is foolishly pitied by the folk from the point of view of their narrow 'unwitting lives'. The Wanderer is he who bears a knowledge they could not bear:

> ... knowing the world how limitless and the way how long,
> and the home of man how feeble and builded on the winds..
>
> (93)

But his voice carries an apocalyptic prophecy of the destruction of the folk's fragile comfortable world, a destruction the folk will suffer but not understand:

> I cry to you as I pass your windows in the dusk;
> .   .   .   .
> But I, who have come from the outer night, I say to you
> the winds are up and terribly will they shake the dry wood:
> .   .   .   .
> And when ye come forth at dawn, uncomforted by sleep,
> ye shall stand at amaze, beholding all the ways overhidden
> with worthless drift of the dead and all your broken world.
>
> (94)

The compassion is lofty; the poet's arrogation to himself of superknowledge could provoke some cheerful Australian sarcasm. In the separate sequence, *The Burden of Tyre,* written in 1902 but not included in *Poems,* the bardic voice of superknowledge becomes one of prophetic denunciation in a specific political situation, the Boer War; like Blake, Brennan tries to unify this topical theme with his Eden myth and with his lofty concern (and contempt) for the folk, who ignore or attack their spiritual masters. This sequence does, however, also show the poet trying to rise above 'the foolish spirit of ire' that breathes hate and denunciation instead of sounding 'some note of love'. 'The foolish spirit of ire' unfortunately had it all its own way in *A Chant of Doom* (1918), in which the German foe is rabidly denounced.

Poems represents the work mainly of the years 1894-1902, with the years 1897-99 as the period of most intense activity. Briefly in 1923-25 his love for 'Vie' (Violet Singer) and grief for her accidental death produced a few poignant poems, the sonnet 'You, the one woman' (p. 55) among them.[5]

COMMENTARY

Passages from the writings of Christopher Brennan

Poetry is ... a mediator; it presents us with embodiments of the total reality and the perfected reality; it uses the facts of our broken life as elements with which to fashion images of the life that is complete ... The first thing to explain is the word 'moods' — a word definitely brought into circulation by the editors of Blake ... A mood is a movement of the total self as opposed to any of its broken surface manifestations: an energy on its way to become broken, but still whole ... It is a movement of the energy of the self, but in a certain direction ... The mood gathers the doctrine or emotion into the unity; and this is what I meant when I said that poetry could keep a doctrine alive because it let the argument go and held by the mood ... For a mood, resuming into itself and transcending the imperfections of our manifested soul, brings, as embodiment, an image into which the scattered beauty of many material things runs together and burns more vividly. The law of correspondences has a double action. It charges the outer world with meaning and it awakens meaning within ourselves, helping the mood to disengage itself. When a man lets his soul wed itself to some unified aspect of nature, the vastness of the dawn, the wonder of the woods, or the royal passing of the day, all the pettinesses and vexing trifles drop away: what is left is the purer, intenser mood, the rhythm that is ample enough to sing in tune with that of nature ... There are, as most of us keenly feel, two lives: that lies in the brightness of truth, this stumbles in error; that is radiant with love and beauty, this is vexed with its own littleness and meanness; that is unfettered, lying beyond good and evil, this is caught in the quagmire. That, in short, is our health and this our disease: or one might call these two facts of poetry by their simple names — our happiness and our unhappiness ... Poetry, mediating between the two, necessarily enters into the conflict, and as I said at the beginning of this lecture, its part is both to exasperate and reconcile that war. Hence a double attitude of poetry towards the imperfect world, an attitude which we shall find running through Blake, exemplified in Novalis's and his fellows' theory of irony, and in Mallarmé's definition of poetry as consisting of lyrism or enthusiasm and satire ... Out of this symbol of Eden or the Golden Age [as an image of perfect life] grows a myth, for every symbol naturally produces a myth — this time a myth as to the relation between the two worlds [the perfect and the imperfect], a relation which must naturally be

imagined in terms of time. The myth is that of the fall of man —
in Blake that of his redemption as well — the decay of the Golden
Age and its restoration. But this myth is to be read in the same
sense as that in which the Gnostics and Neoplatonists reshaped
it: the fall is the birth of the soul into matter, which is its
bondage.

'Symbolism in Nineteenth Century Literature', *The
Prose of Christopher Brennan*, ed. A. R. Chisholm
and J. J. Quinn, pp. 84-9 (passages from the second
of six lectures given in 1904)

Since, then, we must accept our humanity, since we cannot
always, or even often, live the perfect life, since there is in our
existence a great residue of imperfect days, it follows that our
poetry has largely beauty not as its direct subject, but as its
justifying aim. We use poetry to express not the perfect beauty
but our want of it, our aspiration towards it. Setting it far off
in some imagined empyrean, the poet may even, by a paradox,
treat with fierce irony of life devoid of all shadow of it or desire
for it. More often his theme will be the tragedy of such beauty
as this world affords, or the fate that dogs the soul intoxicated
with perfection.

Introduction to *From Blake to Arnold* — *Selections
from English Poetry, 1783-1853* ed. C. J. Brennan,
J. P. Pickburn, and J. Le Gay Brereton, 1900;
reprinted in *Prose*, p. 19

I suppose I'd be called 'pessimistic' by the sagacious critic;
but I can't help that. I only know that I allow something in me
to speak that gazes for ever on two heavens far back in me: one
a tragic night with a few expiring stars, the other an illimitable
rapture of golden morn over innocent waters and tuneful boughs.
I merely tell the news of these as it comes; and I'm responsible
for the manner of the telling.

Letter to J. Le Gay Brereton, undated, Mitchell
Library MS., quoted by G. A. Wilkes, *New Perspectives on Brennan's Poetry*, 1953, p. 39n.

I'm NOT a symbolist (I've simply some tendencies that way &
of my contemporaries—for one must live in one's age—I get on
best with the so called ((for looking at Symbolism one way it's
hard to tell who is, another, who isn't a Symbolist)) symbolists)

Letter written in 1898 quoted by A. G. Stephens in his
Christopher Brennan, 1933, p. 38. Stephens dated his

copy of the letter 29 September 1898 (see Harry F. Chapin, *A Brennan Collection: an Annotated Catalogue*, 1966, p. 60)

To explain my theory of metaphor.

  Poem consists (for me) of union brought about between emotion and physical beauty

  E.g. Daley's sunset rose of passion

  Therefore of a harmony, a correspondence between soul & world (this accounting for form of poetry—rhythm, harmony, rhyme, outer signs of *that* harmony.)

Now the ideal of style would be to embody *directly* in verse that union

  not to let it be seen in the making

  This union I choose to call the *image* the work of imagination

  Inside this image poetry begins & ends *(cf.* my metaphor about 'drawing' of poem)

Simile is plainly a mere workshop 'state' of the work: a first shaping of the material.

(The grass is green
& so am I)

Metaphor is a longer step towards complete fusion but even now too often used in patches

  nor are writers careful of a harmony of metaphors

What we (I) want

  "Absorption of metaphor into essential phrase"

  (or change place of the nouns here, it means the same thing)

i.e. a phrase caught out of the heart of the image, building this latter up around itself, to music, as it proceeds

or, as Mallarmé puts it, to let the thing unfold like a flower &c.

(You might compare the signification of the poem to the perfume of the flower, to music, not in the ivories (words), to the soul, everywhere implied in the body, nowhere runnable-to-earth)

To do this,

  more work must be put on the living part of the phrase, the Verb

  The nuptials of soul and nature must be a moment of the action.

  Cf. for richer use of the Verb, Mallarmé in *l'après-midi* & in the later sonnets

Once more incompletely & obscurely put, I fear, in haste . . .

Letter to A. G. Stephens, 1898,
ibid., pp. 38-9

On the third or upper plane, it is true, a man who writes verse should have nothing to say.

I'm afraid I'm very unpatriotic. I've written nothing about the horse or the swagman. As far as 'national' traits go, I might have made my verse in China.

Some people say I have not the afflatus, that I have made myself write poetry. I am prepared to agree with that to a certain extent.

I know nothing of the public. Who are the public? Poetry requires that the reader should be in training for it — 'keyed' to it. For that reason probably people read prose; it is so much easier, and human nature has a loveable tendency to slackness.

> Answers by Brennan in an interview with D. J. Quinn,
> the *Sydney Mail*, 9 June 1909, illustrated section, p. 35

It was appointed that I should use a language which must seem foreign to me; that I should be almost entirely cut off from the legendary tradition of my Celtic ancestors: and, as many an Irishman in other days found a new home in France, so I have found in her literature a spirit, in her writers a style, to which I feel myself instinctively drawn, as some are drawn towards home. In sending you this slight book, Sir, I would, if I might, at least mark my gratitude — to you, especially, as the poet whose works have been to me the greatest renewal, the greatest revelation.

> Letter to Mallarmé, 9 August 1897 (with a copy of
> *XXI Poems*), printed in the *Australian Quarterly*,
> vol. 19, no. 2, 1947, p. 27

Passages from the writings of other authors

... beyond doubt there is an affinity of imaginative insight between you and me ... *Towards the Source* is no empty title; carried along by its force, you trace to its rarest source powerfully, limpidly the ordinary current of poetry. The words of your choice you use exactly as they ought to be used, tempered and purified at some original spring of existence, blown through with the breath of life. Beyond doubt, though it is pure English, I am deeply aware that your song has crossed mine; but it gives the impression also that this is what it would have been by its own nature and by it alone.

> Letter to Brennan from Mallarmé, in Mitchell
> Library MS., quoted by Robin B. Marsden, 'New
> Light on Brennan', *Southerly*, vol. 31, no. 2, 1971,
> p. 132. (This is Brennan's translation: he was
> fond of quoting in French the first phrase, '*il y a de
> vous à moi certainement une parenté de songe*'.)

Brennan's is a bush of poetry that smoulders and never really burns; an apparatus of patient craft that seldom becomes an artistic engine. Always busy with himself, his images remain external for others; they rarely make the decisive escape of poetry from the composer. Tolerable displays; some good sonorities; many efficient ideas; yet we sit in a theatre to watch a performance we do not often join.

A. G. Stephens, *C. J. Brennan,* 1933, p. 42

At the same time, along with the intellectual quality of Brennan's poetry, and both vivifying and deepening it, there runs a quality of intense feeling. On this point Hughes as well as Stephens has gone badly astray. Stephens declared that Brennan lacked poetic feeling; he 'wanted heat to set his words in motion, and he wanted sense of melody to make their motion musical'. You may remember that other opinion of Stephens' that I have quoted that Brennan's was 'a bush of poetry that smoulders and never really burns'. And Hughes declared that Brennan lacked 'the particular singing faculty...that (was) pre-eminently Swinburne's and Shelley's, and for which it were desirable that the word lyrical should be reserved', and that he lacked also the elegiac music that with Keats 'rises into a rhapsodic cry'. Now I think Stephens has indeed found the right term for Brennan's poetry; it does smoulder rather than burn; it shows no flame. But I think also that Hughes is wrong and that Stephens has misused his term and quite misunderstood the quality of feeling in the poetry. I believe you will agree with me, even from what you have already heard, that at times in Brennan's poetry the smouldering covers as intense a heat as any flame could give. At such times the poetry is extremely passionate; it is true that the passion is not that of love; Brennan's most passionate lyrics are not love lyrics. But in certain other poems, as in the one about his 'vast and impotent dreams', there is heat enough. There is more still in *O desolate eves,* and most of all perhaps in the last poem that I read as a whole, *O white wind numbing the world.* It would be hard to find anything more passionately intense than that. And are none of these poems lyrical? All Brennan's poetry moves to music, usually a slow and rather heavy music, brooding, monotonous, laboured sometimes, but always rich and sonorous, breaking out now and then in a bold phrase or passage that strikes directly home, but carrying the reader for the most part only gradually forward, as it were upon slow wave after slow wave. But a lyric need not necessarily be light and swift, and some of these poems are as musical as they are passionate; if they are not lyrical, then I don't know what a lyric is. To my mind a great part of Brennan's poetry belongs to a lyrical as well as a reflective mood, so that I should describe him as an emotional intellectual, in whom brain and blood are in intimate co-partnership, and whose utterance is a lyrical as well as a reflective cry.

Yet, more important than all these things is the personality that is revealed in the poems. In the last resort, in poetry as in all other forms of literature, other things being anywhere near equal, it is personality that counts; and it is very largely for this reason that, although the vicissitudes and the moods arising out of them to which Brennan has given expression are such as we ordinary people can sympathise with because they are of the same type as our own, yet their poetic representation has a value which ours would not possess, even if they were expressed with an art which we do not possess either, because in them is reflected a personality that is greater than ours. Bearing all these things in mind, and bearing in mind also Brennan's isolation in the Australia of his day, and how few Australian poets may be ranked even within a long distance of him, we can understand how Hugh McCrae—himself one of those few poets—has called Brennan, in a phrase which I must borrow because I cannot better it, 'a star in exile, unconstellated at the south'.

H. M. Green, *Christopher Brennan*,
1939, pp. 74-7

... a work deprived of classic status only because it is trapped in the iconography and diction of an age too early.

Frank Kermode, 'The European View of Christopher Brennan', *Australian Letters,* vol. 3, no. 3, 1961, p. 60

The impression that remains after we close *Poems 1913* is of a simple and rather callow sensibility, in which irony and tough intelligence had no part. There is no sign of the irony that would have involved *self*-appraisal as well as a critical attitude to life and letters, or of the tough intelligence that would have been needed before World War I to make a new start in English verse. There is not even much sign in Brennan's poetry of any unusual feeling for language; in fact quite the reverse.

A. L. French, 'The Verse of C. J. Brennan', *Southerly,*
vol. 24, no. 1, 1964, p. 17

POEMS

from *Towards the Source*

The yellow gas is fired from street to street
past rows of heartless homes and hearths unlit,
dead churches, and the unending pavement beat
by crowds — say rather, haggard shades that flit

round nightly haunts of their delusive dream,
where'er our paradisal instinct starves:—
till on the utmost post, its sinuous gleam
crawls in the oily water of the wharves;

where Homer's sea loses his keen breath, hemm'd
what place rebellious piles were driven down —
the priestlike waters to this task condemn'd
to wash the roots of the inhuman town! —

where fat and strange-eyed fish that never saw
the outer deep, broad halls of sapphire light,
glut in the city's draught each nameless maw:
— and there, wide-eyed unto the soulless night,

methinks a drown'd maid's face might fitly show
what we have slain, a life that had been free,
clean, large, nor thus tormented — even so
as are the skies, the salt winds and the sea.

Ay, we had saved our days and kept them whole,
to whom no part in our old joy remains,
had felt those bright winds sweeping thro' our soul
and all the keen sea tumbling in our veins,

had thrill'd to harps of sunrise, when the height
whitens, and dawn dissolves in virgin tears,
or caught, across the hush'd ambrosial night,
the choral music of the swinging spheres,

or drunk the silence if nought else — But no!
and from each rotting soul distil in dreams
a poison, o'er the old earth creeping slow,
that kills the flowers and curdles the live streams,

that taints the fresh breath of re-risen day
and reeks across the pale bewilder'd moon:
— shall we be cleans'd and how? I only pray,
red flame or deluge, may that end be soon!

from *The Twilight of Disquietude*

What do I know? myself alone,
a gulf of uncreated night,
wherein no star may e'er be shown
save I create it in my might.

What have I done? O foolish word,
and foolish deed your question craves!
think ye the sleeping depths are stirr'd
tho' tempest hound the madden'd waves?

What do I seek? I seek the word
that shall become the deed of might
whereby the sullen gulfs are stirr'd
and stars begotten on their night.

from *The Quest of Silence*

A gray and dusty daylight flows
athwart the shatter'd traceries,
pale absence of the ruin'd rose.

Here once, on labour-harden'd knees,
beneath the kindly vaulted gloom
that gather'd them in quickening ease,

they saw the rose of heaven bloom,
alone, in heights of musky air,
with many an angel's painted plume.

So, shadowing forth their dim-felt prayer,
the daedal glass compell'd to grace
the outer day's indifferent stare,

where now its disenhallow'd face
beholds the petal-ribs enclose
nought, in their web of shatter'd lace,

save this pale absence of the rose.

from *Lilith*

She is the night: all horror is of her
heap'd, shapeless, on the unclaim'd chaotic marsh
or huddled on the looming sepulchre
where the incult and scanty herb is harsh.

She is the night: all terror is of her
when the distemper'd dark begins to boil
with wavering face of larve and oily blur
of pallor on her suffocating coil.

Or majesty is hers, when marble gloom
supports her, calm, with glittering signs severe
and grandeur of metallic roof of doom,
far in the windows of our broken sphere.

Or she can be all pale, under no moon
or star, with veiling of the glamour cloud,
all pale, as were the fainting secret soon
to be exhaled, bride-robed in clinging shroud.

For she is night, and knows each wooing mood:
and her warm breasts are near in the charm'd air
of summer eve, and lovingly delude
the aching brow that craves their tender care.

The wooing night: all nuptials are of her;
and she the musky golden cloud that hangs
on maiden blood that burns, a boding stir
shot thro' with flashes of alluring pangs,

far off, in creeks that slept unvisited
or moved so smoothly that no ripple creas'd
their mirror'd slip of blue, till that sweet dread
melted the air and soft sighs stole, releas'd;

and she the shame of brides, veiling the white
of bosoms that for sharp fulfilment yearn;
she is the obscure centre of delight
and steals the kiss, the kiss she would return

deepen'd with all the abysm that under speech
moves shudderingly, or as that gulf is known
to set the astonied spouses each from each
across the futile sea of sighs, alone.

All mystery, and all love, beyond our ken,
she woos us, mournful till we find her fair:
and gods and stars and songs and souls of men
are the sparse jewels in her scatter'd hair.

from *The Wanderer*

The land I came thro' last was dumb with night,
a limbo of defeated glory, a ghost:
for wreck of constellations flicker'd perishing
scarce sustain'd in the mortuary air,
and on the ground and out of livid pools
wreck of old swords and crowns glimmer'd at whiles;
I seem'd at home in some old dream of kingship:
now it is clear grey day and the road is plain,
I am the wanderer of many years
who cannot tell if ever he was king
or if ever kingdoms were: I know I am
the wanderer of the ways of all the worlds,
to whom the sunshine and the rain are one
and one to stay or hasten, because he knows
no ending of the way, no home, no goal,
and phantom night and the grey day alike
withhold the heart where all my dreams and days
might faint in soft fire and delicious death:
and saying this to myself as a simple thing
I feel a peace fall in the heart of the winds
and a clear dusk settle, somewhere, far in me.

from *The Burden of Tyre*

EPILOGUE

O life, O radiance, love, delight,
O nuptial rose and valley of bliss
renew'd in maiden bloom and bright
with morn each time thou stoop'st to kiss;

Eden, whence only life is whole
and healing, when thy angel-flowers
sigh the dew's silence into our soul
what hast thou with these wars of ours?

We slay and die: thou art not scarr'd
nor dimm'd with battle-smoke; the din
stirs thee as little as when the hard
God spake the foolish word of sin

o'er foolish souls of men that fear'd,
but thou didst shine in changeless glee
and joy of fruitful strife, endear'd
—and yet our wars are all from thee.

Thou torturing, when thy love invades,
this body of death and hate and greed
gibbers and writhes and frantic raids
break over it and the nations bleed:

and I, who love thee, how oft have I
dream'd of that foolish spirit of ire
riding the mass'd prophetic sky
that breaks in sleet and hail of fire

above the hated citadels,
or done the holy abysms this wrong
to array their ghost, the voids and hells,
against the turrets of the strong:

nor minded me that thou, when spite
and hate have won all they may win,
changing thy shape to Death and Night
(for these and thou are subtle kin),

resumest all our waste and new
conceiving, bring'st to better birth
in thy glad lap where fire and dew
wed in the war that brightens earth.

Thee with whose name in bitter jest
these songs began, to thee at the end
I turn, that all their hate confess'd
as worthless, yet if thou befriend

some note of love, crying in pangs
of wrath and grief, may echo higher
than the derided bow that twangs
against the spectre-walls of Tyre.

[*To V.S.*]

You, the one woman that could have me all
because you would, because it multiplied,
all that I was and did, your joy and pride
to have and hold me; you, Love's gladsome thrall
and hence exactress, that you must forestall
nor yet remit to all the world beside
love of that lover whom your love defied
to rate himself less than itself should call:

Death, that is dire to all, most dreadful here
to you the smitten and this stricken man
you made and call'd your own, let him have done
that thing he can, the one, no more to fear,
since late or soon himself undoes, nor can
that thing you made, the only, be undone.

SELECT BIBLIOGRAPHY

XXI Poems (1893-1897): Towards the Source, Angus & Robertson, Sydney, 1897.
Poems [*1913*], G. B. Philip, Sydney, 1914; reprinted in a facsimile edition, with an Introduction by G. A. Wilkes, 1972.
A Chant of Doom and other Verses, Angus & Robertson, Sydney, 1918.
The Verse of Christopher Brennan, ed. A. R. Chisholm and J. J. Quinn, Angus & Robertson, Sydney, 1960.
The Prose of Christopher Brennan, ed. A. R. Chisholm and J. J. Quinn, Angus & Robertson, Sydney, 1962.

Stone, Walter and Anderson, Hugh, *Christopher John Brennan, a Comprehensive Bibliography and Annotations*, Stone Copying Company, Sydney, 1959.

Chisholm, A. R., *Christopher Brennan: The Man and His Poetry*, Angus & Robertson, Sydney, 1946.
——— *A Study of Christopher Brennan's 'The Forest of Night'*, 1970.
Docker, John, *Australian Cultural Elites*, Angus & Robertson, Sydney, 1974, chapters 1 and 5.
FitzGerald, R. D., 'Communication and the Exhaustion of a Style', *Southerly*, vol. 16, no. 1, 1955.

E

French, A. L., 'The Verse of C. J. Brennan', *Southerly,* vol. 24, no. 1, 1964. Reprinted in *The Australian Nationalists: Modern Critical Essays,* ed. C. Wallace-Crabbe, Oxford University Press, Melbourne, 1971.

Green, H. M., *Christopher Brennan,* Angus & Robertson, Sydney, 1939.

Hughes, Randolph, *C. J. Brennan: an Essay in Values,* P. R. Stephensen, Sydney, 1934.

King, Alec, 'Thoughts on the Poetry of Brennan', *Westerly,* no. 3, 1961.

McAuley, James, *Christopher Brennan* (Australian Writers and their Work series, revised edition), Oxford University Press, Melbourne, 1973.

Moore, T. Inglis, *Six Australian Poets,* Robertson & Mullens, Melbourne, 1942.

Sturm, T. L., 'The Social Context of Brennan's Thought', *Southerly,* vol. 28, no. 4, 1968.

Wilkes, G. A., *New Perspectives on Brennan's Poetry* (reprinted from *Southerly,* vols 13 and 14), 1953.

―――― 'Brennan and his Literary Affinities', *Australian Quarterly,* vol. 31, no. 2, 1959; reprinted in *Australian Literary Criticism,* ed. Grahame Johnston, Oxford University Press, Melbourne, 1962.

―――― 'Christopher Brennan' in *The Literature of Australia,* ed. Geoffrey Dutton, Penguin Books, Melbourne, 1964.

Wright, Judith, *Preoccupations in Australian Poetry,* Oxford University Press, Melbourne, 1965, ch. 6; reprinted in *The Australian Nationalists,* ed. C. Wallace-Crabbe, Oxford University Press, Melbourne, 1971.

NOTES

[1] *The Prose of Christopher Brennan,* ed. A. R. Chisholm and J. J. Quinn, 1962, p. 370.

[2] Leonie Kramer has remarked in seminar discussions that a thorough lexical and syntactical study of Brennan's language is needed, to establish its sources more accurately; such a study would be the basis for a clearer view of why Brennan chose to work in this way, what he thought he was achieving poetically, and why the greater part of his work is a defeat rather than a victory.

[3] *The Verse of Christopher Brennan,* ed. A. R. Chisholm and J. J. Quinn. Numerical references in brackets refer to the editors' numbering of *Poems* [*1913*].

[4] *Poems* [*1913*] is designed to be a *livre composé,* a structured whole. The poem 'Lilith', which is quasi-epical, occurs in the second part, called *The Forest of Night.* Brennan's intentions are discussed by G. A. Wilkes in his Introduction to the facsimile edition published in 1972.

[5] A sidelight on Violet Singer and her relation with Brennan is contained in Richard Singer, 'A Forgotten Poet — or Two', *Southerly,* vol. 21, no. 2, 1961.

3

John Shaw Neilson

INTRODUCTION

The precise dating of Neilson's work is difficult.[1] Some critics have assumed that this does not matter because, as Chisholm put it, his 'work is practically timeless; there are no "periods of development" in his career, such as we find in the case of poets with a more consciously intellectual background; some of his best work was done early, some late . . .'.[2] Certainly there are no periods of the sort that are determined in other poets by changes in formulated artistic aims or intellectual doctrines. But such dating as is possible seems to bear out what Neilson told Devaney: 'Up till about forty I wrote a great deal of rubbish. Since then I have been more particular'.[3]

Every critic of Neilson has to admit the defects which are widely present in his work: uncertain control of diction and tone, veering towards stock poeticisms, sentimentality or bathos; expressions too stereotyped, and others too arbitrary and odd. It is easy to dismiss Neilson unless one looks closely and finds the right poems.[4]

As Harold Oliver has pointed out, not only is Neilson the one poet of his generation to have grown, not declined, in the esteem of later critics and general readers, but also he is the first poet of literary worth (setting aside the popular balladists) 'to use the Australian background with no self-consciousness whatsoever'.[5]

The story of Neilson's life as an unskilled labourer with little schooling and, from his thirties, poor eyesight (he had to rely on amanuenses much of the time) has been traced in some detail by Hugh Anderson and L. J. Blake.[6] Much of his intimate emotional life remains obscure. Mary Gilmore has acknowledged[7] that her poem 'The Spade' refers to Neilson:

Once there was one, who, in creative mood,
Sang words like jewels on a silver air;
Entranced my whole heart listened as I stood;
Then died the sound, and there was nothing there.
Instead I heard a slow spade strike the earth,
In hungry toil that slew the song at birth.

The verses that Neilson wrote for the American poet Stephen
Foster cannot but remind us of himself:

Who was the man? he was not great or wise,
He lived in sore distress,
Always he went with pity in the eyes
For burnt-out Happiness.

He who was poor had melodies of gold,
He had the rude man's Art,
No one can deny him — he could hold
The quick roads to the heart.

The first thing necessary in reading Neilson is to separate out
his finest lyric achievement, when the verse is sensitively musical,
the phrasing delicate and suggestive, often peculiarly oblique.
'Song Be Delicate' (p. 68) deserves the high praise given it by
A. R. Chisholm[8] as an example of the *'symbolisme sans doctrines'*
of this intuitively symbolist poet. It is not a formal *ars poetica*
laying down a prescription for others, but an expression of the
poet's own individual artistic and emotional need, and metaphysical sense.

Having identified Neilson's enduring achievement in a few
lyrics, it is not necessary to disregard everything else or ignore
his variety. In many inferior lyrics there are gleams of the true
opal. And there is a secondary strength in a few of the many
poems Neilson wrote in the popular recitation-ballad vein. His
ability in this genre was not, as he confessed,[9] in the handling
of narrative; but there are moments in which his abhorrence
of man's inhumanity and his deep compassion create an authentic
pathos. In 'The Soldier is Home', written looking back on the
Boer War, he sees the returned soldier who has lost his legs
in a bad cause; the poem ends:

Now shall he sit in the dark, his world shall be fearfully small —
  He shall sit with old people, and pray and praise God for fine
                                        weather;
Only at times shall he move for a glimpse away over the wall,

Where the men and the women who make up the world are
                                              striving together!
                                    Oh! yes, the soldier is home!

Simple, salt tears, full often will redden his eyes;
    No one shall hear what he hears, or see what he sees;
He shall be mocked by a flower, and the flush of the skies!
    He shall behold the kissing of sweethearts — close by him,
                                    here under the trees —
                                    Oh! yes, the soldier is home![10]

A longer poem, moving when recited, is 'The Ballad of Remembrance' in which the poet impersonates a 'new chum Englishman'
arguing the merits of English law and fair play with a convict's
son who remembers the lashmarks on his father's back:[11]

He was a convict forced to work, when the squatter ruled the land.
For some slight fault his master put a letter in his hand
And he said, 'Take this to Bathurst Gaol, they'll make you
                                              understand.'

Too well the law, my father knew, the law of Lash and Chain,
That day he walked to Bathurst Gaol, 'twas in the blinding rain,
And they flogged his flesh into his bones — then he walked back
                                              again.

Neilson's varied production also encompasses satirical and
humorous verses including limericks. Nevertheless it is the
perfect and near-perfect delicate lyrics that matter supremely.
In regard to them, Neilson's devoted editor, A. G. Stephens, was
wrong when he told Neilson that his later work was becoming
too rarefied: 'You mustn't get so fine and thin that you can't
be heard by ordinary ears sometimes'.[12] It is when Neilson is
working in the half-private language of his sensibility — not
divorced from common feeling but carrying his peculiar version
of it to the limits of audibility, as it were — that his idiom is
artistically most successful. He rarely passes over into unintel-
ligibility, though one of his admired poems, 'The Orange Tree',
may have to be admitted as an exception, in spite of the
commentary it has already attracted.[13]

However difficult to decipher Neilson's idiom can be at times,
he knew what he was trying to express, and was never intentionally enigmatic — though we have to allow for the fact that what
he was trying to express may lie on the verge of the unsayable,
as in 'The Crane is My Neighbour', where the bird stands not
merely in a lake but in a metaphysical 'centre', receiving a
celestial communication, of which the poet is able to catch only

the outermost intimations, symbolized by the ripples coming out of the edge of the lake. He told Devaney about the origin of this image of the crane in connection with an earlier poem about his religious experience, 'The Gentle Water Bird':

> I didn't just make it up about that bird. It was that bluey swamp bird, the blue crane. I used to see it in the swamp near where we lived. It seemed so confident and happy, without any fear. It wasn't frightened about God like me. That's what gave me my first idea for the rhyme, and my first idea of right religion too.[14]

Neilson reacted from the notion of a frowning vengeful God that oppressed his childhood. His later beliefs were tentative and unsystematic. Interpreters have sought to make explicit the intuitively held metaphysic they discern in the poetry;[15] and Oliver finds Neilson 'philosophically more interesting than many who try more obviously to reason' (p. 42). He is very seriously metaphysical, and agnostically religious; but he is certainly not 'an arrogant drummer' (a phrase in 'The Crane is My Neighbour', connected with the Salvation Army experiences of his mother and sister); nor does he covet the preacher's black gown, associated with his Presbyterian upbringing, for like his blue crane in the same poem,

> His gown is simplicity — blue as the smoke of the summer.

Of secular ideology — such as the socialist utopianism or the Nietzschean élitism that captured many of his generation — he shows no trace. Keenly alive to social evil and injustice, he took a rather pessimistic and quietist view of the prospect of improvement, as implied in one of the 'notions' he recorded in 1907 in a notebook:

> The Earth is scarcely even in the remotest sense a better place through the life of an honest man, but the example he sets to other men less honest is at least wholesome.[16]

But however dark its underside, Neilson's vision is not dispirited: his dominant colours are not grey and black, but living tender green, sky blue, and red and yellow and white.

COMMENTARY

(i) *Passages from the writings of John Shaw Neilson*

When a man is on poor tucker and loading spawls,* he doesn't have much spare time for rhyming...Please don't think I'm grumbling. I'm merely stating facts.

> Letter to A. G. Stephens, 24 May 1926, Mitchell
> Library MS.; quoted by Oliver, p. 9

I trust that my friends will not expect too much of my last little Booklet [*New Poems*]. I have scarcely any education, and as I am 55 years of age, my rhymes must be going back.

> Letter to Dr James Booth, 18 December 1927,
> La Trobe Library MS.; quoted by Oliver, p. 13

Some people seem to think that it [a poem] should be as definite as an ironmonger's catalogue, and as dogmatic as a Calvinist sermon.

> Letter to James Devaney, 19 August 1934, National
> Library MS.; quoted by James Devaney, *Shaw
> Neilson*, 1944, p. 176

When a critic says that I become monotonous and that I have a very limited range of words he is not far from the truth.

> Autobiography, National Library MS.; quoted by
> Oliver, p. 31

Note your advice about keeping 'em short. I am really only a sprinter — something under forty lines is about my distance.

> Letter to A. G. Stephens, 26 May 1927, Mitchell
> Library MS.; quoted by Oliver, p. 36

(ii) *Passages from the writings of other authors*

John Shaw Neilson's verses embody genuine poetical emotion, and some of them have won wide credit. The work of Shaw Neilson is sometimes pathetic, sometimes humorous, and at its best expresses the essence of lyric poetry in a way which few modern writers can excel... We go farther; and say that we

---

* or 'spalls', pieces of broken stone.

see no poet now writing who approaches so nearly as Neilson
to the quality of Blake. Neilson reminds us of Blake's crystal
vision; he reminds us of Blake's spontaneous expression. His
work is uneven; but in its most successful passages vision and
expression are so matched that we receive a perfect intuition of
poetry.

A. G. Stephens, 'Shaw Neilson',
Bookfellow, 1 October 1912, p. 77

In a roomful of clever and distinguished people he was
always notable. Yet I have seen the faintly patronizing attitude
at a literary gathering where he was incomparably the biggest
figure present. This was because of the modernist notion that
simple poetry is simple. The truth is that Shaw Neilson's subtle
and delicate art must be the despair of the most cultured
imitators. Its simplicity is that rare and difficult thing which the
most ambitious and industrious artificers still find unattainable.

James Devaney, *Shaw Neilson,*
1944, p. viii

When Furnley Maurice dropped in about five, Neilson was
talking of the few poets he had been able to read. In his good
days, he came on Padraic Colum's *Wild Earth* and it meant a lot
to him, perhaps giving him confidence to use naive rhythms and
simple themes that suit him. But through the years the bulk of
his reading has undoubtedly been the letters pouring in from
A.G.S.

Nettie Palmer, *Fourteen Years,* 1948 (journal
entry for 9 December 1929), p. 57

Nineteenth century Australia did not ask for a derivative minor
English poetry; it asked for 'Australian poetry' — something
altogether peculiar and even absurd; and it asked for bardic
poetry, something never well written except by poets of genius.
One of the reasons, I think, why Neilson is so satisfying is that,
by a happy accident, Australian meant to him, not absurd
demands on insufficient genius, but almost total isolation from
influences. He was isolated physically, he was insulated from
prolonged schooling, he was almost deprived of books. But he
carried in his memory the world of ballads which his father had
given to him, and more precious, an unspoilt, childlike, folk-
inherited, imagination, full of natural generic metaphor. He was
derivative in the sense that he makes his poetry nearly always
from the old song-measures and their lucent outlining, kept to the

most ancient preoccupations of sentient man: love and desire,
death, growing and fading, seasonal changes in all living things,
sky, earth, animals, young, old, man, woman; and he used the
most deep-rooted forms of symbol and emblem. I do not find his
poetry delicate, as so many seem to do. It is clear, spare, and rich,
at its best. And how well he keeps to the poetic life that as a minor
poet of genius he could serve, singleminded, and unambitious.
He does not know the nineteenth century langour, soft-centred
elevations, clotted verboseness. At his best his verbs are active, his
adjectives few, his syntax direct, his metaphor bold and un-
explained, the pleasures and pains he handles unmuffled.

> Alec King, review of Shaw Neilson selection,
> 'Australian Poets' series, *Australian Literary
> Studies*, vol. 1, no. 4, 1964, p. 276

I think this is Neilson's real secret — the unshieldedness of his
inner eye. Lacking what almost all men require to drive them on
— an idea of self and its importance, to which everything must
be referred to test its value — he was free to accept his perceptions
and use them without betraying their immediacy. The light fell
on him unfiltered. From that fact, perhaps, comes his chief fault,
his lack of self-criticism which led to occasional banality; but
from it also come those phrases and cadences which strike home
with so surprising a twist of the knife, or touch off a flare of light
by which we see again something we have not seen since childhood.

> Judith Wright, *Preoccupations in Australian
> Poetry*, 1965, p. 114

Neilson is a haunting and elusive figure. The uneducated poet
of the Wimmera who has written some of the most delicate poems
in our literature appears at one moment to be a genuine
primitive, at another as sophisticated and as consciously-
unconsciously achieved a writer as some of the French Symbolists
. . . That Neilson is a superb lyricist in a handful of poems is
beyond doubt: he has 'a way with words' characteristic of the
born poet; his best work casts an authentic and unmistakable
spell and enchantment . . . To read Neilson in bulk is a deeply
rewarding and moving experience. One has contact with a
remarkable sensibility and mind, with a spirit capable of the most
exceptional attentiveness to the mysterious details of reality which
form the fabric of his verse. But his successes are intermittent.
His limitations have to be faced.

Neilson uses only two or three shapes; the bulk of his work consists of songs and ballads. With this limited range goes an abuse of repetitions and repeated stanzas which frequently do not reinforce but dissipate the total impact of individual poems. Rhythmically Neilson is unadventurous; and his poorer poems suffuse the book at times with a certain muffled languor.

No one will question Neilson's delicacy of ear: his poems never jar and they rarely fail in tone. His weakness is rather a certain visual smudging, a melodious melting and merging. In his unsuccessful poems his images neither focus nor fuse; what we are left with is a mellifluous blur. Professor Chisholm comments on Neilson's lack of sound constructive technique and I think it is true that where Neilson's vision fails him he has hardly any external strengths to fall back on. We are left instead with rather stilted and willed pieces like the 'Sundowner'. But Neilson has some constructive power. 'The Ballad of Remembrance' is an astonishing performance.

Neilson is frequently described and discussed as a writer of timeless songs, but a great deal more of the external world gets into his poems than this description might suggest. The world of nature of course — trees and water-birds, honey and light; but also — though less successfully — the contemporary world of picture-shows and blonde typists; poor pensioners and the sick in the city. It is fascinating to watch Neilson trying to expand and develop— sad too: his gift was too absolute for him to be a successful experimenter or manipulator of modes, and when he tries to organise ideas or consciously develop an argument or sustain an image with variations throughout the whole course of a poem he frequently lapses into gentle jingle. For all his unconscious sophistication Neilson remains a primitive of genius.

One wonders if, paradoxically enough, Neilson wasn't made or saved as a poet by his lack of professional skills, his technical limitations. There is a tendency to prettify throughout his work, a genuine primitive brightness and charm which a smoother technique could empty of all resonance and turn into something like commercial art. As it is, his slight awkwardnesses grip into the mind: they become a way of speaking — intensely individual and real inflexions. Even in poems that fail as totals there is usually an amazing image, a felicitous phrase. Technical limitations are limitations; but better an honest awkwardness than a display of empty skills . . . Neilson at his sentimental unhappiest reminds one of the Victorian writers of album verses or the composers of Victorian parlor songs:

The elder was a five years girl
With the blue eyes of the mother,
And younger by a year there ran
A flaxen-headed brother ...

These two fell ill with a quick fever
— 'Twas in the red ripe weather —
Kind neighbors came with flowers for them
When they lay dead together.

Neilson is especially sentimental and coy when he writes of young girls and children; ('He sold himself to the daisies'); the misty realms of fairy-land and the 'little creatures'. Like many nature poets he reveals a strange embarrassment in front of human events and facts; and the word that best characterises him is the one Professor Chisholm has chosen — shyness. Shy of life, shy of the harsh light, shy of noise, Neilson's is the misty half-lit inner world of frail emotions and fragile feelings and awarenesses. He is at his calmest, sweetest and strongest in moments of rapt contemplation of the external world: as in 'The Smoker Parrot', 'Native Companions Dancing', 'The Crane is My Neighbor', 'The Gentle Water Bird', 'May'; and in his passive alertness to the mysterious as in 'The Orange Tree', and the sheer lyrical inwardness of the well-known 'Love's Coming' and 'Song be Delicate'.

Vivian Smith, 'A Haunted Primitive',
the *Bulletin*, 10 April 1965, p. 53

In drawing attention to work of such very poor quality, I seek not to damage Neilson's reputation but, paradoxically, to enhance it by challenging two widely-received and misleading ideas: that his poetic impulse was so idiosyncratic, so 'timeless', that he was almost untouched by the work of his predecessors and contemporaries; and that his work was 'timeless' in the sense of showing — and needing — no development. By displaying, on the contrary, how thoroughly 'literary' (in a bad sense) was his early work and how slowly but completely he outgrew it, one can hope to throw a sharper focus on the qualities of his best poems.

The first idea finds its most influential expression in a well-known essay by Miss Judith Wright ... her main thesis is both untenable and misleading. Borrowing colour, as she says, from the brevity of Neilson's formal education and from the limits imposed on his reading by the partial blindness that overtook him when he was a young man, Miss Wright suggests that these handicaps become something very like an advantage to a poet of his temperament: for in him we see one who preserved always the 'unshielded eye' of childhood, lost to most of us, if we ever had it, in the sophistication and self-consciousness of adulthood.

To the extent that this argument depends upon Neilson's poor education and poor sight, it has been rebutted before now. Whatever he did or did not learn at school, there is clear and ample evidence of his admittedly scattered reading in the English, Australian, and even American writing of the nineteenth century especially... It is too often forgotten, one may add, that Neilson's eyesight did not begin to trouble him until 1905, when he was thirty-three. And, in any case, the whole question of his access to other poetry is altered when one recalls the popularity of singing and recitation at a time when people were obliged to supply their own entertainment... A still more important consideration remains: behind all these questions of biographical fact and of the manner in which they have been argued lie central and less widely-canvassed questions of judgment. To accept, with Miss Wright, that the 'unshielded eye' is the heart of Neilson's mystery is to lay a strong emphasis upon his unquestionable gift for fantasy, for parable, and for a kind of nature-mysticism akin to Miss Wright's own more recent poetry. It might be argued, however, that Neilson has other gifts to which the 'unshielded eye' is less responsive — for a simpler kind of nature poetry, for the comic and satirical poetry neglected by almost everyone except Neilson himself and Professor Oliver, and for the poetry of social concern that Professor McAuley stresses more than others have done. Again, the 'unshielded eye' is inclined to overlook what is massed in the foreground, the conventionally literary work in the manner of the period which makes up a very large proportion of the verse printed in the largest collection generally available, that of Professor Chisholm.

J. F. Burrows, 'Shaw Neilson's Originality',
Southerly, vol. 32, no. 2, 1972, pp. 122-5

POEMS

The Man Who Prayed

'Twas in the time when oranges surrender all their green for
    gold;
'Twas in the time when lemon-trees are bitten by the bitter cold.

'Twas in the time when butterflies seek in the wilted earth a
    home,
And the bewildered honey-bees sleep in the heavy honeycomb.

'Twas in the time when buttercups move shyly to the face of day,
And silver-hatted mushrooms rise like little people in a play.

'Twas in this time my love fell ill, because of evil winds that
    blew;
Her sister and her father prayed, and I — I fell a-praying too.

Not as the holy did I pray — with their closed eyes they cannot
    see —
But in a rage to God I prayed to leave my little love with me.

I looked straight up into the sky, I shut no eye, I bent no knee;
With all my being long I cried to God to give my love to me.

Oh, many a night good neighbours came, and many a cheery tale
    they told
Of the bright world and market days, and all that people bought
    and sold.

One night my dear love spoke my name. I said, 'What is it
    aileth thee?'
She whispered, 'All the air is dark.' It was the last she said
    to me.

The Smoker Parrot

He has the full moon on his breast,
The moonbeams are about his wing;
He has the colours of a king.
I see him floating unto rest
When all eyes wearily go west,
And the warm winds are quieting.
The moonbeams are about his wing:
He has the full moon on his breast.

May

Shyly the silver-hatted mushrooms make
   Soft entrance through,
And undelivered lovers, half awake,
   Hear noises in the dew.

Yellow in all the earth and in the skies,
   The world would seem
Faint as a widow mourning with soft eyes
   And falling into dream.

Up the long hill I see the slow plough leave
   Furrows of brown;
Dim is the day and beautiful; I grieve
   To see the sun go down.

But there are suns a many for mine eyes
   Day after day:
Delightsome in grave greenery they rise,
   Red oranges in May.

Song be Delicate

Let your song be delicate.
   The skies declare
No war — the eyes of lovers
   Wake everywhere.

Let your voice be delicate.
   How faint a thing
Is Love, little Love crying
   Under the Spring.

Let your song be delicate.
   The flowers can hear:
Too well they know the tremble
   Of the hollow year.

Let your voice be delicate.
   The bees are home:
All their day's love is sunken
   Safe in the comb.

Let your song be delicate.
   Sing no loud hymn:
Death is abroad ... Oh, the black season!
   The deep — the dim!

The Hour of the Parting

Shall we assault the pain?
  It is the time to part:
Let us of Love again
  Eat the impatient heart.

There is a gulf behind
  Dull voice and fallen lip,
The blue smoke of the mind,
  The gray light on the ship.

Parting is of the cold
  That stills the loving breath,
Dimly we taste the old
  The pitiless meal of Death.

The Orange Tree

The young girl stood beside me. I
  Saw not what her young eyes could see:
— A light, she said, not of the sky
  Lives somewhere in the Orange Tree.

— Is it, I said, of east or west?
  The heartbeat of a luminous boy
Who with his faltering flute confessed
  Only the edges of his joy?

Was he, I said, borne to the blue
  In a mad escapade of Spring
Ere he could make a fond adieu
  To his love in the blossoming?

— Listen! the young girl said. There calls
  No voice, no music beats on me;
But it is almost sound: it falls
  This evening on the Orange Tree.

— Does he, I said, so fear the Spring
  Ere the white sap too far can climb?
See in the full gold evening
  All happenings of the olden time?

Is he so goaded by the green?
  Does the compulsion of the dew
Make him unknowable but keen
  Asking with beauty of the blue?

— Listen! the young girl said. For all
  Your hapless talk you fail to see
There is a light, a step, a call
  This evening on the Orange Tree.

— Is it, I said, a waste of love
  Imperishably old in pain,
Moving as an affrighted dove
  Under the sunlight or the rain?

Is it a fluttering heart that gave
  Too willingly and was reviled?
Is it the stammering at a grave,
  The last word of a little child?

— Silence! the young girl said. Oh, why,
  Why will you talk to weary me?
Plague me no longer now, for I
  Am listening like the Orange Tree.

The Sweetening of the Year

When old birds strangely-hearted strive to sing
and young birds face the Great Adventuring:

When manna from the Heaven-appointed trees
bids us to banquet on divinities:

When water-birds, half-fearing each blue thing,
trace the blue heavens for the roving Spring:

When school-girls listening hope and listening fear:
They call that time the sweetening of the year.

　　　　*　　　　*　　　　*

When schoolboys build great navies in the skies
and a rebellion burns the butterflies:

Sunlight has strange conspiracies above
and the whole Earth is leaning out to Love:

When joys long dead climb out upon a tear:
They call that time the sweetening of the year.

The Poor, Poor Country

Oh 'twas a poor country, in Autumn it was bare,
The only green was the cutting grass and the sheep found little
    there.
Oh, the thin wheat and the brown oats were never two foot high,
But down in the poor country no pauper was I.

My wealth it was the glow that lives forever in the young,
'Twas on the brown water, in the green leaves it hung.
The blue cranes fed their young all day — how far in a tall tree!
And the poor, poor country made no pauper of me.

I waded out to the swan's nest — at night I heard them sing,
I stood amazed at the Pelican, and crowned him for a king;
I saw the black duck in the reeds, and the spoonbill on the sky,
And in that poor country no pauper was I.

The mountain-ducks down in the dark made many a hollow
    sound,
I saw in sleep the Bunyip creep from the waters underground.
I found the plovers' island home, and they fought right valiantly,
Poor was the country, but it made no pauper of me.

My riches all went into dreams that never yet came home,
They touched upon the wild cherries and the slabs of honey-
    comb,
They were not of the desolate brood that men can sell or buy,
Down in that poor country no pauper was I.

*   *   *

The New Year came with heat and thirst and the little lakes
    were low,
The blue cranes were my nearest friends and I mourned to see
    them go;
I watched their wings so long until I only saw the sky,
Down in that poor country no pauper was I.

F

The Walking of the Moon-Woman

'Twas moonlight in the ripe barley,
And she was half concealed;
Perchance she was a Moon-Woman,
Below the barley field.

For Moon-Women they never dance,
They neither laugh nor sing;
They are made up of old wishes
That fear not anything.

Perchance she was a Moon-Woman
Who stole from east to west;
Her feet were in the white barley,
And a child was on her breast.

Perchance she was a Moon-Woman,
Whose wishes all were sighs,
For the child was all too beautiful,
And the blue was in his eyes.

Perchance she was a Moon-Woman
Who in her day did burn,
And now in moonlight courage stood,
But would not yet return.

*   *   *

'Twas long ago — my eyes are dim —
I fear too much the cold;
Perchance she was a Moon-Woman,
Down in the barley gold.

You Cannot Go Down to the Spring

The song will deceive you, the scent will incite you to sing;
You clutch but you cannot discover: you cannot go down to the
    Spring.

The day will be painted with summer, the heat and the gold
Will give you no key to the blossom: the music is old.

It is at the edge of a promise, a far-away thing;
The green is the nest of all riddles: you cannot go down to the
    Spring.

The truth is too close to the sorrow; the song you would sing,
It cannot go into the fever: you cannot go down to the Spring.

The Old Man in the Autumn

The calm is unceasing,
The soul would delay;
He the Unseen in Autumn
Steps not far away

How gentle the children!
Softly they pass
In a faint merriment
On the scented grass.

As Love half defeated
The flowers seek the dim;
Oh, the Unseen — I like not
The long talk with him.

He shall not dare to come
Down to my rhyme;
He is of God, and surely
A kinsman of Time.

He offered wisdom; already
I am too wise,
With all my years counted up
At the back of my eyes.

Too cold is the beauty,
The love burns dim;
That old man I like not,
Nor the long talk with him.

The Poor Can Feed the Birds

Ragged, unheeded, stooping, meanly shod
The poor pass to the pond; not far away
The spires go up to God.

Shyly they come from the unpainted lane;
Coats have they made of old unhappiness
That keeps in every pain.

The rich have fear, perchance their God is dim;
'Tis with the hope of stored-up happiness
They build the spires to Him.

The rich go out in clattering pomp and dare
In the most holy places to insult
The deep Benevolence there.

But 'tis the poor who make the loving words.
Slowly they stoop; it is a sacrament:
The poor can feed the birds.

Old, it is old, this scattering of the bread,
Deep as forgiveness, or the tears that go
Out somewhere to the dead.

The feast of love, the love that is the cure
For all indignities — it reigns, it calls,
It chains us to the pure.

Seldom they speak of God, He is too dim;
So without thought of after happiness
They feed the birds for Him.

The rich men walk not here on the green sod,
But they have builded towers, the timorous
That still go up to God.

Still will the poor go out with loving words;
In the long need, the need for happiness
The poor can feed the birds.

Beauty Imposes

Beauty imposes reverence in the Spring,
Grave as the urge within the honeybuds,
It wounds us as we sing.

Beauty is joy that stays not overlong.
Clad in the magic of sincerities,
It rides up in a song.

Beauty imposes chastenings on the heart,
Grave as the birds in last solemnities
Assembling to depart.

The Crane is My Neighbour

The bird is my neighbour, a whimsical fellow and dim;
There is in the lake a nobility falling on him.

The bird is a noble, he turns to the sky for a theme,
And the ripples are thoughts coming out to the edge of a dream.

The bird is both ancient and excellent, sober and wise,
But he never could spend all the love that is sent for his eyes.

He bleats no instruction, he is not an arrogant drummer;
His gown is simplicity — blue as the smoke of the summer.

How patient he is as he puts out his wings for the blue!
His eyes are as old as the twilight, and calm as the dew.

The bird is my neighbour, he leaves not a claim for a sigh,
He moves as the guest of the sunlight — he roams in the sky.

The bird is a noble, he turns to the sky for a theme,
And the ripples are thoughts coming out to the edge of a dream.

The Little Militant

Of waterbirds that in my youth I did admire,
Can I forget that crafty little islander
Whose home I did full many a time desire?

So keen was he, he did all day discover
The enemy in every passer-by;
I love that little militant, the plover.

At night he did the world about awaken.
Shrill was his cry; go to the topmost heaven,
His doubt in mankind still remained unshaken.

Always he was both general and lover;
Loud were his falsehoods to the enemy!
I love that little militant, the plover.

SELECT BIBLIOGRAPHY

Heart of Spring, Bookfellow, Sydney, 1919.
Ballad and Lyrical Poems, Bookfellow, Sydney, 1923.
New Poems, Bookfellow, Sydney, 1927.
Collected Poems of John Shaw Neilson, ed. R. H. Croll, Lothian, Melbourne, 1934.
Beauty Imposes: Some Recent Verse, Angus & Robertson, Sydney, 1938.
Unpublished Poems of Shaw Neilson, ed. James Devaney, Angus & Robertson, Sydney, 1947.
The Poems of Shaw Neilson, ed. A. R. Chisholm, Angus & Robertson, Sydney, 1965.
Witnesses of Spring: Unpublished Poems by Shaw Neilson, ed. Judith Wright from material assembled by Ruth Harrison, Angus & Robertson, Sydney, 1970.

Anderson, Hugh, *Shaw Neilson: An Annotated Bibliography and Checklist 1893-1964* (Studies in Australian Bibliography No. 14), Wentworth Press, Sydney, 1964.

Anderson, Hugh, and Blake, L. J., *John Shaw Neilson,* 1972.
Burrows, J. F., 'Shaw Neilson's Originality', *Southerly,* vol. 32, no. 2, 1972.
Devaney, James, *Shaw Neilson,* Angus & Robertson, Sydney, 1944.
———— 'One of the Rare People,' *Makar,* vol. 8, no. 2, 1972 (edited text of taped recollections of Neilson).
Douglas, Dennis, 'The Imagination of John Shaw Neilson', *Australian Literary Studies,* vol. 5, no. 1, 1971.
King, Alec, review of Australian Poets series selection by Judith Wright, *Australian Literary Studies,* vol. 1, no. 4, 1964.
McAuley, James, 'Shaw Neilson's Poetry', *Australian Literary Studies,* vol. 2, no. 4, 1966.
Moore, T. Inglis, *Six Australian Poets,* Robertson & Mullens, Melbourne, 1942.
Oliver, H. J., *Shaw Neilson* (Australian Writers and their Work series), Oxford University Press, Melbourne, 1968.
Wright, Judith, *Preoccupations in Australian Poetry,* Oxford University Press, Melbourne, 1965, 'John Shaw Neilson'. (An earlier version of this essay, 'The Unshielded Eye', was published in *Quadrant,* vol. 3, no. 4, 1959 and reprinted in *Australian Literary Criticism,* ed. Grahame Johnston, Oxford University Press, Melbourne, 1962.)

NOTES

1 The order of the poems in the selection is as chronological as the present state of the evidence permits; 'The Man who Prayed' was written in a notebook of 1906-07, 'The Little Militant' in a notebook of 1936. On the matter of dating I am most grateful for the guidance very generously given me by J. F. Burrows and Ruth Harrison, whose work on the MSS. is providing a firmer basis for Neilson studies.

[2] A. R. Chisholm, *The Poems of Shaw Neilson*, 1965, p. 271.

[3] James Devaney, *Shaw Neilson*, 1944, p. 6. See also J. F. Burrows, 'Shaw Neilson's Originality', *Southerly*, vol. 32, no. 2, 1972. In a letter to J. K. Moir, 3 September 1939 (quoted with other extracts in *Southerly*, vol. 7, no. 1, 1956, p. 36) he says: 'I was always about ten years younger than my actual age. I was about thirty before I got out a decent piece of verse, and most men manage it about twenty'.

[4] A. D. Hope in *Southerly*, vol. 6, no. 4, 1945, reviewing James Devaney's *Shaw Neilson*, found Neilson's verse to be 'mannered and literary' with rhythms 'of epicene delicacy' . . . 'a language as charming, as feminine in its sensibility, as exotically poetical as the pictures of dresses in the *Modes Parisiennes* of the eighteen-nineties' (p. 43). Hope did not, however, regard this artificial style as incompatible with 'natural and direct expression or with simplicity and sincerity of feeling'. The immigrant English critic Charles Higham, reviewing *The Penguin Book of Australian Verse* (1958) in *Quadrant*, vol. 3, no. 1, 1959, found nothing to distinguish Neilson's poems from those of McCrae, McCuaig and Mathew, dismissing them all as 'amiable, nice, but too easy on the eye and spirit to matter at all' (p. 99). But the selection of Neilson's work in that volume was poor.

[5] H. J. Oliver, *Shaw Neilson*, 1968, pp. 3 and 41 (hereinafter cited as Oliver). Judith Wright in *Preoccupations in Australian Poetry*, 1965, p. 111, contrasts the selfconsciousness of Harpur, Kendall and Brennan with the unself-conscious spontaneity of Neilson.

[6] *John Shaw Neilson*, 1972, (hereinafter cited as Anderson and Blake).

[7] *Southerly*, (Shaw Neilson Issue) vol. 17, no. 1, 1956, p. 41.

[8] Introduction to *The Poems of Shaw Neilson*, pp. 12-13. Neilson's self-critical artistry — real and deliberate, even though uncertain and imperfect — is shown in the verses he discarded from this poem, which are reproduced by Chisholm (p. 12) from Devaney in *Unpublished Poems*, 1947.

[9] Letter to J. K. Moir, quoted in Anderson and Blake, p. 209.

[10] The over-exclamatory punctuation is probably due to his editor A. G. Stephens (see Oliver, p. 23).

[11] The origin of this poem is discussed in Anderson and Blake, pp. 161-2, and Oliver, p. 17, on the basis of Neilson's autobiographical MS. (It is a good illustration of how Neilson could start from a suggestion and imaginatively create a situation. It is perilous to try to discern experiences in Neilson's life behind incidents in his poems.)

[12] Letter to Shaw Neilson, 18 May 1926, McKinon Collection MS.; quoted by Oliver, p. 22, and Anderson and Blake, p. 157.

[13] See Chisholm's introduction to *The Poems*, pp. 22-5; James McAuley, *Australian Literary Studies*, vol. 2, no. 4, 1966, p. 249; Annette Stewart, 'A New Light on "The Orange Tree"?' *Australian Literary Studies*, vol. 5, no. 1, 1971, pp. 24-30. The origin of the poem is discussed in Anderson and Blake, pp. 122, 124-5, and in Oliver, p. 10, on the basis of Neilson's autobiographical MS.

[14] James Devaney, *Shaw Neilson*, 1944, pp. 198-9.

[15] A. R. Chisholm, 'Shaw Neilson's Metaphysic', *Southerly*, vol. 17, no. 1, 1956, finds an intuition of a primordial unity behind all multiplicity. Clifford Hanna, 'The Dual Nature of Shaw Neilson's Vision', *Australian Literary Studies*, vol. 5, no. 3, 1972 stresses Neilson's unease and uncertainty about the divine, and the ambivalence of his concept of Love. He relates this to the fusion in Neilson's vision of 'the primitive faith in the natural cycle and Christian belief in the Son of God'.

[16] Mitchell Library MS., quoted by Oliver, p. 40.

4

The Earlier Twentieth Century

INTRODUCTION

In their different ways, Brennan and Neilson stand apart early in the period. The other dominating figure is Slessor, whose best work belongs to the thirties. The rest of the scene contains some curious features needing comment, but very little poetry of distinction. Mary Gilmore is an important lesser poet whose life and writing span a great deal of our history; and one of the latest-born in the period, the difficult poet Bertram Higgins, deserves attention.

At the beginning of the century Victor Daley and Roderic Quinn would probably have been the first names to be mentioned as 'literary' poets. Roderic Quinn's lyrical work was generally set above that of Daley in the critical comment of his period. His two early volumes, *The Hidden Tide* (1899) and *The Circling Hearths* (1901) were joined together in the volume *A Southern Garland* (1904). There is a touch of lyric grace, and occasionally a phrase or an image:

> In streaks and twists of sudden fire
> Among the reeds
> The bream went by, and where they passed
> The bubbles shone like beads.
>
> ('The Fisher')

But in general one must agree with Harold Oliver's opinion that his work is weaker than Daley's.[1]

Daley's *At Dawn and Dusk* (1898) and *Wine and Roses* (published in 1911 after Daley's death in 1905, with a memoir by A. G. Stephens) have a wan charm.[2] Norman Lindsay wrote of him:

> Though I illustrated a great deal of his verse in the *Bulletin,* it was to me only that kind of poetry which is derived from poetry, not life. Good facile verse, and an essential contribution to his period, which was that middle period between the folk-lore balladist, and the arrival of great poetry. That, as Daley's period perished, was arriving with the poetry of Hugh McCrae — with some of the greatest lyrical poetry written in the English language.[3]

Daley's other side is the satirical and topical verse he wrote, some of it published under the pseudonym 'Creeve Roe'.[4] One of Daley's best skits is 'Narcissus and Some Tadpoles', which the victim, A. G. Stephens, published in the *Bookfellow* in 1899.

> I am the Critic set on high,
> The Red Page Rhadamanthus I.

Norman Lindsay's extravagant praise of McCrae, quoted above, is echoed in a more restrained fashion by Kenneth Slessor in his 1954 lectures on Australian poetry.[5] As with Lindsay, the indelible impression in Slessor's mind was that McCrae had brought on the real thing at last:

> it is not until . . . the publication of Hugh McCrae's *Satyrs and Sunlight* (or, as it was originally called, *Silvarum Libri*) in 1909, that poetry can be considered to have begun any consistent growth in Australia (p. 74) . . . *Satyrs and Sunlight* is a book so stuffed with riches, so pierced by the naked flame of poetry through almost every line, that it is difficult to come to an estimate of its total worth by examining it piecemeal (pp. 98-9).

Slessor's references to favorite poems show the sort of thing he rejoiced in as 'projectiles of lusty, leaping, dancing, heel-kicking and completely irrepressible raw poetry' (p. 99). This is from 'I Blow My Pipes':

> I blow my pipes, the glad birds sing,
> The fat young nymphs about me spring,
> The sweaty centaur leaps the trees,
> And bites his dryad's splendid knees . . .

In 'Fantasy' the poet dreams of dryads dancing on his lawn to Pan's fluting, until centaurs come rushing in:

> They seize on the dancing wood-women,
> And kick poor Pan over
> The back of his fat spotted leopard
> Amid the lush clover.

Slessor dwells particularly on the merits of the fragments of
McCrae's unfinished drama, *Joan of Arc,* such as this passage
from la Fol's dream of grandeur:

> The tears you spill, the drops of sweat
> Are jewels for my carcanet,
> Each groan proclaims the near approach
> Of running footmen and a coach.
> Figs barrelled, sucket, and conserves . . .
> Marry, and shall, when weather serves,
> Wind my own horn and carry fair
> Hawks of the tower through the air,
> Ride in long stirrups with stiff legs . . .
> Drink Greek or Spanish, to the dregs;
> And spitting, in gold basins, yerk
> Down carpets of rich Turkey-work.

We see one of the important sources of Slessor's early fantasias
with his delight in 'clusters of exciting and almost physically
palpable images'.[6] Slessor's gratitude to McCrae is such that he
defends the poet quite fiercely against detractors. But alas, the
whimsy, the pastiche, the divertimenti, the macabre, the guignol,
the vaudeville, do not work for everyone, and seem to have
quite faded for the generation that did not know him personally.
Philip Martin, reviewing R. G. Howarth's selection, *The Best
Poems of Hugh McCrae* (1961), speaks for many more recent
judgements:

> One can make Wordsworth look silly by careful selection; but with
> McCrae, all the care has to be used in the other direction. Most of
> the book is mere rhyming, and one is left gasping at the sustained
> lack of control, over imagery, for example (producing the most
> unfortunate association), and even over syntax (with like results);
> at the lack of mere coherent thought, and the imaginative chaos
> ensuing at the utter lack of tact, poetic and every other kind, cease-
> lessly begetting the ludicrous or the offensive, or both. A great
> mistake has been made, and it's to be hoped that the appearance of
> this collected edition will begin to make that clear.[7]

McCrae must be given some prominence from the point of
view of literary history, but whatever gift he had was lost in
dilettantism, an inability or refusal to let his talent engage with
life.[8]

Bernard O'Dowd is another figure that must be given prominence in an historical survey, but is an embarrassment to the
anthologist because he was a clumsy utopian bard, not a poet.[9]
His mind was filled with democracy, socialism, evolution, secular
religiosity, Nietzsche, Whitman. The poet, he decided, must be
the Poet Militant, playing his part in bringing in the millennium

in which 'the Coming Race, Australia' would play the leading role. In his best-known poem, 'Australia', a sonnet which won a prize which the *Bulletin* offered to commemorate the Federation, he hails the continent as

> Last sea-thing dredged by sailor Time from Space

and asks, are you

> A new demesne for Mammon to infest?
> Or lurks millennial Eden 'neath your face?

Elsewhere, in *The Bush,* he is more certain:

> She is Eutopia, she is Hy-Brasil.

Judith Wright has commented on O'Dowd, placing him accurately as representing a certain kind of ideological ferment:

> Clearly, 'Poetry Militant' is, as it were, the expression of nineteenth-century demagogic rationalism in the face of the situation summarized by Nietzsche as 'The death of God'. It was the optimism, the air of accepting the challenge of a universe suddenly become the sole property of man, that roused the enthusiasm of the youthful. But it was an optimism which was merely the obverse of the pessimism which Boake and Gordon had felt in the face of the same mental situation.[10]

If O'Dowd has some importance because he was influential at the time, the poet who called himself William Baylebridge (born William Blocksidge) need not detain us because his bardic prophetism has had virtually no influence, and he possessed if possible even less talent than O'Dowd. Baylebridge's doctrine was a derivation from Nietzsche,[11] developed in a nationalistic way to an antipodean Nazi-like vision of 'the over-running of Earth by Australians, strong, hot-necked, natural men'.[12] Baylebridge also wrote love poems of which R. G. Howarth felt able to say: 'It can be claimed without fear of contradiction that Baylebridge is the supreme Australian poet of love.'[13]

> I worshipped, when my veins were fresh,
> A glorious fabric of this flesh,
> Where all her skill in living lines
> And colour (that its form enshrines)
> Nature had lavished; in that guess
> She had gathered up all loveliness.
>
> .   .   .   .
>
> The shape I had so oft embraced
> Was sealed up, and in earth was placed —
> And yet not so; for hovering free
> Some wraith of it remained with me . . .

The influence of Nietzsche, straight or garbled, is visible at several points in twentieth-century Australian literature. It is prominent in the writings of Norman Lindsay, especially in his main doctrinal essay, *Creative Effort* (1920). Though not a poet, Lindsay influenced a number of poets.[14] He used Nietzschean doctrine to exalt the artist as the higher man who embodies Life while the common herd have mere Existence. He differed from Nietzsche, however, in rejecting the idea that the higher men should assume a political function, to exercise power over the herd: for Lindsay, the higher man becomes degraded by concerning himself with such matters. Lindsay's influence on the development of Australian art was slight — artists have not been much impressed by him; but upon some poets who came under the spell of his personality, Lindsay's vitalist doctrine and his drawings and paintings, with their arrested juvenility of eroticism and bookish fantasy, worked with remarkable effect. In the 1920s Lindsay's influence was extended by his son Jack, who absorbed his father's doctrine, but later, in England, moved on to Communism. Jack Lindsay's editing of the four issues of *Vision* (1923-24) was a significant moment in what is now 'the legend of the twenties'. The magazine was conceived by Jack Lindsay as an organ for the expression of Norman Lindsay's ideas and for work by others consonant in spirit.[15]

The First World War was the event of greatest moment in the period under review, followed by the Great Depression in the 1930s.[16] Neither of these experiences left much durable trace in our poetry. Of the poetry visibly connected with the First World War, a few pieces by Leon Gellert are of some merit, the best of them being 'These Men', though it falters in the conclusion:

> Men moving in a trench, in the clear noon,
> Whetting their steel within the crumbling earth;
> Men moving in a trench 'near a new moon
> That smiles with a slit mouth and has no mirth;
> Men moving in a trench in the grey morn,
> Lifting bodies on their clotted frames;
> Men with narrow mouths thin-carved in scorn
> That twist and fumble strangely at dead names.
>
> These men know life — know death a little more.
> These men see paths and ends, and see
> Beyond some swinging open door
> Into eternity.

Other poets in this period are features on the map, but present problems to the anthologist. Of these the most important is Frank Wilmot, who wrote under the name 'Furnley Maurice'.

His pacifist poem 'To God: From the Warring Nations' attracted
some attention in 1917. He achieved some prominence again in
1934 when his 'Melbourne and Memory' won a poetry competition
at the time of the Melbourne Centenary. This poem was included
in *Melbourne Odes* (1934). Here Wilmot essayed an amiable
semi-modernism; the verse is partly free in form, and there are
patches of everyday detail freshly observed, though the idiom is
uncertain, the diction not consistently free of old habit. Perhaps
his best poem is a longish episodic piece, 'The Agricultural Show,
Flemington'[17] which opens:

> The lumbering tractor rolls its panting round,
> The windmills fan the blue; feet crush the sand;
> The pumps spurt muddy water to the sound,
> The muffled thud and blare of a circus band.

The selections for this period begin with Mary Gilmore. Her
occasional strength lies in truth stated directly in ordinary
language. In a poem called *'Los Heridos'* she wrote:

> I have not written mad things,
> For mad things do not enchant me;
> But I have written the small and simple,
> Lest the mad things haunt me.

The 'small and simple' can have power. An interesting example
lies in a vignette called 'The Vineyard'. No other poet in Australia, not even Slessor, could write so simply and well at the
time — it was published in her volume *Battlefields* (1939) — and
few since could match its rendering of a scene.

> Scented and old was the vineyard, and there, when the vines
> Were in leaf, and the moon rode full in the height,
> If a wandering puff of the wind came running over,
> Like a lifting of fingers the leaves were up-flung,
> And the light rays shot from their tips in spears.
> And always under the vines were the aisles of shadow,
> That darkling reached through the lines of stakes,
> Where, row after row, they stood; while, etched on the clods between,
> The leaves lay patterned in black, and shaped like our human hands,
> Hands that made movement in each little wind as it passed,
> Then clung to the earth, so still, they seemed to be part of it.

Unfortunately Mary Gilmore would not leave well alone, but had
to add the following false note as coda:

> God made a garden, O long long ago;
> Out of the garden came toil;
> But out of the toil came beauty.

Everywhere in Mary Gilmore, one step beyond the truly and immediately experienced brings back the vices of sentimentality, pretension, romantic rhetoric. What matters is that there are true things to be found in her work: simply told situations and thoughts arising directly from experience, with at times a gnomic quality that grips the mind and feelings. Her work is varied, and cannot be adequately shown in limited space. For example, I have omitted a very enjoyable recitation piece, 'The Brucedale Scandal', because it doesn't work so well in print as in a reading aloud. The plangent lyricism of the black swan poems is not represented; nor are the poems interpreting Aboriginal culture and feeling; nor poems with implications of social protest or political attitude, except for the striking brief poem 'Nationality' (p. 92).

From three lesser poets I have selected poems which, even unexpectedly, rise for a moment above the mediocrity and worse of the period. Dorothea Mackellar's 'My Country' has been known to every child, but the sudden flash of sharp feeling in 'Once When She Thought Aloud' has gone almost unnoticed. The poem is not autobiographical: after a disappointment in love, which is recounted by Adrienne Matzenik in her edition of *Poems* (1971), Dorothea Mackellar never married. Though the scholarly L. H. Allen's work was in general graceful but undistinguished, 'The Reaper' (p. 94) is a moment of vision. J. A. R. McKellar[18] died at twenty-eight years of age of pneumonia contracted after a football match: he is different from his Australian contemporaries, and one wishes that one could guess from his surviving work what might have come. Perhaps nothing much more; yet there was a strong critical mind and sense of artistic form, working within the eminent respectabilities of classical scholarship, sporting achievement, and banking. The poem 'Nominis Umbra' does not exhaust its theme, but challenges attention, as poetry and as a meditation on a political theme.

No previous anthology of Australian poetry has included work by Bertram Higgins. A brief outline of his career will help to explain this. He left Melbourne in 1919 to go to Oxford University. His most brilliant period of literary work was as the writer of important critical articles in Edgell Rickword's *The Calendar of Modern Letters* (1925-27)[19] where he also published some poems. He returned to Melbourne in 1930 for three years and took part in the literary activity of that time. In the first of the three issues of *Stream* (edited by Cyril Pearl) he published two poems. The difficulty of one of them, 'The Confrontation', caused him to write an extensive explanation in the second issue, where he also published a new poem 'The Two Angels' which in turn evoked in the third issue a commentary by A. R. Chisholm, written without consultation with the poet but later substantially endorsed by him; from which Chisholm concluded that:

> the exegesis which is worked out below clearly shows that so-called hermetic poetry, so long as it is real poetry and sincere thought, is quite accessible to the careful reader: it is not obscure, but merely difficult.[20]

A glimpse of Higgins and the impression he made at the time is contained in an entry for 26 September 1931 in Nettie Palmer's journal *Fourteen Years* (1948):

> For as a poet Bertram believes in having a strong basis of fact and learning and philosophy (Aquinas and sunspots and spectrum and *The Golden Bough*) but such basis is to remain invisible, implied, never explicit in the actual words of the poem. His readers must dig, dig for their experiences; I heard one admirer say proudly, 'I got that last poem of Bertram's "out" first time.'
>
> This deliberate secrecy (hermetism?) comes as part of the reaction in England against the Georgian poets, the Georgian readers, and their easy hopes that more and more people may read and hear more and more poetry with less and less effort. I can't guess how Bertram would have developed as poet or critic if he had remained in this country. As it is, having spent his years since the age of seventeen in Oxford and London, he dedicated his remarkable powers to a movement akin to that of Valéry's followers in France. This English movement found expression chiefly in the London periodical, *The Calendar of Letters*, in which Bertram assiduously collaborated for its duration, as well as in *Scrutinies*, a subsequent collection of residual essays, searching and critical. The *Calendar* round 1927 undertook the task of revaluing widely accepted reputations, its withering bleak wind and cold light blasting Galsworthy, Arnold Bennett, Masefield, and other too easy victims . . . This habit has led the Scrutineers — led Bertram at any rate to turn his deadly ray on his own fastidious poems of a few years earlier.

Higgins returned briefly to Australia in 1938 and then not again until 1946. From that time till his death in 1974 he remained in Australia but published very little poetry and scarcely re-entered literary life except for the short-lived venture of a literary fortnightly, *The Australian Week-End Review,* which ran from March 1950 to February 1951.[21] Articles on him by A. R. Chisholm and some contributions by himself in *Meanjin* and *Quadrant* aroused little interest. In his last years he revised a selection of his poems which he intended to publish under the title *The Haunted Rendezvous.*

The two poems chosen for the selection are 'The Confrontation', which originally appeared in *Stream* in 1931 and was republished by *Poetry* (Chicago) in 1932, and the shorter companion piece 'The Chance Encounter', dedicated to his brother, and written thirty-five years later, in 1966. These poems are grouped by the title 'Under the Sign of the Fisher'. The Fisher refers in the first instance to St Peter, and these two poems are, like all Higgins's main work, movements of a dialectic in which the poet's assumptions are Christian.

Higgins's work challenges criticism by its difficulty and its refusal of superficially attractive inducements. The place it will finally win will depend on the assessments of its poetic value made when a greater number of readers have learned his idiom and absorbed his meaning. Apart from Chisholm's articles, only one interpretive study has so far been made; this is contained in a thesis by Robert King, the substantial accuracy of which has been endorsed by Higgins.[22]

COMMENTARY

Passages from writings by Gilmore and Higgins

Mary Gilmore

As to verse, I think we are due for a return to the simple and direct. We have had a long period of the inverted, the contorted, and even the pretentious, but in that time we have not improved on any of the older forms of verse, nor, as America has done, have we developed from the hackneyed something fresh, and at times even new. Moreover, Australia has been neglected for the sectional, the individually personal, and the emotional. But this land is not contained in these. Something greater is required. If it is simple, so much to the good, since folk-song, psalm, and balladry are, of all forms of literature, the most lasting. Indeed it is perhaps in these that nationality is most truly expressed; and it may be that publishers have ceased to foster verse, and readers to buy it, because the simple and direct have not been written, at least sufficiently by those whose writing is the most worthwhile. Here I except Hugh McCrae and now, in 1948, some of the younger ones.

Extract from a note on 'The Ringer',
Selected Verse, 1948, pp. 289-90

Bertram Higgins

[Commentary on 'The Confrontation']: The 'Voice' in the poem is, of course, Conscience — or whatever psychological term may be thought fit to describe what is indicated by that word . . . it is Conscience, personified, that is suffering from Man, rather than this man from conscience . . . In effect, the theme of the poem, and the object of its emotional basis, is the tragic destiny of the voice itself . . . Now, as to the status of the other being in the poem, the man addressed by the Voice throughout . . . he is not given the opportunity to speak and defend himself, and consequently we only know him at a remove, through the representatives of the Voice . . . Its [the Voice's] destiny is tragic because, although it is absolute in truth and will, in power it is limited — in fact, doomed to frustration, because the material it works on, Mankind, allows, no more than does a wave of the sea, the possibility of a constant form in which a final principle could be manifested (Stanza 12, line 1). These two elements in Man's nature are as irreconcilable as Night and Day appear to be, to the sense; Night finds him amenable to the Voice, which, like a moon-glint, may ride by the wave of his spirit only until dawn (Stanza 12, lines 2-4), when the other order reasserts itself — the order of the Day, in which the values that the Voice stands for (and which are subscribed to by Man himself during its short reign) are regularly eclipsed (Stanza 13), or even, by a horrible process natural to that order, assimilated into the movements of its brutalities and automatisms (Stanza 14). This is the tragedy of the Voice: unimpaired energies, but a reduced function (Stanzas 10 and 11); tied to Matter, powerless to direct it continuously, often enslaved by it (Stanza 8, lines 3-4).

In this vision of its intolerable humiliations the Voice has a moment of despair and rebellion against God Himself . . . And one can readily see how an attitude like the Voice's could easily resolve itself into an attack on the very nature of life — the very Yeast and Flourish of things! However, the Voice does not appear to be an 'irreconcilable' of this kind. As the context shows, the 'automatic' incidents in human behaviour are those that it finds most detestable. And in the last stanza — where the imagery, as it applies to the particular case of the listener, is singularly vehement — another strain of feeling, which culminates in the final image, discloses the Voice's sympathy with the human aspiration towards happiness, and its horror at the murder of Joy.

Stream, vol. 1, no. 2, 1931, pp. 14-17

G

Passages from the writings of other authors

  On Mary Gilmore

I find as I go on reading them that my respect for them grows
and my objections diminish. It is partly a matter of getting used
to the idiom, and so sliding over the occasional infelicities of
language. As with Thomas Hardy, the awkwardnesses of expression can become almost endearing, and perhaps it is for the
same reason. They are the evidence of unsophisticated honesty.
Both are provincial writers: Hardy climbed out of the rural
lower middle class in nineteenth-century England, and Mary
Gilmore was born to a Gaelic-speaking Scots father in the early
days of settlement around Wagga, only a generation later. For
neither was an education conducive to literary sophistication
possible. Literary fashions were not available to them, nor an
environment where there was frequent, easy and informed
discussion of books. They had to find out for themselves by hard
labour, trial and error, what in other circumstances might have
been learned with ease. That Mary Gilmore was herself acutely
aware of this, and of the loss of talent under the hard demands
of circumstance, appears from the chapter 'The Bent Twig' in
Hound of the Road. She cites many examples of talents denied
or wasted by circumstance.

> I knew a boy in Victoria. He could tell you when the first tiger-orchid
> came out, miles away from his home, and the kind of grass that
> showed its most likely place of growth. He discovered the first white
> boronia in his district, and knew the cry and call of every wandering
> bird. But he had no name for the flowers, and no classification for
> the birds. He had dumb knowledge, depending on the pointing of a
> finger or the production of a plant, and but dumb thoughts, because
> none had come to give him language . . .
> A naturalist? . . . At eighteen he was shearing. At twenty-three he was
> dead on the fields of France. (pp. 32, 34).

And in conclusion,

> There is no real exchange in these things. There is only the terrible
> loss of the subverted and the destroyed, and the cruelty of waste
> unhallowed by any compensating return of values. (p. 37).

It need not be doubted, I think, that she felt this acutely in her
own person: 'The oven has baked many a woman's song to hard
crusts'. Her very late arrival at the peak of her ability as a writer
is evidence of the same kind, along with her being taken in by
the false-heroic of Henley and the bogus-romantic of Frankau.
Although she has very fine lyric or meditative poems — 'The

Whinnying Mare of Bronte' for example — even in these there are a few uneasy locutions or halting rhythms. Her stated preference for the ballad and the hymn perhaps reflects in part her own long acquaintance with, and consequent ease in, those popular forms.

F. H. Mares, 'Dame Mary Gilmore', *Southerly*, vol. 25, no. 4, 1965, pp. 240-1

On Hugh McCrae

Those who think, incidentally, that McCrae picked up his outlook from Norman Lindsay, or that he and Lindsay worked out together some conspiracy to import the nymph, the satyr and the faun into our sacred groves of gumtrees, are mistaken. It was because McCrae, quite independently, was writing poems similar in outlook to Lindsay's early pen-drawings that they first came together in Melbourne. Though his subsequent friendship with Lindsay may well have confirmed him in his bent, the origin of McCrae's poetry is, generally, the spirit of the 'Nineties in the form in which it filtered through to Australia; specifically, the French Parnassians whose influence is stated clearly in Lionel Lindsay's translations of Hérédia... It was a kind of Renaissance. The movement was not, as it has often been described, a conscious reaction against the naturalistic Australian school represented in the bush ballads — McCrae himself wrote at least one bush ballad, which was printed in the *Bulletin;* Norman Lindsay illustrated Paterson as well as McCrae — but simply a parallel movement of the period.

Douglas Stewart, 'An Introduction to McCrae', *Southerly*, vol. 22, no. 1 ,1962, pp. 2-3

On Bertram Higgins

I had read 'The Confrontation' in manuscript, and had been deeply impressed by it. It is curious to think that in those days it needed an explanation in a later issue. For I am sure that nowadays there is nothing very puzzling about it, though its idiom is highly condensed and its imagery, like that of the French Symbolists, is more suggestive than descriptive.

On reading it, I felt immediately that we had here a poet who had grasped the importance of the 'explosive' phrase, of the tightly packed image that expands in the mind of the reader — a method of communication whereby the periphery of a poet's thought illuminates without 'explanation' or definition, its inner, incommensurable vitality.

I select an illustration from the 1931 text, which has since undergone several alterations, and to which the poet recently added a sequel. The 'subject' of the poem is Conscience, kept under by a guilty man's diurnal well-being; a voice that at moments comes up from the silent and seemingly tranquil depths of his mind ... The sense of guilt is packed into the short phrase 'an ancient hull', a hull which Conscience, like a river-lock, lifts to the level of the present. And the single word 'heart' reveals what the hull is, and what the lock: the 'flood' is the healthy bloodstream that helps a man to live at peace with his crime; but like a lock, the heart, the seat of Conscience, quietly discolours it with the still unabolished sediment of the past.

Such tightly-packed imagery, beautiful though it is, can become poetic habit, and therefore be over-used; and I frankly think that Bertram Higgins sometimes yields to this temptation, so that his poetry, here and there, becomes too esoteric ... However, I hesitate to condemn these esoteric methods, for several reasons. The first is that for many years I thought some of Mallarmé's sonnets were undecipherable, and then discovered that the fault was mine, not Mallarmé's — he had shot too far ahead of me. And I don't want to fall into that kind of trap again.

The second reason involves a question of communication. The social mind can express itself easily — any blatant extrovert demonstrates that *ad nauseam*. But the deeper mind is not social, and yet it has, in order to express itself, to fall back upon language, a social medium and consequently an inadequate one for such a purpose. In what results, there is necessarily an esoteric element, which I condemn only when it consists of private imagery; when the poet uses, as it were, a personal code and keeps his code-book locked away. And I have elucidated for myself a sufficient proportion of Bertram Higgins's work to know that he has no code-book; that he is honestly trying to solve a linguistic problem in order to express genuine but difficult thought.

My third reason is that Bertram Higgins, following (perhaps unconsciously) the classical method, reaches the universal through the particular. When he speaks of a man, he is thinking also of Man, and justifiably makes the reader find a stairway for himself between these two conceptual levels.

A. R. Chisholm, 'The Poetry of Bertram Higgins',
Quadrant, vol. 11, no. 4, 1967, pp. 90-1

MARY GILMORE

Nurse No Long Grief

Oh, could we weep,
And weeping bring relief!
But life asks more than tears
And falling leaf.

Though year by year
Tears fall and leaves are shed,
Spring bids new sap arise,
And blood run red.

Nurse no long grief,
Lest the heart flower no more;
Grief builds no barns; its plough
Rusts at the door.

Penelope

Twice I waked in the night,
　Feeling if you were there —
Softly touched your cheek,
　Softly kissed your hair;
Then turned to sleep again,
　Lying against your arm,
Just as a child might do,
　Fearing nor hurt, nor harm.

No fastened windows, now,
　No bolting down the door,
Shaking at every sound
　Of creaking chair and floor;
No watchful, wistful sleep,
　Anxious, ever on guard,
Waked if only a dog
　Moved in a neighbour's yard!

No start at a rattling blind,
　No holding back the breath,
Fearful of some menace
　Crueller far than death!

All of it gone! and why?
   Somebody's home at last!
. . . Strange how real the fear;
   Stranger still that it passed.

Out on the Hillside

Summer will come with its warm, clear light,
   And the long grasses wave;
But O, may the rain fall soft tonight
   On that little last grave.

Nay! He is wrapped and warm in his nest,
   He would not hear the rain;
It is only I would know no rest,
   If it beat on the pane.

But, rain, if thou fall, O softly fall,
   Wet not too soon the mould,
Lest I should listen to hear him call,
   Crying out in the cold.

The Tenancy

I shall go as my father went,
A thousand plans in his mind,
With something still held unspent,
When death let fall the blind.

I shall go as my mother went,
The ink still wet on the line;
I shall pay no rust as rent,
For the house that is mine.

Nationality

I have grown past hate and bitterness,
I see the world as one;
But though I can no longer hate,
My son is still my son.

All men at God's round table sit,
And all men must be fed;
But this loaf in my hand,
This loaf is my son's bread.

HUGH McCRAE

Leaf out of a Rhyming Diary

Somebody under my window
    Is digging an April bed
For stocks and sweet anemones,
    Pink, yellow, and white and red.

And in at the open casement
    A shower of loam-dust floats,
Which mottles the sheet I write on,
    My books and my hundred notes.

And I leave off work to wonder
    At seeing a wild wasp bring
Buff-coloured clay to build with
    A home for its brood in Spring.

And up in the furthest corner
    The locust I found last year
(The ants had eaten him hollow)
    Clings tight to a Queensland spear.

Bees have made hives in a lion,
    At least, so the Good Book saith . . .
Spiders have built in the skulls of
    Kings in the bosom of Death:

But I can tell of the locust
    (Drawing-room, dining, and bed)
Transformed to the country mansion
    Of Vespa, the newly wed.

Vespa's a wasp in the Latin;
    Vespa, the beautiful thing
But (Vespa or Wasp) it cannot
    Change her immutable sting.

Someone is digging the garden,
    And in at the window floats
A shower of dust all over
    My books and my hundred notes.

L. H. ALLEN

The Reaper

Under the dying sun
And the moon's frail shell,
The fields are clear as glass:
I love them well.

A horse's amber flanks
Shine in the grain.
The wheel of the reaper cleaves
A yellow lane.

The reaper is ruddy gold,
Unearthly bright,
Driving an amber cloud,
Touched with its light.

They say the earth's a stone
Wrinkled and old,
Yet she has steeds of fire
And men of gold!

DOROTHEA MACKELLAR

Once When She Thought Aloud

I've had all of the apple, she said,
Except the core.
All that many a woman desires —
All and more.
Children, husband, and comfort enough
And a little over.
Hungry Alice and Bitter Anne
Say I'm in clover.

I've had all of the apple, she said.
— All that's good.
Whiles I feel I'd throw it away,
The wholesome food,
Crisp sweet flesh snowy-cool, and skin
Painted bright —
To have a man that I couldn't bear
Out of my sight.

J. A. R. McKELLAR

Nominis Umbra

Caesar is dead, and cannot see the sun.
When it is dark, my lord, no more can I,
But Caesar's march on earth is not yet done,
The sun not gone for ever from the sky.

Children at books that stumble on his name,
The new barbarians entering into Gaul,
Receive the long transmission of his fame,
And feel the chains of his ambition fall

Upon them, and are bound as Rome was bound
To one who smiles, thin-lipped, beyond the Law —
Strike at him, stab him, bleeding to the ground,
And tremble in your shoes. For Caesar saw.

Who talks of stabbing Caesar? It is done —
Let it be so, my lord. 'Tis done too late,
For Caesar's eagle flies before the sun,
And shadows all our Commonwealth, our State.

For slaves and merchants, citizens and lords,
The governed and the governors, aspire
To arts of war, go beating into swords
Their ploughshares, for a single man's desire.

Is there a soldier for the working day
Recites his cause, and knows his quarrel just,
Except that he's for England, and his pay
Is fifteenpence, so fights because he must?

Take then this England, split it into parts,
King, Clergy, Lords, the Commons, and the rest —
Somewhere among that thousand thousand hearts
The heart that might be Caesar's burns its breast.

The voice that might be Caesar's speaks his will
With honey tongue, with golden, or of brass.
The air of council is a moment still —
The rest resign, the rods to Caesar pass.

BERTRAM HIGGINS

Under the Sign of the Fisher
(i) The Confrontation

Under the lintel at midnight
A Voice was coiled. Whirring and warm,
Darting a rootless tongue of light.
Like the puff of sand that starts a storm

It turned the drift of the cool dews;
Rearing in the heart's deep lull,
'Once more the lock shall lift,' it whispered,
Flush with the flood, an ancient hull.

'Outside, the tips of trees dilate
 (Open your senses and lean down)
And seeds stir like a next estate —
Insurgence in a scene of brown!

'Here where the bald boughs, lunging, clear
The air for unborn green;
Under those locking antlers, here
Where the sap discards its screen,

'The forest tingling with its heirs
Knows, at the last anointing, small
Festivals in its scars commingling
With the huge innocence of that Fall.

'Since your compunction seeks a sign
And one pure sigh demands its mood,
Mild theorist of the condign —
Whose million smiles should salve the deed

'If, lighting on the abandoned suture,
Arachnid of the rankling edges,
Incorrigible Hope bind past and future
With a dissolving gut of pledges?

'Do you think to, by not harming,
Attach me? Am I of female nature?
Bond of your deasil* arm
My homeland's the discarded date.

* 'It is a Celtic word meaning "clockwise: in the direction of the sun".'
(Note by Higgins, *Stream*, vol. 1, no. 2, 1931, p. 147.)

'I am the Sun-spot whose charred roses
Leaven his prime — I am that Juno
Fostering for war on the low clime
The cretins of the Noon!

'Before the fire and flood, before
The smoking flax, the rain of tongues,
Before the ichor on the axe,
Sole redeemer, had sprung.

'Before the Manichee — entire,
Total I burned! as the light
Exiled inwards, in whom
The glimmer vests, after the fire.

'To climb, to crest the incessant soul!
Throned! but a throne that reels towards dawn,
Collapsing on the crystal mole
Where the bled crescent dips its horn.

'O Moon, how long? Your reflex power
Abides the smothering glass
As eternally from the dark tower
I see the murdered princes pass

'Through the crass veins of their seducers,
Jerked metabolically, bandied
Where the diurnal well-being sluices
From the fermenting crimes of Man!

'. . . Waif of the storm-encrusted villa,
The infra-red commands the door!
Crawl, clutch at the sill,
Lift up your roots against the floor!

'The heart was calm, the last word said.
An octave higher than the ears
My voice still plucks the conquering head,
The head trepanned by fiery fears.

'For I felt all, the fang, the lash,
And heard the stifled shout and saw
The filament behind the flash
Blackening as the smile blew out.'

(ii) The Chance Encounter
(To Geoff)

With less delay than an insect hovering,
Then sheering off from an indurated skin,
With a message more like a memory, so soon
The sibilance that silked the traffic's din
Said its day within the chimes of noon.

'Well met, by chance. A junior case is waiting.
I must be with him while the illusion still
Protracts the crisis of his own creating
Known as such only to his crystal will.

'In the rolls that already are being prepared
Your name has moved to the margin. Your dossier
That in the first few years was sometimes aired
Is now almost inaccessibly filed away.

'Was it for this I plagued the Dominations,
Importuned Principalities and Powers?
A belly of wind subsumed the brash orations;
The impotent missives fall to earth in showers.

'In grey groves, as in abattoirs, the felling
Proceeds. Surprisingly, perhaps too late,
A few shoots point or buds protest their swelling.
I shall be with you on the darkling date.'

SELECT BIBLIOGRAPHY

MARY GILMORE

Marri'd, G. Robertson, Melbourne, 1910.
The Passionate Heart, Angus & Robertson, Sydney, 1918.
The Tilted Cart, Worker, Sydney, 1925.
The Wild Swan, Robertson & Mullens, Melbourne, 1930.
The Rue Tree, Robertson & Mullens, Melbourne, 1931.
Under the Wilgas, Robertson & Mullens, Melbourne, 1932.
Battlefields, Angus & Robertson, Sydney, 1939.
The Disinherited, Robertson & Mullens, Melbourne, 1941.
Pro Patria Australia, W. H. Honey, Sydney, 1945.

Selected Verse, Angus & Robertson, Sydney, 1948; enlarged edition 1969.

Fourteen Men, Angus & Robertson, Sydney, 1954.

Selected Poems (Australian Poets series), Angus & Robertson, Sydney, 1963.

Lawson, Sylvia, *Mary Gilmore* (Great Australians series), Oxford University Press, Melbourne, 1966.

Wilde, W. H., *Three Radicals* (Australian Writers and their Work series), Oxford University Press, Melbourne, 1969.

Mares, F. H., 'Dame Mary Gilmore', *Southerly,* vol. 25, no. 4, 1965.

Cusack, D.; Moore, R. I.; Ovenden, B.; *Mary Gilmore: A Tribute,* with a bibliography by Walter Stone, 1965.

HUGH McCRAE

Satyrs and Sunlight: Silvarum Libri, John Sands, Sydney, 1909.

Colombine, Art in Australia, Sydney, 1920.

Idyllia, Norman Lindsay Press, Sydney, 1922.

The Mimshi Maiden, Angus & Robertson, Sydney, 1938.

Poems, Angus & Robertson, Sydney, 1939.

Forests of Pan, sel. R. G. Howarth, Meanjin, Brisbane, 1944.

The Best Poems, ed. R. G. Howarth, 1961.

Selected Poems (Australian Poets series), Angus & Robertson, Sydney, 1966.

'Hugh' McCrae Number', *Southerly,* vol. 17, no. 3, 1956. (Contains articles by D. N. Burgess, R. G. Howarth, Norman Lindsay, Lionel Lindsay, Kenneth Slessor, Douglas Stewart.)

Moore, T. Inglis, 'Hugh McCrae' in *Six Australian Poets,* Robertson & Mullens, Melbourne, 1942.

Stewart, Douglas, 'An Introduction to McCrae: For a Proposed *Selected Poems',* *Southerly,* vol. 22, no. 1, 1962.

Wright, Judith, 'The Affirmation of Hugh McCrae', in *Preoccupations in Australian Poetry,* Oxford University Press, Melbourne, 1965.

DOROTHEA MACKELLAR

The Witch Maid, Dent, London, 1914.

Poems, with a Memoir by Adrienne Matzenik, Rigby, Adelaide, 1971.

L. H. ALLEN

Gods and Wood Things, Angus & Robertson, Sydney, 1913.

Phaedra, Macdonald, London, 1921.

Araby, Dymock's, Sydney, 1924.

Patria, Melbourne University Press, Melbourne, 1941.

J. A. R. McKELLAR

Twenty-Six, Frank Johnson, Sydney, 1932.

Collected Poems, Angus & Robertson, Sydney, 1946.

BERTRAM HIGGINS

Commentary on 'The Confrontation', *Stream,* vol. 1, no. 2, 1931.

Chisholm, A. R., 'The Poetry of Bertram Higgins', *Quadrant*, vol. 11, no. 4, 1967.

—'Notes on Bertram Higgins' "Under the Sign of the Fisher" ', *Meanjin Quarterly*, vol. 30, no. 1, 1971.

NOTES

1 Harold Oliver, 'Victor Daley and Roderic Quinn', *Meanjin*, vol. 10, no. 1, 1951.

2 See also the selection and Introduction by H. J. Oliver in the Australian Poets series (1963).

3 *Bohemians of the Bulletin*, 1965, pp. 46-7.

4 A collection edited by Muir Holburn and Marjorie Pizer, with a Foreword by E. J. Brady, *Creeve Roe: Poetry by Victor Daley*, was published in 1947.

5 *Bread and Wine*, 1970.

6 *ibid.*, pp. 107-8.

7 *Quadrant*, vol. 6, no. 2, 1962, p. 93.

8 R. D. FitzGerald in his Foreword to *The Letters of Hugh McCrae* (1970) remarks on the change from a plain to a florid style in handwriting that occurred around 1927, and relates it to a change in attitude — quoting Lindsay's assessment that 'after the failure to complete the *Orleans and Isabella* narrative poem he threw aside any effort to take poetry, himself, or anyone else seriously. He defended himself against the stress of life by making a joke of it' (p. xiv).

9 See the selection and Introduction by A. A. Phillips in the Australian Poets series (1963); and the discussion of O'Dowd by W. H. Wilde, *Three Radicals* (Australian Writers and their Work series, 1969), by Hugh Anderson, *The Poet Militant: Bernard O'Dowd* (1969), and by Victor Kennedy and Nettie Palmer, *Bernard O'Dowd* (1954).

10 *Preoccupations in Australian Poetry*, 1965, p. 75. In the O'Dowd number of *Southerly*, vol. 14, no. 2, 1953, R. G. Howarth says: 'All O'Dowd's curious intellectual-emotional idiom belongs to the past, when a poet, following the example of Blake and Shelley, and even of the black-caped Tennyson, could still regard himself as a prophet' (p. 85). Slessor makes fun of O'Dowd in reference to 'the heavy sententious by Ishmael Dare, S. Elliott Napier, or Bernard O'Dowd' (*op. cit.*, p. 99). Vincent Buckley says: 'poetically he was a reactionary, an arthritic yet ambitious Shelley' (*Essays In Poetry*, 1957, p. 11). S. E. Lee, in *Southerly*, vol. 18, no. 4, 1957, rejecting Buckley's view, says that O'Dowd improves on acquaintance, emerging as 'one who probably deserved the high praise lavished on him by such critics as Tom Inglis Moore, Walter Murdoch and Brian Elliott' (p. 227).

11 Also from Shaw who drew upon Nietzsche. In any case, Baylebridge assimilated only part of Nietzsche's doctrine. These qualifications are carefully made in an article by N. L. Macainsh, 'Baylebridge, Nietzsche, Shaw: Some Observations on the New Nationalism', *Australian Literary Studies*, vol. 7, no. 2, 1975.

12 This phrase is quoted by F. T. Macartney in his *Australian Literary Essays* (1957), p. 96, from the first version of a poem in *National Notes*. When Baylebridge reprinted *National Notes* in *This Vital Flesh* (1939) he toned the phrase down.

[13] *Southerly*, William Baylebridge number, vol. 16, no. 3, 1955, p. 127.

[14] John Docker, 'Norman Lindsay's *Creative Effort*: Manifesto for an Urban Intelligentsia', *Australian Literary Studies*, vol. 6, no. 1, 1973, attacks the tendency to minimize Lindsay's influence on McCrae, Slessor, FitzGerald, and gives a useful list of references. Douglas Stewart has written that 'it is beyond question that the majority of Australian writers — and especially the poets — have accepted him from the beginning not only as an artist but as the fountainhead of Australian culture in our time' (*The Flesh and the Spirit*, 1948, p. 275). Slessor makes a list of poets influenced profoundly or slightly, directly or indirectly: Hugh McCrae, Rupert Atkinson, Leon Gellert, Jack Lindsay, Robert D. FitzGerald, Ronald McCuaig, Kenneth Mackenzie, Douglas Stewart, Francis Webb (*Bread and Wine*, 1970, p. 111). Influence does not, of course, mean that all these poets adopted the full range of Lindsay's ideas. Most of those named (but certainly not Webb) shared a vitalist attitude, toned differently by temperament.

[15] Jack Lindsay gave his version of the enterprise in *The Roaring Twenties* (1960), and in an article, 'Vision of the Twenties', *Southerly*, vol. 13, no. 2, 1952, where he says: 'We believed fiercely in an Australian Renascence, and considered that the clue to world-culture now lay in Australia; yet we denounced nationalist art as a betrayal of the great tradition' (p. 67). He commented slightingly on Slessor's later development. Slessor was stung to a reply in which he denied having shared in Jack Lindsay's views, saying that, in using the pronoun 'we', 'Mr. Lindsay is making use of the prerogative generally reserved for crowned heads, editors, and people suffering from tapeworm' (*Southerly*, vol. 13, no. 4, 1952, p. 217).

[16] See J. T. Laird, *Other Banners, an Anthology of Australian Literature of the First World War* (1971); and also Laird's essay, 'Australian Poetry of the First World War: a Survey', *Australian Literary Studies*, vol. 4, no. 3, 1970.

[17] Wilmot's work, together with that of Mary Gilmore and O'Dowd, is discussed in the monograph by W. H. Wilde already cited, and in monographs by Vance Palmer, *Frank Wilmot* (1942), a booklet published by the Frank Wilmot Memorial Committee (reprinted in *The Writer in Australia*, ed. John Barnes 1969); and by Frederick T. Macartney, *Furnley Maurice (Frank Wilmot)*, (1955).

[18] See Geoffrey Lehmann's poem, 'For J. A. R. McKellar' (p. 322).

[19] The 'Scrutiny' articles in this journal, some of which were written by Higgins, were an important influence on the English critic F. R. Leavis. In a journal entry for 5 April 1936 Nettie Palmer records a visit to the Leavis household during which Leavis expressed his admiration for and indebtedness to Higgins's contributions to the 'Scrutiny' series and spoke of him as 'a wonderfully sound and shrewd critic' (*Fourteen Years*, 1948, p. 206). It was at Leavis's suggestion that the 'Scrutiny' series was republished separately.

[20] *Stream*, vol. 1, no. 3, p. 43.

[21] *Southerly*, vol. 12, no. 4, 1951, announced the demise of *The Weekend Review* in the following austere terms: 'The idea behind it — to assess current publications for the benefit of readers — was good, but unfortunately the tone suffered from bias and even spleen. Little trouble was taken to understand and to evaluate fairly extra-Melbourne publications. The paper's demise, therefore, cannot be greatly regretted' (p. 239).

[22] Letter to Robert King, 7 January 1972 (quoted by permission): 'I think your thesis is extraordinarily perceptive, and in exegesis almost impeccable'. This thesis was presented for the M.A. degree in Monash University.

5

Kenneth Slessor

INTRODUCTION

Appreciation of Slessor's poetry has remained remarkably constant. There has been a normal range of critical difference about its merits, but the durability of the best pieces seems assured. The garnered output is small, but it is densely worked. Not only do the good poems renew their pleasures and disclose new features on re-reading, but also the poems of lower or mixed quality offer various kinds of interest.

In one way, the reason for the success is obvious. Slessor had exceptional poetic powers: a gift for handling words, for creating bright, clear, startling images, varied and exciting sensuous textures, rhythms and cadences well-timed and tuned. Yet in another way the case is mysterious. A good deal goes on in the poems which is not wholly explicit. And there is some discontinuity between the brilliant virtuoso surface effects and the dark sentiment that lurks below them and appears more distinctly from time to time: the pain, the harshness, a subdued stridency of rage and desperation. It is a poetry that has much to do with blankness, frustration, bafflement, yet is busy with the diversions and affections life requires.

Slessor fell silent after publishing *Five Bells* in 1939. In 1944 he published *One Hundred Poems* as the selected body of work he wished to preserve. Two war poems, 'An Inscription for Dog River' and 'Beach Burial' (p. 120), and an inferior divertimento, 'Polarities', were added to the canon when in 1957 the volume was re-named *Poems* on its fourth re-printing.

In the early poems Slessor's talents are mainly in the service of exotic fantasies with scenic properties drawn from books and pictures. 'Nuremberg' (p. 114) is the finest of these; the poetic artisanship evident in the handling of the poem has as its thematic equivalent the image of Dürer at work on his engravings, in a town which is itself a work of art. Some of the early poems make a flourish of erotic sensuality, which is actually, as Charles Higham has noted, superficial and frigid;[1] others indulge in a roistering bravura which is purely verbal, as in the Elizabethan pastiche in 'Thieves Kitchen':

> Good roaring pistol boys, brave lads of gold,
> Good roistering easy maids, blown cock-a-hoop
> On floods of tavern steam, I greet you!

These poems are set in the 'mapless country of the mind',[2] in Cuckooz Contrey, whether the décor be Oriental, or Renaissance, or eighteenth-century Rococo. In several early poems the significantly recurring image first appears of the watcher at the window-pane. In 'Earth-Visitors', dedicated to Norman Lindsay, the gods descend as exotic strangers to feast at an inn: the common folk peer in at them through the windows:

> Men, staring outside
> Past watery glass, thick panes, could watch them eat,
> Dyed with gold vapours in the candleflame,
> Clapping their gloves, and stuck with crusted stones,
> Their garments foreign, their talk a strange tongue,
> But sweet as pineapple — it was Archdukes, they must be.

In 'The Ghost', the watcher is the ghost vainly looking in upon the feast of life. In 'Winter Dawn' it is the poet looking out at the city at dawn, wishing he could be wakened into real life. In 'The Night-Ride' (p. 114) it is the passenger peering out half-awake at the activity on the railway station. In the final lyric of the sequence 'Music' there is a somewhat obscure image, in the mode of de la Mare, in which music is a spiritual presence at the window able to wake the sleeper (if he dares be woken) from everyday life into a different kind of existence:

> Look up! Thou hast a shining Guest
> Whose body in the dews hath lain,
> His face like a strange wafer pressed
> Secret and starry at thy pane . . .

Captain Dobbin looks out at the harbour from his retirement; and also, peering at maps through a reading glass, brings into view the vanished life of the seas. In 'Five Bells' the poet stands at the window looking out on the harbour which is, symbolically, both past and present, life and death; and the dead man Joe is momentarily imagined as trying vainly to communicate with the living, as through a port-hole in our space-time ship.

H

The early poems that survived Slessor's critical scrutiny may leave the impression that at the beginning of his career he was little concerned with direct observation of Australian scenes. 'Pan at Lane Cove' gives a local setting only to fill it with dancing gods and centaurs evoked by the music of the stone flute and pan-pipes played by the statue of a faun in the garden of an old colonial house. 'Winter Dawn' is a first attempt at a vision of Sydney. 'Mangroves' has local reference to 'black bush-waters' but is otherwise smothered in literary images. Yet if one looks at the poems Slessor discarded, it becomes evident that Slessor was from the start trying to deal with directly observed Australian scenes as well as with exotic fantasias: this was not a new development of his later period. But the early poems with a local basis were not very successful. One reason for this was that the poet felt the need to infuse into them romantic exotic effects which did not easily combine with his genuine observation.[3]

Throughout his work Slessor has viewed poetry as essentially made out of images. This tendency was reinforced by Norman Lindsay's demand that art should give 'the image of actual experience' (however difficult it may be to find that in Lindsay's own work). Slessor acknowledged the importance for him of Lindsay's influence in this respect: 'Lindsay's doctrine insists on the concrete image, and it is not without significance that most of the Australian poets whom he may be considered to have influenced show the same abhorrence of abstraction'.[4]

Already in some of the early poetry emerges the theme of the individual isolated and lost in a menacing or meaningless cosmic darkness, as in 'Stars':

> But I was beating off the stars, gazing, not rhyming.
>   I saw the bottomless black cups of space
> Between their clusters, and the planets climbing
>   Dizzily in sick airs, and desired to hide my face.
> But I could not escape those tunnels of nothingness,
>   The cracks in the spinning Cross, nor hold my brain
> From rushing for ever down that terrible lane,
>   Infinity's trap-door, eternal and merciless.

The later work has moments of exhilarating pleasure and entertainment. In the sequence 'Music', the poem (section V) connected with Stravinsky's *Petroushka* is one such divertimento:

> In and out the countryfolk, the carriages and carnival,
>   Pastry-cooks in all directions push to barter their confections,
> Trays of little gilded cakes, caramels in painted flakes,
>   Marzipan of various makes and macaroons of all complexions,

Riding on a tide of country faces.
Up and down the smoke and crying,
Girls with apple-eyes are flying,
Country boys in costly braces
Run with red, pneumatic faces;
Trumpets gleam, whistles scream
Organs cough their coloured steam out . . .

But in that sequence there are other moods, including section IV with its strange, listless, desolate vision of the empty outback with the drying river.

In the other large sequence, 'The Old Play', the themes of anguish and sardonic disillusionment are sounded urgently through the highly manneristic performance. There is (section VIII) an ironical biography (autobiography?) of a quixotic hero who never manages to engage with the enemy:

This is really a Complete Life and Works,
The memorial of a great man
Who was born with Excalibur in his fist
And finished by asking questions.

.   .   .

So he began to use Excalibur in the kitchen,
Or on occasion as a hay-rake.

.   .   .

However he managed to live very tolerably,
And now, in a substantial villa,
Having saved enough to purchase an annuity,
Is piously glad he never found anyone.

The sense of a lost buried self, of pain and despair, is nakedly expressed in the adjoining lyric 'A bird sang in the jaws of night' (section IX), where the pressure of feeling threatens the poem with incoherence. In one of the later poems presenting Australian scenes, 'Crow Country', the dry desolation becomes a country of the mind:

Over the huge abraded rind,
Crow-countries graped with dung, we go,
Past gullies that no longer flow
And wells that nobody can find,
Lashed by the screaming of the crow,
Stabbed by the needles of the mind.

'Gulliver' presents an allegory of the individual tied down in a humiliating actuality:

Hair over hair, I pick my cables loose,
But still the ridiculous manacles confine me.
I snap them, swollen with sobbing. What's the use?
One hair I break, ten thousand hairs entwine me.
Love, hunger, drunkenness, neuralgia, debt . . .

Slessor's fine tribute, 'To the Poetry of Hugh McCrae', has a stanza in parenthesis, with a phrasing reminiscent of T. S. Eliot, expressing his own sense of man baffled in time:

> (Look in this harsher glass, and I will show you
> The daylight after the darkness, and the morning
> After the midnight, and after the night the day
> After the year after, terribly returning.)

One of Slessor's finest poems, 'Cock-Crow' (p. 116), though marred, again perhaps through pressure of feeling, with what seems a slight incoherence,[5] eerily presents loss and grief and hopeless bafflement. Such poems as these lead towards 'Five Bells', which on a larger scale rehearses the same themes.

In 'Five Bells', the poet begins, however, by referring to another feature of his art which we have not yet considered, his interest in the presentation of characters. At the outset of 'Five Bells' he undertakes to re-create Joe, to re-live his life by a process of poetic resurrection which he has used on others:

> I have lived many lives, and this one life
> Of Joe, long dead, who lives between five bells.

The backward reference is to such studies as 'Heine in Paris', Laurence Sterne in 'The Man of Sentiment', 'Captain Dobbin', 'Five Visions of Captain Cook', and on a smaller scale the re-creation of William Hickey in 'The Nabob', and of John Benbow in 'Metempsychosis', and the satirical impersonation contained in 'The Vesper-Song of the Reverend Samuel Marsden'. These do not seem to me to be among Slessor's best achievements. The larger ones take too long for anything they manage to do, the extra space being filled up with picturesque incidentals. The most ambitious of them is 'Five Visions' where Cook is seen in different situations from different points of view. Slessor here opened up a vein of poetry which others have continued to work: dramatic or narrative presentation of historical themes of exploration and discovery, or of seafaring or land-journeying with its hazards and goals.[6] As already hinted, he also showed something of the artistic problems that can occur. Such poems can fall into an irritating routine of allusive wordiness, intended as a device for creating a context. Picturesque detail is accumulated with a kind of nudging insistence and relish. This can be particularly tedious when it is strung out in loose co-ordination by a repetitive syntax. Slessor does not provide examples as copious as some others, but consider the expense of fifteen lines in introducing the blind Alexander Home, reminiscing in old age about Cook while bored listeners have quietly left:

After the candles had gone out, and those
Who listened had gone out, and a last wave
Of chimney-haloes caked their smoky rings
Like fish-scales on the ceiling, a Yellow Sea
Of swimming circles, the old man,
Old Captain-in-the-Corner, drank his rum
With friendly gestures to four chairs. They stood
Empty, still warm from haunches, with rubbed nails
And leather glazed, like aged serving-men
Feeding a king's delight, the sticky, drugged
Sweet agony of habitual anecdotes.
But these, his chairs, could bear an old man's tongue,
Sleep when he slept, be flattering when he woke,
And wink to hear the same eternal name
From lips new-dipped in rum.

The significant difference between the earlier character-studies
and 'Five Bells' is that in 'Five Bells' the promised poetic
revivification of Joe does not effectively take place and this is
admitted. Memory can retrieve only profitless scraps, a medley of
chance impressions: corresponding to the name 'Joe Lynch' there
is no one, only a few fading vestiges. What the poem is really
about is the triumph of time and the apparent meaninglessness
of life. Joe is just an example:[7] he started with bohemian energy
and yet before his accidental death he had already begun 'living
backward', retreating from the present and brooding about the
past, represented by the photographs of his family on the wall,

> . . . those frames
> And shapes of flesh that had perplexed your youth . . .

The poet, too, has turned away from actuality, from clock-time,
and retreated into 'my time', which is memory, the still tideless
depth of the past — only to find that the mind cannot dredge up
any sustaining reality from the past. Enclosing this theme is the
apparent meaninglessness of life and a sense of utter darkness
and nothingness beyond life.[8] It is remarkable but characteristic
that one of Slessor's most brilliant virtuoso performances is the
final harbour vision, which is an image of life's surface glitter, its
weary repetitiveness, its loneliness, surrounded by the dark.

Slessor's critical powers were expended on editorial policy in
Southerly which he edited 1956-61, and on short newspaper
reviews of individual works. He was not strong in general critical
argument. Of the extracts from his critical prose given here, the
first is a proper defence of standards, the second an echo of the
meaningless romantic cliché about the shape of a poem matching

the shape of an emotion; but it is part of the record and can at least draw attention to the versatility of Slessor's work in fixed and freer forms, to which the third extract refers.

COMMENTARY

Passages from the writings of Kenneth Slessor

But we can establish a basis for the poetry of the present and the future only by a clear-sighted appraisal of the past — that is to say, only by exercising unflinching honesty and severity and by refusing to make allowances for the passage of time or the ageing of 'expressions' that become out of date.

Making allowances is a poor foundation for appreciating poetry . . . if poetry is present it will not require indulgence. It must be cultivated in this 'new continent', not by a policy of 'not expecting too much', but on the contrary by expecting everything.

> From a Commonwealth Literary Fund Lecture series 1954; printed in *Bread and Wine,* 1970, p. 91

My own belief is that good poetry will dictate its own form. Six years ago, in a broadcast discussion, I remarked that 'by form I mean that shape of a work, whether in music, words or design, which seems most nearly to reflect the shape of the emotion which produced it. Thus, for example, a sonnet, one of the severest formal forms of poetry, is particularly suited in its mechanism for the kind of feeling which possessed Michael Drayton when he wrote the poem beginning 'Since there's no help, come, let us kiss and part'. On the other hand there is another kind of emotion which can be matched only by the paradox of disciplined formlessness.

> *ibid.,* p. 128

With these attempts to unify a poem's emotion with its form, I have also had no hesitation in using experiment. By experiment, I mean a considered breaking of rules where the fracture can suggest even a shadow of the effect desired. The traditional grammar of rhyme, metre and formality must be learnt by a poet as earnestly as the pianist learns his five-finger exercises. But he must not be shackled by academic rules once he has learnt their discipline. The colour and texture of vowel-sounds, the infinite rhythm of consonants, the emotional effects obtained by avoiding a rhyme, approaching a rhyme or by subtly altering it — all these are experiments in anarchy of which poets today know very little except by intuitive feeling.

> From A Radio Talk, November 1947; reprinted as an appendix in Max Harris, *Kenneth Slessor*, 1963, p. 45

Passages from the writings of other authors

What is chiefly disappointing in Slessor's best verse is the promise it seems to give, which is not completely fulfilled. I am led to expect the poetic revelation, and I find it does not come. And then I hear those echoes, poetic sphere-music, which float indistinctly and vaguely in Slessor's atmosphere . . . It is impossible, I find myself objecting, to achieve poetry by aiming at the poetic. The result too easily — indeed too inevitably — slips into the dazzlement of clever effects. These effects can be quite admirable, but in cumulation they convey an impression of heartless calculation. This is in my opinion Slessor's chief fault; and if it were not for the feeling that brilliance of effect — whether in vocabulary, phrase, rhetoric, rhyme and pattern, learned and bizarre reference or dramatic concept — has had more scope than the heartfelt imagination, there would be little to stand in the way of giving him a place among the highest.

> Brian Elliott, review of *One Hundred Poems*, in *Meanjin Papers*, vol. 4, no. 2, 1945, p. 135

Vincent Buckley has observed of Slessor that he is 'a man with a feeling for the grotesque', and that the element of the grotesque is 'not simply a foible of his early days, but is rather a recurring and directing element in his poetry';* but he produces no other evidence to support his contention than to detect a 'hint of romantic grotesquerie' in the titles of Slessor's poems. Max Harris also finds in Slessor's poetry a penchant for the grotesque,† and Charles Higham‡ and A. D. Hope§ support the view by inference.

* *Essays in Poetry, Mainly Australian*, 1957, pp. 113-14.
† Max Harris, *Kenneth Slessor*, 1963.
‡ Charles Higham, 'The Poetry of Kenneth Slessor', *Quadrant*, vol. 4, no. 1, 1960.
§ A. D. Hope, 'Slessor Twenty Years After', *Bulletin*, 1 June 1963.

Close examination shows that Slessor's poetry is in fact characterized by this element of the grotesque, an element which appears
in the early poems (primarily those written in the early nineteen
twenties) as a garish and superficial ornamentation, a precious
style, and a deliberate search for the unconventional, but which
he learns to control and utilize with considerable effectiveness
about the time he writes 'Captain Dobbin'.

A likely origin of this grotesque element can be found in
Slessor's association with the 'Vision' school, despite the fact that
he himself discounts the significance of this association. His poetry
shows the influence of this school in a number of ways. One of
the dominant influences on the group was the art of Peter Rubens,
either directly or through Norman Lindsay, and it becomes
evident that Slessor's imagery is in part a conscious imitation of
the grotesque as it appears in Rubens's paintings and consequently in Lindsay's sketches and etchings. The fact that two of
his poems are directly concerned with Rubens suggests that
Slessor had some knowledge of Rubens's art.

Secondly, many of the attitudes of the 'Vision' school can be
traced back to the English nineties. Charles Higham has
emphasized in his discussion of Slessor's poetry that

> . . . the resemblance to the London literature of the eighteen-nineties
> is clear: the emotions foppish and desiccated, the physicality puerile
> and diffused, the discipline imposed rather than operating from
> within . . .*

John Tregenza in *Australian Little Magazines* (Adelaide, 1964)
has also noticed that the work of the younger contributors to
Vision, particularly Slessor's, is imbued with ideas and attitudes
derived from the nineties. The most immediate aspect of this
influence is the decadence of Aestheticism, and this is the
resemblance that Charles Higham finds in Slessor's work. Yet
the influence of the nineties is much more pervasive, for the
Aesthetic Movement provides the basis for a number of assumptions about art and society made by the 'Vision' school, and
directs its fundamental poetic attitudes. The two groups share
essentially the same aesthetic principles, although these are rarely
thought out with much clarity by the contributors to the second
movement, and remain for the most part unquestioned assumptions. Thus the romantic approach to literature is not questioned
in any detail, but it is implicitly a fin-de-siècle romanticism, and
Pater's remarks in the Postscript to *Appreciations* (1889) show
just how true this is of Slessor's romanticism in particular:

* *op. cit.,* p. 67.

Its [Romanticism's] desire is for a beauty born of unlikely elements, by a profound alchemy, by a difficult initiation, by the charm which wrings it even out of terrible things; and a trace of distortion, of the grotesque, may perhaps linger, as an additional element of expression, about its ultimate grace. Its eager, excited spirit will have strength, the grotesque, first of all . . .*

Pater's contemporaries may not have acknowledged this concern with the romantic grotesque, but it is present in their art — in Wilde's and Beardsley's for example, to name two of the more important exponents. Similarly, although Slessor may never have read Pater, his poetry nevertheless subscribes to the romantic spirit outlined in the above quotation. The combination of 'unlikely elements' is a characteristic of his poetic technique, but it is some time before he develops this technique to a stage where we are more impressed by the beauty of the combination than by the unlikeliness of its elements . . .

Much of Slessor's imagery can be understood as a poetic rendering of the grotesque, not in any concern with a play on conventional imagery, although there are examples of this, but in the incongruous combination of 'unlikely elements'. And while the following discussion tends to concentrate on Slessor's imagery, his themes can also be considered in the light of the grotesque. In his imagery we can see this effect operating in two distinct ways. The profusion or agglomeration of images characteristic of his early poetry is in many cases grotesque, but more significantly many of the individual images are grotesque in themselves, either from the association of incongruous ideas as metaphors, or from the combination of such ideas in a symbol. Of course it might be argued that this use of imagery is in fact the use of conceits. But the point is that Slessor's conceits (if such they be) are conceits with a difference. There is something in their content, in the way they are used, that is peculiar to Slessor. Although he is attempting to be ingenious, he is not so much concerned with being fantastic; with him this is not, ultimately, an affectation.

Many of the early poems, such as 'Thieves' Kitchen', 'The Ghost', and several of the series entitled 'Music', seem to exist only as a profusion of images without much coherent intellectual content, apart from that imposed somewhat desultorily in the final line or two. Of all the early poems it may be said that they exist primarily in so far as they express through their imagery that peculiar animated gaiety associated with the 'Vision' school. (It will be recalled that the professed object of *Vision* was 'to liberate

* W. Pater, *Appreciations*, 1924, p. 260.

the imagination by gaiety or fantasy'.) Even Slessor's later, maturer
poems, such as 'North Country' 'Last Trams', 'William Street',
and especially 'To the Poetry of Hugh McCrae', rely heavily on
the sudden fusion of unusual components in the images for their
effectiveness.

A. C. W. Mitchell, 'Kenneth Slessor and the Grotesque',
Australian Literary Studies, vol. 1, no. 4, 1964, pp. 242-4

Such, then, is the supposed 'Dionysiac' yearning in Slessor's
[early] work which attracted or repelled his contemporaries;
nothing Dionysiac at all, for all its pretence at that, but an aloof
and dilettanteish preoccupation with pretty nothings in an art
bloodless but spry. The resemblance to the London literature of
the eighteen-nineties is clear: the emotions foppish and desic-
cated, the physicality puerile and diffused, the discipline imposed
rather than operating from within. The decadence and puerility
were to fall away with increasing maturity; so, too, the preoccupation with literature and drawings as sources of inspiration. But
the nostalgia for a romanticized past, the lack of realism and
sternness in the poetic outlook, long remained. In 'Thieves'
Kitchen', with its jaunty evocation of an orgy, he comes out
crudely but importantly with the first open statement of a theme
which will recur to the very end: that life is short and to be
enjoyed with a vigorous indiscipline; that flesh, which decays,
must be indulged while it, and time, are ripe. He speaks, in many
poems of these early days, about an ideal eighteenth-century
world, the world of William Hickey, back from India and bent
on capricious diversion; or of Boswell, scampering after a pretty
leg. The world of these verses is populated with fat kitchen-boys,
flagons, wenches being tossed in white beds; yet these figures in a
masquerade are scarcely more real than the sweets and bottles
which preceded them. There is continually the sense that the
ideal world they inhabit cannot be reached, that the poet frets
after it in vain. In 'The Ghost', wild revels are summoned up,
but in the last two lines the summoner is revealed as an evanes-
cent spirit, pressing its face on a pane from which the light, the
glow of human comfort and company has gone forever, gazing
into a relinquished and empty house. And in 'Stars', where the
astral myriads are compared to berries in harvest, candles, link-
boys, and other such fruitful and glowing things, there is
suddenly the shocked realition of the black cups of space
between the heavenly bodies, opening 'Infinity's trap-door, eternal
and merciless'.

This is the logical result of Slessor's love for externals, for surfaces. The actual fruits and splendours of human love, the bearing of children, the changing beauties of the consequent seasons, of growing up and growing old, are nowhere to be found in these poems. There is no blessedness, no calm and permanence and tranquillity. Instead, there is a passion for those very things which are least substantial and most quickly extinguished in human life.

That these are poems without faith—sad and despairing poems for all their jollity, written in a darkness of being — becomes increasingly clear as Slessor's art develops. 'The Night-Ride', about a train's pause at a country station in the early morning, is full of the darkness which Slessor believes will envelop us all; full of

> Hurrying, unknown faces,—boxes with strange labels—
> All groping clumsily to mysterious ends,—
> Out of the gaslight, dragged by private Fates.

There is, in poems of this kind, nothing so positive as a dialectic; they assert the pain and futility of the physical world simply through familiar images . . . and the energy of the lines springs from instinctive passion rather than intellectual force.

Charles Higham, 'The Poetry of Kenneth Slessor',
Quadrant, vol. 4, no. 1, 1960, pp. 67-8

Slessor's early poems manifest less the simple 'love for externals, for surface' that Mr Higham says they do than the unsatisfactoriness of such a worshipping of 'mere things'. These are moral poems, and their morality resembles that in terms of which Higham condemns them. There is concern in the poems with the limitation of 'things' that point only to Existence, rather than 'a passion *for* things', and Higham lags behind Slessor himself in seeing that these are 'those very things which are least substantial and most quickly extinguished in human life'. It is Lindsay doctrine which speaks of 'things' as belonging to the lower order of Existence, the order of 'eternal recurrence', and of creative art as transcending that order and entering the order of Life. Slessor's early poems are at one, however variously, with the doctrine. It is also Lindsay doctrine which speaks of 'the eternal paradox of that effort to conquer the problem of intellect by the senses which obstruct the effort, but without which the effort cannot be made' *(Creative Effort*, p. 132) — a statement which has, I suggest, more bearing on Slessor's poems, early and later, than anything Mr Higham advances.

W. M. Maidment, 'Australian Literary Criticism',
Southerly, vol. 24, no. 1, 1964, p. 38

POEMS

Nuremberg

So quiet it was in that high, sun-steeped room,
So warm and still, that sometimes with the light
Through the great windows, bright with bottle-panes,
There'd float a chime from clock-jacks out of sight,
    Clapping iron mallets on green copper gongs.

But only in blown music from the town's
Quaint horologe could Time intrude . . . you'd say
Clocks had been bolted out, the flux of years
Defied, and that high chamber sealed away
    From earthly change by some old alchemist.

And, oh, those thousand towers of Nuremberg
Flowering like leaden trees outside the panes:
Those gabled roofs with smoking cowls, and those
Encrusted spires of stone, those golden vanes
    On shining housetops paved with scarlet tiles!

And all day nine wrought-pewter manticores
Blinked from their spouting faucets, not five steps
Across the cobbled street, or, peering through
The rounds of glass, espied that sun-flushed room
    With Dürer graving at intaglios.

O happy nine, spouting your dew all day
In green-scaled rows of metal, whilst the town
Moves peacefully below in quiet joy . . .
O happy gargoyles to be gazing down
    On Albrecht Dürer and his plates of iron!

The Night-Ride

Gas flaring on the yellow platform; voices running up and down;
Milk-tins in cold dented silver; half-awake I stare,
Pull up the blind, blink out — all sounds are drugged;
The slow blowing of passengers asleep;
Engines yawning; water in heavy drips;
Black, sinister travellers, lumbering up the station,
One moment in the window, hooked over bags;
Hurrying, unknown faces — boxes with strange labels —
All groping clumsily to mysterious ends,

Out of the gaslight, dragged by private Fates.
Their echoes die. The dark train shakes and plunges;
Bells cry out; the night-ride starts again.
Soon I shall look out into nothing but blackness,
Pale, windy fields. The old roar and knock of the rails
Melts in dull fury. Pull down the blind. Sleep. Sleep.
Nothing but grey, rushing rivers of bush outside.
Gaslight and milk-cans. Of Rapptown I recall nothing else.

Country Towns

Country towns, with your willows and squares,
And farmers bouncing on barrel mares
To public-houses of yellow wood
With '1860' over their doors,
And that mysterious race of Hogans
Which always keeps General Stores . . .

At the School of Arts, a broadsheet lies
Sprayed with the sarcasm of flies:
'The Great Golightly Family
Of Entertainers Here To-night' —
Dated a year and a half ago,
But left there, less from carelessness
Than from a wish to seem polite.

Verandas baked with musky sleep,
Mulberry faces dozing deep,
And dogs that lick the sunlight up
Like paste of gold — or, roused in vain
By far, mysterious buggy-wheels,
Lower their ears, and drowse again . . .

Country towns with your schooner bees,
And locusts burnt in the pepper-trees,
Drown me with syrups, arch your boughs,
Find me a bench, and let me snore,
Till, charged with ale and unconcern,
I'll think it's noon at half-past four!

Cock-Crow

The cock's far cry
From lonely yards
Burdens the night
With boastful birds
That mop their wings
To make response —
A mess of songs
And broken sense.

So, when I slept,
I heard your call
(If lips long dead
Could answer still)
And snapped-off thoughts
Broke into clamour,
Like the night's throats
Heard by a dreamer.

South Country

After the whey-faced anonymity
Of river-gums and scribbly-gums and bush,
After the rubbing and the hit of brush,
You come to the South Country

As if the argument of trees were done,
The doubts and quarrelling, the plots and pains,
All ended by these clear and gliding planes
Like an abrupt solution.

And over the flat earth of empty farms
The monstrous continent of air floats back
Coloured with rotting sunlight and the black,
Bruised flesh of thunderstorms:

Air arched, enormous, pounding the bony ridge,
Ditches and hutches, with a drench of light,
So huge, from such infinities of height,
You walk on the sky's beach

While even the dwindled hills are small and bare,
As if, rebellious, buried, pitiful,
Something below pushed up a knob of skull,
Feeling its way to air.

Five Bells

Time that is moved by little fidget wheels
Is not my Time, the flood that does not flow.
Between the double and the single bell
Of a ship's hour, between a round of bells
From the dark warship riding there below,
I have lived many lives, and this one life
Of Joe, long dead, who lives between five bells.

Deep and dissolving verticals of light
Ferry the falls of moonshine down. Five bells
Coldly rung out in a machine's voice. Night and water
Pour to one rip of darkness, the Harbour floats
In air, the Cross hangs upside-down in water.

Why do I think of you, dead man, why thieve
These profitless lodgings from the flukes of thought
Anchored in Time? You have gone from earth,
Gone even from the meaning of a name;
Yet something's there, yet something forms its lips
And hits and cries against the ports of space,
Beating their sides to make its fury heard.

Are you shouting at me, dead man, squeezing your face
In agonies of speech on speechless panes?
Cry louder, beat the windows, bawl your name!

But I hear nothing, nothing . . . only bells,
Five bells, the bumpkin calculus of Time.
Your echoes die, your voice is dowsed by Life,
There's not a mouth can fly the pygmy strait —
Nothing except the memory of some bones
Long shoved away, and sucked away, in mud;
And unimportant things you might have done,
Or once I thought you did; but you forgot,
And all have now forgotten — looks and words
And slops of beer; your coat with buttons off,
Your gaunt chin and pricked eye, and raging tales
Of Irish kings and English perfidy,
And dirtier perfidy of publicans
Groaning to God from Darlinghurst.

Five bells.

Then I saw the road, I heard the thunder
Tumble, and felt the talons of the rain
The night we came to Moorebank in slab-dark,
So dark you bore no body, had no face,
But a sheer voice that rattled out of air
(As now you'd cry if I could break the glass),
A voice that spoke beside me in the bush,
Loud for a breath or bitten off by wind,
Of Milton, melons, and the Rights of Man,
And blowing flutes, and how Tahitian girls
Are brown and angry-tongued, and Sydney girls
Are white and angry-tongued, or so you'd found.
But all I heard was words that didn't join
So Milton became melons, melons girls,
And fifty mouths, it seemed, were out that night,
And in each tree an Ear was bending down,
Or something had just run, gone behind grass,
When, blank and bone-white, like a maniac's thought,
The naphtha-flash of lightning slit the sky,
Knifing the dark with deathly photographs.
There's not so many with so poor a purse
Or fierce a need, must fare by night like that,
Five miles in darkness on a country track,
But when you do, that's what you think.

Five bells.

In Melbourne, your appetite had gone,
Your angers too; they had been leeched away
By the soft archery of summer rains
And the sponge-paws of wetness, the slow damp
That stuck the leaves of living, snailed the mind,
And showed your bones, that had been sharp with rage,
The sodden ecstasies of rectitude.
I thought of what you'd written in faint ink
Your journal with the sawn-off lock, that stayed behind
With other things you left, all without use,
All without meaning now, except a sign
That someone had been living who now was dead:
'At Labassa, Room 6 x 8
On top of the tower; because of this, very dark
And cold in winter. Everything has been stowed
Into this room — 500 books all shapes
And colours, dealt across the floor

And over sills and on the laps of chairs;
Guns, photoes of many different things
And differant curioes that I obtained . . .'

In Sydney, by the spent aquarium-flare
Of penny gaslight on pink wallpaper,
We argued about blowing up the world,
But you were living backward, so each night
You crept a moment closer to the breast,
And they were living, all of them, those frames
And shapes of flesh that had perplexed your youth,
And most your father, the old man gone blind,
With fingers always round a fiddle's neck,
That graveyard mason whose fair monuments
And tablets cut with dreams of piety
Rest on the bosoms of a thousand men
Staked bone by bone, in quiet astonishment
At cargoes they had never thought to bear,
These funeral-cakes of sweet and sculptured stone.

Where have you gone? The tide is over you,
The turn of midnight water's over you,
As Time is over you, and mystery,
And memory, the flood that does not flow.
You have no suburb, like those easier dead
In private berths of dissolution laid —
The tide goes over, the waves ride over you
And let their shadows down like shining hair,
But they are Water; and the sea-pinks bend
Like lilies in your teeth, but they are Weed;
And you are only part of an Idea.
I felt the wet push its black thumb-balls in,
The night you died, I felt your eardrums crack,
And the short agony, the longer dream,

The Nothing that was neither long nor short;
But I was bound, and could not go that way,
But I was blind, and could not feel your hand.
If I could find an answer, could only find
Your meaning, or could say why you were here
Who now are gone, what purpose gave you breath
Or seized it back, might I not hear your voice?

I looked out of my window in the dark
At waves with diamond quills and combs of light

J

That arched their mackerel-backs and smacked the sand
In the moon's drench, that straight enormous glaze,
And ships far off asleep, and Harbour-buoys
Tossing their fireballs wearily each to each,
And tried to hear your voice, but all I heard
Was a boat's whistle, and the scraping squeal
Of seabirds' voices far away, and bells,
Five bells. Five bells coldly ringing out.

Five bells.

Beach Burial

Softly and humbly to the Gulf of Arabs
The convoys of dead sailors come;
At night they sway and wander in the waters far under,
But morning rolls them in the foam.

Between the sob and clubbing of the gunfire
Someone, it seems, has time for this,
To pluck them from the shallows and bury them in burrows
And tread the sand upon their nakedness;

And each cross, the driven stake of tidewood,
Bears the last signature of men,
Written with such perplexity, with such bewildered pity,
The words choke as they begin —

'*Unknown seaman*' — the ghostly pencil
Wavers and fades, the purple drips,
The breath of the wet season has washed their inscriptions
As blue as drowned men's lips,

Dead seamen, gone in search of the same landfall,
Whether as enemies they fought,
Or fought with us, or neither; the sand joins them together,
Enlisted on the other front.

El Alamein.

SELECT BIBLIOGRAPHY

Thief of the Moon (privately printed), Sydney, 1924.
Earth-Visitors, Fanfrolico Press, London, 1926.
Cuckooz Contrey, Frank Johnson, Sydney, 1932.
Darlinghurst Nights and Morning Glories, Frank Johnson, Sydney, 1933.
Five Bells, Frank Johnson, Sydney, 1939.
One Hundred Poems, Angus & Robertson, Sydney, 1944 (enlarged edition, *Poems,* 1957).

Bread and Wine, Angus & Robertson, Sydney, 1970.

Buckley, Vincent, 'Kenneth Slessor: Realist or Romantic', in *Essays in Poetry, Mainly Australian,* Melbourne University Press, Melbourne, 1957.
Docker, John, *Australian Cultural Elites,* Angus & Robertson, Sydney, 1974, ch. 2.
Grono, William, review of Semmler (q.v.) in *Westerly,* no. 4, 1966.
Harris, Max, *Kenneth Slessor* (Australian Writers and their Work series), Lansdowne Press, Melbourne, 1963.
Higham, Charles, 'The Poetry of Kenneth Slessor', *Quadrant,* vol. 4, no. 1, 1960; reprinted in *Australian Literary Criticism,* ed. Grahame Johnston, Oxford University Press, Melbourne, 1962.
Hope, A. D., 'Slessor Twenty Years After', *Bulletin,* 1 June 1963.
Jaffa, Herbert C., *Kenneth Slessor,* New York, Twayne Publishers Inc., 1971.
McAuley, James, 'An Imprint of Slessor', *Quadrant,* vol. 17, no. 1, 1973.
———— 'On Some of Slessor's Discarded Poems', *Southerly,* vol. 33, no. 2, 1973.
Mitchell, A. C. W., 'Kenneth Slessor and the Grotesque', *Australian Literary Studies,* vol. 1, no. 4, 1964.
Semmler, Clement, *Kenneth Slessor* (Writers and their Work series), Longmans, Green, London, 1966.
Sturm, T. L., 'Kenneth Slessor's Poetry and Norman Lindsay', *Southerly,* vol. 31, no. 4, 1971.
Smith, Vivian, 'The Ambivalence of Kenneth Slessor', *Southerly,* vol. 31, no. 4, 1971.
Thomson, A. K., ed., *Critical Essays on Kenneth Slessor,* Jacaranda Press, Brisbane, 1968.
Wallace-Crabbe, Chris, 'Kenneth Slessor and the Powers of Language', in *The Literature of Australia,* ed. Geoffrey Dutton, Penguin Books, Melbourne, 1964.
Wright, Judith, 'Kenneth Slessor — Romantic and Modern', in *Preoccupations in Australian Poetry,* Oxford University Press, Melbourne, 1965.

NOTES

1 Charles Higham, 'The Poetry of Kenneth Slessor', *Quadrant,* vol. 4, no. 1, 1959-60; reprinted in *Australian Literary Criticism,* ed. Grahame Johnston, 1962.

2 The phrase is applied by Slessor to the imagined scenes in McCrae's poetry in *Bread and Wine* (1970), p. 103.

3 See my article 'On Some of Slessor's Discarded Poems', *Southerly,* vol. 33, no. 3, 1973.

4 *Bread and Wine,* p. 124.

5 The analogy concerning the cry and the confused response is muddled in the second stanza by the application of the word 'answer' to the calling voice that elicits the poet's frustrated response.

6 For example, R. D. FitzGerald's 'Heemsckerck Shoals' and, in part, *Between Two Tides;* Rosemary Dobson's *The Ship of Ice;* William Hart-Smith's *Colombus Goes West;* Francis Webb's *A Drum for Ben Boyd, Leichhardt in Theatre,* and 'Eyre All Alone'; Douglas Stewart's *Fire on the Snow,* 'Worsley Enchanted', 'D'Albertis', 'Mungo Park'; my *Captain Quiros;* J. M. Couper's *The Book of Bligh.* In reviewing Couper's poem, Geoffrey Lehmann points out the way in which the protagonist can become representative: 'The subject of the poem is more than a simple voyage through time and space. Bligh is mankind travelling through a metaphysical dimension . . .' (*Bulletin,* 30 May 1970, p. 51). Douglas Stewart collected together an anthology called *Voyager Poems* (1960); a more comprehensive term might be 'traveller poems'.

7 In a comment on 'Five Bells' in the *Daily Telegraph,* 31 July 1967, reprinted in *Bread and Wine: Selected Prose* (1970), pp. 196-9, Slessor says: 'The poem therefore is on two planes. First it attempts to epitomize the life of a specific human being, but fundamentally it is an expression of the relativeness of "time". Considered in this light, the personal allusions are unimportant.' (He goes on to give some details of Joe Lynch, the black-and-white artist who was accidentally drowned.) What Slessor meant in 1967 by 'the relativeness of "time" ' is not clear: what is clear is that it is not a satisfactory statement of the fundamental theme of the poem he published in 1939. What poets say in retrospect about their poems is often useful and illuminating, but can also be disappointing and sometimes even misleading. For example, in his comment, in the same place, on 'Beach Burial' Slessor explains the phrase 'the other front' in a surprising way. He gives the 'superficial' meaning of the words as referring to the 'second front' which was in 1942 being discussed as a matter of strategy. Then he says: 'However, there is a deeper implication which is really the theme of the poem. It is the idea that all men of all races, whether they fight with each other or not, are engaged together on the common "front" of humanity's existence. The absolute fact of death unites them. Their hatreds, quarrels and wars should be dwarfed by the huger human struggle to survive against disease and cataclysms on this dangerous planet.' This is a fine platitude, but it has no point of support in the text. The poem does not have anything to say about the need for the living to unite for survival. It plainly means that these particular seamen, whether friends or enemies or neutrals, have all, involuntarily, joined the ranks of the dead, where earthly differences are irrelevant. The French poet René Arcos made the same point a generation earlier: '*Les morts sont tous d'un seul côté*'. Slessor's post-interpretation unhappily obliterates the peculiar force of the words 'enlisted' and 'front' when applied not to the living but the dead.

8 Not all interpretations of 'Five Bells' are in accord with the one I have offered. Max Harris in his *Kenneth Slessor* (1966) finds in it a 'quasi-religious' development; Vivian Smith, in 'The Ambivalence of Kenneth Slessor', *Southerly*, vol. 21, no. 4, 1971, finds a balance of positive and negative, so that the poem affirms that 'life is full of profoundly significant, but fleeting and baffling experience' (p. 266). T. L. Sturm, in 'Kenneth Slessor's Poetry and Norman Lindsay' in the same issue of *Southerly*, and John Docker in *Australian Cultural Elites*, ch. 2, after rightly stressing the importance of Norman Lindsay's doctrine for Slessor's early work are led to reading Lindsay doctrine into 'Five Bells' without, it seems to me, real support from the text. The critical issue is whether the poet does effect the re-living of Joe that the poem offers at the outset. It may be that the poem changed direction.

6

The Ferment of the Forties

INTRODUCTION

Connections between social change and literary development are difficult to trace. One can agree that the social circumstances of Australia between the 1890s and the late 1930s must have conditioned the style and subject and orientation of early twentieth-century Australian poetry, but how far, and how inevitably? The poetry of Brennan and Neilson and Slessor arose in a particular context, but is obviously to a large extent determined from within. In the same way, the cultural quickening of the 1940s invites but eludes sociological analysis. The Second World War was a period of national danger, of new challenges, of quickening industrialization; the atmosphere was vibrant with the realization that Australia was going to be different from now on, in a very different post-war world. The emergence of new poetic activity in the forties seemed to many of us to be a natural part of this ferment, yet the accidents of birth possibly had much more to do with it. Something of the atmosphere of the time is caught in an early poem by Judith Wright, 'The Trains':

> Tunnelling through the night, the trains pass
> in a splendour of power, with a sound like thunder
> shaking the orchards, waking
> the young from a dream, scattering like glass
> the old men's sleep; laying
> a black trail over the still bloom of the orchards.
> The trains go north with guns.

Not much of the poetry dealing directly with incidents of war now looks durable. Slessor was moved by his experience as a war correspondent to break silence and write 'Beach Burial'

(p. 120) and the sardonic comment on General Blamey, 'An Inscription for Dog River'. David Campbell's 'Men in Green' uses some of the techniques of popular narrative verse effectively. Geoffrey Dutton's 'Abandoned Airstrip, Northern Territory' is a monologue evoking feelings and reminiscences. One of John Manifold's best poems is his elegy 'The Tomb of Lieutenant John Learmonth, A.I.F.' (p. 149). In making the tally it must be remembered that only a few poets had combat experience. The one poet of some reputation whose death was due to the war was James Picot, who died of illness while a prisoner in Burma: his posthumous volume *With a Hawk's Quill* (1953) reveals a graceful derivative talent. An anthology of poems, not all on war themes, by men and women serving in the Australian forces, *Poets at War*, was compiled by Ian Mudie and published in 1944.

Just before and in the early part of the Second World War, the most noticeable literary movement was that of the Jindyworobaks,[1] which was a symptom not a substantive poetic event. Rex Ingamells founded the Jindyworobak Club in Adelaide in 1938, expounded his aims in *Conditional Culture* (1938), and also in 1938 began publication of an annual gathering of Australian verse called *Jindyworobak Anthology* which was continued by various editors until 1953. In 1948 he published a collection of retrospective comments by himself and various contributors, *Jindyworobak Review 1938-1948*.

Poets associated in varying degrees and for different periods of time with his activity included Flexmore Hudson, Max Harris, Ian Mudie, Victor Kennedy, William Hart-Smith, Roland Robinson, Gina Ballantyne, and Nancy Cato.

There was an inner and an outer circle of Jindyworobak tenets. The inner doctrine is thus described by F. H. Mares:

> Recognizing the rootlessness of Australian culture, hooked uneasily to the heels of a Europe and America widely different in their attitudes and requirements, their social and political organization, and — not least important — their climate and scenery, the leaders of the movement determined to find roots at home, and set out to look for them in the by-that-time (1938) very scattered fragments of Aboriginal myth and ritual. The cure was as romantic as the diagnosis was acute, but it did oblige other writers to face a real problem, the significance of the Aborigines in 'White Australia's' past, present, and future. One critic has remarked that Judith Wright has inscribed the epitaph of the Jindyworobaks in her poem 'Bora Ring'.[2]

The idea of basing a modern Australian literary culture on the utterly alien Aboriginal culture was too absurd to be taken seriously by most people.[3] The outer doctrine was the familiar resistance to European cultural domination, the demand for a national character in art and letters. Ingamells in *Conditional Culture* did not deny that some good literature, and painting too, might have no distinctive local colour or manner, but went on to say:

> The real test of a people's culture is the way in which they can express themselves in relation to their environment, and the loftiness and universality of their artistic conceptions raised on that basis (p. 6).

The best Jindyworobak poet, and the one most persistent in the line of Jindyworobak concern with Aboriginal culture in particular and the Australian natural scene in general, is the immigrant Irishman Roland Robinson.[4] Many of his poems are vivid and attractive in individual images more than in what they memorably achieve. 'Altjeringa'[5] is an example of his best work:

> Nude, smooth, and giant-huge,
> the torsos of the gums
> hold up the vast dark cave
> as the great moon comes.
>
> Shock-headed black-boy stands,
> with rigid, thrusting spear,
> defiant and grotesque
> against that glistening sphere.
>
> In clenched, contorted birth
> black banksias agonise;
> out of the ferns and earth,
> half-formed, beast-boulders rise;
>
> because The Bush goes back,
> back to a time unknown;
> chaos that had not word,
> nor image carved on stone.

This concluding quatrain gestures insistently, yet vaguely, in contrast to the acute vision of the earlier quatrains.

In retrospect the Jindyworobak movement belongs with P. R. Stephensen's strident essay, *The Foundations of Culture in Australia* (1936),[6] as the last outburst of the assertive nationalism which had been with Australian poetry from the beginning. The prose in early issues of *Meanjin Papers* was also much concerned with the nationalist theme — No. 6 in 1941 was given over to a 'Nationality Number'. It was in this context that A. D.

Hope's well-known ambiguously questioning poem 'Australia' (p. 8) first appeared;[7] and Max Harris, having moved away to become chief Angry Penguin, in an amusing article in the next issue cited examples of nationalist assertion and poured scorn on the amount of 'talk about Australian Kulchewer, environmental values, national beauty' which *Meanjin Papers* contained, charging the nationalists with neglect of the one thing that matters, the question of sheer poetic quality.[8] The nagging omnipresence of this issue in the forties made it hard to believe that the time of release could be close at hand.. The obsession faded during the next decade, and in the sixties it ceased to be an important issue for most poets.[9]

Meanjin has been a register of the change and development of interests over its period. It was begun by C. B. Christesen in December 1940 as *Meanjin Papers*.[10] The first issue was devoted entirely to the work of four Queensland poets, 'Brian Vrepont' (B. A. Truebridge), James Picot, Paul Grano, and Christesen himself. Gradually it developed as a vehicle for prose as well as verse, and its scope became national, indeed to some degree international. In 1944 the name of 'Miss Judith Wright' appeared as Secretary. In 1945 the journal moved to a new home in Melbourne University and became *Meanjin;* it was re-named *Meanjin Quarterly* in 1961, but *Meanjin* it remains in common reference.

A concurrent ingredient in the ferment was represented by the Adelaide-based journal *Angry Penguins* (1940-46), whose main editor was Max Harris. In retrospect Max Harris has described it as expressing 'a noisy and aggressive revolutionary modernism'. He has compared it in its time with the later American magazine *Evergreen Review,* as a 'vehicle for literary talents at an immature stage of development... For these modernists passion, brio, and romantic obsession are enough: form, organization, and a disciplined concept of literary communication are either irrelevant, haphazard, or secondary'.[11] The achievement of this valiant magazine was not merely to assert the claims of local writers — and painters like Sidney Nolan — impatient of 'bush-balladry and outbackery', of 'tired and mediocre nationalism', and of the 'cultural illiberalism' deeply entrenched in Australia (exemplified, Harris says, in due course by attacks by the Communist Party and by 'the cultural wing of the newly formed Catholic Action'), but also to set up communication with modern movements in Britain and America, and to open paths into modern European literature and art, in an endeavour to overcome the isolation and isolationism which were evident in Australian culture.

Max Harris remarks in his *Quadrant* article that it was a pity that the brashly experimental and neo-romantic side of *Angry Penguins* alienated people like A. D. Hope and Harold Stewart and myself, who from a different quarter were equally critical of literary Australianism and provincial narrowness, and wanted to appeal to universal values and keep communication open with European culture:

> They were fighting, if silently, the same enemies as the *Angry Penguins*. But for all this, the very energy and egoism of the experimentalists goaded Professor Hope into his famous Whelan-the-Wrecker job on myself in *Meanjin,* and Professor McAuley into his Ern Malley masquerade.[12]

Poetic schools are rarely as cohesive and formalized as later history can make them seem; manifestos, if they appear, do not for long represent the actual tendencies of those who subscribe to them. And the best work of good poets has more in common than the opposed slogans and labels suggest; it transcends nationalist, traditionalist, modernist or other categories.[13]

It is in this spirit that John Pringle's chapter on poetry in his *Australian Accent* (1958), entitled 'The Counter-Revolution' must be interpreted. He says that a counter-revolution against nationalism and modernism occurred, and that 'This counter-revolution is almost entirely the work of three men: A. D. Hope, James McAuley and Harold Stewart' (p. 139). There was in this case no movement, no plan, no manifesto, merely the somewhat similar opinions of three poets who were acquainted with one another and not at that time much in contact with other writers or groups.

Harold Stewart's path diverged early into a more totally 'traditionalist' commitment in literature and philosophy than Hope or I were inclined to follow. Under the initial influence of the writings of René Guénon and Ananda K. Coomaraswamy, his work became increasingly dedicated to the expression of attitudes appropriate to oriental metaphysical doctrine, and in later years he has lived in Japan studying Buddhism. His influence on Australian poetry was not great and has altogether ceased. His expatriate published work consists of translations of Japanese haiku and original poems in that form.[14] The concluding part of his finely executed early poem, 'A Flight of Wild Geese', is included in the selection (p. 150). The text given is not as it appears in *Phoenix Wings* (1948); it is a revised version supplied by the author.

As between Hope and myself, the literary conservatism has

been stricter in his case, the philosophical and political conservatism in mine. A considerable similarity of literary views
continued into the fifties, and undoubtedly had its main influence
at that time,[15] though the dissimilarities in practice, then and
later, are obvious.

The groupings so far considered resulted from a fairly definite
position-taking, even though the amount of firm doctrine and
exclusiveness should not be exaggerated.[16] *Meanjin* continued
to maintain open house to all literary tendencies in accordance
with its stated policy of eclecticism. The Sydney *Bulletin,* also,
under the literary editorship of Douglas Stewart from 1941 to
1961, was not the organ of a doctrine or intentionally narrow in
range. If something of a new 'Bulletin School' of poets grew
up, as Vincent Buckley later claimed in his *Essays in Poetry*
(1957),[17] this was by natural accretion. Stewart and R. D.
FitzGerald were friends with much in common in their literary
sympathies. Ronald McCuaig was on the staff. A number of
Sydney-connected poets tended to group themselves by congruity
and acquaintance around Stewart and the Red Page (the inside
of the red cover of the old *Bulletin,* which was its literary page).
Preferences for Australian colouring, or Browningesque historic-
ally based dramatizations or lyrical and light verse, emerged.
David Campbell and Rosemary Dobson became frequent contributors. Others were Nan McDonald, Ray Mathew, William
Hart-Smith, Nancy Keesing, and Roland Robinson. Francis Webb
made his debut in the *Bulletin.* Judith Wright's work fitted in
to this environment. But this grouping, to the loose extent it
occurred, was quite informal.

R. D. FitzGerald began writing in the twenties and has had
an important place in Australian poetry from the thirties to
the seventies. It seemed best to place him at the head of this
section because his influence on other writers was strongest in
the forties, even though some of his best poems were written later.
He first became well known in 1938, not just because his 'Essay
on Memory' won a *Sydney Morning Herald* prize in a literary
competition marking the 150th anniversary of the First Settlement, but also because the poem had great impact: it seemed
to many the best thing in weight and extent and strenuous
energy since Brennan. FitzGerald's work is always meditative,
but also partly dramatic or narrative. There are lyrics, but
the later ones are less fluently lyrical, more angular and reflective.
The difficulty felt by many readers is that, if one looks at the
work as an artistic achievement, it becomes necessary to bring
in aid a conviction of the value and importance of the ideas;

and if one looks at the ideas, it becomes necessary to bring in aid a conviction of the artistic worth of their embodiment. Those who are deeply impressed by both the ideas and the poetic art have had no trouble in placing FitgGerald among the foremost Australian poets likely to endure; but those who in varying degrees are less impressed by the ideas, or by the expression, or by both, differ in their assessment of his work.

The emphasis upon FitzGerald's ideas which is apparent in many commentaries on his work does not mean that he is an intellectualist, or that his poems develop a complex structure of argued statements. The ideas that emerge are few, simple and recurring; they express a basic romantic vitalism. As Harold Oliver has observed:

> A strong anti-intellectualism, paradoxically, is always prominent in FitzGerald . . . and never yet in FitzGerald has it been poetically or logically — if I may use his dichotomy — *justified*.[18]

Oliver analyses the ideas into three, which appear in 'An Essay on Memory' and persist in later poems:'(i) memory as continuity, (ii) action as virtue, or the necessity of translating virtue into action and (iii) Australia as opportunity'. Thus, he says, 'Fitz-Gerald's development is not, particularly, in thought' — a judgement which does not seem to need modification in the light of the work published since it was made. Not surprisingly, Oliver appears uncomfortable with what he has uncovered in the realm of ideas, and leans for his conclusion upon the artistic achievement, in words that have a somewhat uneasy largeness:

> he is a poet who in splendid meditative verse has worked out for himself a few genuine ideas and expressed them with forceful originality — perhaps even with genius (p. 48).

There is most agreement among critics on the merits of a few short poems, and some longer poems which have an historical situation presented by a monologue or narrative. Among these longer poems are 'Fifth Day' (p. 138) about the trial of Warren Hastings; the long narrative poem *Between Two Tides* (1952), based on the story of Will Mariner in Tonga; and the personal meditation on his ancestors, 'The Wind at Your Door'. There is least agreement among FitzGerald's critics about the quality of his language and versification, which often tend to be harsh and ungainly. The quality in FitzGerald which evokes the strongest response in most readers is the sense of integrity, the steady preservation of personal values without parade and with an unsolemn endurance.

It seemed to many people in the forties that there were a large number of talented poets around. Of course, every period tends to feel this about itself — time unhappily reveals that not all the season's favorites are hardy perennials. Yet it still seems to me that it was a flourishing time for an unusual number of talents. One modestly distinctive poet, for example, was the English-born William Hart-Smith, whose writing life has been divided between New Zealand and Australia. Many of his poems are what might be called humoresques, often free in form, with sharply observed images and a quirkish wit. Alec King has written of 'the bare poetic stare' of his poetry: 'it is spare, negative, and artfully a little flat'.[19] Hart-Smith himself commented on the imagistic quality of many of his poems: 'my mind makes, or takes, photographs, and these remain extra-clear, concisely detailed, vivid visual memories; and provide the core of an idea around which a poem may grow later, sometimes much later'.[20] Thus in his poem 'Kangaroos':

> Brown out of the brown tussock a darker brown
> head rises as if thrust up cautiously on a pole.

> A green bird on a feathering grass-stem
> That bends under its weight, flutters

> And sinks out of sight. It is the only disturbance
> except for the reiterated clicking of castanets

> and the fife-notes of insects.

The forties also had its share of oddities. One was Peter Hopegood, who came to Australia from England in 1924. His work combined indiscriminate dippings into what Philip Larkin has called 'the myth-kitty' with an off-key humoristic vein. A. D. Hope summed the result up in a review of Hopegood's *Circus at World's End* (1947):

> The myth is grandiose; the vision is profound but the poetry is too often a collection of grotesque tags and a jumble of incoherent clichés. The humorous poems are too often merely irritating clowning when they are meant to give the sense of heroic and elemental laughter.[21]

Another oddity was Harry Hooton, an anarchist whose writings were without talent or coherent ideas.

Among the poets whose work is included in the selection the earliest born is Ernest G. Moll, much of whose poetry belongs to Australia in theme though for his working life he was an expatriate. He left Australia in the 1920s, and later became

Professor of English in the University of Oregon. In 1939 under an exchange arrangement he returned to teach for a year in the Sydney Teachers' College. Thereafter, his poems were written out of Australian rural memories, refreshed by further visits, and successive volumes were published in Australia. Robert Frost is an evident influence.[22] Many of the poems are careful in a blunt unexciting way,[23] but sometimes expression matches observation and feeling more notably, as in 'Eagles over the Lambing Paddock' (p. 143).

Ronald McCuaig published his first volume, *Vaudeville,* in 1938. He wrote light but sharp verse, with wit and pathos, a deftness of handling and a keeness of aesthetic sense. I think these qualities have caused him to be underrated,[24] and that time will keep some of his best poems remarkably fresh.

Kenneth Mackenzie's *The Moonlit Doorway* (1944) established a reputation which its facile romanticism would not long have sustained. Indeed his work was disappearing from sight until attention was revived by Evan Jones's monograph, followed by an edition of the poems including previously unpublished work.[25] It is among the later poems that one must look, especially those written between 1951 and 1954 within the shadow of alcoholic dereliction and impending death. The two poems chosen for the selection represent two kinds of theme handled objectively, with a sure organization of subject and feeling and expression which he did not often attain. This estimate is distinctly below the claims made for Mackenzie by Evan Jones and some other critics.

Nan McDonald published her first volume, *Pacific Sea,* in 1947. There is a depth of observation and feeling in her work, though sometimes the reader is not drawn in readily enough: the poem spreads out, the rhythm is at times too slack. Yet if one is not impatient what one arrives at is poignancy and truth and poetic life. Some of the poems evince a strong religious feeling.

COMMENTARY

Passages from the writings of Robert D. FitzGerald

There are voices, too, indisputably modern in pitch, that lack nothing in strength, that make statements of marked originality, and whose tone is strikingly conscientious — perhaps the finest and fullest being that of Day Lewis. These in their scope and intention have usually little in common with recognizable poetry, but their vitality is as unquestionable as their sincerity.

'An Attitude to Modern Poetry', *Southerly*,
vol. 9, no. 3, 1948, p. 153 [written in 1939]

Certainly it will be fair to warn such a student not to be deceived by labels such as that stuck on my work long ago: 'Intellectual' — a term I can only accept as a general classification covering also several other poets with whom I may have certain affinities. But so many have followed suit since that great critic A. G. Stephens, shown some early rhymes of mine by a friend, made but the single comment 'All head; no heart,' that by reaction I have become now first an 'anti-intellectual', which is bearable because inaccurate and more recently a 'so-called intellectual' which seems gratuitously contemptuous — only one degree less so than 'pseudo-intellectual' which I await with no great qualms.

Study of these poems, if they are paid that compliment, will surely show that they neither advance nor argue out any concept, shallow or profound, purely as an exercise of the intellect; nor is it ever the function of poetry to do so. Poetry of ideas, poetry of purpose and poetry of thought do pursue truth, if not as directly as science or with the meticulous detail of philosophy; but it is a different kind of truth, that of innate significances in objects, scenes and relationships considered as unique wholes rather than as evidences of general principles; and such significances are realized in the first place through the emotions and developed by the imagination. The use of intellect in any poem is normal, however, though secondary, and occurs in the rationalizing and synthesis of these relationships and in their ordering within the framework of craftsmanship. So that a poem can only specifically be called intellectual when it goes beyond this into an analysis of fundamentals, whereby there is danger of it ceasing to be poetry at all, or when it makes use of some exceptional dialectic or scholarship to beat out its conclusions; and then it is in danger of running into a very vicious kind of obscurity. My own verse has sometimes been thought obscure, but not in that way.

There can be other defects besides unjustified obscurity; and where they are found in my own work it is not my purpose to defend them. Any reply to adverse criticism is inexcusable. Charges against artistic integrity, however, are another matter; and to imply that any artist is indifferent to his medium is such a charge. It has been said or inferred quite often of myself that I am little concerned with technique so long as my verse makes its required statement. I trust that this selection will refute that charge by showing how technique has had attention from the outset. Techniques are at the foundation, and composition and construction are of the very essence, of every work of art; it would be nonsensical for any conscientious executant to believe he could despise or dispense with them.

It is true though that I lay stress on content; and the label 'Philosophical Poet' which has also been put on me probably derives from the fact. And if I wear it a little more comfortably than the other, though somewhat under false pretences, it is only because the term philosophy is a wide one and can cover, though loosely, most expression of thought. Of formal philosophy I know very little, and very little of the kind really appears in my verses on close examination.

Introduction to Selected Poems (Australian Poets
series) 1963, pp. viii-ix

On Fifth Day

The prosecution at the impeachment of Warren Hastings (1788) was led by the great liberal statesman Edmund Burke. The trial was a failure for Burke in that after seven years' intermittent hearing it ended in acquittal for Hastings; and a failure too in that Burke's violent detestation of Hastings somewhat clouded his judgment and proportions; but a triumph in that it resulted indirectly in the destruction of the worst features of British exploitation in India under the system which Hastings had represented. Part of Burke's intemperate attitude is probably attributable to his being misled in many matters by Sir Phillip Francis, the bitter personal enemy of Hastings and almost certainly the author of the notorious 'Letters of Junius'.

'Another hour' refers to Burke's effective opposition to any kind of compromise with the revolutionaries of France — no small factor in the later determined resistance to Napoleon.

Note in Selected Poems (Australian Poets series)
1963, pp. 58-9

Passages from the writings of other authors

What FitzGerald has to say, as well as the way in which he chooses to say it, has little in common with other poets of the present time, whether in Australia or elsewhere. As with his language, the origins of his ideas can be found in the Sydney of his youth. The materialism, the praise of energy and action without very much regard for what kind of action is seen all through his work. He does not, like many modern writers, retreat to religion for comfort, or fall into despair at the prospect of man's possible self-annihilation, or writhe in self-disgust at the gap between his idealism and his sensual nature. He asserts, steadily and calmly, the value of work well done, of pleasure enjoyed; and he asserts too the potential dignity of man. It is easy to see how FitzGerald's views, pushed a little in the direction of caricature, could seem in some ways like a restrained version of W. E. Henley's 'Invictus'. It is not without some justification that Judith Wright (in her essay on FitzGerald in *Preoccupations in Australian Poetry*) refers, after a quotation from 'Heemskerck Shoals', to 'the Kipling notion of the universe'. Her whole essay shows a curious struggle between her repugnance for FitzGerald's ideas (as she conceives them) and her recognition of the quality of his poetry. She cuts the Gordian knot by saying 'Philosophies, however, are not poetry; and even if FitzGerald's man-of-action viewpoint on the world does not always convince us, the poetry remains'; and she concludes with a generous tribute.

But with FitzGerald, it seems to me, the philosophy to a large extent *is* the poetry: he is a 'poet of statement' and his poetry stands up to re-reading because of the truth and wisdom of what it says, sometimes in spite of some ungainliness in the saying. Miss Wright's remark 'FitzGerald seems a poet for the man-of-action in need of a faith for everyday-use' (p. 161) disparaging in its context, is all the same true . . . the strict integrity of FitzGerald's report on experience in *Forty Years' Poems* is one of the strongest impressions that comes from reading. There is a steady progress, a development of mood and understanding as the poet moves from early manhood through maturity; though the vista changes, past experience does not have to be denied, and there is no flinching from the harder truths of approaching old age. In this process the sometimes disordered or overstuffed syntax can seem itself a virtue, as in the epigram 'Experience':

> In always a fumbled and strange task,
> Not scribed to a template, squared or planned,
> and never drafted at the desk,
> this tool shapes clumsily to the hand.   (p. 86)

K

The sense that the poet (or his persona) is thinking aloud, is with effort making his way to the understanding of his own experience, is often felt in FitzGerald. For this the dancer's elegant stance would not be apposite, and we have instead (to use the most obvious analogy) the heavy-booted surveyor's stride, over rough and unknown country.

F. H. Mares, 'The Poetry of Robert FitzGerald',
Southerly, vol. 26, no. 1, 1966, pp. 4-6

FitzGerald once told me that he dropped upon the theme of another of his finest poems, 'Fifth Day', about the trial of Warren Hastings, when he was up at the Sydney Public Library for no other purpose than to study different systems of shorthand . . . Joseph Gurney, who reported the Hastings trial was the inventor of a shorthand system . . .

Douglas Stewart, 'Robert D. FitzGerald: a Background
to his Poetry', in *The Literature of Australia,*
ed. Geoffrey Dutton, 1964, pp. 334-5

The poems are close-knit and introspectively treat of various philosophical and historical themes. They require close attention and repay the trouble taken. They do not rush out into their subjects but as it were withdrawn from them to ponder and contain them in carefully wrought forms of imagery and thought. They have a quality of knobbled stoicism, are slow-moving and painstakingly conscientious. But, above all, they give a sense of inner development and of personal integration such as is rarely found elsewhere . . . He is often turgid, lacking in lyricism, seems in no way concerned to dramatize himself, or make any claims on the world; his language is frequently awkward, his philosophizing is wearying. There is something old-fashioned and restrictive about him. Yet he is plainly one of the best writers in Australia — and that by virtue of his imaginative honesty, by the way in which he reveals himself as a man who has sought to stabilize his world, not from outside, but from the painstaking development of his own inner resources.

Noel Macainsh, review of *Southmost Twelve,*
in *Overland,* no. 26, 1963, p. 40.

The 'Fifth Day' . . . deals with the fifth day of the trial of Warren Hastings; and, unlike, 'Heemskerck Shoals', it is not a third-person dramatic monologue. It is rather like the first scene of a film scenario, written in verse. We see Hastings, the victim; Edmund Burke, the prosecutor; Francis, the informant; the two

Houses of Parliament assembled; the fashionable onlookers, eaten with curiosity. We see all this, now through the eyes of Joseph Gurney, a clerk whose only part in the proceedings is to record them, and who is quite relieved when Burke collapses under the strain, because it gives him the opportunity to go home early.

Again, the theme is that of the continuity of human experience. But now it is played with variations. Every man, says FitzGerald, is responsible for the actions of all his fellow-men . . . Men are actors in the drama of life, and so 'Attitude matters; bearing'. It is only by the recorded gesture and pose that we can assess events which have long ago become part of the stream of time. The changing fortunes of men are insignificant compared with the revealing externals which Joseph Gurney's pen, the witless instrument of the disinterested paid scribe, can record for us:

> Results mean little; they cancel and coalesce.
> A gesture will outweigh them, a trick of dress.

In such a view of life as this, the hero is not any one man, but mankind. The presumptive hero, be he Hastings or Burke, is there to endure for the sake of posterity; it is not his role to triumph . . . To act is to endure the rigours of one's representative role in time.

'Fifth Day' is a very intelligent, beautifully balanced and mature poem. One would understand, however, if the bulk of modern readers found it arid and boring; its value is not guaranteed by any staple in their reading; it is, in fact, a completely new mode in contemporary poetry. FitzGerald's theme has not really changed, except in depth and complexity. His basic method, however, has altered entirely . . . he is concerned with a poetry of statement, a poetry of ideas; and his method is to take an historical character, place him in some imaginative context which has possibilities for his dramatic development and, by analysing either his own thoughts or FitzGerald's comments on him, to show the philosophical significance of the adventure in which he is engaged. It is, as I have said, a quite new method. The modern poets, Pound and Eliot for example, who have attempted to extend our conception of drama in short poems have done nothing like it. Nor has any Australian poet, with the exception of Francis Webb, who probably learnt much of his technique from FitzGerald in any case. The nearest parallel is with Browning, a poet who shares much of his joyful, realistic spirit with FitzGerald. Yet even Browning has contributed little, if indeed he has contributed anything save personal example, to 'Fifth Day' and 'Transaction'.

Vincent Buckley, Essays in Poetry, 1957, pp. 133-5

ROBERT D. FITZGERALD

Fifth Day

In William Rufus's hall the galleries reached
half to the rafters like a roost for lords,
perching the fashion of England; back seats fetched
more than a nabob's bribe. The season affords
nothing so sought as these hard boards;
so rustling ladies, crush your muslin frocks . . .
There's Mrs Fitzherbert in the royal box.

Scarlet and ermine judges, wigs, gold laces,
canopies, woolsacks, drapings in red and green
for Peers' benches and Commons'—the culprit faces
a canvas not a court, a painted scene;
and from the obsolete frame there lean
figures trapped for tomorrow: history hooks
the observer into its foreground while he looks.

The proclamation for silence! Silence lies deep
under two hundred years. Almost you would say
the heralds are varnished over, standing asleep,
and the voice demanding silence has echoed away
far into silence. As if that day
were flat, still surface at last. But there survives
a hand in the midst, turning old thoughts, old lives.

Quill-marks migrate across a writing-block—
it is Joseph Gurney's hand. He heads his page:
'Fifth day: it wants a quarter of twelve o'clock:
the Chancellor presides'; so sets a stage
where words must jostle and engage
and die on utterance. But as they pass
paper shall catch their breaths like fog on glass.

'Warren Hastings Esquire, come forth in court
to save thee and thy bail' . . . Seven years shall run;
but a verdict will not end it—would a report
settle affairs in India, cool that sun
that policies well and ill begun
curve about since da Gama? Britain was built
round India and on Hastings—prove his guilt!

'Charges of misdemeanours and high crimes'—
prove—if proved, share them! Long ago, far hence,
they are drowned under the influx of new times.
What's done goes on for ever as consequence;
but there's some blurring of evidence
by happenings more at elbow. Why try this man?
Hastings is no concern of Pakistan.

But it concerns all men that what they do
remains significant unbroken thread
of the fabric of our living. A man spoke so,
and acted so; and everything done or said
is superseded and overlaid
by change of time and pattern. Be that as it may,
there was need he lift his finger, say his say.

Attitude matters: bearing. Action in the end
goes down the stream as motion, merges as such
with the whole of life and time; but islands stand:
dignity and distinctness that attach
to the inmost being of us each.
It matters for man's private respect that still
face differs from face and will from will.

It is important how men looked and were.
Infirm, staggering a little, as Hastings was,
his voice was steady as his eyes. Kneeling at the bar
(ruler but late of millions) had steeled his poise;
he fronted inescapable loss
and thrown, stinking malice and disrepute,
calmly, a plain man in a plain suit.

Undersized, spare, licked dry by tropic heat;
one, with severe forehead and hard lips,
who had taken age's shilling and complete
grey uniform though not its grey eclipse—
with movements like commands, like whips:
here is the centre, whether for applause or loathing,
when evidence and acquittal alike mean nothing.

But the eye strays from centre. The axle's part
is just to endure the play and spin of the spokes.
It is another figure rouses the heart,
a scholar loving his nation above his books,

who, pushed by a conscience that provokes
past reason or discretion, steps, half blind,
to darkness of anger from great light of his mind.

A compact, muscular man warms to the work
which will embitter him in another's feud,
his own mission and error. Edmund Burke
for right's clear sake is hounding his pursued,
inveterate, through this seven years' cloud
where subtle poison—Francis—steeps him whole;
he stands at the middle of the floor and twists his scroll.

'My lords, the gentlemen whom the Commons appoint
to manage this prosecution direct me thus
to inform your lordships' . . . The cool phrases joint
one into other, and clause links on clause
wrought arguments whereby the cause
of justice and upright dealing may extend
from Westminster to India, and beyond.

Pitt sits near Fox and the managers, listens and learns.
Burke's heavy features liven with that magic
under them and their spectacles, which turns
knowledge to vision, and vision to strategic
marshalling of words and march of logic
through illustrations like landscapes and up steep
Quebec heights of statistics. Fox is asleep.

Francis is awake—behind the mask of his face,
inscrutable . . . as Junius. 'I have found,'
Hastings had said, 'in private as in his place,
he is void of truth and honour.' But cards go round;
brilliant, elegant as unsound,
he is one to hold them craftily, lead them well;
Hastings is now his victim, Burke his tool.

Something is eternal in the tugging of minds
which is not in mountains or monuments maturing
through day and darkness of centuries; something
    that binds
life into tensions and balances enduring
amid flowers withering and years flowering;
whereby in the instant of contest men outlive
upshots that melt in hot hands that achieve.

The fifth day wore to its close. On his feet still,
Burke was become tired body, who was cold brain
of impersonal Accusation. Suddenly ill,
he suddenly was himself, forcing through pain
words that seemed far off and in vain—
empty things scattered about by someone else,
a child dressed up in a bob-wig, playing with shells.

That moment swallows everything, like the gulf
two hundred years are hushed in: the fatigues
that buzzed like sickness in his brain; the trial itself
which was a swarming of motives and intrigues.
All the antagonisms, leagues,
plots and pamphlets are folded up, collapse;
but still the persons move, the drama shapes.

Here is displayed failure. Though there ensues
a recovery, a tomorrow that shall atone—
another hour, when Burke's voice shall cry: 'Choose!'
and he shall stand in England almost alone,
weighing a guillotine and a throne—
results mean little; they cancel and coalesce.
A gesture will outweigh them, a trick of dress.

The common work outweighs them—the anonymous gift
to the future, living, widening. What indeed
of that old struggle matters or would be left
but for an ordinary fellow's simple need,
who had a family to feed
and liked going to church looked up to, known
as a man with a tidy business of his own?

Fox hurried to Burke's aid. The court adjourned.
Gurney stoppered his inkhorn, wiped his pen ...
Poor Mr Burke! But it was money earned
lightly and sweetened labour, for lesser men,
to go home early now and then.
Tuck today under an arm—though Hastings bent
that frown, there remained but shorthand. He bowed
    and went.

Song in Autumn

Though we have put
white breath to its brief caper
in the early air,
and have known elsewhere
stiff fingers, frost underfoot,
sun thin as paper;

cold then was a lens
focussing sight, and showed that riggers' gear,
the spider's cables,
anchored between the immense
steel trusses of built grass. The hills were so near
you could pick up pebbles.

It is different at evening: damp rises
not crisp or definite like frost
but seeping into the blood and brain—
the end of enterprises.
And while, out of many things lost,
courage may remain,

this much is certain
from others' experience
and was indeed foretold:
noon's over; the days shorten.
Let there be no pretence;
none here likes the cold.

Beginnings

Not to have known the hard-bitten,
tight-lipped Caesar
clamped down on savage Britain;
or, moving closer,
not to have watched Cook
drawing thin lines across
the last sea's uncut book
is my own certain loss;

as too is having come late,
the other side of the dark
from that bearded sedate
Hargrave of Stanwell Park,

and so to have missed, some bright
morning, in the salty, stiff
north-easter, a crank with a kite—
steadied above the cliff.

Beginnings once known
are lost. Perpetual day,
wheeling, has grown
each year further away
from the original strength
of any action or mind
used, and at length
fallen behind.

One might give much
to bring to the hand
for sight and touch
cities under the sand
and to talk and trade
with the plain folk met
could we walk with the first who made
an alphabet.

But more than to look back
we choose this day's concern
with everything in the track,
and would give most to learn
outcomes of all we found
and what next builds to the stars.
I regret I shall not be around
to stand on Mars.

ERNEST MOLL

Eagles Over the Lambing Paddock

The business of the lambing ewes would make me
At times a trifle sick. The strain and quiver
Of life just squeezed past death to stand and shiver
Wet in the cold on wobbly legs would shake me
With pity for these accidents of lust,
Sometimes with mere disgust.

But I would watch the wedge-tailed eagle wheeling
In skies as biting blue as ocean spaces,
Great wing above the messy commonplaces
Of birth and death and the weak sprawl of feeling;
And coolly then would flow through heart and brain
Respect for life again.

RONALD McCUAIG

Au Tombeau de mon Père

I went on Friday afternoons
Among the knives and forks and spoons
Where mounted grindstones flanked the floor
To my father's office door.

So serious a man was he,
The Buyer for the Cutlery . . .
I found him sketching lamps from stock
In his big stock-records book,

And when he turned the page to me:
'Not bad for an old codger, eh?'
I thought this frivolous in him,
Preferring what he said to them:

They wanted reparations paid
In German gold and not in trade,
But he rebuked such attitudes:
'You'll have to take it out in goods.'

And what they did in time was just,
He said, what he had said they must:
If Time had any end in sight
It was, to prove my father right.

The evening came, and changed him coats,
Produced a rag and rubbed his boots,
And then a mirror and a brush
And smoothed his beard and his moustache;

A sign for blinds outside to fall
On shelves and showcases, and all
Their hammers, chisels, planes and spades,
And pocket-knives with seven blades.

Then, in the lift, the patted back:
'He's growing like you, Mr Mac!'
(The hearty voices thus implied
A reason for our mutual pride.)

And so the front-door roundabout
Gathered us in and swept us out
To sausage, tea in separate pots,
And jellies crowned with creamy clots.

And once he took me on to a
Recital, to hear Seidel play,
And Hutchens spanked the piano-bass,
Never looking where it was.

When I got home I practised this,
But somehow always seemed to miss,
And my cigar-box violin,
After Seidel's, sounded thin.

And once he took me to a bill
Of sporadic vaudeville.
A man and woman held the stage;
She sneered in simulated rage,

And when he made a shrewd reply
He'd lift his oval shirt-front high
And slap his bare and hairy chest
To celebrate his raucous jest.

Then, as the shout of joy ensued,
Uniting mime and multitude,
And mine rang out an octave higher,
A boy-soprano's in that choir,

My father's smile was half unease,
Half pleasure in his power to please:
'Try not to laugh so loudly, Ron;
Those women think you're catching on.'

But far more often it was to
The School of Arts we used to go;
Up the dusty stairway's gloom,
Through the musty reading-room

And out to a veranda-seat
Overlooking Hunter Street.
There in the dark my father sat,
Pipe in mouth, to meditate.

A cake-shop glowed across the way
With a rainbow-cake display;
I never saw its keeper there,
And never saw a customer,

And yet there was activity
High in the south-western sky:
A bottle flashing on a sign
Advertising someone's wine.

So, as my father thought and thought
(Considering lines of saws he'd bought,
Or, silence both his church and club,
Feeling close to Nature's hub,

Or maybe merely practising
Never saying anything,
Since he could go, when deeply stirred,
Months, at home, without a word,

Or pondering the indignity
Of having to put up with me),
I contemplated, half awake,
The flashing wine, the glowing cake:

The wine that no one can decant,
And the cake we didn't want:
As Mr Blake's Redeemer said,
'This the wine, and this the bread.'

KENNETH MACKENZIE

The Wagtail's Nest

Moulded in cobweb, horse-hair, cow-hair, grass and soft, stray
feathers
the nest is a cup shaped by the beak of desire and the breast of
love
accurately yet with a careless look set in the joint of a slender
sloping branch of the dying pepper tree. The hen's touch is
tender,
she smooths the lip of the cup with her black throat and every
amorous move
she makes is a pledge of the nest's strength against time and all
weathers.

The eggs in the bowl of the grey nest are the fruits of love that
flowered apart
in a petalled spreading of wings when the wind was cold and the
days came blue and bright
and the dying tree with a gallant desperate gesture plumed its age
with green
feathery pinnate leaves more perfectly curved than even its
youth's had been
so that when the increasing moon of the month shone stronger
late at night
fluttering shadows touched the sitting bird with dark and delicate
art.

The cock unsleeping sings all night in the besom crown of the
dead tree
stripped of its bark last year and sweeping still the floor of the
moonlit sky.
He says without fail *You sweet innocent creature* in clearly
whispering notes.

Night Duty

Old Young who sleeps by day by night
   talks madly in his rested brain
where in his bed he sits upright
   drugged against movement, against pain;
   shouts whispers moans and shouts again.

The nurse holding the lantern low
  hears every cry or sigh but his
as she goes lightly to and fro.
    His unrelenting memories
    are of what was: he knows no is

and she with difficult restraint
  goes past and on and bends to hear
some too-familiar poor complaint
    from sleepless lips that cannot bear
    the tides of darkness, and the fear.

She is the conscience of the place
  when lights are out or screened away.
Her shadowy averted face
    is like an empty mask of clay
    cast in the mould of yesterday

unrecognisable now; her hands
  emerged from chaos reassure
the night's distortion; while she stands
    momently near, the shapeless hour
    takes shape, is momently secure.

Old Young, the nurse, the night, the flame
  within the shielded globe of glass
pause like the players in a game
    held by some delicate impasse;
    and while they pause the seconds mass

to break the half-cast spell, to whirl
  the hour apart once more in night.
The nurse becomes a simple girl
    who with a desolate air of flight
    goes swiftly treading out in light.

J. S. MANIFOLD

The Tomb of Lieutenant John Learmonth, A.I.F.

At the end of Crete he took to the hills, and said he'd fight it out with
a revolver. He was a great soldier.

—One of his men in a letter

This is not sorrow, this is work: I build
A cairn of words over a silent man,
My friend John Learmonth whom the Germans killed.

There was no word of hero in his plan;
Verse should have been his love and peace his trade,
But history turned him to a partisan.

For from the battle as his bones are laid
Crete will remember him. Remember well,
Mountains of Crete, the Second Field Brigade!

Say Crete, and there is little more to tell
Of muddle tall as treachery, despair
And black defeat resounding like a bell;

But bring the magnifying focus near
And in contempt of muddle and defeat
The old heroic virtues still appear.

Australian blood where hot and icy meet
(James Hogg and Lermontov were of his kin)
Lie still and fertilize the fields of Crete.

*   *   *

Schoolboy, I watched his ballading begin:
Billy and bullocky and billabong,
Our properties of childhood, all were in.

I hear the air though not the undersong,
The fierceness and resolve; but all the same
They're the tradition, and tradition's strong.

Swagman and bushranger die hard, die game,
Die fighting, like that wild colonial boy—
Jack Dowling, says the ballad, was his name.

He also spun his pistol like a toy,
Turned to the hills like a wolf or kangaroo,
And faced destruction with a bitter joy.

His freedom gave him nothing else to do
But set his back against his family tree
And fight the better for the fact he knew

He was as good as dead. Because the sea
Was closed and the air dark and the land lost,
'They'll never capture me alive,' said he.

       *   *   *

That's courage chemically pure, uncrossed
with sacrifice or duty or career,
Which counts and pays in ready coin the cost

Of holding course. Armies are not its sphere
Where all's contrived to achieve its counterfeit;
It swears with discipline, it's volunteer.

I could as hardly make a moral fit
Around it as around a lightning flash.
There is no moral, that's the point of it,

No moral, but I'm glad of this panache
That sparkles, as from flint, from us and steel,
True to no crown nor presidential sash

Nor flag nor fame. Let others mourn and feel
He died for nothing: nothings have their place.
While thus the kind and civilized conceal

This spring of unsuspected inward grace
And look on death as equals, I am filled
With queer affection for the human race.

HAROLD STEWART

from *A Flight of Wild Geese*

Down the sky in file the wild geese tack,
Slanting their obliquely angled track
To reach the estuary's banks of sand,
Where basalt blocks have sunk along the strand.
The leader there comes skidding in, to sit
On a long splash, for the sheer sport of it:
His broad tail-feathers fan to brake the flight,
His webbed feet splay, and his red legs alight,

Fixed in the instant's clear aquamarine,
So still the surface-water is, and green.
To wash his travel-dusty feathers clean,
He ducks, and ladles over back and head
Wingfuls of water, till its trickles spread.
Next he stands upright in the water-rings,
Throws out his breast, and flaps his wide wings;
Then sits again, and shakes his tail to shed
Stray superfluous drops that diamonded
His oily coverts; then, with beak depressed,
Worries the grey pin-plumage at his breast,
Restoring comfort with a fluffed unrest;
And last, his bathing over, preens and grooms
Down smooth and trim his toilet-ruffled plumes.
More glide in after him. The others land,
Pinions aloft, and settle upon the sand;
Where flatly snapping bills hiss and contest
Scraps of aquatic weed not long possessed.
Pushing a fold of glass against the stream,
One paddles in pursuit of his own gleam.
Another stoops his pliant neck to sip
This running ripple with the glassy lip,
And cranes to swallow after every dip.
A third, whose bill tugged at the wavering weeds,
Lifts their dripping ribbons up, and feeds.
Riding its undulated calm, the fleet
Of geese sets sail upon the glaucous sheet;
But a snapped stick startles one among
The floating flock. Instantly all are sprung!
As low over the water skims each pair,
The wing-tip beaten downward through the air
Touches its upward-beaten image there.
Once in the central sky, they travel south
Beyond the sandspit at the river's mouth,
Beyond the dim horizon. All are gone.
But, like a drift of feathers dropped upon
The refluent air after their motion has flown,
A soft grey flocculence of cloud is strown,
Hovering, while invisible waves of wake
Diverge and on the mountains, sprayless, break.

Wu Tao-tzŭ

'They have migrated toward a warmer clime.'

Chang Chih-ho

'They will be here now till the end of time.'

A fitful breeze that springs up off the bay,
Bending the plume-topped grasses all one way
And carrying silver-seeded fluff astray,
Just as suddenly drops. At once the rushes'
Thicket of dried whispers thins and hushes
To a faint rustle. Nothing stirs the brake.
Chang winds his fishing-line in from the lake:
Wu's face is lost in an astonished look,
For dangling thence is neither bait nor hook!

Wu Tao-tzǔ

'How can you ever hope to catch a stray
Tadpole, though you angle here all day?
That is no way to get a bite! You need
A tempting bait: some juicy worm or weed
To hide the hook of cunning, if you wish
To cast the right enticement for a fish.'

Chang Chih-ho

'Ah! But that's not what I was fishing for!'

He poles his lean black punt away from shore.
The layered streaks of vapour, closing in,
Leave no trace that he has ever been . . .

Into infinite distance, sad and clear,
Recede the miles of autumn atmosphere:
With pale citrine tone, the watery light
That shines out after rain, washes their height.
The autumn mountain, swept as neat and clean
As the tidy winds can, reclines serene:
No twig is out of place; no leaf is seen
Of all the tarnished ruin of gold that lay
So densely underfoot but yesterday,
Claimed by the earth as tribute to decay.

Upon its sides the naked forests brood,
Locked in a crystalline disquietude;
And looped with sleeping vines and beards of moss,
Despair for want of leaves, the season's loss.
Each tall gauntly calligraphic tree,
Forked against the light's sour clarity,
Soars with static branches, sparse and bare,
In that remote and disappointed air.
An empty vast, the autumn waters lie,
Merging into the open sea of sky.
Slowly the ebb goes out, and from the height
Drains away the westering tide of light.

Ah! The evening's mood is growing late.
The peasant enters now his brushwood gate.
The garden, overgrown with grass and weed
Wher: spires of wilding lettuce run to seed,
Lies drenched with recent rain, and desolate.
A sulphur-coloured butterfly chases its mate
Over the fence with devious flutterings:
They are the only autumn leaves with wings.
The altered air that chills the end of day
Makes the fishing-nets and tackle sway
Gently over on their bamboo poles.
And now a temple-bell remotely tolls
The still and solemn hour; now holds its peace.
The work of men, the year's affairs decrease.
Now lamps are lit in windows, far and near:
See! Through the yellow dusk their flames appear.
Within the peasant's hut two suppers wait.
Ah! The evening's mood is growing late.

A smooth moon in the laminated fog
Whose levels weave above the stagnant bog
Their trails of gossamer, is hanging low
Its pallid disc, too early yet to glow.
Beside this languid marsh the artist walks.
Still to the old and withered lotus stalks
The rattling seeds in conic pods adhere;
The round leaves droop, their flounces tattered, sere;
And sere the willow-leaves spin as they sift
On the despondent pond a falling drift.
There, like yellow sampans, they are thrust
Aimlessly along by a tired gust

To strand in a backwater. There some dust
Is spent, and settles, where the waste becalms
Among an undergrowth of roots with arms.
For now the world of nature grows subdued
And grave with long autumnal lassitude.

Out on the lake, one solitary sail
Goes home into the world. With this detail
The old recluse aboard his fishing-smack
Sketches in the landscape's only lack:
Its blind of mat, diminished, outward blown.
One last goose wings on its way alone:
A flick of ink against the silken sky,
Gone with the echo from a far high cry . . .

Wu Tao-tzŭ

'A lone goose and a lone sail depart:
They do not leave the shore, they leave the heart.'

NAN McDONALD

Wet Summer: Botanic Gardens

Under the low dark sky and the sodden leaves
Poor Summer bared her shoulder with coy grace,
Her marble flesh streaked with mortality,
Her sheaf of wheat lay mildewed on her arm,
Her eyes stared vacant from her tear-stained face
On paths empty at noon, on glooms beneath
Great fig-trees, where the drop of rotting fruit
Broke the warm, damp hush, on unbelievable green
Of wet grass still unfaded by the sun
In this strange season. Once we laughed to see
That foolish white thing named for the brazen queen
Whose sword we knew, the fierce and splendid one.

But tonight, alone with the steady sound of rain,
I do not smile, seeing her image there
On the haunted edge of sleep — the blackening marble,
The blind and weeping eyes, the ruined grain —
Seeing this season of the world's despair.

Photograph of an Actress, c. 1860

Long schoolroom days, drowsy with chanting voices
And heat from the iron roof, and on the wall,
Flesh drought-devoured and eyes set on despair,
The explorers come to their last camp. Recall
That picture when you look on this, for there—
In the pack in the foreground? In the leader's rags?—
This small flat case lay hidden. When night came
He drew it out and kissed, late and alone,
Her young round throat, smooth cheek, and curled
    dark hair . . .
Then, being mortal, may have known love's flame
Dying within him by the dying fire;
Merely to live became his heart's desire.

As for her, her heart broke, but was joined once more
And served her well enough in later years
(Her talent was too slight for tragedy)
Yet a flawed heart reflects a different light,
At times a double scene. So on nights long after
When the rain murmured like remembered tears
On the high theatre roof, she still might see
The desert sun strike downward, hot and white,
Blinding the gaslight, showing the crack in the gilt,
Moth-graze in plush, melting the paint she wore—
See players mime and mouth like phantoms then
Against the rock-hewn figures of doomed men.

No doubt the applause of London crowds was sweet
But it would have an undertone for ears
That had learnt first in Melbourne how the walls
May reel to wave on bursting wave of cheers
Bearing the rider on down the long street
(His eyes still seeking hers); how the sound falls
Away so soon, and faintly out of silence
Comes to the few who listen the northward tread
Of horses and of camels, then human feet
Stumbling in dust, and last the tiny whisper
Of running ants over dry sand, dry skin,
And in the sockets where those eyes had been.

She died of fever in New Orleans, still young,
Far indeed from the land of her Irish hero's sleeping.

How should her light foot print so harsh a ground,
Her smile find place in that grim tableau hung
On schoolroom walls? Yet it may be when sickness
Had burned her body gaunt as his, and dried
Her lips enough to take the poor kiss given
Her pictured face so long ago, she found
His camp at last, and there, too great for weeping,
Held to her breast the adder of that country,
Felt the fangs bite, the intricate knot untied,
Set her crown straight, and lay down at his side.

SELECT BIBLIOGRAPHY

ROBERT D. FITZGERALD

The Greater Apollo (privately printed), 1927.
To Meet the Sun, Angus & Robertson, Sydney, 1929.
Moonlight Acre, Melbourne University Press, Melbourne, 1938.
Heemskerck Shoals, Mountainside Press, Melbourne, 1949.
Between Two Tides, 1952.
This Night's Orbit, 1953.
The Wind at Your Door, 1959.
Southmost Twelve, 1962.
Selected Poems (Australian Poets series), Angus & Robertson, Sydney, 1963.
Forty Years' Poems, 1965.
R. D. FitzGerald Reads from his own Work (Poets on Record series), University of Queensland Press, Brisbane, 1971.

The Elements of Poetry, University of Queensland Press, Brisbane, 1963.

Van Wageningen, J. M., and O'Brien, P.A., *R. D. FitzGerald: A Bibliography*, Libraries Board of South Australia, 1970.

Buckley, Vincent, 'The Development of R. D. FitzGerald', in *Essays in Poetry, Mainly Australian*, Melbourne University Press, Melbourne, 1957.
Oliver, H. J., 'The Achievement of R. D. FitzGerald', *Meanjin*, vol. 13, no. 1, 1954; reprinted in *Australian Literary Criticism*, ed. Grahame Johnston, Oxford University Press, Melbourne, 1962.
Stewart, Douglas, 'Robert D. FitzGerald, a Background to his Poetry', in *The Literature of Australia*, ed. Geoffrey Dutton, Penguin Books, Melbourne, 1964.
Todd, F. M., 'The Poetry of R. D. FitzGerald,' *Twentieth Century*, vol. 9, no. 1, 1954.
Wright, Judith, 'R. D. FitzGerald', in *Preoccupations in Australian Poetry*, Oxford University Press, Melbourne, 1965.

HAROLD STEWART

Phoenix Wings, Angus & Robertson, Sydney, 1948.
Orpheus and Other Poems, 1956.
A Net of Fireflies, Tuttle, Vermont & Tokyo, 1960.
A Chime of Windbells, Tuttle, Vermont & Tokyo, 1969.

KENNETH MACKENZIE

Our Earth, Angus & Robertson, Sydney, 1937.
The Moonlit Doorway, Angus & Robertson, Sydney, 1944.
Selected Poems, ed. Douglas Stewart, Angus & Robertson, Sydney, 1961.
The Poems of Kenneth Mackenzie, ed. Evan Jones and Geoffrey Little, Angus & Robertson, Sydney, 1972.

Jones, Evan, *Kenneth Mackenzie* (Australian Writers and their Work series), Oxford University Press, Melbourne, 1969.

ERNEST MOLL

Cut from Mulga, Melbourne University Press, Melbourne, 1940.
Brief Waters, Australasian Publishing Co., Sydney, 1945.
Beware the Cuckoo, Australasian Publishing Co., Sydney, 1947.
The Waterhole, Angus & Robertson, Sydney, 1948.
The Lifted Spear, Angus & Robertson, Sydney, 1953.
Poems 1940-1955, Angus & Robertson, Sydney, 1957 (comprises the five preceding volumes).
Below These Hills, Melbourne University Press, Melbourne, 1957.
The Rainbow Serpent, Angus & Robertson, Sydney, 1962.
Briseis, New York, 1965.
The Road to Cactus-Land, Edwards & Shaw, Sydney, 1971.

RONALD McCUAIG

Vaudeville (privately printed), Sydney, 1938.
The Wanton Goldfish (privately printed), Sydney, 1941.
Quod Ronald McCuaig, Angus & Robertson, Sydney, 1946.
The Ballad of Bloodthirsty Bessie, Angus & Robertson, Sydney, 1961.

J. S. MANIFOLD

The Death of Ned Kelly and Other Ballads, Favil Press, London, 1941.
Trident (with David Martin and H. Nicholson), Fore Publications, London, 1944.
Selected Verse, Day, New York, 1946, and Dobson, London, 1948.
Nightmares and Sunhorses, Overland, Melbourne, 1961.
Opus 8: Poems 1961-69, University of Queensland Press, 1971.

NAN McDONALD

Pacific Sea, Angus & Robertson, Sydney, 1947.
The Lonely Fire, Angus & Robertson, Sydney, 1954.
The Lighthouse, Angus & Robertson, Sydney, 1959.
Selected Poems, Angus & Robertson, Sydney, 1969.

NOTES

1 Ingamells took the word from the glossary of James Devaney's *The Vanished Tribes* (1928), with the meaning 'to annex, to join' and he defined his peculiar use of it thus: 'The Jindyworobaks, I say, are those individuals who are endeavouring to free Australian art from whatever alien influences trammel it, that is, to bring it into proper contact with its material', (*Conditional Culture*, section III; reprinted in *The Writer in Australia*, ed. John Barnes, 1969, p. 249).

2 F. H. Mares, 'The Poetry of Judith Wright', *Australian Letters*, vol. 2, no. 1, 1960, p. 26. The relevant first stanza of 'Bora Ring' is quoted in the Introduction to Judith Wright on p. 161. The comment on it referred to by Mares is by R. F. Brissenden, 'The Poetry of Judith Wright', *Meanjin*, vol. 12, no. 3, 1953, p. 258.

3 R. H. Morrison coined the phrase 'Jindyworobakwardness' in a review of the 1946 *Jindyworobak Review* in *Southerly* vol. 9, no. 1, 1948 in a Pro and Con debate he staged.

4 See his autobiographical volume, *The Drift of Things* (1973).

5 The author explains the word as 'chaos, creation time'.

6 Reprinted in *The Writer in Australia*, ed. John Barnes, 1969. Ingamells acknowledges in his *Conditional Culture* his indebtedness to Stephensen.

7 *Meanjin Papers*, vol. 2, no. 1, 1943, p. 42.

8 'Dance Little Wombat', *Meanjin Papers*, vol. 2, no. 2, 1943.

9 An exception must be recognized in the oscillating bulletins on the state of our national consciousness issued at intervals by Judith Wright, some of which are quoted on pp. 163-5.

10 'Meanjin' (as explained in the first issue and more fully in No. 6) is an Aboriginal word for the site of Brisbane. The adoption of an Aboriginal name is in keeping with the time.

11 'Angry Penguins and After', *Quadrant*, vol. 7, no. 1, 1963, p. 5. The name of the magazine was taken from section VIII of a poem called 'Growth' in Max Harris's volume *The Gift of Blood* (1940). It refers to revellers in dinner suits:

> We know no mithridatum of despair
> as drunks, the angry penguins of the night . . .

12 *ibid.*, p. 7. Hope's article referred to is his review, under the heading 'Confessions of a Zombi', of Max Harris's prose work *The Vegetative Eye* in *Meanjin Papers*, vol. 3, no. 1, 1943. In 1944 Harold Stewart and I sent the Ern Malley poems to Max Harris, as coming from the dead poet's sister Ethel. They were burlesque exercises in the manner of the neo-romantic semi-surrealistic poetry of the Apocalyptic movement in England and *Angry Penguins* in Australia — starting with one or two relatively straight 'early' poems and ending with the late profundities of:

> And in conclusion:
> There is a moment when the pelvis
> Explodes like a grenade. I
> Who have lived in the shadow that each act
> Casts on the next act now emerge
> As loyal as the thistle that in session
> Puffs its full seed upon the indicative air.
> I have split the infinitive. Beyond is anything.

(The word 'infinitive' was printed as 'infinite' in *Angry Penguins*, and corrected in the statement by Stewart and myself published in *Fact*, the supplement to the *Sunday Sun*, 25 June, 1944.) The poems, entitled *The Darkening Ecliptic*, were the occasion of a special '1944 Autumn Number to commemorate the Australian poet Ern Malley'. Sidney Nolan provided a painting for the cover, illustrating one of the poems. The texts and the history of the hoax and the discussion surrounding it are given in *Ern Malley's Poems* (1961) with an introduction by Max Harris. Sir Herbert Read gallantly backed Max Harris's judgement even after the truth was known. A number of subsequent comments have taken the form that the hoax was unfortunate because it strengthened the philistines and frightened poets and critics into timid conformity. This is probably a myth. Philistinism has retreated, not advanced; and there is no evidence that any writer of consequence was affected in any way. It is reasonable to wonder how feeble the talent would have to be that could be deflected from serious aims in this way — or how feeble the critical mind that could be thus daunted.

13 In an essay on 'Literature and the Arts' in *Australian Civilization* (ed. Peter Coleman, 1962), I wrote: It is very pleasant to find how much in common poets have whether they have taken up opposing positions in critical discussions or not. . . Hope's 'Death of the Bird' and Douglas Stewart's 'The Silkworms' are spiritually and stylistically not so far from one another' (p 133).

14 *A Net of Fireflies* (1960) and *A Chime of Windbells* (1969), published by Tuttle.

15 See the further discussion in the Introduction to 'Continuity and Change in the Fifties' (p. 262).

16 Most of those concerned recognized that in poetry theory can never bind practice, that in the end the poet takes his good where he finds it, and does what he can, not what he or anyone else prescribes. This is made explicit by Hope in his article 'Literature Versus the Universities': 'All I know of writing at first hand and at second hand suggests to me that real creative originality and the sources of literary imagination are imperilled by too much critical theorizing. . .' (*The Cave and the Spring*, 1965, pp. 170-1; the essay is not reprinted in the 1974 edition).

17 This is further discussed under 'Continuity and Change in the Fifties' (p. 262).

18 'The Achievement of R. D. FitzGerald', *Meanjin*, vol. 13, no. 1, 1954, p. 42; reprinted in *Australian Literary Criticism*, ed. Grahame Johnston, 1962.

19 Review of *The Unceasing Ground* (1946) in *Meanjin*, vol. 7, no. 3, 1948, p. 201.

20 *Australian Poets Speak*, ed. Colin Thiele and Ian Mudie, 1961, p. 91.

21 *Meanjin*, vol. 6, no. 3, 1947, p. 199.

22 'Moll has been accused of being "Frost-bitten",' H. M. Green remarked in *Southerly*, vol. 2, no. 1, 1941, p. 18.

23 'One may doubt if Ernest G. Moll's work ever showed anything so immature as promise' said R. D. FitzGerald in *Southerly*, vol. 15, no. 2, 1954, p. 109, in a rare flash of pointed wit.

24 This may seem a strange remark, but there is a glumness in much of our criticism, a suspicion of anything entertaining.

25 Evan Jones, *Kenneth Mackenzie* (Australian Writers and their Work series), 1969; and *The Poems of Kenneth Mackenzie*, ed. Evan Jones and Geoffrey Little, 1972.

7

Judith Wright

INTRODUCTION

No recent Australian poet has won wider appreciation and critical regard than Judith Wright. A small number of her poems inevitably recur in anthologies because they are by common consent her best, and are among the finest poems we have. There is, however, disagreement about the merits of the bulk of her verse; a final assessment of her achievement will depend not merely on the undisputed best poems but on one's reaction to the rest. This is because many of these poems make high claims for themselves by the nature of their themes and language: they play for high stakes.

Judith Wright comes from a grazier family long established in New England, and on the paternal side her connections go back to early settlement in the Hunter Valley, at 'Dalwood'. This background is lovingly re-created in her book *The Generations of Men* (1959). Her encounter with the natural environment and rural life is not from an urban basis. Yet her work strikes one as the product of an observer endowed with unusual sensibility rather than a participator. Judith Wright's encounter with nature is meditative, intuitive, emotional, with strong metaphysical searching.

In some poets a personal history is the main argument of the poetry: a particular and identifiable problem or crisis — events, disasters, resolutions and despairs. Judith Wright's poetry certainly arises from personal experience; but the personal experience is not (as a rule) the theme, rather it is the accidental means to a theme which is typically general — concerned with the human condition, with what it is like to be subject to time and change, having and losing, knowing and feeling, in a world which never ceases to be strange though familiar. What also strikes one is that, though there are positives and negatives within this personal experience — unresolved conflicts in the signals that come from the outer world — there is very little interior conflict. The whole person seems to react integrally to each situation or problem; the self is not a divided one, and the poet has had little need for the ironies and ambiguities or dramatizations that many modern poets have required.

Although a personal history is not the main concern of most of the poems, it is nevertheless helpful to trace it in the poetry as a means of gaining a general view. In the first two volumes especially, there is the world of childhood and youth, as in 'Northern River':

> Where your valley grows wide in the plains
> they have felled the trees, wild river.
> Your course they have checked, and altered
> your sweet Alcaic metre.
> Not the grey kangaroo, deer-eyed, timorous,
> will come to your pools at dawn;
> but their tamed and humbled herds
> will muddy the watering places.

The sense of local history is strong: for example the memory of Aboriginal tribes driven out and exterminated haunts the poem 'Bora Ring':[1]

> The song is gone; the dance
> is secret with the dancers in the earth,
> the ritual useless, and the tribal story
> lost in an alien tale.

The world of the convicts and bushrangers is evoked in 'Country Town':

> This is no longer the landscape that they knew,
> the sad green enemy country of their exile,
> those branded men whose songs were of rebellion.
>
> .   .   .
>
> Thunderbolt was killed by Constable Walker
> long ago; the bones are buried, the story printed.

The pioneers are remembered, the bullocky with his team is commemorated; and grandmother May Wright is seen in old age walking in the garden she made in the great property she founded ('The Garden'):

> Walking slow along her garden ways,
> a bee grown old at summer's end, she dips
> and drinks that honey.

The pattern includes the impact of war, the meeting and parting of 'The Company of Lovers' under its shadow:

> and round us, round the company of lovers,
> Death draws his cordons in.

The scene has shifted to Brisbane. New England is now the land of memory, 'south of my day's circle'. The poet's new range of observation includes the city's outcasts, as in 'Metho Drinker' where the derelict in winter clutches his 'white lady' (methylated spirits laced with ammonia),

> His white and burning girl, his woman of fire . . .

There follows the experience of love, and the gestation and birth of the child which are recorded especially in the most admired of all her poems, 'Woman to Man', but also in others: for example in 'Woman's Song':

> O wake in me, my darling.
> The knife of day is bright
> to cut the thread that binds you
> within the flesh of night.[2]

Later there is also the experience of losing an unborn child, a theme which occurs also, very poignantly, in the work of Rosemary Dobson. Judith Wright expresses it in 'The Unborn', with the child's imagined voice:

> Neither awake nor asleep
> on the rack of dark I lie,
> hearing my own not-voice.
> 'What was I? I? I?'

The scene has changed to Mount Tamborine, where a new landscape had to be learned, gradually becoming another landscape of the heart. The poem 'The Cycads' (p. 171) is one result. There was a particular cycad called Grandfather Peter in the locality, a specimen, itself immensely old, of this very primitive kind of plant. In 'Sanctuary' she mentions how it was destroyed:

> . . . here the old tree stood
> for how many years? that old gnome tree
> some axe-new boy cut down.[3]

The poem 'The Forest' (p. 174) also refers to this landscape.

The private poetry during these years becomes more explicitly and insistently metaphysical in its assertion or in its seeking. At times the poet seems to succumb to the temptation that afflicts some modern writers — to try to make the words create and enact a gnosis and transfiguration desired but not attained. But more often the theme is the search, not a claim to fulfilment. There is the sense of being 'on the periphery of truth' ('For Precision'), and the poet cries out ('The Wattle-Tree'):

> Oh, that I knew that word!

In the later poetry public themes emerge more frequently. Sometimes the 'hear-the-voice-of-the-bard' note is sounded: it seems to be claimed that poets have privileged insight into current problems of war, pollution and conservation. In 'Advice to a Young Poet' it is implied that the situation is too serious for cautious restraint; the young poet is encouraged to adopt 'a prophetic stance'. The poet certainly takes her own advice. But the best poems are not those with bardic pretensions; they are those which stay close to immediate experience. There is the maternal experience as the daughter grows into a separate person; the grief of bereavement[4] which evoked a number of poems more particularly personal than usual; the strength that accepts all kinds of later growth and knowledge, as in 'Portrait':

> It was a heartfelt game, when it began —
> polish and cook and sew and mend, contrive,
> move between sink and stove, keep flower-beds weeded —
> all her love needed was that it was needed,
> and merely living kept the blood alive.
>
> Now an old habit leads from sink to stove,
> mends and keeps clean the house that looks like home,
> and waits in hunger dressed to look like love
> for the calm return of those who, when they come,
> remind her: this was a game, when it began.

COMMENTARY

Passages from the writings of Judith Wright

Since poetry has so small an audience, the notion has begun to grow up that it is a kind of survival from more primitive times, a form of communication no longer needed by modern man. The fact is rather that modern man is something like a survival of poetry, which once shaped and interpreted his world through language and the creative imagination. When poetry withers in us, the greater part of experience and reality wither too; and when this happens, we live in a desolate world of facts, not of truth — a world scarcely worth the trouble of living in.

Walt Whitman put the distinction between fact and truth succinctly, when he said:

> Logic and sermons never convince,
> The damp of the night drives deeper into my soul.

Poetry is concerned with what drives deepest into the soul. However much we may learn academically about night and dampness, unless we have experienced them we do not know the truth about them. This kind of truth is the business of poetry.

Poetry deals first of all, that is, with experience — physical experience, or emotional experience, or mental experience — and nothing that the poet learns from books or from other poets can teach him to make a poem, unless he experiences the things he writes of, and knows them so deeply that they become his personal truth.

> Introduction to *Selected Poems* (Australian Poets series), 1963, p. vi

Australia is still, for us, not a country but a state — or states — of mind. We do not yet speak from within her, but from outside; from the state of mind that describes, rather than expresses, its surroundings, or from the state of mind that imposes itself upon, rather than lives through, landscape and event . . . For we are the Antipodes, the Opposites, the Under-dogs. We still live in a hut that's upside down. Only now, gradually, is the love-hate relationship we have with this country beginning to become clear to us. Some day we will be able to think of Europe as *our* antipodes. Only then will the theme of exile, sacrifice, hope be finally worked out, and our house be right-side up at last.

> 'The Upside-down Hut', *Australian Letters,* vol. 3, no. 4, 1961, p. 30 and p. 34; reprinted in *The Writer in Australia,* ed. John Barnes, 1969

We are becoming identified with this country; we are beginning to know ourselves no longer exiles, but at home here in a proper sense of the term.

> Introduction to *Preoccupations in Australian Poetry,* 1965, p. xxi

The trouble with our relationship to Australia is that we still don't live here. I was brought up in it, you might say, and have succeeded in absorbing it, to some extent, but there's a tremendous amount still outside . . . We've really got no indigenous anything.

> Taped comment quoted by W. N. Scott, *Focus on Judith Wright,* University of Queensland Press, 1967, p. 39

John Thompson: Do you think ... that there is any intrinsic inbuilt difference between men and women, a sort of difference which will always colour male and female poetry?

Judith Wright: Oh, I think that's necessarily so, because women are much more inclined to rely on their basic experience. They're more in touch, as it were, with life in the raw. They're not dealing with it in the same way that men are. They're coping more day-to-day, and I think that women *have* to rely and should rely a good deal, on their emotional reaction to life, rather than their intellectual reaction to life; and I feel that one has, one's really walking a knife-edge there. One can't over-develop one's intellect or one loses the emotional reaction. The basic touch with life probably is women's main strength.

'Poetry in Australia: Judith Wright' interviewed by
John Thompson, *Southerly,* vol. 27, no. 1, 1967, p. 38

Passages from the writings of other authors

She is not the only modern Australian whose work reveals this unselfconscious acceptance of Australia; but she is, I believe, the first in whose poetry it has been present from the very beginning. In years to come Judith Wright will almost certainly be regarded as the typical poet of the forties: the decade in which Australian poetry came of age and learned to forget that it was adolescent and antipodean.

R. T. Brissenden, 'The Poetry of Judith Wright',
Meanjin, vol. 12, no. 3, 1953, p. 258; reprinted in
Critical Essays on Judith Wright, ed. A. K. Thomson, 1968

... She has written some fifteen poems, which seem to me as good, in their kind, as one would meet in English, and that is a considerable achievement. Her success has been all in short poems, and mainly in a sort of intensely felt still life ... [In regard to some middle-period poems]: it is what I would term ink-blot writing. And I am a dull prosaic fellow who cannot read teacups. When I look into the bottom of my cup I see a mass of tea leaves. And when I read this sort of poetry, I note a welter of strongly emotive words.

R. G. Hay, 'Judith Wright's Achievement',
Australian Letters, July 1960, p. 33 and p. 32;
reprinted in Thomson *op. cit.*

Her powers, then, are very considerable. They consist of a brilliance of image, a rhetorical facility which assists her in her image-making, an elevated sense of her mission both as woman and poet, and a strikingly strong lyrical impulse. Her experience of man's life and of the natural world is a rich one; and in her best poems it is presented in a direct, vital way, without the myriad hesitations and circumlocutions which so many modern poets use, from fear of looking too closely at the human state. When all these powers act together as agents of the one immediate and personal emotion, we get a very fine and exciting poetry. Yet, apart from a few powerful and homogeneous poems in *Woman to Man*, they have acted together all too seldom . . . Her weaknesses, too, are as obvious as her proficiencies; and they seem to arise from three separate but complementary sources: from too great a reliance on (even imitation of) other poets; from a confusion of themes and attitudes coming from her own confusion of aim, which results first in a pessimism of which the cause is inadequately defined, and secondly in the too facile optimism of the person who is a contemplative-at-will; and from a straining after original or forceful effects plus a reliance on her own facility as a maker of images. The balance is undoubtedly in her favour.

Vincent Buckley, *Essays in Poetry*, 1957, pp. 175-6

The best of Judith Wright's later poetry is not an attempt to reproduce the 'primitive' intensity of the earlier successes but represents the emergence of a more critical awareness, and a fuller conscious control. 'For My Daughter' is a return to the subject-matter of 'Woman to Child'; it is better articulated, though not as sensuously rich. 'Sports Field' develops an extended allegory, which is not a mode used earlier. It has a poignancy which is a gift of the experienced heart. In the most recent volume, *The Other Half* (1966), 'Portrait' and 'Naked Girl and Mirror' and 'Document' stand out for continuing conquest of personal experience — I must admit that I shy away from some other poems which go on about poetry and being a poet. A close formal analysis of the best of the later work would certainly reveal some continuity with the earlier work, but also some difference in spirit, reflected in change and development in method and organization.

James McAuley, 'Some Poems of Judith Wright', *Australian Literary Studies*, vol. 3, no. 3, 1968, p. 213; reprinted in Thomson *op. cit.*, and in James McAuley, *The Grammar of the Real* (1975)

The recognition so quickly won by Judith Wright's early work, in *The Moving Image* (1946) and *Woman to Man* (1949), has proved strangely prejudicial to her later verse. *The Moving Image* was a volume in which sense perceptions were held and explored, the titles of the poems reading like a series of talismans — 'Trapped Dingo', 'Bullocky', 'The Surfer', 'Nigger's Leap: New England' — and their impact coming from the sheer individuality of perception:

> South of my days' circle, part of my blood's country,
> rises that tableland, high delicate outline
> of bony slopes wincing under the winter;
> low trees blue-leaved and olive; outcropping granite —
> clean, lean, hungry country.

The same immediacy and vitality was felt in the lyrical poetry of her second book, in the set of love poems on the woman, the man and the unborn child — 'the third who lay in our embrace'.

The collections that followed, *The Gateway* (1953) and *The Two Fires* (1955), were received with less enthusiasm, if not with positive misgivings at the 'increasing impersonality' of Judith Wright's work, its movement towards the general and the abstract. To the reader who valued *The Moving Image* and *Woman to Man, The Gateway* could well seem like a collection of the poems rejected from those earlier books. Criticism of the later verse in general has been influenced by an assumption that Judith Wright was still trying to write the kind of poetry she had written before, but was now failing in the attempt. I should argue, to the contrary, that in *The Gateway* and *The Two Fires* she is attempting poetry of another kind.

It had been clear in *The Moving Image* itself that Judith Wright was not content merely to write poems of observation, however acute and sensitive: there had been a constant effort to reach beyond the immediate experience, to probe its significance. This effort was felt in the strained endings of 'The Surfer' and 'Bullocky', and in the forcing of the Homeric parallel in 'Trapped Dingo'; it was felt also in the title-poem in the attempt at a large philosophical pronouncement on Time, as 'a moving image òf eternity'. *Woman to Man,* interpreted in the light of its epigraph, upheld love ('the summary or collective law of nature . . . imposed by God upon the original particles of all things') as a counter to the destructiveness of Time, a force of renewal and regeneration. The tendencies pursued in the later verse are tendencies present from the beginning, but they confront Judith Wright with dilemmas that compel a departure from her earlier manner.

M

The surface change — the one repeatedly noted — is that the world as perceived, hitherto the main source of her poetic inspiration, ceases to dominate her field of vision. Instead it offers now a starting-point for reflection, as in 'Phaius Orchid'; or a symbolic situation to be explored, as in 'The Pool and the Star'; or it is translated from literal reality into a sphere of imagination and dream, as in 'Lion'. A poem like 'The Cycads' in *Woman to Man* already indicates the change. The trees are seen as enduring through the centuries, surviving generation after generation of other forms of life:

[stanzas 4-5 quoted, see pp. 171-2]

but the cycads are not here 'observed' as they would have been in *The Moving Image*. The reader could not learn from the poem that cycads are palm-like, or discover much else of their physical appearance as Macrozamia.* The cycads figure only as part of the reverie of the poet, as a symbol of time itself . . .

[stanzas 2-3 quoted]

Judith Wright's earlier poetry had been established in one world, the finite world available to the senses, and had drawn its strength from the clarity and vitality of her sense perceptions. The effort of the later poetry is to reach beyond that world — an effort that is always arduous and most often frustrated, but that leads Judith Wright into regions unexplored before. In *The Gateway* and *The Two Fires* the contingent world has become both an earnest of the ideal world and a denial of it, at times a prison and at a times a means of release . . .

At other moments again, the world is seen with the particularity characteristic of *The Moving Image,* but with the difference that its beauty now symbolises the plight of existence subject to time. For whom does the phaius orchid flower? For the lizards and the ants merely, in a purposeless splendour?

> Out of the brackish sand
> see the phaius orchid build
> her intricate moonlight tower
> that rusts away in flower.
>
> For whose eyes — for whose eyes
> does this blind being weave
> sand's poverty, water's sour,
> the white and black of the hour

---

* cf. the notes on the poem in Judith Wright's selection from her verse in the Australian Poets series (1963).

into the image I hold
and cannot understand?
Is it for the ants, the bees,
the lizard outside his cave,

or is it to garland time —
eternity's cold tool
that severs with its blade
the gift as soon as made?

These later poems betray an increasing consciousness of dualities that refuse to be resolved into singleness — the duality of life in time and life beyond it, of disorder and harmony, of flesh and spirit, of reason and unreason.

G. A. Wilkes, 'The Later Poetry of Judith Wright',
Southerly, vol. 25, no. 3, 1965, pp. 163-7; reprinted
in Thomson, *op. cit.*

POEMS

Bullocky

Beside his heavy-shouldered team,
thirsty with drought and chilled with rain,
he weathered all the striding years
till they ran widdershins in his brain:

Till the long solitary tracks
etched deeper with each lurching load
were populous before his eyes,
and fiends and angels used his road.

All the long straining journey grew
a mad apocalyptic dream,
and he old Moses, and the slaves
his suffering and stubborn team.

Then in his evening camp beneath
the half-light pillars of the trees
he filled the steepled cone of night
with shouted prayers and prophecies.

While past the campfire's crimson ring
the star-struck darkness cupped him round,
and centuries of cattlebells
rang with their sweet uneasy sound.

Grass is across the waggon-tracks,
and plough strikes bone beneath the grass,
and vineyards cover all the slopes
where the dead teams were used to pass.

O vine, grow close upon that bone
and hold it with your rooted hand.
The prophet Moses feeds the grape,
and fruitful is the Promised Land.

Woman to Man

The eyeless labourer in the night,
the selfless, shapeless seed I hold,
builds for its resurrection day —
silent and swift and deep from sight
foresees the unimagined light.

This is no child with a child's face;
this has no name to name it by:
yet you and I have known it well.
This is our hunter and our chase,
the third who lay in our embrace.

This is the strength that your arm knows,
the arc of flesh that is my breast,
the precise crystals of our eyes.
This is the blood's wild tree that grows
the intricate and folded rose.

This is the maker and the made;
this is the question and reply;
the blind head butting at the dark,
the blaze of light along the blade.
Oh hold me, for I am afraid.

The Bull

In the olive darkness of the sally-trees
silently moved the air from night to day.
The summer-grass was thick with honey-daisies
where he, a curled god, a red Jupiter,
heavy with power among his women lay.

But summer's bubble-sound of sweet creek-water
dwindles and is silent; the seeding grasses
grow harsh, and wind and frost in the black sallies
roughen the sleek-haired slopes. Seek him out, then,
the angry god betrayed, whose godhead passes,

and down the hillsides drive him from his mob.
What enemy steals his strength—what rival steals
his mastered cows? His thunders powerless,
the red storm of his body shrunk with fear,
runs the great bull, the dogs upon his heels.

The Cycads

Their smooth dark flames flicker at time's own root.
Round them the rising forests of the years
alter the climates of forgotten earth
and silt with leaves the strata of first birth.

Only the antique cycads sullenly
keep the old bargain life has long since broken;
and, cursed by age, through each chill century
they watch the shrunken moon, but never die,

for time forgets the promise he once made,
and change forgets that they are left alone.
Among the complicated birds and flowers
they seem a generation carved in stone.

Leaning together, down those gulfs they stare
over whose darkness dance the brilliant birds
that cry in air one moment, and are gone;
and with their countless suns the years spin on.

Take their cold seed and set it in the mind,
and its slow root will lengthen deep and deep
till, following, you cling on the last ledge
over the unthinkable, unfathomed edge
beyond which man remembers only sleep.

The Old Prison

The rows of cells are unroofed,
a flute for the wind's mouth,
who comes with a breath of ice
from the blue caves of the south.

O dark and fierce day
the wind like an angry bee
hunts for the black honey
in the pits of the hollow sea.

Waves of shadow wash
the empty shell bone-bare,
and like a bone it sings
a bitter song of air.

Who built and laboured here?
The wind and the sea say
—Their cold nest is broken
and they are blown away.

They did not breed nor love.
Each in his cell alone
cried as the wind now cries
through this flute of stone.

Night Herons

It was after a day's rain:
the street facing the west
was lit with growing yellow;
the black road gleamed.

First one child looked and saw
and told another.
Face after face, the windows
flowered with eyes.

It was like a long fuse lighted,
the news travelling.
No one called out loudly;
everyone said 'Hush.'

The light deepened; the wet road
answered in daffodil colours,
and down its centre
walked the two tall herons.

Stranger than wild birds, even,
what happened on those faces:
suddenly believing in something,
they smiled and opened.

Children thought of fountains,
circuses, swans feeding:
women remembered words
spoken when they were young.

Everyone said 'Hush;'
no one spoke loudly;
but suddenly the herons
rose and were gone. The light faded.

Extinct Birds

Charles Harpur in his journals long ago
(written in hope and love, and never printed)
recorded the birds of his time's forest—
birds long vanished with the fallen forest—
described in copperplate on unread pages.

The scarlet satin-bird, swung like a lamp in berries,
he watched in love, and then in hope described it.
There was a bird, blue, small, spangled like dew.
All now are vanished with the fallen forest.
And he, unloved, past hope, was buried,

who helped with proud stained hands to fell the forest,
and set those birds in love on unread pages;
yet thought himself immortal, being a poet.
And is he not immortal, where I found him,
in love and hope along his careful pages?—
the poet vanished, in the vanished forest,
among his brightly tinted extinct birds?

The Forest

When first I knew this forest
its flowers were strange.
Their different forms and faces
changed with the seasons' change—

white violets smudged with purple,
the wild-ginger spray,
ground-orchids small and single
haunted my day;

the thick-fleshed Murray-lily,
flame-tree's bright blood,
and where the creek runs shallow,
the cunjevoi's green hood.

When first I knew this forest,
time was to spend;
and time's renewing harvest
could never reach an end.

Now that its vines and flowers
are named and known,
like long-fulfilled desires
those first strange joys are gone.

My search is further.
There's still to name and know
beyond the flowers I gather
that one that does not wither—
the truth from which they grow.

Sports Field

Naked all night the field
breathed its dew until
the great gold ball of day
sprang up from the dark hill.

Now as the children come
the field and they are met.
Their day is measured and marked,
its lanes and tapes are set;

and the children gilt by the sun
shoulder one another;
crouch at the marks to run,
and spring, and run together—

the children pledged and matched,
and built to win or lose,
who grow, while no one watches,
the selves in their sidelong eyes.

The watchers love them in vain.
What's real here is the field,
the starter's gun, the lane,
the ball dropped or held;

and set towards the future
they run like running water,
for only the pride of winning,
the pain the losers suffer,

till the day's great golden ball
that no one ever catches,
drops; and at its fall
runners and watchers

pick up their pride and pain
won out of the measured field
and turn away again
while the star-dewed night comes cold.

So pride and pain are fastened
into the heart's future,
while naked and perilous
the night and the field glitter.

A Document

'Sign there.' I signed, but still uneasily.
I sold the coachwood forest in my name.
Both had been given me; but all the same
remember that I signed uneasily.

Ceratopetalum, Scented Satinwood:
a tree attaining seventy feet in height.
Those pale-red calyces like sunset light
burned in my mind. A flesh-pink pliant wood

used in coachbuilding. Difficult of access
(those slopes were steep). But it was World War Two.
Their wood went into bomber-planes. They grew
hundreds of years to meet those hurried axes.

Under our socio-legal dispensation
both name and woodland had been given me.
I was much younger then than any tree
matured for timber. But to help the nation

I signed the document. The stand was pure
(eight hundred trees perhaps). Uneasily
(the bark smells sweetly when you wound the tree)
I set upon this land my signature.

SELECT BIBLIOGRAPHY

The Moving Image, Meanjin Press, Melbourne, 1946.
Woman to Man, Angus & Robertson, Sydney, 1949.
The Gateway, Angus & Robertson, Sydney, 1953.
The Two Fires, Angus & Robertson, Sydney, 1955.
Birds, Angus & Robertson, Sydney, 1962.
Five Senses (selected poems), Angus & Robertson, Sydney, 1963.
Selected Poems (Australian Poets series), Angus & Robertson, Sydney, 1963.
The Other Half, Angus & Robertson, Sydney, 1966.
Collected Poems, 1942-1970, Angus & Robertson, Sydney, 1971.
Alive: Poems 1971-72, Angus & Robertson, Sydney, 1973.
Judith Wright Reads from her own Work, Poets on Record series, University of Queensland Press, Brisbane, 1974.

Preoccupations in Australian Poetry, Oxford University Press, Melbourne, 1965.
'Meaning, Value and Poetry', *Meanjin Quarterly*, vol. 27, no. 2, 1968.
'Poetry in Australia: Judith Wright', interviewed by John Thompson, *Southerly*, vol. 27, no. 1, 1967.

O'Brien, P. and Robinson, E., *Judith Wright: A Bibliography*, Libraries Board of South Australia, 1968.

Brissenden, R. F., 'The Poetry of Judith Wright', *Meanjin*, vol. 12, no. 3, 1953; reprinted in *Australian Literary Criticism*, ed. Grahame Johnston, 1962 and in A. K. Thomson (*q.v.*).
—— review of *Five Senses* in *Australian Quarterly*, vol. 36, no. 1, 1964.
Buckley, Vincent, 'The Poetry of Judith Wright' in *Essays in Poetry, Mainly Australian*, Melbourne University Press, Melbourne, 1957.
Harris, Max, 'Judith Wright', in *The Literature of Australia*, ed. Geoffrey Dutton, 1964.
Hay, R. G., 'Judith Wright's Achievements', *Australian Letters*, July 1960: reprinted in A. K. Thomson (*q.v.*).
Higham, Charles, 'Judith Wright's Vision', *Quadrant*, vol. 5, no. 3, 1961.
Hope, A. D., *Judith Wright* (Australian Writers and their Work series), Oxford University Press, Melbourne, 1975.
Jurgensen, Manfred, 'The Poetry of Judith Wright', *Makar*, vol. 7, no. 2, 1971.
McAuley, James, 'Some Poems of Judith Wright', *Australian Literary Studies*, vol. 3, no. 3, 1968; reprinted in A. K. Thomson (*q.v.*).
Mares, F. H., 'The Poetry of Judith Wright', *Durham University Journal*, vol. 50, no. 2, 1958; reprinted in *Australian Letters*, July 1960, and A. K. Thomson (*q.v.*).
Moore, T. Inglis, 'The Quest of Judith Wright', C.L.F. Lecture at Melbourne University, in A. K. Thomson (*q.v.*).
Scott, Robert Ian, 'Judith Wright's World View', *Southerly*, vol. 17, no. 4, 1956.
Scott, W. N. *Focus on Judith Wright*, 1967 (includes taped interviews).
Thomson, A. K. (ed.), *Critical Essays on Judith Wright*, 1968.
Walker, Shirley P., 'A Note on Sense-Perception in the Poetry of Judith Wright, *Westerly*, no. 4, 1973.
Wilkes, G. A., 'The Later Poetry of Judith Wright', *Southerly*, vol. 25, no. 3, 1965, reprinted in A. K. Thomson (*q.v.*).

NOTES

[1] A bora ring is the circle within which an initiation rite is performed.
[2] Compare the phrase 'the blaze of light along the blade' in 'Woman to Man'.
[3] Information related to this poem is given by A. K. Thomson in his introductory essay to the volume he has edited, *Critical Essays on Judith Wright*, 1968, p. 14.
[4] J. P. McKinney, the poet's husband, died in 1966. His philosophical work *The Challenge of Reason* (1950) indicates one source of the poet's meditative interests.

8

A. D. Hope

INTRODUCTION

Because Hope published poems fugitively and rarely in the 1940s, the nature and range of his gifts was not at first widely understood. He had a growing reputation but chiefly as a satirist, and it was only when he published his first volume, *The Wandering Islands* (1955), that he began to be generally seen as a major poet. The delay in publication was partly caused by a publisher's hesitations: the subject matter and treatment of some of the poems could have brought it within the legal category of indecency as the law was then applied. But in any case Hope was a relatively late developer. The poetry he wrote up to about his thirtieth year has mostly remained unpublished; it showed a talent in search of a theme and style. Even when his talent began to wrestle with his essential subject matter, sureness and power still developed rather slowly. The importance of poems written between 1938 and 1943, with their varied brilliance and intensity, must not be minimized, but 'Ascent into Hell' (which the poet has dated 1943-44) marks the first real conquest of the poet's difficult material; and it took the poems written from 1948 onwards to provide the basis for his later eminence.

What Hope offers is large and complex in conception and execution. Some of the most important elements can be identified by using the conventional Apollonian-Dionysian polarity,[1] but this is a device for dealing with the Protean metamorphoses of the poetry, not a scheme which the poet has proposed or might want to endorse.

The Dionysian strain consists in an assertion of will or power transcending normal limitation. It is associated with characteristic words such as passion, pride, will, instinct, power, night, demonic, god, captain, king, prince, poet. This might be said to be a kind of vitalism, but not anti-intellectual in intention.

The Apollonian strain is not so strongly affirmed. It has to do with the norms of daily existence, with the ordinary, the social and established, the morally defined. Some of the language associated with this is used with slighting intention: habit, custom, compromise, 'the frantic devotees of good and ill'. Yet some of it is more affirmative, acknowledging claims that must be met: the poet speaks of 'daylight vision', 'the real world, plain sight and common truth', 'the appointed season', 'the festivals of love, the rites of kind' — the implications are social as well as poetic.

> There was a time the poet's mission
> Was to give men their daily bread
>
> .   .   .
>
> Long narratives are out of fashion;
> Sustained invention does not please;
> And sacred truth and moral passion
> Belong to former centuries.

('Conversation with Calliope')

Some poems are one-sided in proclaiming the prerogative of godlike transcendent power for the individual who has the 'intemperate will and incorruptible pride' to exercise it — whether the man of genius be a Pharaoh lashing an enslaved nation into building a pyramid, or a genius whose 'demonic mind' refuses normal limit to build 'the great incredible monuments of art' ('Pyramis, or the House of Ascent'). The lover, too, fulfils himself only by a divinizing ascent beyond the all-too-human:

> . . . there with the mark
> Of blood upon his breast and on his brow,
> An unknown king, with my transfigured face,
> Bends your immortal body to his delight.

('The Lamp and the Jar')

Other poems are two-sided in granting some validity to the claims of the Apollonian, and acknowledging the need somehow to reconcile them with the Dionysian contraries. This is clearly the meaning of the conclusion of that obscurely contorted poem, 'An Epistle from Holofernes', in which the demonic life is (at least verbally) reconciled with the normal life:

> There's a hard thing, and yet it must be done,
> Which is: to see and live them both as one.

> The daylight vision is stronger to compel,
> But leaves us in the ignorance of hell;
> And they, who live by starlight all the time,
> Helpless and dangerous, blunder into crime;
> And we must learn and live, as yet we may,
> Vision that keeps the night and saves the day.

Entwined in this Dionysian-Apollonian antinomy is a third strain which may be called the Orphic, without which the full range of this complex poetry cannot be grasped. The Orphic gift penetrates beyond the apparently random particulars and accidents of everyday experience: it gains a sense of cosmic order, of a 'Great Design', of the 'shapes and creatures of eternity'. It is above all the poet who has access to the mysteries and the mythic patterns, and can celebrate 'the whole/Just order of the random world'.[2] The poet suffering the pain of hopeless love can turn it into vision:

> . . . These torments mind and heart approve,
> And are the sacrifice of love.
> The soul sitting apart sees what I do,
> Who win powers more than Orpheus knew,
> Though he tamed tigers and enchanted trees
> And broached the chthonic mysteries.

> ('An Epistle: Edward Sackville to Venetia Digby')

Orphic vision of cosmic order and mythic pattern is not daylight vision of human social order and moral law: nor is it a further insight springing from recognition of these. It is linked rather with Dionysian assertion of will and power:

> Yet myth has other uses: it confirms
> The heart's conjectures and approves its terms
> Against the servile speech of compromise,
> Habit which blinds, custom which overlies
> And masks us from ourselves — the myths define
> Our figure and motion in the Great Design,
> Cancel the accidents of name and place,
> Set the fact naked against naked space,
> And speak to us the truth of what we are.

> ('An Epistle from Holofernes')

It will be seen that Hope's effort to reconcile these competing elements, or somehow settle accounts with them, requires a good deal of declaration, of eloquence, even a touch of grandiloquence.

There is a characteristic note of rhetorical suasion, the verbal
enactment of an assurance that insight has now at last been
achieved.

The themes prominent in Hope's poetry can be seen reflected
in prose essays collected in *The Cave and the Spring* (1965). One
of his most interesting essays from this point of view is 'The
Argument of Arms', a study of Marlowe's *Tamburlaine,* in which
a philosophy of power is presented as valid both for the world
of action and for the world of art. It affirms a 'humanism of
war, a view in which all human values are determined by war
alone', a theory of a universe 'in which order is the creation of
strife and values are determined by strife'. Hope shows how
critics have shied away from this implication in Marlowe's work:

> The mere notion of accepting, even for the sake of argument, a
> thorough-going morality of power, aesthetics of power and logic of
> power, with its implication that only one man can achieve the end
> of life and that society is entirely subordinated to producing and
> promoting that man, these are ideas that the mind boggles at enter-
> taining (p. 122).

Hope does not, any more than Marlowe, boggle at entertaining
the idea of 'a thorough-going morality of power, aesthetics of
power and logic of power'. He quotes a striking passage from
Hazlitt about the resemblance between poetic imagination and
the operations of absolute tyrannical power, and concludes that
'the Argument of Arms and the Argument of Poetry are in their
essence the same' (p. 128).

It will be noted that in justification of Dionysian excess it is
claimed that order arises from it. Hope claims that such a
philosophy is 'not a modern theory of "might is right"; it is not
a Nietzschean view of the will to power' (p. 120).[3] He seeks rather
to reconcile it with Apollonian sobriety by deriving it from the
Aristotelian principle that every creature strives towards the
perfection of its nature. But the conclusions drawn are quite
remarkably un-Aristotelean:

> [Tamburlaine] has the natural genius for power and he actually tests
> it out against all possible contenders. He achieves the perfection of
> human nature in a world in which only one man can be perfect.
> This standard of values means that the man who imposes his will on
> all others is, in a sense, the only fully human being among them . . .
> It means in fact that the man who can achieve this and maintain
> his position must have gifts and qualities above the human. He
> partakes of the divine, a claim that Tamburlaine makes more than
> once (p. 120).

It should not be surprising if the Dionysian, Apollonian, and

Orphic tendencies in Hope's poetry give some of it an ambiguous character, or threaten it with incoherence under the increasingly masterful imposition of formal unity. I do not myself think that all the reconciliations or solutions proposed are convincing; nor that the poet necessarily regards them as more than provisional or hypothetical as a means of developing an attitude which does not grow out of a doctrine but seizes on a doctrine as a possible means of self-explanation. But at least the problem is rehearsed in exciting ways. Hope has himself, in his essay 'The Practical Critic', made an important comment:

> Why should every poem which presents us with a problem be required to offer a solution of the problem? Why should a poem be a failure if it presents an ambiguous situation but not a resolution of the ambiguity? . . . The intellectual joy of apprehending the mystery of things as they are may in fact be the very 'resolution' at which the poet aims (p. 89).

This defence of the value of rehearsing the problem can be extended to include attempts at a solution, even if these are not final or fully successful.[4]

It is as a method of containing the forces competing within his themes that Hope's poetic procedures can best be appreciated: the value he finds in adopting a definite genre (for example, formal satire, epistle, Ovidian elegy, ballad, narrative); and with this an appropriate style with traditional features, sometimes even deliberately based on a particular model (Byron, Pope, Dryden, Yeats); and in keeping with these the speaking through a *persona,* or the setting up of a situation (historical, mythical, biological) which is a means of expressing the essential subject analogically. It is because of the prominence of neo-formalist elements in Hope's poetic practice, and in his essays on poetry, that the label 'classical' has been applied to him. But romantic elements are evident in his work as well.

There is a literariness of language and a considerable dependence on subject matter derived from reading which is part of these procedures. The style is unmistakably personal and original yet also imitative and traditional. Only a writer of unusual gifts could assimilate and effectively use so many styles. (An early absorption in Leconte de Lisle and Hérédia has left its trace — Hope has remarked to me that he could once recite a good deal of these poets by heart: there is indeed a good deal in Hope that one could call Parnassian.) To some, this literariness of style and subject requires *ipso facto* an adverse assessment. Before making such a judgement such readers might ponder Hope's essay 'Frost at Midday', in *The Cave and the Spring,* in which he contrasts Wordsworth as a poet of 'the sensory imagination', dependent on direct observation, with Coleridge whose greatest gift was 'the verbal imagination', which operated by transforming impressions, derived mainly from reading, into a brilliant new creation. That Hope feels himself to be more on Coleridge's side than on Wordsworth's (as he presents them) is evident. But the fact that he explains the title of his book by saying that the Cave and the Spring stand for the sensory and the verbal imagination respectively (p. vii), and elsewhere says that these are 'the two essential gifts of the poet' (p. 105), indicates that he is well aware of the need to cultivate both gifts.

COMMENTARY

Passages from the writings of A. D. Hope

> The climate of the mind at last had changed;
> Something in human nature seemed deranged;
> Vast fogs of feeling sundered Man from men;
> Romantic swamps oozed thickly from the pen;
> And now the woolly-witted flocks protest
> That Pope lacked vegetable interest!
> And not alone mere critic foes he had,
> But mighty poets in their misery mad:
> Wordsworth the most erected spirit that fell,
> Coleridge that wrote the metaphysic of hell,
> Though great and gifted joined the general rant,
> The cant of Nature and the cant of Kant,
> Decried the clear dry light of classic art
> Which lacked 'essential passions of the heart'.

Dunciad Minor, Book III, 105-18

The first step in intelligent regeneration of the soil of poetry may well be to re-establish the discursive mode, in particular to restore the practice of formal satire.

'The Discursive Mode', *Quadrant,* vol. 1, no. 1, 1956;
reprinted in *The Cave and the Spring* (1965), p. 9

The language itself provides continual new resources for rejuvenating the traditional patterns and providing them with new and yet traditional music. The whole notion that the capital

N

resources of poetry were limited and would one day be exhausted is no more than a bogy based on ignorance of the real nature of language. Not only is the remedy of free verse a bogus remedy, the disease it pretends to cure is a popular delusion.

'Free Verse: a Post-Mortem', *Quadrant*, vol. 4, no. 2, 1960; reprinted in *The Cave and the Spring*, pp. 49-50

Thompson: What do you feel about poetry for public recitation and poetry for the study? Do you feel poetry should be read aloud?

Hope: Yes. I think that too little poetry is written to be read aloud, but I do rather agree with Robert Graves' distinction of what he calls 'eye' poems and 'ear' poems. I think there are some poems which read better on the page, and some which read better when they're read aloud.

Thompson: Yes. You feel that with your own poems, perhaps?

Hope: I'm not quite sure about that. I'm not much of a judge.

Thompson: There's another aspect. You've often been — I don't know whether criticized — but regarded as a very much a satirical and ironic poet. I don't think it's fair, but there are people — I think the English publisher of your recent book, has it on the puff that your poetry has 'a fierceness seldom felt in English literature since Swift'?

Hope: Oh yes.

Thompson: How do you feel about that?

Hope: This is something that's been pursuing me all my life, and it does puzzle me a bit sometimes. I don't feel that I'm especially savage or ironic or anything like that, but even if I were, I would say that this is not the thing at which I was aiming. My own view of what a poet is usually trying to do — what I'm trying to do — is what I'd call in general terms 'celebration of the world'. Now, celebration is an act of joy. I think the qualification I'd make there is that, you know, you can also celebrate the evil and the things that you get angry about ...

Thompson: Do you feel, for instance, that poetry should be able to handle almost any subject?

Hope: Yes. Perhaps I could best illustrate this by a remark that W. B. Yeats made, when he was similarly attacked for being savage and angry and so on. He said, 'On the contrary, this is meant to be joyful poetry' and he illustrated it by a remark from Swift, which was one of Swift's most savage remarks, 'If somebody,' said Swift, 'tells me that so-and-so is a fellow Protestant, I remember that the rat is my fellow creature.' Well, it's a pretty savage thing to say, 'That,' said Yeats, 'seems to me a thoroughly joyous remark.' Now this is the kind of feeling I would have about things that people think are purely savage, or angry, or ironical.

'Poetry in Australia: A. D. Hope', interviewed by
John Thompson, *Southerly*, vol. 26, no. 4, 1966, pp. 245-6

Passages from the writings of other authors

Every significant artist has a fundamental axis about which his work revolves, a basic perspective from which, in which, he sees the world and himself. (This is true even — perhaps especially — when the central attitude is composed of different, and maybe opposing elements.)

The aim of the following essay is to attempt to demarcate this 'frame of reference' in the poetry of A. D. Hope, as far as it has been published in *The Wandering Islands* (1955) and *Poems* (1960), and to discuss some of the implications of such a position.

The poem which gives its title to Hope's first collection expresses this basic perspective with simple directness: human isolation. 'Wandering islands' are by no means without points of possible, and sometimes even actual contact, but the meetings are in principle external, temporary only: for the ship-wrecked sailor there is no hope of rescue. (Compare here the island image in 'Ascent into Hell', and also the penultimate stanza of 'X-ray Photograph'.)

Because of its awkwardly yoked images, roughnesses of rhythm, because of its mode of statement which is at once too abstract and too explicit, this poem expresses only imperfectly the central attitude of isolation. The latter emerges in a clearer and poetically much more satisfying manner in what is doubtless one of Hope's finest poems, 'The Death of the Bird'. The bird is a natural creature, a motif in its own right, and its destiny — its lostness and final death — natural to it. At the same time it may be seen as a concrete image of Hope's view of the 'human condition':

[see poem on p. 191]

The theme of isolation which appears in the above poem in a general form (though expressed in specific, concrete images) is particularized in numerous others.

It is seen in an estrangement from his own country, his image of which (in 'Australia') is not the traditional one of a young land of promise, but an immensely aged land, lacking any real future, its cities and people depleted and unoriginal, clinging to an alien soil.

He is estranged also from much of contemporary life, to various aspects of which he has devoted a number of satirical pieces: the husband-hunting female, and especially the mild and virtuous variety ('The Brides', 'The Explorers'), 'successful' men and 'Technocratic man' ('Toast for a Golden Age', 'The Kings'), vicarious emotions ('Sportsfield'), TV and advertising ('A Commination'), religion ('Easter Hymn', 'The House of God', 'Lambkin: A Fable'), levelling ('The Age of Innocence'), and even contemporary complaints about contemporary life ('Standardization').

W. A. Suchting, 'The Poetry of A. D. Hope: a Frame of Reference', *Meanjin Quarterly*, vol. 21, no. 2, 1962, pp. 154-5

... there is little evidence in his own poetry that he has found any direct inspiration from his actual environment. His imagination is aroused not by the particularities of a place and time, but by other men's minds from other times and other places. Hope is not an observer of nature or men; he is a witness rather, and a purveyor of ideas about them. These ideas he frequently filters through literature or fables, the accumulated wisdom of mankind ... Hope's persistent tendency is away from the local, the particular and the detailed, and towards the general statement or argument ... The precision of detail which is missing from his descriptions of objects or scenes is missing too from his arguments and themes. He is adept at the large gesture, the summarizing statement ... Hope's poems present a smooth and orderly surface. While their tone moves between the extremes of facetiousness and learned gravity, the characteristic speaking voice is measured and deliberate, sometimes moving into an elevated and even declamatory utterance. Beneath the controlled surface there is sharp, sometimes savage conflict — between lust and love, fear and hopeful expectation, the desire for beauty and the recognition of ugliness, between man as predator and man as victim, the world as a joke, and as a place of torture. Images of brutality, cruelty and destruction are balanced against images of fruitfulness, harmony, and, though infrequently, fulfilment, but the former are developed with a power and precision that the latter rarely display, and greatly reinforce the darker side of Hope's work ... In temper his work is romantic, rather than classical. In reading it one is conscious of a man who knows what it is to be at odds with himself. The admiration expressed in the poems for the qualities of will and pride might argue not their presence in the poet himself, but their absence ... The poet who creates the world of these poems recognizes a conflict between desire and action, between attempt and achievement. He is aware that will is susceptible to false judgment, and takes the view that man can look for no sustenance or comfort except from a recognition of his own nature. The prayer offered in 'A Bidding Grace'

> Grant that we may, still trembling at the bar
> Of Justice in the thud of fiery rain,
> Acknowledge at last the Truth of what we are ...

may point to man's only way of 'strengthening those powers that fence the failing heart'.

Leonie Kramer, Introduction to *Collected Poems 1930-1970*,
second edition, 1972, pp. viii-xiv

There is something operatic about the way his more-than-life-size figures sing out their arias against exotic backdrops. Defiant energy rather than delicate perception is commonly the distinguishing mark. His essential poet can be the epic lover, as Sigurd with Gudrun, the impassioned high priest of 'The Lamp and the Jar', the old, stoical king viewing his city from midnight battlements, Lot in his drunkenness, or the crudely eloquent bard-elect of 'Invocation':

> Damnation still hangs on that naked act
>
> By which the few, the free, the chosen light
> Our way, and deeply live and proudly move,
> Renew the uncompromising choice of love,
> Engender power and beauty on our night.
>
> That breed is in my bones: in me again
> The spirit elect works out its mighty plan—

The engendering of *power* and beauty comes, I presume, from Yeats's 'Leda and the Swan', where knowledge and power are thrust upon beauty, but the whole situation is considerably more abstract and wilful in Hope's poem. It is hard to forget one critic's sour comment on these lines: 'Half his luck!' At worst, Hope's voices can claim too much grandeur for themselves and merely come out sounding shrill.

Yet I would argue that Hope's representations of the creative man are by no means simply programmatic; they do not illustrate a settled thesis about ways of life and hierachies of value. Many complexities are introduced because he tends to present art and love as analogically parallel. The tropes involving these two elements are so common and so highly developed in his poetry that we often find it hard to decide which element is primary and which secondary. Is the artist like a lover or is the lover like an artist, or are we being asked to view some general aspect of human nature which is both artist-like and lover-like?

We come upon such complexity in Hope's very playful 'Pseudodoxia Epidemica'. The poem ends by describing itself as a 'parable of love', but its direction as a parable can be thoroughly baffling, as it is in the second stanza:

> Our questions choose the answers they think good:
> What shape is wine? The shape of any cup.
> Since what we fancy serves to keep us human,
> To keep love circulating in the blood
> Its addicts, when they they start to sober up,
> Reach out and pour themselves another woman.

The epigrammatic leap-and-dash tends to leave the reader in some confusion, but surely the main concern here, as, I suspect, throughout the poem, is with epistemology: the sentimental education turns out to be an education in language and logic.

Another — a stranger and, so far as I can discern, a clumsier — version of the art-love analogy is found in Hope's poem written in homage to Yeats. The first four stanzas of this poem consist of direct literary tribute, and worthily exemplify the 'noble, candid speech' to which they are giving praise. Yeats is admired in turn for his eloquence, for his naked prophecy, for his Swiftian toughness and for his Blakean intolerance of humbug. Then we come to the last two stanzas which shoot off at an astonishing tangent from all that has gone before:

[see poem on p. 192]

That Platonic Year is presumably only a figurative bit of play with Yeats's materials. But what is the status of his book, his poetry? At a simple level the lines tell us that lovers go to Yeats's poems and recognize themselves there. But the book is also 'the glass of the Great Memory' and their recognitions are also 'eternal moments'. The poetry of Yeats becomes another consummation, over and above the all-night blessing of the lovers; both love and art offer an ascent into the Great Memory, the *Anima Mundi,* but it is the work of a poet which can provide identification for lovers, showing them, figured in the artifice of eternity, what they have grown to be.

In this example, art would appear to stand higher among the orders of being than love. On another occasion they seem to be quite equal. This is in the essay, 'All for Love, or Comedy as Tragedy'. Here, in comparing Dryden's *All for Love* with its

Shakespearean forebear, Hope considers the nature of truly heroic beings and the gap between genius and 'the temperament of the trader'. In the course of this discussion, the art-love analogy bubbles up again:

> Nearly all human beings have the power of love and many of intense passion. But there are types of persons who when they meet and fall in love produce a new quality of experience as great poetry transcends ordinary powers of language.

Hope is, then, preoccupied with the capacity which human beings possess to rise above the ordinary mortal condition. The danger in his concern with 'a new quality of experience' is that he is apt to pay insufficient attention to the common intensities of experience: his verse tends to harden in places and to ride grandly over the natural fluctuations of sensibility; his protagonists are rather too often large marmoreal figures in grand operatic situations. For all this, we should do well to remember that the heroic *is* a realm of human aspiration and action: poetry has other tasks than numbering the streaks on the tweed jacket. In the best poems an action is deeply rooted in common feelings . . .

Chris Wallace-Crabbe, 'Three Faces of Hope',
Meanjin Quarterly, vol. 26, no. 4, 1967, pp. 398-401

POEMS

Ascent into Hell

Little Henry, too, had a great notion of singing.
History of the Fairchild Family

I, too, at the mid-point, in a well-lit wood
Of second-rate purpose and mediocre success,
Explore in dreams the never-never of childhood,
Groping in daylight for the key of darkness:

Revisit, among the morning archipelagoes,
Tasmania, my receding childish island;
Unchanged my prehistoric flora grows
Within me, marsupial territories extend:

There is the land-locked valley and the river,
The Western Tiers make distance an emotion,
The gum trees roar in the gale, the poplars shiver
At twilight, the church pines imitate an ocean.

There, in the clear night, still I listen, waking
To a crunch of sulky wheels on the distant road;
The marsh of stars reflects a starry croaking;
I hear in the pillow the sobbing of my blood

As the panic of unknown footsteps marching nearer,
Till the door opens, the inner world of panic
Nightmares that woke me to unawakening terror
Birthward resume their still inscrutable traffic.

Memory no more the backward, solid continent,
From island to island of despairing dream
I follow the dwindling soul in its ascent;
The bayonets and the pickelhauben gleam

Among the leaves, as, in the poplar tree,
They find him hiding. With an axe he stands
Above the German soldiers, hopelessly
Chopping the fingers from the climbing hands.

Or, in the well-known house, a secret door
Opens on empty rooms from which a stair
Leads down to a grey, dusty corridor,
Room after room, ominous, still and bare.

He cannot turn back, a lurking horror beckons
Round the next corner, beyond each further door.
Sweating with nameless anguish then he wakens;
Finds the familiar walls blank as before.

Chased by wild bulls, his legs stick fast with terror.
He reaches the fence at last — the fence falls flat.
Choking, he runs, the trees he climbs will totter.
Or the cruel horns, like telescopes, shoot out.

At his fourth year the waking life turns inward.
Here on his Easter Island the stone faces
Rear meaningless monuments of hate and dread.
Dreamlike within the dream real names and places

Survive. His mother comforts him with her body
Against the nightmare of the lions and tigers.
Again he is standing in his father's study
Lying about his lie, is whipped, and hears

His scream of outrage, valid to this day.
In bed, he fingers his stump of sex, invents
How he took off his clothes and ran away,
Slit up his belly with various instruments;

To brood on this was a deep abdominal joy
Still recognized as a feeling at the core
Of love — and the last genuine memory
Is singing 'Jesus Loves Me' — then, no more!

Beyond is a lost country and in vain
I enter that mysterious territory.
Lit by faint hints of memory lies the plain
Where from its Null took shape this conscious I

Which backward scans the dark — But at my side
The unrecognized Other Voice speaks in my ear,
The voice of my fear, the voice of my unseen guide;
'Who are we, stranger? What are we doing here?'

And through the uncertain gloom, sudden I see
Beyond remembered time the imagined entry,
The enormous Birth-gate whispering, *'per me,
per me si va tra la perduta gente.'*

The Death of the Bird

For every bird there is this last migration:
Once more the cooling year kindles her heart;
With a warm passage to the summer station
Love pricks the course in lights across the chart.

Year after year a speck on the map, divided
By a whole hemisphere, summons her to come;
Season after season, sure and safely guided,
Going away she is also coming home.

And being home, memory becomes a passion
With which she feeds her brood and straws her nest
Aware of ghosts that haunt the heart's possession
And exiled love mourning within the breast.

The sands are green with a mirage of valleys;
The palm-tree casts a shadow not its own;
Down the long architrave of temple or palace
Blows a cool air from moorland scarps of stone.

And day by day the whisper of love grows stronger;
That delicate voice, more urgent with despair,
Custom and fear constraining her no longer,
Drives her at last on the waste leagues of air.

A vanishing speck in those inane dominions,
Single and frail, uncertain of her place,
Alone in the bright host of her companions,
Lost in the blue unfriendliness of space,

She feels it close now, the appointed season:
The invisible thread is broken as she flies;
Suddenly, without warning, without reason,
The guiding spark of instinct winks and dies.

Try as she will, the trackless world delivers
No way, the wilderness of light no sign,
The immense and complex map of hills and rivers
Mocks her small wisdom with its vast design.

And darkness rises from the eastern valleys,
And the winds buffet her with their hungry breath,
And the great earth, with neither grief nor malice,
Receives the tiny burden of her death.

William Butler Yeats

To have found at last that noble, candid speech
In which all things worth saying may be said,
Which, whether the mind asks, or the heart bids, to each
Affords its daily bread;

To have been afraid neither of lust nor hate,
To have shown the dance, and when the dancer ceased,
The bloody head of prophecy on a plate
Borne in at Herod's feast;

To have loved the bitter, lucid mind of Swift,
Bred passion against the times, made wisdom strong;
To have sweetened with your pride's instinctive gift
The brutal mouth of song;

To have shared with Blake uncompromising scorn
For art grown smug and clever, shown your age
The virgin leading home the unicorn
And loosed his sacred rage —

But more than all, when from my arms she went
That blessed my body all night, naked and near,
And all was done, and order and content
Closed the Platonic Year,

Was it *not* chance alone that made us look
Into the glass of the Great Memory
And know the eternal moments, in your book,
That we had grown to be?

Imperial Adam

Imperial Adam, naked in the dew,
Felt his brown flanks and found the rib was gone.
Puzzled he turned and saw where, two and two,
The mighty spoor of Jahweh marked the lawn.

Then he remembered through mysterious sleep
The surgeon fingers probing at the bone,
The voice so far away, so rich and deep:
'It is not good for him to live alone.'

Turning once more he found Man's counterpart
In tender parody breathing at his side.
He knew her at first sight, he knew by heart
Her allegory of sense unsatisfied.

The pawpaw drooped its golden breasts above
Less generous than the honey of her flesh;
The innocent sunlight showed the place of love;
The dew on its dark hairs winked crisp and fresh.

This plump gourd severed from his virile root,
She promised on the turf of Paradise
Delicious pulp of the forbidden fruit;
Sly as the snake she loosed her sinuous thighs,

And waking, smiled up at him from the grass;
Her breasts rose softly and he heard her sigh —
From all the beasts whose pleasant task it was
In Eden to increase and multiply

Adam had learned the jolly deed of kind:
He took her in his arms and there and then,
Like the clean beasts, embracing from behind,
Began in joy to found the breed of men.

Then from the spurt of seed within her broke
Her terrible and triumphant female cry,
Split upward by the sexual lightning stroke.
It was the beasts now who stood watching by:

The gravid elephant, the calving hind,
The breeding bitch, the she-ape big with young
Were the first gentle midwives of mankind;
The teeming lioness rasped her with her tongue;

The proud vicuña nuzzled her as she slept
Lax on the grass; and Adam watching too
Saw how her dumb breasts at their ripening wept,
The great pod of her belly swelled and grew,

And saw its water break, and saw, in fear,
Its quaking muscles in the act of birth,
Between her legs a pigmy face appear,
And the first murderer lay upon the earth.

Sportsfield

Goddess of light, Renewer of the mind,
Now, as of old, Desire of gods and men,
Return to earth, shine, bless and bring again
The festivals of love, the rites of kind!

Since now no more in field or sacred grove
Do men perform them, naked, fervent, proud:
Packed in a plush arena now, the crowd
Sit chewing or gape to see the sports of love.

The Olympian game brings all together at last;
For Lonely Heart today may join the team,
Lover by proxy now enact his dream,
Ex-player once more live over all the past.

The amateurs who practise in parked cars
Gather to watch the smooth professional game.
What if real life is never quite the same —
An orchestra accompanies the stars.

An umpire watches for the least mistake,
The ambulance is there if they should fall;
These players only have to watch the ball,
Hero and heroine in the brilliant fake.

See the hot favourite who always wins
Lead out the Bedroom Harriers with trained ease;
The Golden Girls run on with twinkling knees;
The Love Team takes the field, the sport begins.

The sexual athlete takes her by the hand,
Crosses the line and scores the first embrace:
Fountains of youth and reservoirs of grace,
The schoolgirls cheer them from the Members' Stand.

See how they run! With what delicious airs
She leads him on! Now Villainy makes a pass,
Tackles her low and lays her on the grass;
Still chewing, the crowd lean forward in their chairs.

All will be well: the muscular child of light
Arriving just when she seems doomed to yield,
As Lust, disqualified, limps from the field,
Kisses away her tears and holds her tight.

Now in the final play their lips are met —
The grandstand holds its breath, the field grows dark,
The ball between the bed-posts finds the mark
To win the match, love all, love game and set!

The watchers all go wild, they leap and scream;
The flabby muscles that never learned to play,
Now tense, now drunk with make-believe, obey
The all-compelling, all-compensating dream:

Winner take all! all win where none take part,
All play at love where love is only play;
Who cares if, grace and violence drained away,
This debt is charged against the bankrupt heart?

Goddess of kind, whom twilight and the dawn
Bare to our eyes, if, as of old, you still
Keep holiday with men, descend and fill
The loins with light, with honey the curving horn.

Meditation on a Bone

A piece of bone, found at Trondhjem in 1901, with the
following runic inscription (about A.D. 1050) cut on it:
*I loved her as a maiden; I will not trouble Erlend's detest-
able wife; better she should be a widow.*

Words scored upon a bone,
Scratched in despair or rage —
Nine hundred years have gone;
Now, in another age,
They burn with passion on
A scholar's tranquil page.

The scholar takes his pen
And turns the bone about,
And writes those words again.
Once more they seethe and shout,
And through a human brain
Undying hate rings out.

'I loved her when a maid;
I loathe and love the wife
That warms another's bed:

Let him beware his life!'
The scholar's hand is stayed;
His pen becomes a knife

To grave in living bone
The fierce archaic cry.
He sits and reads his own
Dull sum of misery.
A thousand years have flown
Before that ink is dry.

And, in a foreign tongue,
A man, who is not he,
Reads and his heart is wrung
This ancient grief to see,
And thinks: When I am dung,
What bone shall speak for me?

Moschus Moschiferus

A Song for St Cecilia's Day

In the high jungle where Assam meets Tibet
The small Kastura, most archaic of deer,
Were driven in herds to cram the hunters' net
And slaughtered for the musk-pods which they bear;

But in those thickets of rhododendron and birch
The tiny creatures now grow hard to find.
Fewer and fewer survive each year. The search
Employs new means, more exquisite and refined:

The hunters now set out by two or three;
Each carries a bow and one a slender flute,
Deep in the forest the archers choose a tree
And climb; the piper squats against the root.

And there they wait until all trace of man
And rumour of his passage dies away.
They melt into the leaves and, while they scan
The glade below, their comrade starts to play.

Through those vast listening woods a tremulous skein
Of melody wavers, delicate and shrill:
Now dancing and now pensive, now a rain
Of pure, bright drops of sound and now the still,

Sad wailing of lament; from tune to tune
It winds and modulates without a pause;
The hunters hold their breath; the trance of noon
Grows tense; with its full power the music draws

A shadow from a juniper's darker shade;
Bright-eyed, with quivering muzzle and pricked ear,
The little musk-deer slips into the glade
Led by an esctasy that conquers fear.

A wild enchantment lures him, step by step,
Into its net of crystalline sound, until
The leaves stir overhead, the bowstrings snap
And poisoned shafts bite sharp into the kill.

Then, as the victim shudders, leaps and falls,
The music soars to a delicious peak,
And on and on its silvery piping calls
Fresh spoil for the rewards the hunters seek.

But when the woods are emptied and the dusk
Draws in, the men climb down and count their prey,
Cut out the little glands that hold the musk
And leave the carcasses to rot away.

A hundred thousand or so are killed each year;
Cause and effect are very simply linked:
Rich scents demand the musk, and so the deer,
Its source, must soon, they say, become extinct.

Divine Cecilia, there is no more to say!
Of all who praised the power of music, few
Knew of these things. In honour of your day
Accept this song I too have made for you.

SELECT BIBLIOGRAPHY

The Wandering Islands, Edwards & Shaw, Sydney, 1955.
Poems, Hamish Hamilton, London, 1960, and New York, 1961.
Selected Poems (Australian Poets series), Angus & Robertson, Sydney, 1963.
Collected Poems, Angus & Robertson, Sydney, 1966 (expanded paperback edition with Introduction by Leonie Kramer, 1972).
New Poems, 1965-1969, Angus & Robertson, Sydney, 1969.
Dunciad Minor, Melbourne University Press, Melbourne, 1970.
A. D. Hope Reads from His Own Work, Poets on Record series, University of Queensland Press, Brisbane, 1972.
'Poetry in Australia: A. D. Hope', interview with John Thompson, *Southerly,* vol. 26, no. 4, 1966.
The Cave and the Spring, Essays on Poetry, Rigby, Adelaide, 1965, and Chicago, 1970 (reprinted omitting 'Literature versus the Universities' and with three new essays, 1974).
Native Companions, Angus & Robertson, Sydney, 1974.

O'Brien, Patricia, *A. D. Hope: A Bibliography,* 1968.

Argyle, Barry, 'The Poetry of A. D. Hope', *Journal of Commonwealth Literature,* no. 3, 1967.
Brissenden, R. F., 'A. D. Hope's New Poems', *Southerly,* vol. 30, no. 2, 1970.
Buckley, Vincent, 'A. D. Hope: The Unknown Poet', *Essays in Poetry, Mainly Australian,* Melbourne University Press, Melbourne, 1957.
Campbell, David, review of *The Wandering Islands,* in *Southerly,* vol. 17, no. 2, 1956.
Cross, Gustav, 'The Poetry of A. D. Hope', in *The Literature of Australia,* ed. Geoffrey Dutton, 1964.
Docker, John, 'The Image of Woman in A. D. Hope's Poetry', in *Australian Cultural Elites,* 1974.
Fuller, Roy, 'A. D. Hope's Collected Poems', *Meanjin Quarterly,* vol. 25, no. 2, 1966.
Goldberg, S. L., 'The Poet as Hero: A. D. Hope's *The Wandering Islands*', *Meanjin,* vol. 16, no. 2, 1957; reprinted in *Twentieth Century Australian Literary Criticism,* ed. Clement Semmler, Oxford University Press, Melbourne, 1967.
Hartman, Geoffrey H., review of *Poems,* in the *Kenyon Review,* vol. 25, no. 4, 1963.
Heseltine, H. P., 'Paradise Within: A. D. Hope's *New Poems*', *Meanjin Quarterly,* vol. 29, no. 4, 1970.
Hutchings, P. Æ., 'Letter from Australia', in *Islands* (New Zealand), vol. 1, no. 1, 1972.
Jones, T. H., review of Australian Poets series selection, in *Quadrant,* vol. 8, no. 2, 1964.
Lehmann, Geoffrey, review of *New Poems,* in the *Bulletin,* 10 January 1970.
McAuley, James, 'The Pyramid in the Waste: an Introduction to A. D.

O

Hope's Poetry', *Quadrant*, vol. 5, no. 4, 1961; reprinted in *Australian Literary Criticism*, ed. Grahame Johnston, Oxford University Press, Melbourne, 1962.

Nagarajan, S., 'Aspects of the Poetic Thought of A. D. Hope', *Journal of Commonwealth Literature*, vol. 6, no. 1, 1971.

Suchting, W. A., 'The Poetry of A. D. Hope: a Frame of Reference', *Meanjin Quarterly*, vol. 21, no. 2, 1962.

Wallace-Crabbe, Chris, 'Three Faces of Hope', *Meanjin Quarterly*, vol. 26, no. 4, 1967.

Webb, Edwin, 'Dualities and their Resolution in the Poetry of A. D. Hope', *Southerly*, vol. 32, no. 3, 1972.

Wright, Judith, 'A. D. Hope', in *Preoccupations in Australian Poetry*, Oxford University Press, Melbourne, 1965.

NOTES

1 'The attitude from which his themes arise is Dionysian or tragic, disturbed, romantic, existentialist at least in its premises; on the other hand, the sense of tradition and order implicit in his art — an order he has always insisted on as a critic as well as a poet — is decidedly Apollonian or classical, and intellectual rather than freely organic' (S. L. Goldberg, 'The Poet as Hero: A. D. Hope's *The Wandering Islands*', *Meanjin*, vol. 16, no. 3, 1957, p. 127).

2 R. F. Brissenden, 'A. D. Hope's *New Poems*', *Southerly*, vol. 30, no. 2, 1970, stresses the increasing importance in Hope's work of this celebration of a natural order. H. P. Heseltine, 'Paradise Within: A. D. Hope's *New Poems*', *Meanjin Quarterly*, vol. 29, no. 4, 1970, also remarks on the theme of celebration. Both refer in this connection to two essays in *The Cave and the Spring* (1965): 'Poetry and Platitude' and 'Poetry, Prayer and Trade'. This theme emerges especially in some of the larger poems of the middle and later periods, such as the two Epistles mentioned above, and 'Soledades of the Sun and Moon', 'Ode on the Death of Pius the Twelfth', 'On an Engraving by Casserius', and 'Vivaldi, Bird and Angel' (see for example the conclusion to section I). Such work, like Hope's satires, had to be under-represented in the selection.

3 The Nietzschean character of this doctrine of the artist is not disclaimed in Hope's essay 'Henry Handel Richardson's *Maurice Guest*', *Meanjin*, vol. 14, no. 2, 1955. S. L. Goldberg, in tracing the same doctrine in the poems, has commented: 'It is an attitude typical of this century, with analogues to make it familiar enough; but it has certain dangers for a poet, and especially, for one so concerned with traditional values as Hope' (*Meanjin*, vol. 16, no. 3, 1957, p. 133). See also the comment by W. A. Suchting, 'The Poetry of A. D. Hope: a Frame of Reference', *Meanjin Quarterly*, vol. 21, no. 2, 1962.

4 The essay from which the passage is quoted contains Hope's comment on three interpretations of his poem 'Imperial Adam', by Vincent Buckley, S. L. Goldberg, and myself — all three critics being guilty of misreading. Another commentary is that of Evan Jones in *The Literature of Australia*, ed. Geoffrey Dutton (1964), pp. 114-15. So far as I am aware none of the critics has recanted or shown a sign of being impressed by Hope's own retrospective explanation. I do not myself think that Hope has read my contribution aright. This curious argument need not be pursued here. It may point towards a more general situation in Hope's work, where its apparently solid declaratory substance proves oddly elusive and ambiguous. This is part of its challenge to criticism.

9

James McAuley

INTRODUCTION

The earliest phase from which I have retained any poems, 1936-39, was influenced by some aspects of the work of Stefan George and R. M. Rilke. What I most wanted to do was to write short poems with a delicacy of texture, lyrical, intimate, based on personal experience. One example of these early intentions is a poem published in the Sydney University literary magazine *Hermes,* and not re-published, in which there is an exploration of childhood feeling stimulated by Rilke, and a form of punctuation borrowed from Stefan George:

> The late sky clears · wet pavements shine
> With hard blue light · shrill mother-cries
> Twang on quick ears · then fading sight
> Intense, intenser dusk till down the line
> Soft yellow station-lamps bud for the night.
>
> And then the breathing walls · the womb
> Where childhood grew · where life recalls
> The ritual magic good-night kiss . . .
> Remembers dream and growth now in this room
> Dry-eyed and sleepless · having come to this.[1]

In the years that followed, another impulse emerged strongly: an interest in cultural and historical crisis and a search for means to express its meaning poetically. The somewhat Blakean and Expressionist poem 'Blue Horses', is an early example. 'The Incarnation of Sirius' and 'Philoctetes' some years later are results of an increasingly critical reaction to the myth of revolution which has been so powerful in this century. The chief product of the years just after the Second World War was 'The

Hero and the Hydra', a group of poems using Greek myth as a means of encountering the agony of a civilization which seemed to have lost its principle of coherence, unable to bring together the twin themes of order and justice in the *polis* and order and justice in the soul. Later poems, up to and including the narrative *Captain Quiros* which was written 1958-59, were concerned with seeing the world in the light of a recovered acceptance of Christian tradition and orthodoxy.

My first volume of poems, *Under Aldebaran* (1946), had a favorable critical reception. Its elements of tension, wryness, serious comedy, the vivacity of unusual imagery, as well as the lyricism and personal feeling, made it acceptably modern, though traditional in verse-form. But some poems in fact were symptoms of a dissatisfaction with the precariousness inherent in my method or lack of method. The poem 'Henry the Navigator' arose from a deliberate decision to try writing a poem of a narrative and discursive kind; while the short poem 'Marginal Note' protested at the turbid quality of much modern poetry:

> So poetry that moves by chance collision
> Scatters its brightness at each random mote
> And mars the lucid order of its vision.

This was echoed by 'An Art of Poetry' in my second volume:

> Let your literal figures shine
> With pure transparency:
> Not in opaque but limpid wells
> Lie truth and mystery.

Such statements are of course in their turn one-sided, or at least do not encompass the full complexity of the problem.

My second volume, *A Vision of Ceremony* (1956), did not chime so well with prevailing preferences. It was felt to have sacrificed too much of the qualities offered by the first volume. The emergence of a Christian basis was not in itself a hindrance; but some felt disappointment with the way it emerged. On the one hand it was acknowledged that there were some beautiful lyrics in the volume, but they were felt to be serene rather than tense and unresolved, too clarified of the messy substance of life.[2] On the other hand the discursive poem 'A Letter to John Dryden' displeased some by its aggressive polemic.

The subsequent decade was a difficult one in my poetical development. I had an inner necessity — the word is not too strong — to move still further away from contemporary critical preferences in order to grow in my own way. I felt the need to re-absorb some residues of nineteenth-century poetry which were part of my experience: Byron's lyrics, Tennyson, William Morris; Eichendorff, Heine, Mörike. In the midst of dryness and uncertainty I suddenly took up again an almost forgotten project of writing a long narrative poem about Quiros. The experience is described in 'The Inception of the Poem':

> Midnight once more; the untended fire sinks low;
> The lamp stares down upon the book unread;
> The papers on my desk have nothing to show:
> I have not learned the things I wish to know,
> The things I wished to say remain unsaid.
>
> Again the dead pause, the need for a new start;
> The vanishing of every name and form
> That seemed the very contours of the heart;
> And all the working mystery of art
> A queenless hive deserted by the swarm.
>
> Then suddenly, unbidden, the theme returns
> That visited my youth; over the vast
> Pacific with the white wake at their sterns,
> The ships of Quiros on their great concerns
> Ride in upon the present from the past.

Captain Quiros, which was not published until 1964, was written for reading aloud. It takes about two hours, and by repeated test holds its audience very effectively. But in silent reading on the page the deliberately flatter parts are more noticeable; and in any case long narratives are not particularly welcome nowadays, nor does the language they require meet the taste of those who look for the intensities of short poems. Chris Wallace-Crabbe, in regard to some of the writing of this period, has spoken of 'a species of deadened language'.[3] It was at any rate clear that I had moved to a position as opposite as possible to prevailing expectations — not by a wilful intransigence but by the need to follow a path intuitively sensed and dimly descried. In spite of the difficulties, in the late fifties and early sixties I produced a number of poems which I still consider among my best, including 'Pietà' (p. 212).

An unexpected turn in development came late in 1966 when I suddenly began to write some autobiographical poems about childhood and youth, which in the volume *Surprises of the Sun* (1969) were grouped under the title 'On the Western Line'.[4]

These poems caused some surprise when they appeared, but were well received. Inevitably they were compared with the kind of 'confessional' poetry Robert Lowell had been writing.[5] I had no sense of influence from that quarter. Oddly enough, a vivid stimulus, rather than influence or model, was provided during those months by constantly reading in English translation the late poems of Pasternak.[6]

In 1970 I had a serious illness and emerged with that exquisitely keen sense of life and its fragility which such experiences give. The result was a number of short poems which use a language of sense-impressions to render aspects of a world. Two of the poems in the selection are among several that share the same locality: for example, the clock that chimes in 'Morning Voluntary' is in the church-tower mentioned in 'St John's Park'. Occasionally there are echoes of earlier poems: for example, the star Vega in 'St John's Park' appears in an early poem, 'Landscape of Lust'. An influence of the poems of Georg Trakl[7] is evident, stronger and more identifiable than any other poet has exercised on my work since the attraction of Rilke faded; yet the effect has been to liberate, not to deflect, my native impulse.[8] It seems that in the last decade I have come full circle back to the kind of poem I began with, but with a greater depth of experience which has brought me closer to fulfilling the persistent desire to write poems that are lucid and mysterious, gracefully simple but full of secrets, faithful to the little one knows and the much one has to feel.

COMMENTARY

Passages from the writings of James McAuley

. . . in a remote and general way, 'the impressive ideas of traditional religion' *are* fundamental for great art and literature. These ideas may work at some distance: they mould the culture, and thus at one or more remove communicate a certain dignity and vitality and mystery to works, even heterodox works, formed within that culture and employing its symbolic language. They haunt the greater minds of this latter age, even when these minds are 'disinherited', having but a poor and distorted notion of the stupendous vision and vitality which orthodoxy forever conserves. It is not, let me add, a matter of demanding a conversion of art and literature exclusively to religious themes. Nor does it follow that any individual artist or writer will solve his difficulties by an individual act of faith, for he remains to a large extent the child of his time; indeed his difficulties may increase, for to attempt to be normal in an abnormal phase of civilization is a kind of eccentricity.

Preface to The End of Modernity, 1959, p. viii

The way forward to a post-modern poetry cannot be simply in a return behind the Romantic deviation to the eighteenth century. The so-called classical formulae of the eighteenth century represent too great a narrowing of the spiritual resources on which it is necessary to draw. In any case we cannot act as if the intense experiences of the past one hundred and fifty years had never been; we cannot suppress and deny the voices of that period that continue to speak in us. It is necessary to understand what happened, to experience it deeply, to absorb and master its results, before one can pass beyond it. ·

'The Magian Heresy', Quadrant, vol. 1, no. 4, 1957, p. 71;
reprinted in The End of Modernity, 1959, p. 159

Subtlety, complexity and balance are all on the side of the traditional verse. It provides the best combination of freedom and order. Other proposed forms all sacrifice some part of the maximum interplay between metrical expectation and actual sound which the traditional verse provides . . . Free verse, since it surrenders all the advantages of the traditional form, has not proved very useful in English, though in German it has had a more distinguished career, for reasons I am not sure of: it has more weight, and at the same time seems closer to classical verse.*

'From a Poet's Notebook', Quadrant, vol. 2, no. 4,
1958, pp. 50-1; reprinted in The End of Modernity,
1959, pp. 170-1

When I look over my poems and see various themes and images — voyages, maps, stars, birds, instinctual patterns, and so on — I know that these things are there as part of the imaginative means I have found of exploring, ordering, and expressing the sentiments connected with certain recurring subjects. (The term 'sentiment'

---

* Brennan, commenting on Novalis' *Hymns to the Night,* offered a reason: 'These free rhythms will not do in English — Arnold's failure is proof of that — because our language is too loose: the inflected nature of German holds the words closely together from line to line and corrects the looseness of the rhythm' (*Prose,* p. 114).

suggests pretty accurately that fusion of ideas, memories, images, feelings and judgments of value which is the stuff of poetry.)

The subjects that seem, in looking back, to recur in my poetry are: love, human and divine; order and crisis in the soul and in the city of man; creative energy in life and art; the heroic virtues. Yet if I had to state in a phrase what was my constant concern, I should say it has been the search for, and the struggle to express, an intuition of the True Form of Man.

The figures presented or implied in much of my poetry are the lover, the saint, the artist, the ruler, the hero. The poems measure experience against such figures, instead of taking a sensitive, non-committal, rather passive, modern ego as the sole measure of all things . . .

I also came by trial and error to the conviction that attempts to 'free' poetic imagination from the frame of rational order were an artistic mistake. The reason is quite simple, that poetry is of the whole man. Wordsworth's remark to the astronomer Hamilton is well justified: 'The logical faculty has infinitely more to do with poetry than the young and inexperienced, whether writer or critic, ever dreams of . . .'. Putting a phrase of the Fathers to another use, I would call poetry 'the rational paradise'.

The hardest problem confronting the poet in my time has not, I think, greatly changed or become less urgent: it is the struggle for an adequate symbolism. I use the word in a wide sense. Even a selective stress upon certain details in a realistic account of a situation can charge those details with meaningfulness beyond themselves. Or such details may be separated out of any particular occasion and used in a more general and abstract way.

Introduction to *Selected Poems* (Australian Poets series), 1963, pp. vii-viii

Passages from the writings of other authors

His best writing is evenly distributed over the whole of his poetic career; and, while certain central ideas and images have persisted throughout this period, each successive volume has seen a change of manner, and a new exploration of the resources of his language.

McAuley's firm formulation of and adherence to his poetic manifesto has certainly not meant inflexibility. After the cele-bratory poems of the 'fifties, and the bringing together in 'Captain Quiros' of his ideas of spiritual exploration, the relationship between the natural and supernatural worlds, and the nature of political activity, he turned in *Surprises of the Sun* to an explora-tion of his own past. The autobiographical poems of the 'sixties are conducted in a manner very different from anything he had attempted before. The intimacy of his recollections surprised those readers who had thought of him — wrongly in my opinion — as a public poet given to narrowly formal pronouncements. In fact, however, their interest lies only partly in what they reveal about the poet's boyhood and youth. Individually, the poems are concerned with issues larger than their immediate subjects. They are not basically confessional poems, but deal, in their concrete particulars, with such subjects as the acquisition of different kinds of knowledge, the impingement of mystery upon ordinary life, the nature of judgment, the stirring of the imagination and its relationship to desire and hope, the education of the heart, and the puzzles of self-knowledge. Fine adjustments of tone enable him to move easily from colloquial simplicity to evocative imagery.

The last poems in this collected volume show that again, though without deserting his broad poetic aims, McAuley is breaking new ground. Under the title 'The Hazard and the Gift' is a group of poems which he has described as an attempt 'to define a world'. The use of the indefinite article is significant. There is here no arbitrary or doctrinaire labelling, no assertion that the world must be regarded in a certain light. These new poems are short, some only two or three small stanzas. The language is pared down to absolute simplicity. He creates an actual world carefully observed and moving in time. He pays great attention to the seasons and the time of day, the weather, the color of light and trees.

'St John's Park', for example, moves literally from morning through a colorful late afternoon in early spring to dusk and faint starlight. But against this actual temporal progression, the poem plots a counterpointing emotional course, between forces of beauty and ugliness, despair and hope, loss and promise. 'Wet Day' presents a world that 'has never been redeemed'; 'At Rushy Lagoon' counters with 'a world of sense and use'. In 'Pastoral' a springtime scene shows the wattle, 'tree of grace', in a setting where earth holds 'an image of the sky'. But the scene is scored across by 'cruel white-eyed shadows' of ravens wheeling above new lambs. In three brief stanzas McAuley creates a remarkably complex sense of an actual pastoral world threatened by its natural predators; and of a world beyond to which 'the book of hours' points — one which both is, and is not, under the protection of heaven.

In some of these poems natural images lead to or incorporate a direct statement. 'St John's Park' is built upon contrasts between vitality and decay. Though its season is spring, its world is peopled by the rotting old and the indifferent young. The images validate the direct statement 'Loss is what nothing alters or annuls', while at the same time the statement itself works back into the imagery, sharpening its impact. Other poems carry more explicit religious references, but these, too, are controlled by interrelated images of time, place, color and movement, resolved into startling clarity. In method and subject matter these most recent poems represent a new direction in McAuley's writing, but they also point to the consistency of his poetic preoccupations. In many of the earlier poems, too, a subtle dialectic shapes the structure. Positives and negatives are held in balance through the interplay of images, and the poems offer neither a simple resolution nor foggy ambiguity, but a clear rendering of complex meanings.

Leonie Kramer, review of *Collected Poems 1936-1970*,
in the *Bulletin*, 29 May 1971, pp. 46-7

The corrupting stink of man's 'old self' and the despair which it generates permeate the world of McAuley's poetry. 'Despair', indeed, is a word which recurs at key points throughout his work... The atmosphere of McAuley's poetic universe is not, of course, one of all-pervading and unrelieved gloom. 'Living is thirst for joy;/That is what art rehearses', is the assertion he makes 'to any poet'; and it is the note of strong and simple joyfulness which distinguishes some of his most successful and individual pieces... But in the context of his work as a whole this happiness appears all the more precious because it so clearly occurs in, has been won from, an imperfect and at its worst inimical environment. There are occasions when love, or domestic tranquillity, or merely a feeling of personal well-being coincide with and are reinforced by our sense of some deep and pervasive natural order; and McAuley can render such occasions with a rare tact and authenticity... It *is* a world of sense and use — or it has been or it can be. But the possibility of our realizing this, both in the intellect and the imagination, and in actuality, is continually being threatened by our own irrationality and perversity, our capacity for stupidity and misuse — and also by something more subtly and fundamentally awry in the nature of things themselves... Running through McAuley's poetry there is a persistent note of radical disquiet and uneasiness, of dissatisfaction not only with the nature of man but with the nature of the world in which he finds himself or has been placed. It is much deeper and more disturbing than the con-

ventional modern lament for the fact that we live in an age
in which the traditional bases of faith have been eroded . . .
basically I would suggest his despair has nothing to do with the
specific problems of the twentieth century. The muted horror,
outrage and bewilderment of 'A Leaf of Sage', a tale from the
Decameron, for instance, are intensely personal; at the same time
one feels that they have been evoked through the forced contemplation of a problem which the poet reluctantly acknowledges as perennial, as inherent in the inscrutable order of the
universe . . . his quarrel is as much with the nature of things as
it is with the twentieth century; and the great strength of his
poetry is the honesty with which he faces up to this.

R. F. Brissenden, 'The Wounded Hero:
James McAuley's *Collected Poems', Southerly*,
vol. 32, no. 4, 1972, pp. 267-77

POEMS

In the Huon Valley

Propped boughs are heavy with apples,
Springtime quite forgotten.
Pears ripen yellow. The wasp
Knows where windfalls lie rotten.

Juices grow rich with sun.
These autumn days are still:
The glassy river reflects
Elm-gold up the hill,

And big white plumes of rushes.
Life is full of returns;
It isn't true that one never
Profits, never learns:

Something is gathered in,
Worth the lifting and stacking;
Apples roll through the graders,
The sheds are noisy with packing.

The Incarnation of Sirius

In that age, the great anagram of God
Had bayed the planets from the rounds they trod,
And gathered the fixed stars in a shining nation
Like restless birds that flock before migration.

For the millennial instinct of new flight
Resolved the antinomy that fixed their light;
And, echoing in the troubled soul of Earth,
Quickened a virgin's womb, to bring to birth

What scarce was human: a rude avatar
That glistened with the enclosed wrath of a star.
The woman died in pangs, before she had kissed
The monstrous form of God's antagonist.

But at its showing forth, the poets cried
In a strange tongue; hot mouths prophesied
The coolness of the bloody vintage-drops:
'Let us be drunk at least, when the world stops!'

Anubis-headed, the heresiarch
Sprang to a height, fire-sinewed in the dark,
And his ten fingers, bracketed on high,
Were a blazing candelabrum in the sky.

The desert lion antiphonally roared;
The tiger's sinews quivered like a chord;
Man smelt the blood beneath his brother's skin
And in a loving hate the sword went in.

And then the vision sank, bloody and aborted.
The stars that with rebellion had consorted
Fled back in silence to their former stations.
Over the giant face of dreaming nations

The centuries-thick coverlet was drawn.
Upon the huddled breast Aldebaran
Still glittered with its sad alternate fire:
Blue as of memory, red as of desire.

The Tomb of Heracles
from *The Hero and the Hydra*

A dry tree with an empty honeycomb
Stands as a broken column by the tomb:
The classic anguish of a rigid fate,
The loveless will, superb and desolate.

This is the end of stoic pride and state:
Blind light, dry rock, a tree that does not bear.

Look, cranes still know their path through empty air;
For them their world is neither soon nor late;
But ours is eaten hollow with despair.

Mating Swans

A pair of black swans on the lake
Twine their necks in amorous play.
The cob turns in a swirling wake,
Treading the maze of love's delay
Till she receives him, sinking low;
Then both their urgent necks lift high
United in a strident cry
Forced from love's exultant throe.
Parting as excitement ebbs,
They fuss their plumes with busy nebs,
Shake them smooth, and gently glide
On the water side by side.

They crease the angle of their wake
Along a liquid depth of sky;
White clouds inverted in the lake
Quiver as they paddle by
Towards a reed-fringed island, where
Green willows arch their springing shoots
And a frog croaks beneath the roots,
And shags hold synod, beaks in air.
Soon the swan will heap her nest,
Drawing reeds against her breast,
Whilst the watchful cob near by
Forbids the world with bright red eye.

Merry-Go-Round

Bright-coloured, mirror-plated, strung with lights,
With swan-shaped cars and prancing wooden horses,
The silent waiting merry-go-round invites
A swarm of eager riders for its courses.

It moves: a painted miniature cosmos, turning
With planetary music blaring loud.
The riders lean intent, lips parted, faces burning;
Brief smiles float out towards the watching crowd.

On their brass poles the horses rise and fall
In undulant flight; the children ride through dreams.
How faery-bright to them, how magical,
The crude and gaudy mechanism seems!

Almost I see the marvel that they see,
And hear like them the music of the spheres;
They smile out of the enchanted whirl to me.
The lights and colours suddenly dim with tears.

But now their turning world is slowing, slowing;
Horses and music stop: how brief the ride!
New-comers clamber on as these are going
Reluctantly to join the crowd outside.

Pietà

A year ago you came
Early into the light.
You lived a day and night,
Then died; no-one to blame.

Once only, with one hand,
Your mother in farewell
Touched you. I cannot tell,
I cannot understand

A thing so dark and deep,
So physical a loss:
One touch, and that was all

She had of you to keep.
Clean wounds, but terrible,
Are those made with the Cross.

St John's Park

The mountain is streaked white, the air is cold.
Under a pure blue sky the players begin.
Thickly-clotted prunus lines the way in,
And wattles put on helmets of heavy gold.

A dark-green gum bursts out in crimson flowers.
Old people slowly rot along the wall.
The young ones hardly notice them at all.
Both live in the same picture-book of hours.

Four-turreted a square tower balks the sky,
Casting a shadow; an organ softly plays.
The afternoon wears out in a gold daze.
On ragged wings, uttering its carking cry

A raven scavenges; a flock of gulls
Flies from the tip. The last teams leave the park.
The old have crept inside to meet the dark.
Loss is what nothing alters or annuls.

At nightfall glaring traffic rushes by
Filling the air with reek and the scream of brakes.
Faint stars prick out a sign. And Vega wakes
Liquid and trembling on the northern sky.

Wet Day

Rain sweeps in as the gale begins to blow,
The water is glaucous-green and mauve and grey.
A pelican takes refuge on the bay;
Snow-white and black it rides the complex flow.

A child stands in a yellow mackintosh.
Gulls lift away and circle round about.
Cans, bottles, and junk appear as the tide runs out.
Wind cannot sweep away nor water wash

The dreck of our vulgarity. I think
The world has never been redeemed; at least
The marks it bears are mostly of the Beast —
The broken trust, the litter, and the stink.

At Rushy Lagoon

Wet mirrors covering soft peat.
Swag-bellied graceful mares in foal.
Red-umber bulls on plashing feet
With mild white face and curly poll.

Crutching time; each heavy ewe
Is trimmed and slides off down the chute.
The mountains are cut out in blue.
An opalescent sky is mute.

Ducks loiter. Children play before tea.
In the home paddock a lone goose
Follows the cows for company.
It is a world of sense and use.

Because

My father and my mother never quarrelled.
They were united in a kind of love
As daily as the *Sydney Morning Herald,*
Rather than like the eagle or the dove.

I never saw them casually touch,
Or show a moment's joy in one another.
Why should this matter to me now so much?
I think it bore more hardly on my mother,

Who had more generous feelings to express.
My father had dammed up his Irish blood
Against all drinking praying fecklessness,
And stiffened into stone and creaking wood.

His lips would make a switching sound, as though
Spontaneous impulse must be kept at bay.
That it was mainly weakness I see now,
But then my feelings curled back in dismay.

Small things can pit the memory like a cyst:
Having seen other fathers greet their sons,
I put my childish face up to be kissed
After an absence. The rebuff still stuns

My blood. The poor man's curt embarrassment
At such a delicate proffer of affection
Cut like a saw. But home the lesson went:
My tenderness thenceforth escaped detection.

My mother sang *Because,* and *Annie Laurie,*
White Wings, and other songs; her voice was sweet.
I never gave enough, and I am sorry;
But we were all closed in the same defeat.

People do what they can; they were good people,
They cared for us and loved us. Once they stood
Tall in my childhood as the school, the steeple.
How can I judge without ingratitude?

Judgement is simply trying to reject
A part of what we are because it hurts.
The living cannot call the dead collect:
They won't accept the charge, and it reverts.

It's my own judgement day that I draw near,
Descending in the past, without a clue,
Down to that central deadness: the despair
Older than any hope I ever knew.

In Northern Tasmania

Soft sodden fields. The new lambs cry,
And shorn ewes huddle from the cold.
Wattles are faintly tinged with gold.
A raven flies off silently.

Bare hawthorn thickets pearled with rain
Attract the thornbill and the wren.
Timber-trucks pass now and then,
And cows are moving in the lane.

At dusk I look out through old elms
Where mud-pools at the gatepost shine.
A way of life is in decline,

And only those who lived it know
What it is time overwhelms,
While they must gradually let go.

P

Morning Voluntary

Morning comes with milk and bread.
Wind-blown puddles seem to flow.
Clouds have a brown look of snow.
Cat comes limping from the shed.

The white birch with arms upspread
Having changed its wealth for gold
Drifts it down into the mould.
Stalky vines glow darker red.

News that no-one wants to know
Comes in with the milk and bread.
Turn the music loud instead,
Finish waking up and go.

Flat strokes dinned out overhead
Dropping through the red and gold
Tell the tale that must be told.
Friday's child is full of dread.

Very little can be said.
Cold inconstant breezes blow.
Starlings comment in a row.
Spots of black invade the red.

In Aeternum

Soft rainbows, tumbling fleeces of grey cloud,
Lagoons of blue. The mountainside is dark.
Crabapple flowers deep red in the old park.
Each breath we draw draws in the time allowed.

The churchtower clock beats out six metal strokes.
A wavering bird-flight scribbles far and wide.
I think that I could read it if I tried,
The sentence our delinquency invokes.

SELECT BIBLIOGRAPHY

Under Aldebaran, Melbourne University Press, Melbourne, 1946.
A Vision of Ceremony, Angus & Robertson, Sydney, 1956.
Selected Poems (Australian Poets series), Angus & Robertson, Sydney, 1963.
Captain Quiros, Angus & Robertson, Sydney, 1964.
Surprises of the Sun, Angus & Robertson, Sydney, 1969.
James McAuley Reads from his own Work, Poets on Record series, University of Queensland Press, Brisbane, 1970.
Collected Poems 1936-1970, Angus & Robertson, Sydney, 1971.
Music Late at Night, Angus & Robertson, Sydney, 1975.

The End of Modernity, Angus & Robertson, Sydney, 1959.
A Primer of English Versification, Sydney University Press, 1966 (separately published in U.S.A. as *Versification, a Short Introduction,* East Lansing, 1966).
'Poetry in Australia: James McAuley', interview with John Thompson, *Southerly,* vol. 27, no. 2, 1967.
The Personal Element in Australian Poetry, Angus & Robertson, Sydney, 1970.
The Grammar of the Real, Oxford University Press, Melbourne, 1975.

Brissenden, R. F., 'The Wounded Hero: James McAuley's *Collected Poems*', *Southerly,* vol. 32, no. 4, 1972.
Bradley, David, 'James McAuley—The Landscape of the Heart', in *The Literature of Australia,* ed. Geoffrey Dutton, Penguin Books, Melbourne, 1964.
Buckley, Vincent, 'Classicism and Grace: James McAuley', in *Essays in Poetry, Mainly Australian,* Melbourne University Press, Melbourne, 1957; reprinted in *Australian Literary Criticism,* ed. Grahame Johnston, Oxford University Press, Melbourne, 1962.
Docker, John, 'James McAuley: the Poetry and the Attitude', *Arena,* no. 26, 1971.
———*Australian Cultural Elites,* 1974, ch. 5, pp. 81-2.
Higham, Charles, 'James McAuley's Discipline', *Prospect,* vol. 4, no. 2, 1961.
Hope, A. D., 'Captain Quiros', *Twentieth Century,* vol. 19, no. 2, 1964.
Kramer, Leonie J., 'James McAuley: Tradition in Australian Poetry' (C. L. F. Lecture, Canberra University College), 1957.
——— 'James McAuley's *Captain Quiros*', *Southerly,* vol. 25, no. 3, 1965.
——— review of *Collected Poems,* in the *Bulletin,* 29 May 1971.
Lehmann, Geoffrey, review of *Surprises of the Sun,* in the *Bulletin,* 21 June 1969.
Tulip, James, review of *Surprises of the Sun,* in *Southerly,* vol. 29, no. 4, 1969.
Smith, Vivian, *James McAuley* (Australian Writers and their Work series), 1965 (new edition, Oxford University Press, Melbourne, 1970).

Wallace-Crabbe, Chris, 'Beware of the Past: James McAuley's Early Poetry', *Meanjin Quarterly*, vol. 30, no. 3, 1971; reprinted in *Melbourne or the Bush*, 1974.
Wright, Judith, 'J. P. McAuley', in *Preoccupations in Australian Poetry*, Oxford University Press, Melbourne, 1965.

NOTES

1 *Hermes*, Trinity Term, 1938, p. 10.
2 Vincent Buckley's comment in his *Essays in Poetry* (1957) was along these lines: 'I cannot help feeling that his work at the moment is not sufficiently rooted in the actual: it is not quite earthy enough; there is too little flesh to afford incarnation to the word' (p. 189). I am particularly indebted to an article by R. F. Brissenden, 'The Wounded Hero: James McAuley's *Collected Poems*', *Southerly*, vol. 32, no. 4, 1972, for a view of the work of this period — and indeed of my work generally — which is much closer to my own sense of it.
3 'Beware of the Past: James McAuley's Early Poetry', *Meanjin Quarterly*, vol. 30, no. 3, 1971, p. 329.
4 The poem 'Father, Mother, Son', written in 1962 was included in the group. Along with 'Pietà' it was a precursor of the kind of personal poems I wrote between December 1966 and May 1967.
5 For example, by James Tulip in a review in *Southerly*, vol. 29, no. 4, 1969.
6 *In the Interlude: Poems 1945-60*, tr. Henry Kamen, 1962.
7 An essay on Trakl, with translations of some of his poems, is included in my volume of prose writings *The Grammar of the Real*, Oxford University Press, Melbourne, 1975.
8 K. L. Goodwin's initial reaction to these poems in his review in *Meanjin*, vol. 31, no. 4, 1972, that they are 'essentially minor' (p. 502) and consist in seeking refuge in nature will, I hope, give way on closer consideration.

IO

Douglas Stewart

INTRODUCTION

Descriptions can be accurate as far as they go, yet misleading. For example, the following things can be said, and have been said, of Douglas Stewart. He has pursued the traditional poetic virtues, including a habit of working with well-articulated intelligible themes, though not without ambiguity in the result at times. He has considerable skill in gaining new effects from formal versification; a sense of the value of using certain traditional genres as matrices; a copious use, often in poems of some length, of the discursive mode. His philosophy tends towards a kind of vitalism, which exalts heroic achievement and intellectual discovery, yet accepts that what humans classify as good and evil is indifferently given by the one reality. He is a versatile poet whose range includes the satirical, the ironic, the comic. He often takes a theme derived from human history or natural history and uses it as a way of symbolizing and exploring his own dilemmas and contemporary man's predicaments.

One way of seeing how inadequate these phrases are is to notice that they would apply equally well to some other poets, notably for example A. D. Hope — and it is interesting to find so much common ground in poets ordinarily thought to be far apart. What is wrong with the description as applied to Douglas Stewart is that is misses his specific quality: it makes his work seem more formalized in its approach, more theoretically-based in method and content than it is: it misses the warily intuitive and tentative mode of Stewart's thought and creativity.

The early poetry of Stewart was written in his native New Zealand. *Green Lions* (1936) and *The White Cry* (1939) offer a late outgrowth from the English Georgians, with Edmund Blunden and W. H. Davies an early influence, followed by Roy

Campbell.[1] One notes elements which will persist in later work: a love of pure colour — green, silver, grey, yellow — clear-toned but subdued; a strong feeling for the opposites of the delicate (a hare's print in frosted grass, a starling's song like 'spiralling silver') and the hard and dangerous ('the patient hostility of rock', mountain water calling 'with a cold voice, like iron'); a fluent grace in the fingering of verse; a tendency, when not confined by short lyric forms, to yield to the enticements of concatenated prolixity; an affirmation of life, whether in joy or endurance, yet with a muted ground-tone of disquiet because the ultimate reality is perhaps implacable or meaningless. In the strange poem 'The White Cry', he sees a new-born lamb:

> I saw the youngest lamb in the world
> Beside the oldest tree in the wood.

The poem ends in an intense rather inexplicit moment of vision as he sees the lamb

> Against the tree's dark vastitude
> A dream, a white cry, meaningless,
> Though it were nailed on that huge rood.

Stewart's move to Australia in 1938 coincided with a search for new themes and forms and a widening of his stylistic range, a search which occupied the next ten years, ultimately to good effect but with no first-rate achievement within that decade. He attempted to write directly on war themes, not so much in *Elegy for an Airman* (1940) as in *Sonnets to the Unknown Soldier* (1941). As he himself has remarked,[2] his reaction to contemporary experience was better expressed indirectly in the verse plays which occupied his mind at this time.

His radio play *The Fire on the Snow* was written in 1939 and first performed in 1941. Along with another radio play *The Golden Lover,* a comedy on a Maori theme, it was published in 1944. It is based on Scott's Antarctic expedition and its theme is heroism of a pure unselfish kind. The next poetic drama attempted by Stewart was the stage play, *Ned Kelly*, written in 1940 and published in 1943 where the romantic values of outlaw daring are examined against the values of quiet people — the wild versus the tame. *Shipwreck* was written in 1942 but not published until 1947: it deals with violence and villainy and human weakness, but one does not find oneself involved in the working out of any theme or problem as in earlier plays. Stewart's other use of verse for drama is in *Fisher's Ghost* (1960), a short amusing melodrama which includes ballad-style verse. In attemping to revive poetic drama, Stewart was responding to an overseas phase represented by Eliot, Fry, and Auden.

The non-dramatic poems Stewart wrote in this period were collected in *The Dosser in Springtime* (1946). They show an interest in various kinds of light verse including, under Yeats's influence, the literary use of the popular ballad mode. There is a disabling uncertainty of touch and tone in this volume. Though Stewart was already well-established as a poet (the verse plays had done a great deal to effect this) and his Red Page editing and reviewing had made him influential, it was only in the years that followed that he wrote poems of high quality.

The turning point was *Glencoe* (1947), a narrative sequence about the Glencoe massacre, in which Stewart's strong sense of the ballad tradition is exercised on a theme of violence, treachery and death. At the end, powerful emotion is wedded to tradition to produce a remarkable lyric threnody:

> Sigh, wind in the pine;
> River, weep as you flow;
> Terrible things were done
> Long, long ago.
>
> In the daylight golden and mild
> After the night of Glencoe
> They found the hand of a child
> Lying upon the snow.
>
> Lopped by the sword to the ground
> Or torn by wolf or fox,
> That was the snowdrop they found
> Among the granite rocks.
>
> Oh, life is fierce and wild
> And the heart of the earth is stone,
> And the hand of a murdered child
> Will not bear thinking on.
>
> Sigh, wind in the pine,
> Cover it over with snow;
> But terrible things were done
> Long, long ago.

In the next volume, *Sun Orchids* (1952), Stewart displayed mastery of the things he does best: the short, often lyrical, nature poems, and now and then a longer poem in which an aspect of the human condition is caught and examined.

The best of the nature poems, in *Sun Orchids* and later

volumes, have moved a long way from the anthropomorphic whimsy and pseudo-popular idiom of *The Dosser in Springtime*. They are delicate notations of things observed with an intense fascination. The best of them go beyond the physical: indeed they are the most metaphysical of all Stewart's poems, most profoundly so when there is least comment. Overtly metaphysical questionings are certainly present in some poems: there is for example a rather equivocal consideration of God's point of view ('The Goldfish Pool', 'To Lie on the Grass') in relation to our world of beauty and fear, where the water-scorpion is 'naked evil spiking the luminous pond' and the spider is 'spry with the thought of murder'.

In some poems the metaphysical is present simply in a special sense of being, a sheer awareness of a thing's act of existence: it is this that informs the tranced stillness of 'The Snow-Gum' (p. 231). It comes again in the concentrated vision of 'Sun Orchids':

> Again next spring when the heath blows white and pink
> And ants come out of their holes and run on the rock
> Those clear blue flowers will stand on the blue sky's brink
> And close in rain and open in sun and look
> Except for the cup at the centre, some flecks of sand,
> More like a distillation of sapphire air
> Than anything out of the earth . . .

The image of the flower is exact, precise, yet in the last lines subtly transfigured. This is an interesting poem, because it takes an unexpected and very strange turn, revealing further aspects of the metaphysical mode in Stewart's poems of observation. It tries to say something which is disturbing and cannot be made explicit. Stewart must have attached importance to the poem when he named his 1952 volume after it. He omitted it, however, from his *Selected Poems* (1973); and since it is unblemished in expression one wonders whether this was because of second thoughts about the disturbing strangeness of its content. For the poem goes on to say that next spring he will not look again so intently into the sun orchid:

> . . . somebody else can peer

> As I once did in that deep silky cup
> Whose seed of light would drown in a drop of rain,
> For there's not orchid of gully or mountain top
> But holds some secret knowledge best left alone;
> And small as it was, blue on that sandstone spur,
> Once was enough: it held the sun in there.[3]

Stewart in an interview with John Thompson spoke of an 'exploration of the duality of God, of good and evil in the universe'.[4] Leonie Kramer has traced this theme most attentively in the nature poems, and shown how it gives them a more complex structure than may at first appear:[5] examples in the selection are 'Kindred' and 'The Gully'.[6]

The selection includes three very fine examples of the kind of poem by which Stewart is best known and in which he shows his powers more fully: 'Terra Australis', 'The Silkworms', and 'B Flat'. There is a range of irony, pathos, humour, and quickened imaginative life. The subject matter in each poem provides an emblem or quasi-allegory of an aspect of human experience. The contrasting yet parallel utopianisms of Quiros and William Lane;[7] the life-cycle of the silkworms; the inconsequential curiosity of the Reverend Henry White, brother of the famous eighteenth-century naturalist Gilbert White of Selborne. Each situation is well-constructed and economically presented. Other ruminations, such as 'Rutherford', 'Reflections at a Parking Meter', 'Four-Letter Words', are more prolix and less fully engaging, though not without merit in their serious or serio-comic vein. It is a feature of Stewart's work that a wry or gentle humour may play upon very serious concerns. 'B Flat' is delightful in its lightness of touch (in versification as well as in expression); the whimsical impulse, which does not always function to happy effect in earlier poems, is unerring here. The poet is not poking fun at Henry White: he is celebrating man's virtue of inquiry and originality even in its odd and inconsequential forms. The poem has kinship with 'Rutherford' and 'Professor Piccard' and the celebration of Darwin's genius in 'One Yard of Earth'.

COMMENTARY

Passages from the writings of Douglas Stewart

People are always telling us how poetry should be written and what it ought to be about... Poets should write about what they want to write about. But in the midst of the uproar, which is chiefly instigated by book reviewers because their trade is to criticize and by new poets because they have to make a place for their poetry, how few are the critics who pause to remind us, simply, that poetry is enjoyable... Poetry can be 'enjoyed' of course, in many moods and many styles... one should not lose sight of the true and original meaning of 'enjoyment'. It means giving joy; and in the long run, I feel often enough, that is what poetry is all about... As well as the more exalted virtues in poetry — melody and feeling in the lyric, structure and movement in the narrative — I like things that are alive, odd, humorous, out of the way... The thing I do not enjoy is dullness.

Introduction to *Modern Australian Verse*, Volume II,
ed. by Douglas Stewart, 1964, pp. xxi-xxiv

Flying Crooked

It was a shy poetic person
Wandering zigzag through his garden
Who saw how just by flying crooked,
Rather from habit than from fear,
The butterfly defeats the wicked;
The peewee marked it in the air
But when it dived down sharp and fierce
The butterfly was somewhere else.
And laughed to think that even now
When critics perch on every bough
To pounce, to murder and dissect,
They may not catch what they expect
And poetry still may flutter free
From Dr Peewee, Ph.D.

Thompson: What led you into writing so many of these little miniatures...?

Stewart: I think it had a good deal to do with the pleasure of discovering Australia for myself and it came out of wandering about in the bush, which I've always liked to do. I don't think it was anything more remarkable than that.

Thompson: Is there any philosophy behind these constant contemplations though?

Stewart: Yes, there is. They're all a method of exploring the universe. There's one called 'The Green Centipede' — well, that I got from going through the bush at Norman Lindsay's place at Springwood one time. I saw there, one day, simultaneously, some extraordinarily beautiful yellow flowers in bloom. I don't know what they were — they weren't one of the peas. I could never get the name. And, while I was looking at these, a green centipede came out from under a stone and I had the thought that whatever had created the beautiful flowers had also created this cruel-looking, stinging monster. So that poem is not just about a green centipede. It's an exploration of the duality of God, of good and evil in the universe. Apart from that, I have always thought that one should keep in touch with the earth. You should not lose contact with nature, in case you become too much of a city-type.

Thompson: I feel that you try to get inside the animal or the flower. You don't anthropomorphize the things — that would not be what you're trying to do, would it?

Stewart: No. You try to distil the absolute reality of whatever creature you're writing about. As a matter of fact, every poem is supposed to be about the same size as the creature. If it's a mosquito orchid, well, the poem's got to be just about a quarter of an inch long, and most of them are.

Thompson: Is there any element of mysticism, do you think, creeping into this? Verging on it?

Stewart: I never like to think about mysticism, John. I don't think of myself as a mystic; but the poems are, as I say, an exploration into the truths of the universe.

'Poetry in Australia: Douglas Stewart', interviewed by
John Thompson, *Southerly,* vol. 27, no. 3, 1967, p. 193

Passages from the writings of other authors

Stewart's statement about his 'exploration of the duality of God, of good and evil in the universe' does not fully describe (nor perhaps was it intended to) the cast of his thinking in the nature poems, and especially in those which are concentrated in *Sun Orchids*. Vivian Smith's phrase 'evasive scepticism' (in the article already cited) defines the dominant intellectual tone of his writing in the nature poems which, as R. D. FitzGerald notes,*

---

* *The Elements of Poetry,* University of Queensland Press (1965).

represent 'the real centre' of his 'mode of thought'. Interestingly, FitzGerald goes on to argue that a poet's central work 'is not necessarily his best work as poetry'; and he sees Stewart's best work as occurring in those poems which are 'a little off centre' of his main interests — notably in 'Country of Winter', 'Terra Australis', 'Worsley Enchanted' and the nature poems of *The Birdsville Track* volume. I doubt whether this view will stand up to scrutiny.

FitzGerald argues for the coherence of the whole body of Stewart's work on the grounds that he everywhere acknowledges the unity of creation, and the interlocking relationships within the natural order. Behind the short nature poems he sees the implication 'that every object in the universe both embodies, and is embodied in, an underlying reality'. This is certainly true, but the generalization disguises the detail. Stewart's philosophical preoccupations, if probed further, seem to me to disclose a link between the microscopic and heroic dimensions of his poetry. The nature lyrics give concrete expression to some quite particular notions about the ways in which man and the natural order interact.

The 'duality of good and evil' is everywhere to be seen in the nature poems of *Sun Orchids* and *The Birdsville Track*. 'A Robin', for example, describes the bush robin's illumination of the cold winter landscape. The grey bush is by implication a metaphor for the 'heart's great need', which the robin fills with its flash of crimson:

> The robin darts to bathe
> Breast-deep in the sky's reflection,
> And all that icy trance
> Breaks in most sweet destruction.

In 'The Brown Snake', on the other hand, the poet comes face to face with the aggressive power of nature. The heat of the sun, the green shade of the gum-tree, the 'amber pools' of the river, the blue of the hills are an idyllic picture of a season not yet too hot for human comfort. In the midst of this paradise the serpent rears up

> So brown with heat like the fallen
> Dry sticks it hit among,
>
> I thought the earth itself
> Under the green gum-tree,
> All in the sweet of summer
> Reached out to strike at me.

In both poems, it will be noticed, the poet's observation turns to interpretation of his own experience, but neither poem invites further probing. In 'Kindred', however, a much more complex meaning is suggested: [quotation]. The poet has written himself out of this poem, except as a sign pointing to what needs to be observed. 'Kindred' is unlike 'A Robin' and 'The Brown Snake' in that instead of noting the effects of the natural world on the human observer, it moves towards a theory, though the theory is not allowed to come to the surface abstractly. The notion that forces are at work under the rocky surfaces is frequent in these poems; here, through the comparison between snake and orchid, their suggested common origin, and the association of venom and blood, Stewart seems to be suggesting the possibility of obscure but positive forces ('darkest impulses') which produce the variety of life on the surface.

The nature of earth's creative forces is further explored in 'The Fungus'. Two voices enter this poem. The first utters the common man's view of the brilliant fungus:

> That crimson is nature's warning, those specks that blotch it
> Reek with their leathery stench of corruption and poison.

But this voice seems to withdraw the warning, in the line

> And say it is only a fungus, speckled and crimson

only in order to qualify the withdrawal by directing attention to the fungus's habit of hiding 'in the dark where the grass is thick and sour'. At this point in the poem there is an interesting syntactical device. The phrase 'Leave it alone!' is repeated, but the punctuation requires it to be attached both to what precedes and what follows it. The second half of the poem transfers the scene, by means of the image of the throat and tentacles of the fungus, to the 'oldest ocean'.

> Where, evil and beautiful, sluggish and blind and dumb,
> Life breathes again, stretches its flesh and moves
> Now like a deep-sea octopus, now like a flower,
> And does not know itself which to become.

As in 'Kindred', Stewart suggests a common origin and mysterious relationship between different forms of life. But in 'The Fungus' he makes explicit reference to aesthetic and moral qualities — corruption, evil, beauty — in a context which suggests both the blind purposefulness of creative energy, and its indifference to those qualities. The force of the phrase 'Leave it alone!' when applied to the second section of the poem is thus not a warning to man against the poisonous evil of the fungus, but an injunction not to interfere with the process of life, however inexplicable it may be, or whatever appearance it might present to the human observer.

This poem seems to me to be moving towards a view of a morally neutral universe, or, to put it differently, Stewart seems to be implying, through the two voices in the poem, that man imposes upon the natural world moral and aesthetic categories of his own making. (A similar point is made by White in *Riders in the Chariot* through the contrast between the attitudes of Miss Hare and Mrs Jolley towards the killing of a snake.) This theme is given a new direction in 'The Goldfish Pool' in which the observer looks first through his human eye, and then 'for one clear moment' through the eye of God.

Leonie Kramer, 'Two Perspectives in the Poetry of Douglas Stewart', *Southerly*, vol. 33, no. 1, 1973, pp. 293-5

With the variety that Stewart's output presents, it can only appear hazardous or even wilfully irrelevant to attempt a global generalisation; but I would suggest that the strength of his best lyrics resides in their evasive scepticism — his ability to see both sides of the question and not commit himself to anything beyond the making of the poem itself. This is strikingly the case in 'Terra Australis' with its zestful, energetic tone. The particular success of this poem — and it is among his outstanding pieces — lies in the way the potentially negative energy of mockery is turned into the good-natured refusal to be defeated: the illusions are mocked, but not the persistency of effort. It is, in fact, notable that he is never savage or satirical; and a tone of easy acceptance, even of modest mildness and indulgence, characterizes much of his poetry.

Stewart's evasive scepticism can be seen, too, in his most delicate lyrics, many of which tend to pivot on an expressed or implied 'as if' or 'as though'.

> Leave it alone! For white like the egg of a snake
> In its shell beside it another begins to break,
> And under those crimson tentacles, down that throat,
> Secret and black still gurgles the oldest ocean
> Where, evil and beautiful, sluggish and blind and dumb,
> Life breathes again, stretches its flesh and moves
> Now like a deep-sea octopus, now like a flower,
> And does not know itself which to become.

Many of his later images, like the fungus itself, do not know themselves which to become: 'moth or flower, flower or moth,/ neither moth nor flower but both', as he says of the tongue orchid; and through the juxtaposition and deliberately uncertain interplay of these images the object itself emerges with real precision and clarity.

It is notable that many of Stewart's finest nature poems, and especially those in *Sun Orchids* (1952) and *The Birdsville Track* (1955), are devoted to the slightest of bush creatures and bush plants. There seems little doubt that this preoccupation springs both from an observation of the actual natural scene in Australia as well as temperamentally from the lyric's preference for the slight and delicate, and its belief in the persistence of the frail in whatever shape or form. It may also be related to the need to create a personal native garden where the poet can turn away from the more disturbing and pressing problems of the age, to seek release from the more demanding questions which concern him in his plays.

There are no nature poems in *The Dosser in Springtime* of the kind *Sun Orchids, The Birdsville Track* and *Rutherford* (1962) were later to make us familiar with; and this addition to Stewart's work reflects an important phase in Australian poetry. It was at one stage common to see the whole of Australian poetry in terms of small nature lyrics, but this was in fact a late and quite localised development of the after war years. The late 'forties and the early 'fifties saw the brief development of a 'school' of nature poets whose most distinguished representatives were Judith Wright (in some phases), Roland Robinson, David Campbell and of course Stewart himself, who published these poets in *The Bulletin* at this time. This is the kind of interaction frequent in literary history, and it was clearly an important phase in the ecology of Australian poetry. Perhaps no finer proof of the individuality of these writers is needed than to compare their very different poems — for whatever their similarity of subject matter, they differ considerably in vision, texture and technique. Stewart's nature poems, in particular, differ from both Robinson's, Campbell's and Wright's in their sparseness of emotion, their drier, more etched tone and in the way they tactfully accept the play of image as an end in itself.

Vivian Smith, 'Douglas Stewart: Lyric Poet', *Meanjin Quarterly*, vol. 26, no. 1, pp. 43 and 47

POEMS

The Gully

If life is here how stealthily
It moves in this green hall of rock
Where mosses flourish soft and thick
And lichens imperceptibly
In wrinkled fans and circles shape
A civilization cold as sleep
On wall of stone and fallen tree.

Only in the deep secrecy
Of bracken-fern and maidenhair
One shaft of pink is glowing here
And poised in tiny ecstasy
With all life's hunger in its look
And arm outflung for the sweet shock
The trigger-flower strikes the bee.

Kindred

The rock swallows the snake,
Chilly and black as it vanishes;
In rain and moss the year
Moves in the sandstone crevices
Where like the snake itself
Earth's darkest impulses brood.
Long stems, sharp leaves awake —
O look where the wet moss flourishes
Tall crimson orchids appear,
Snake-headed, with darting tongue,
Now this way striking, now that,
As if indeed they had sprung
From the black snake's rotting side
Under the sandstone shelf
To spill on the green air
Their dewdrops of dark thought
Like venom and like blood.

The Snow-Gum

It is the snow-gum silently,
In noon's blue and the silvery
Flowering of light on snow,
Performing its slow miracle
Where upon drift and icicle
Perfect lies its shadow.

Leaf upon leaf's fidelity,
The creamy trunk's solidity,
The full-grown curve of the crown,
It is the tree's perfection
Now shown in clear reflection
Like flakes of soft grey stone.

Out of the granite's eternity,
Out of the winters' long enmity,
Something is done on the snow;
And the silver light like ecstasy
Flows where the green tree perfectly
Curves to its perfect shadow.

Terra Australis

1

Captain Quiros and Mr William Lane,
Sailing some highway shunned by trading traffic
Where in the world's skull like a moonlit brain
Flashing and crinkling rolls the vast Pacific,

Approached each other zigzag, in confusion,
Lane from the west, the Spaniard from the east,
Their flickering canvas breaking the horizon
That shuts the dead off in a wall of mist.

'Three hundred years since I set out from Lima
And off Espiritu Santo lay down and wept
Because no faith in men, no truth in islands
And still unfound the shining continent slept;

'And swore upon the Cross to come again
Though fever, thirst and mutiny stalked the seas
And poison spiders spun their webs in Spain,
And did return, and sailed three centuries,

Q

'Staring to see the golden headlands wade
And saw no sun, no land, but this wide circle
Where moonlight clots the waves with coils of weed
And hangs like silver moss on sail and tackle,

'Until I thought to trudge till time was done
With all except my purpose run to waste;
And now upon this ocean of the moon,
A shape, a shade, a ship, and from the west!'

2

'What ship?' 'The *Royal Tar*!' 'And whither bent?'
'I seek the new Australia.' 'I, too, stranger;
Terra Australis, the great continent
That I have sought three centuries and longer;

'And westward still it lies, God knows how far,
Like a great golden cloud, unknown, untouched,
Where men shall walk at last like spirits of fire
No more by oppression chained, by sin besmirched.'

'Westward there lies a desert where the crow
Feeds upon poor men's hearts and picks their eyes;
Eastward we flee from all that wrath and woe
And Paraguay shall yet be Paradise.'

'Eastward,' said Quiros, as *San Pedro* rolled,
High-pooped and round in the belly like a barrel,
'Men tear each other's entrails out for gold;
And even here I find that men will quarrel.'

'If you are Captain Quiros you are dead.'
'The report has reached me; so is William Lane.'
The dark ships rocked together in the weed
And Quiros stroked the beard upon his chin:

'We two have run this ocean through a sieve
And though our death is scarce to be believed
Seagulls and flying-fish were all it gave
And it may be we both have been deceived.'

3

'Alas, alas, I do remember now;
In Paradise I built a house of mud
And there were fools who could not milk a cow
And idle men who would not though they could.

'There were two hundred brothers sailed this ocean
To build a New Australia in the east
And trifles of money caused the first commotion
And one small cask of liquor caused the last.

'Some had strange insects bite them, some had lust,
For wifeless men will turn to native women,
Yet who could think a world would fall in dust
And old age dream of smoke and blood and cannon

'Because three men got drunk?' 'With Indian blood
And Spanish hate that jungle reeked to Heaven;
And yet I too came once, or thought I did,
To Terra Australis, my dear western haven,

'And broke my gallows up in scorn of violence,
Gave land and honours, each man had his wish,
Flew saints upon the rigging, played the clarions:
Yet many there were poisoned by a fish

'And more by doubt; and so deserted Torres
And sailed, my seamen's prisoner, back to Spain.'
There was a certain likeness in the stories
And Captain Quiros stared at William Lane.

4

Then 'Hoist the mainsail!' both the voyagers cried,
Recoiling each from each as from the devil;
'How do we know that we are truly dead
Or that the tales we tell may not be fable?

'Surely I only dreamed that one small bottle
Could blow up New Australia like a bomb?
A mutinous pilot I forebore to throttle
From Terra Australis send me demented home?

'The devil throws me up this Captain Quiros,
This William Lane, a phantom not yet born,
This Captain Quiros dead three hundred years,
To tempt me to disaster for his scorn —

'As if a blast of bony breath could wither
The trees and fountains shining in my mind,
Some traveller's tale, puffed out in moonlit weather,
Divert me from the land that I must find!

'Somewhere on earth that land of love and faith
In Labour's hands — the Virgin's — must exist,
And cannot lie behind, for there is death,
So where but in the west — but in the east?'

At that the sea of light began to dance
And plunged in sparkling brine each giddy brain;
The wind from Heaven blew both ways at once
And west went Captain Quiros, east went Lane.

The Silkworms

All their lives in a box! What generations,
What centuries of masters, not meaning to be cruel
But needing their labour, taught these creatures such patience
That now though sunlight strikes on the eye's dark jewel
Or moonlight breathes on the wing they do not stir
But like the ghosts of moths crouch silent there.

Look it's a child's toy! There is no lid even,
They can climb, they can fly, and the whole world's their tree;
But hush, they say in themselves, we are in prison.
There is no word to tell them that they are free,
And they are not; ancestral voices bind them
In dream too deep for wind or word to find them.

Even in the young, each like a little dragon
Ramping and green upon his mulberry leaf,
So full of life, it seems, the voice has spoken:
They hide where there is food, where they are safe,
And the voice whispers, 'Spin the cocoon,
Sleep, sleep, you shall be wrapped in me soon.'

Now is their hour, when they wake from that long swoon;
Their pale curved wings are marked in a pattern of leaves,
Shadowy for trees, white for the dance of the moon;
And when on summer nights the buddleia gives
Its nectar like lilac wine for insects mating
They drink its fragrance and shiver, impatient with waiting,

They stir, they think they will go. Then they remember
It was forbidden, forbidden, ever to go out;
The Hands are on guard outside like claps of thunder,
The ancestral voice says Don't, and they do not.
Still the night calls them to unimaginable bliss
But there is terror around them, the vast, the abyss,

And here is the tribe that they know, in their known place,
They are gentle and kind together, they are safe for ever,
And all shall be answered at last when they embrace.
White moth moves closer to moth, lover to lover.
There is that pang of joy on the edge of dying —
Their soft wings whirr, they dream that they are flying.

B Flat

Sing softly, Muse, the Reverend Henry White
Who floats through time as lightly as a feather
Yet left one solitary gleam of light
Because he was the Selborne naturalist's brother

And told him once how on warm summer eves
When moonlight filled all Fyfield to the brim
And yearning owls were hooting to their loves
On church and barn and oak-tree's leafy limb

He took a common half-a-crown pitch-pipe
Such as the masters used for harpsichords
And through the village trod with silent step
Measuring the notes of those melodious birds

And found that each one sang, or rather hooted,
Precisely in the measure of B flat.
And that is all that history has noted;
We know no more of Henry White than that.

So, softly, Muse, in harmony and conformity
Pipe up for him and all such gentle souls
Thus in the world's enormousness, enormity,
So interested in music and in owls;

For though we cannot claim his crumb of knowledge
Was worth much more than virtually nil
Nor hail him for vast enterprise or courage,
Yet in my mind I see him walking still

With eager ear beneath his clerical hat
Through Fyfield village sleeping dark and blind,
Oh surely as he piped his soft B flat
The most harmless, the most innocent of mankind.

SELECT BIBLIOGRAPHY

Green Lions (privately printed), Auckland, 1936.
The White Cry, Dent, London, 1939.
Elegy for an Airman, Frank Johnson, Sydney, 1940.
Sonnets to the Unknown Soldier, Angus & Robertson, Sydney, 1941.
Ned Kelly (verse play), Angus & Robertson, Sydney, 1943.
The Fire on the Snow and *The Golden Lover* (verse plays), Angus & Robertson, Sydney, 1944.
The Dosser in Springtime, Angus & Robertson, Sydney, 1946.
Glencoe, Angus & Robertson, Sydney, 1947.
Shipwreck (verse play), Shepherd Press, Sydney, 1947.
Sun Orchids, Angus & Robertson, Sydney, 1952.
The Birdsville Track, Angus & Robertson, Sydney, 1955.
Four Plays, Angus & Robertson, Sydney, 1958 (comprising the above verse plays).
Fisher's Ghost (play partly in verse), Wentworth Press, Sydney, 1960.
The Garden of Ships, Wentworth Press, Sydney, 1962.
Rutherford, Angus & Robertson, Sydney, 1962.
Selected Poems (Australian Poets series), Angus & Robertson, Sydney, 1963.
Collected Poems 1936-1967, Angus & Robertson, Sydney, 1967.
Douglas Stewart Reads from his own Work, Poets on Record series, University of Queensland Press, Brisbane, 1971.
Selected Poems, Angus & Robertson, Sydney, 1973.

The Flesh and the Spirit, 1948.
'Poetry in Australia: Douglas Stewart', interviewed by John Thompson, *Southerly,* vol. 27, no. 3, 1967.

Keesing, Nancy, *Douglas Stewart* (Australian Writers and their Work series), 1965 (new edition, Oxford University Press, Melbourne, 1969).
Kramer, Leonie, 'Two Perspectives in the Poetry of Douglas Stewart', *Southerly,* vol. 33, no. 3, 1973.
McAuley, James, 'Douglas Stewart', in *The Literature of Australia,* ed. Geoffrey Dutton, Penguin Books, Melbourne, 1964.
Phillips, A. A., 'The Poetry of Douglas Stewart', *Meanjin Quarterly,* vol. 28, no. 1, 1969.
Smith, Vivian, 'Douglas Stewart: Lyric Poet', *Meanjin Quarterly,* vol. 26, no. 1, 1967.

NOTES

1 Stewart mentions these influences, and also that of Yeats, in the broadcast interview with John Thompson printed in *Southerly,* vol. 27, no. 3, 1967, p. 197.

2 'I suppose that on the whole my reaction to the violence of our time has been chiefly expressed, by image and implication, in the verse and plays and *Glencoe.*' Foreword to *Selected Poems,* 1973, p. vi.

3 Having commented thus on 'Sun Orchids' I mentioned it in conversation with Stewart. Some weeks later he wrote saying he had changed the last line from 'it held the sun in there' to 'all life began in there', because the former phrase was suggested by the common name of the flower whereas, 'actually it was the queer sexual look inside the flower that hit me'.

4 'Poetry in Australia: Douglas Stewart', *Southerly,* vol. 27, no. 3, 1967.

5 'Two Perspectives in the Poetry of Douglas Stewart', *Southerly,* vol. 33, no. 3, 1973.

6 Three features of 'The Gully' are interesting: the way the language of stanza 1 assimilates the gully to the architecture and mural decoration of an ancient civilization, thereby amplifying the possible implications; the erotic undercurrent in stanza 2; and the way the language converts the trigger action of Stylidium laricofolium (the column formed by the long down-bent style united to the stamen-filaments springs up across the bee when touched near its base) from a harmless means of pollination to an act of violence.

7 Lane's expedition is recounted in Gavin Souter's *A Peculiar People* (1968). Mary Gilmore joined William Lane's second utopian socialist settlement in Paraguay, the settlement at Cosme, in 1896. The sources for Quiros's search for Terra Australis and his abortive attempt at a settlement called New Jerusalem are in volumes in the Hakluyt Society series. Recent documents have modified the story from the received version Stewart relied on; the rumour that Quiros lost control and suffered mutiny is now known to be untrue.

I I

David Campbell

INTRODUCTION

David Campbell's fundamental impulse is lyrical. Many of
the poems read like particular actualizations of the same ideal
poem: fluent and graceful, finely shaped, clearly imagined and
sweetly concordant, with an easy relaxed idiom bringing together
the informal and formal — nature turned into art and still
natural, but in an exhilarated trance:

> Where the horse and horseman go
> Iron is clamorous on stone,
> Spark and heavenly bluebell grow.
> World enough for flesh and bone.
> The black mare in the blue pool
> Stamps her image and is still.

> ('Let Each Ripen')

Behind these examples is a sensitivity to older English lyric
and to some modern lyric, including Yeats. The precariously
poised attempt is not always fully successful. Vincent Buckley
in comparing Judith Wright's 'Bullocky' with David Campbell's
early poem 'The Stockman' complains of the latter that it is too
easy a presentation of the Australian's dream of himself: 'the
whole presentation is shallow, because it is based on a cliché;
and its tone is toughly whimsical, bordering on sentimentality'.[1]
I am inclined to agree, yet how visually effective it is, and how
well-tuned:

> The sun was in the summer grass,
> The coolibahs were twisted steel:
> The stockman paused beneath their shade
> And sat upon his heel,
> And with the reins looped through his arm
> He rolled tobacco in his palm.

Like Stewart, Campbell for a time tried to make a new blend of balladry, and in general of a popular mode, with literary qualities. It gives expression to Campbell's good spirits and earthy gusto, but the blend is uneasy. Disappointing, too, are the excursions into modern fabliau, 'The Miracle of Mullion Hill' and 'The Golden Cow': the idea of such a poem, a re-furbishing of an old tradition, is better than the actualization.

Two twelve-poem sequences devoted to the countryman's life stand out for special comment: 'Cocky's Calendar' (from *Poems*, 1962) and 'Works and Days' (from *The Branch of Dodona*, 1970). The form of 'Cocky's Calendar' is more lyrical; the poems are subject occasionally to the temptation to stray unnecessarily from the immediate reality in search of a wider resolution or decorative touch. But the best are very good. Campbell has said 'I do not think of myself as a pastoral poet'.[2] He does not make country matters his particular business or confine himself to them. Nor does he turn his rural material into literary pastoral (at least not in his best poems: one way of saying what is wrong with some of the earlier poems is that they do sophisticate the material in this way). 'Cocky's Calendar' stands worthily with Clare's *The Shepherd's Calendar* as grounded in genuine rural experience and living by it.

'Works and Days' is perhaps the stronger sequence of the two, though less lyrical; one reason is that it stays more confidently close to immediate fact. In invokes the authority of Hesiod's *Works* with its realistic celebration of the countryman's life; and Hesiod's appendix on lucky and unlucky *Days* may be regarded as being represented by fortunate moments of leisure and contemplation, as in the September poem 'Loafing':

> It's good to take a day off late in spring,
> To let the reins hang easy and sheepdogs trot
> At heel in the mare's shadow through cushioning clover
> When instead of the cry of crows, high larks are singing.
>
> They climb the light from nests where hen-quail herd
> Their speckled young. Ducks act a broken wing,
> Splashing downstream through pools to set trout darting
> In slippery flotillas at the tail end of runs.

The special note of Campbell's best work is its yes to life. But the affirmation, the capacity for exhilarated enjoyment, the sheer healthiness, are not maintained in ignorance of the dark and terrible. The poems in 'Works and Days' are not mere notations of fact: implicit is a metaphysical sense of the way of things, and if they say 'it is good' they do so with knowledge of fragility and disaster and pain.

In the series of poems named 'The Branch of Dodona', Campbell tries his hand at a modern treatment of Greek legend. A recent development in Campbell's work is a sequence called 'Starting from Central Station' made up of memories of childhood and youth, centred on his father. The title poem is given in the selection.

COMMENTARY

If *The Miracle of Mullion Hill* is Campbell's most substantial book, *Poems* (1963) is certainly his most perfect. It consists exclusively of songs and sonnets of characteristic freshness and clarity and it marks a break in Campbell's use of the Australian ballad tradition. The songs are predominantly Elizabethan in shape, renewed from within by originality of observation and precision of image — as well as by a discreet use (for the first time in Campbell's work) of explicit Christian imagery.

'Cocky's Calendar' gathers together emblematic images of the countryside throughout the year and returns to Campbell's preoccupation with continuity, timelessness and change:

Bindweed and Yellowtail

November, sweet with secret birds
And thin-voiced weeds that cheat the sun,
For half the season wastes its words,
But when my silent mood comes on

The little blushing flowers that part
The grasses where the sheep-tracks meet,
Go deeper than the morning thought
Of waking lovers or the great;

And those small singers made of light
That stream like stars between the trees,
Sum in an inch the long delight
Of suns and thoughtful centuries.

It is the strength of Campbell's art (as of the lyric in general) to affirm the paradoxical resistance of the small and frail in front of the great and overwhelming, in a poem that avoids both sentimentality and preciosity.

Campbell's poems always suggest a detached yet involved contemplation of the world around him, a mind that responds to the otherness of nature and yet finds human equivalents in it, as in the lovely 'Prayer for Rain', where man's simple and humble dependence on other powers is evoked with a sweet economy of line; or in the sonnet 'When Out of Love' where the self-sufficiency of things in nature imposes calm on the mind. . .

Campbell's development reveals a growth in depth and sophistication, a movement towards refinement, away from the local bush song and ballad tradition to the higher Elizabethan tradition of pastoral elegance and ease. His later landscapes are no longer inhabited by the creatures of Australian tradition and tale; they are landscapes of the mind, places of solitude for communion and awareness. His poems are now smoother and rounder; he no longer writes with the plucked slightly abrupt staccato tension of *Speak with the Sun;* but his poems have retained one quality throughout: the capacity for looking at the commonplaces of nature with a fresh eye. His imagery is never startling, always clear and alertly observed in the manner of folk songs.

Campbell has the gift of writers like Walther von der Vogelweide or the authors of medieval carols, whose mere naming of an object serves to conjure it up concretely without the necessity of that link with another object that creates the image. Their freshness comes from the quality of the vision itself. It is a poetic world in which things exist in and for themselves, while much poetry belongs to a more complicated world where image is related to image in a complex metaphorical pattern.

Campbell's is finally a poetry of the spirit, not of the passions; it engages the sensibility rather than the intellect. But it is certain that he has already given us some poems that are among the finest and most original produced in this country during the last fifteen years.

Vivian Smith, 'The Poetry of David Campbell',
Southerly, vol. 25, no. 3, 1965, pp. 196-8

If 'Cocky's Calendar' and some of the many other landscape poems distil the essence of Campbell's delicate, thoughtful, nature poetry, he shows another side of his poetic talent in the love poems, though some of these too belong to the world of high plains, snowdrifts, droving and the shearers' smoke-ohs. In the love poems Campbell demonstrates the range of tone that he commands — and it is astonishingly wide — from the most gay and light-hearted, through passion and tenderness to worldly cynicism ... One of the most noticeable aspects of his poetry is the sharpness of its definition. He establishes the landscape with a few strokes, etched firmly and clearly. He repeatedly writes of the bare land, the strong light from sun or moon, the magpie singing its song, the hovering hawk, the light shed from wattles in spring, and the snow gums white and clear against the sky. The poetry is full of music. Magpies and thrushes pour their songs from the golden wattles. The crow shouts abuse and threats at John Kelly, the cuckoo 'fills his clear bottles in the dew', and the sounds of men's voices and bridles are heard in the stillness of a frosty evening. This is poetry of clear air, where sounds carry without distortion, moonlight edges the furrows and outlines the snow gums, and sun drenches and fades the yellow hills. Campbell displays a preference for short words (many monosyllabic), lines, stanzas, and poems. Each unit is firm but supple. In a general context of monosyllabic words and normal syntax, the occasional more formal variation — seen in phrases such as 'hillward-munching dams', 'cropped close as parsimony', 'thoughtful centuries' and 'drenching in cloud-burst sunshine' — are particularly effective. The crispness, lightness and freshness of Blake's world of innocence is recalled more than once in lines which have more in common with his than with any Australian poet except, possibly, Shaw Neilson.

Nor is the celebration of natural delight the only common ground between Campbell and Blake. The quality of mysticism mentioned by H. M. Green I should prefer to describe as vision. The sense in which I use this term includes that power, already mentioned, of calling the past and the future before the mind's eye, and of looking, as Willy Gray does, so hard at the objects of memory and present sight that they become alive with feeling and impressed with the marks of a man's individuality. There is nothing extravagant or pretentious in Campbell's exercise of this power. Recurrent images suggest aspects of the poet's vision. The past appears in mirage, an eloquent symbol for life present to the eye yet existing only as a trick of light. The mind at times has to make an effort to shake off the spell or blink away the mirage of the past haunting the present. The imagery of light focuses the inward vision of the poet through his outward eye — 'globes of light' in summer, the dark ignited by the farmer's seed, the light of love laying 'the shadow of our fear', the magpie's song like a shaft of light, and the thrice-repeated question in 'Hear the Bird of Day' — 'What's matter but a hardening of the light?' Campbell may not hear the angels singing 'Holy, Holy, Holy' when he looks at the sun; but he perceives, through the mirages which contain the past, through the light of the present, and the dark which nourishes the life of the future, what it means and how it feels for man to belong to his natural world and to himself. His is an uncommon gospel in a period dedicated to the literature of alienation, and it is peculiarly persuasive coming as it does from a man who has explored his world and his feelings unsparingly.

Faced with these finely wrought, spare poems, the critic's tools of trade seem more than usually clumsy, and more potent to bury than to disclose their virtues. I have deliberately understated the literary connections of the poems, since these, though of considerable interest, are so chiefly because of the ways in which Campbell has placed his individual signature upon them. I have neglected too the satires, and the light frolicsome poems which he turns with great adroitness. 'Multum in parvo' might be placed as an epigraph to this collection. It displays discipline and strength of mind, delicacy of feeling, humour, and a Yeatsian respect for 'walking naked'. Indeed the 'natural tongue' for which he praises Yeats belongs also to him.

Leonie Kramer, 'David Campbell and the Natural Tongue', *Quadrant*, vol. 13, no. 3, 1969, pp. 16-17

POEMS

Who Points the Swallow

Love who points the swallow home
And scarves the russet at his throat,
Dreaming in the needle's eye,
Guide us through the maze of glass
Where the forceful cannot pass,
With your silent clarity.

There where blood and sap are one,
Thrush's heart and daisy's root
Keep the measure of the dance,
Though within their cage of bone
Griefs and tigers stalk alone,
Locked in private arrogance.

Lay the shadow of our fear
With the brilliance of your light,
Naked we can meet the storm,
Travellers who journeyed far
To find you at our own front door,
O love who points the swallow home.

Night Sowing

O gentle, gentle land
Where the green ear shall grow,
Now you are edged with light:
The moon has crisped the fallow,
The furrows run with night.

This is the season's hour:
While couples are in bed,
I sow the paddocks late,
Scatter like sparks the seed
And see the dark ignite.

O gentle land, I sow
The heart's living grain.
Stars draw their harrows over,
Dews send their melting rain:
I meet you as a lover.

To a Ground-lark

from Cocky's Calendar

When I go out to sow the wheat
A freckled bird with sticks for feet
Goes fluttering from sod to sod
And whittles songs of faded light.

The swifts are gathered in a cloud
And now in flights above the ploughed
Lands before there's green to show
Their pointed tongues cry soft and loud.

So let them gather, let them go
With sun and soaring, for I know
That when the wheat's about my waist
I'll stooping find a ground-lark's nest.

Windy Nights

Naked in snowdrifts, we've made love,
In city parks, at the front gate,
And thought no deeper truth to prove
Than this, that lovers cannot wait.
What if the whole world disapprove,
Though it should be a crowded street?
See how instinctive lovers move
To get their clothes off when they meet.
O what do lovers love the best,
Upstairs naked or downstairs dressed?
Windy nights and hot desire
Or an old book and a steady fire?
Ask your mistress. Should she pause,
She has a lover out of doors.

Lambing

from *Works and Days*

Grass cropped to grass-roots, and a few ewes go down,
Like broody hens, with lambing sickness. Thank God
For yellow-tipped oatcrops. The mobs trail slow as clouds
Until they scent new pastures. Watch the barrels run!

Some poor bastard's copping the crows. Then it blows
A blizzard — lambs hunched in cat-humps behind each stump
And boulder; and next day it's like a fall of snow.
There's nothing flatter than a dead lamb. The crows

Move in and it's dawn-to-dusk work. When a ewe's
Cast, crows take the eye first (foxes the tongue)
And their beaks are poison: it's kinder to kill and skin
Than watch sheep stand and swell three days and die.

Delivering Lambs

Skins hang on fence-wires, purple, blue and green.
They turn you up at first, but it's getting through
That matters, getting the ewes through. I have seen
Black crows ride sheep like jockeys. There's one or two

I've settled scores with. Their eyes are a primrose blue
When they turn on the wind with wings like sooty fingers;
But their cry can lead you to ewes cast in the mist
And you thank God when they've eyes and their lambs have too.

Delivering lambs, *you're* god: tug at the forelegs
And drag it, yellow, by the tight lips of the ewe
Until she starts to lick and the lamb starts butting.
Walk home as tall as your shadow in the dew.

Starting from Central Station

A moon hangs in the air,
Its hands at ten past ten:
My father leaps alive
And I shrink to his son.

My father strides ahead
And stops to have a word
With men in caps who laugh.
He slips them a reward.

The trolley rolls behind
With boxes stacked like bricks:
Smoke and a whistle blow
And I am fifty-six.

Houses move through the parks,
Streets run with greens and reds:
Night conjures up the same
Old promises and dreads.

The train is on its way
And daylight gets to work,
Puts father in a box
And shoves him in the dark.

SELECT BIBLIOGRAPHY

Speak with the Sun, Chatto & Windus, London, 1949.
The Miracle of Mullion Hill, Angus & Robertson, Sydney, 1956.
Poems, Angus & Robertson, Sydney, 1962.
Selected Poems 1942-1968, Angus & Robertson, Sydney, 1968 (enlarged edition 1973).
The Branch of Dodona and other Poems: 1969-1970, Angus & Robertson, Sydney, 1970.
David Campbell Reads from his own Work, Poets on Record series, University of Queensland Press, Brisbane, 1975.

Auchterlonie, Dorothy, review of *Poems*, in *Quadrant*, vol. 7, no. 2, 1963.
Kramer, Leonie J., 'David Campbell and the Natural Tongue', *Quadrant*, vol. 13, no. 3, 1969.
Smith, Graeme Kinross, 'David Campbell — a Profile', *Westerly*, no. 3, 1973.

NOTES

[1] *Essays in Poetry*, 1957, p. 166.
[2] Preface to *Selected Poems*, 1973.

P

I 2

Rosemary Dobson

INTRODUCTION

Rosemary Dobson's work is like Douglas Stewart's and David Campbell's in one respect, that the best poems offer little hand-hold to the officious critic and have not attracted much academic commentary. There is some artistic affinity, in the instinct for graceful form, and for holding the moment of delighted vision; at times too there is a good-humoured or comic treatment. These characteristics in fact draw the three poets together, though their work is unmistakably distinct.

Brian Elliott has said 'Rosemary Dobson's most characteristic subject matter is the imaginative interpretation of *choses données* — a symbol, a story, a picture'.[1] This is true enough, but Rosemary Dobson's effective range is not confined to this kind of thing: she can, as some of the poems in the selection show, take her material directly from experience, not mediated by any artefact or pre-existing fiction. A small example one might rescue from neglect is an image in an early poem 'Windfall Apples' in *In a Convex Mirror* (1944) not subsequently reprinted:

> Evening, over the tops of many grasses
> Is a galah's wing flaked with pink and grey
> Feather on feather folding into darkness.

In addition to paintings, there are many other *choses données*: a woodcut, maps, calligraphy, typography, sculpture, illuminated manuscripts, tapestry, theatre, an Antarctic voyage, Greek legends, the story of Eutychus in Acts 20, a jack-in-the-box, Stonehenge, tombs, the scholar Lipsius.

In her use of artefacts there is doubtless an influence from Slessor and from Browning, Keats, and perhaps D. G. Rossetti; but with the distinctive quality that Rosemary Dobson's view is not merely external: it is informed by an intimacy with the processes of craftmanship from her own experience. This comes out in her engaging poem 'Country Press' (p. 257) in regard to printing, and in 'The Missal' in regard to calligraphy.[2]

It is the poems that are based on paintings that first made her reputation. Her imagination is saturated in Florentine, Sienese, and early Netherlandish painting, together with the work of some later artists, especially Vermeer. The poems provide an immediate visual appeal and stimulus to the imagination, and in the handling of phrase and verse they embody the artistry they celebrate. At the same time they are somewhat elusive, and tease the reader's mind as it seeks to establish their meaning and intention. The meaning cannot always be summed up in a single statement: it is often spread over several foci of attention.

This may be illustrated by the poem 'The Raising of the Dead' on which Rosemary Dobson commented in her Introduction to the selected poems in the paperback Australian Poets series (1963). The first three stanzas are as follows:

> Moved by the miracles of saints —
> The child restored, the leper healed —
> Through the black plumes of death I watch
> The intervening angels step
> Down the blue sky, across the field.
>
> To see the young man raised to life,
> The soul return to shuttered eyes
> They crowd in faded radiance
> Where, underneath an orange-tree,
> So inexplicably he lies.
>
> They lift the hand left limp by death
> And stir the stiffly painted gown,
> The wind of life is on their lips,
> The holy gold about their heads:
> Thus has the painter set them down.

The author's commentary establishes that in this case as in others there is no exact correspondence with an actual painting (in some cases there is no single original at all):

The starting-point of the poem for me was a painting of the Sienese school called 'S. Bernadino Resuscitates a Dead Child', and yet there is very little of the painting in the poem except the rather primitive simplicity of it, the wonder of the onlookers, and a strange little tree in the foreground which is hardly likely to be an orange-tree as I have named it in the poem. In fact the painting just started the movement of the poem in my mind (p. vii).

She goes on to show how the meaning and intention of a poem can be multiplied, and distributed over more than one kind of concern:

> . . . at one level, the poem is about a painting, even though the painting is largely an imagined one. At another level the poem is about miracles; at another, about angels and of how humans may envy them their freedom to pass from one world to another while they themselves are bound in their own limited time and space (p. vii).

The last stanza of the poem extends the significance further:

> Angels are free to come and go —
> My pity for the youth who lies
> These seven centuries at least
> Returned to Life; who once had caught
> A wink, a glimpse, of Paradise.

In regard to this she says:

> The poem has yet another meaning which for me is the most important one. It is a theme already unforgettably explored by Browning in his poem 'An Epistle from Karshish'. In this poem the Arab physician writes about the man Lazarus whom he has met, who has been dead and raised again to life, and for whom the whole significance of earthly life is thereafter altered. It is the same idea that I have tried to make explicit in the last stanza of my poem. The young man who has been raised to life from death has my pity since, because he has come to life in a painting, he cannot die again and return to the Paradise he has glimpsed, but must stay alive forever (pp. vii-viii).

It will be seen that the painting-poems play complicated games between the world of the picture and our world. Figures in the picture may look out or speak or step out of their space into ours. The painter or the onlooker may reach into, or step wholly inside, the picture world. The picture itself has levels of reality: heaven, earth, hell. The angels are free to come and go; the mortals are confined; the resuscitated must abide earthly life though he has glimpsed beyond. There is a strange temporal commerce: we travel back into a pictured reality centuries old; the pictured reality moves through time to us in the present. And above all, the picture is an image of eternity: its reality is stilled into an endless Now: it acts and lives and is, but timelessly, without succession or motion; and in this stilled instant outside time our world is transfigured, transformed by art.

The painting-poems are only a special instance of a general habit of Rosemary Dobson's verse: as with pictures, so with memories stopped and stilled so that they become another realm;

so with dream and vision; so with the sense of another reality
which haunts the experience of our actuality.

If we add the increasing sense, in the volumes *Child With a
Cockatoo* (1955) and *Cock Crow* (1965), of human pain and
responsibility, particularly in relation to motherhood, and also a
quick readiness for adroit comedy, we will have begun to see the
main axes of Rosemary Dobson's poetic world. For comments on
her technical artistry the reader is referred particularly to articles
by myself and Hope, from which extracts are given in the critical
section. A number of recent poems have attempted a modern use
of tales from Pausanias, somewhat in the same vein as David
Campbell's treatment of the Jason and Medea story in 'The
Branch of Dodona'.

COMMENTARY

Passage from the writings of Rosemary Dobson

It will be seen that these poems fall readily into groups: poems
about paintings; poems arising from European myths and
legends; poems about what might be termed human responsibility,
and so on. There is also a group of hitherto uncollected poems,
still being added to, which have their beginnings in the writings
of Pausanias. Poems in series are not just substitutes for longer
works that will never be written, as has been suggested. For me
they provide an opportunity to arrange ideas in relation to one
another, as one might arrange objects in space to construct a
harmony, each expressing something by itself and something else
in relation to other objects.

A friend who is a poet in another country, who has another
language and belongs to an older culture, wrote to me defining
poetry as a 'search for roots, for ground whereon to stand, for a
plausible interpretation of the "origin" '. There seems much truth
in this; but then again no one person's definition of poetry is
ever entirely satisfactory to another. What was satisfactory to me
in our interchange was that despite differences in heritage and
equipment (and I mean here culture and language) we could,
nevertheless, converse with clarity about the writing of poetry.
But there is always something that eludes one. I hope it will be

perceived that the poems presented here are part of a search for something only fugitively glimpsed; a state of grace which one once knew, or imagined, or from which one was turned away. Surely everyone who writes poetry would agree that this is part of it — a doomed but urgent wish to express the inexpressible.

Rosemary Dobson, Preface to Selected Poems,
1974, pp. xii-xiii

Passages from the writings of other authors

. . . the statements are not obvious, nor underlined: her poems are often 'communions rather than communications',* and while I would not agree that any of the poems are 'obscure' in the sense that their meanings are clouded by esoteric symbolism or shoddy expression, I am aware that as with the most rewarding poetry the reader needs to work on the texts if he is to go beyond the surface to the emotional and intellectual core of the poetic statement.

Stuart Lee, 'Rosemary Dobson', Quadrant,
vol. 9, no. 4, 1965, pp. 56-7

It must often happen that a reviewer lives long enough to be glad that he is not called upon to review his own reviews, and even more glad that such productions so quickly and mercifully pass into oblivion. Nearly 20 years ago I reviewed Rosemary Dobson's *Child with a Cockatoo* in the pages of *Meanjin*. I would heartily wish that review unwritten now; but the least I can do is to confess its inadequacy and to make some amends for its brashness. I took the poet severely to task for basing her poems so often on other works of art. On the face of it, I argued, there seems no reason why a poet should not take other works of art for his subject any more than the works of nature or ideas and histories and fables which are equally the work of man; there seems no reason why the creative imagination should not feed on the creative imagination of others with as much success as upon the raw materials of experience. Yet such works are always apt to be irritating, however well done, because we feel they are parasitic growths — the life of feeling in them is not drawn from their own roots but from the sap of other bodies than their own; they concoct emotion from ready made or predigested juices and not from the native soil. A poet who turns to this sort of subject too often is in danger of diminishing his original vision and losing himself in facile and meaningless exercises — the ultimate end of the process is the amusing but tedious underworld of whimsy . . .

* John Press, *The Chequer'd Shade*, 1958, ch. 9.

There was more in the same strain: the top-lofty tone of admonition, the glib analogy serving as a specious but inexact argument and the false implication that this argument applied to Rosemary Dobson's art as a whole.

It did not, of course, apply to any of it. It could only have been true of the parasitic sort of mind which cannot find its own subjects, or of the facile imitator whose productions are second-hand even when he can. It is not true of genuine artists who have always drawn their inspiration from the whole range of human experience. They assimilate and create anew whether their subject is a music lesson or Jan Vermeer's painting of a music lesson; whether they recreate the myth of Bacchus and Ariadne from Titian's masterpiece or from the literary sources on which Titian drew for his inspiration. As a matter of fact, some years later Rosemary Dobson in the introduction to a selected edition of her poems, gently pricked the bubble of my offensive criticism by pointing out that a number of her poems had as their subjects pictures which she had simply imagined. Since I could not distinguish these from poems based on actual paintings my discomfiture was complete and deserved. It is, after all, the quality of the poem in itself that is the only and the final test of its worth . . .

The unobtrusive nature of her effects extends in to every part of her poems and is the result of a thorough mastery and instinctive craftsmanship. One is always being taken by surprise by turns of phrase so simple that it is easy to miss the fact that they are meeting places of many sorts of meaning.

> As though some marvellous poetry
> Were making in the air above
> Where minds of poets meet and merge
> Into a single cry of love.

(The Cry)

And this beautiful economy of the means at once preserves the *lucidus ordo* of the poem and makes it glow with a concentrated richness of meaning rare in this day of diffuse effects and verbal fireworks. There are no verbal fireworks in Rosemary Dobson's poetry, everything is subordinated to the main effect and the central theme. It is perhaps the absence of any sort of deliberate cleverness, of using the theme to display the writer's coruscating aptitude with images and allusions, it is the entire *seriousness* of her art, that attracts me in an age of experimental acrobatics in verse.

This is not to say that she is conventional, 'academic', lacking in invention. Experiment for experiment's sake is usually the mark of a second-rate artist. Invention is experiment in the service of vision: the experimental artist lacking vision, tries to replace it by technical novelties. Rosemary Dobson has the reputation of staying close to the traditional forms, but within those forms she is truly and surprisingly inventive. She does not break with the tradition but she does exciting and delightful things in extending its possibilities. Her early verse is full of metrical invention, movements that seem to lead to expected conclusions and end with one catching one's breath at the exquisitely unexpected.

A. D. Hope, 'Rosemary Dobson: a Portrait in a Mirror', *Quadrant,* vol. 16, no. 4, 1972, pp. 10 and 12

In *The Ship of Ice* (1948) there is a poem called 'Still Life', written when her talent was reaching its first maturity.

[see poem on p. 256]

Perfect, except in the eighth line where the vague gesturing use of the word 'some' has been picked up from the bad habit of certain poets, and the word 'sweet' has got a bit tired from the amount of work other poets have made it do.

The poem begins with three lines of pure visual representation, but continues throughout to keep us aware of the physical presence of the picture. Things or impressions are placed with effortless rightness within the logical-grammatical space framed by the verse: there is room enough around them but not too much. The first line presents three objects, the second one, the third two. One might think there is nothing in this: after all, if one is naming objects they have to occur in some order and phrasing. But one has only to look at the work of someone who lacks an instinctive sense of how to dispose things in verbal space to see that a special faculty is involved.

The size and structure of words are also used with instinctive rightness. Throughout the first eight lines there is a series of 'trochaic'-sloping two-syllabled words that refer to some sort of process and create an impression of held movement: 'tumbled', 'leaning', 'guttered', 'flowing', 'welling', 'spreading'. All the other two-syllabled words are of the same 'trochaic' build ('smoky', 'candle', 'Silence', 'canvas', 'feather') so that when the 'iambic'-formed word 'restraint' comes at the end, it comes with appropriate and distinct effect. Again we might think there is nothing in this: of course most words are of one or two syllables, and two-syllabled words are more commonly 'trochaic' in build than 'iambic'. But the fact remains that there are poets for whom words come particularly right because they have a working sense of the expressive value of varying word-build, even when they are not consciously attending to it. So in the later two stanzas: the monosyllables first pick out a tune faintly reminiscent of nursery rhyme ('Whose was the hand that held the brush?/And who the guest who came to break...'); and then they continue on in graceful simplicity, with the sole exception of two adjoining and logically related 'amphibrach'-shaped formations: 'three hundred', and 'belated', which therefore become points of significant emphasis. It can be all accident; but you have to have a talent for the right accidents. A real artificer knows by feel when the words are coming right, and will sometimes consciously attend to such detail, working over it with minute care.

The poem falls into two main parts of two quatrains each. The internal proportioning is nicely varied: in the first half, the first three lines form a subdivision, and then the next five lines flow on to complete the pictorial effect; whereas in the second half the subdivision coincides with the quatrains. If one looks at the phrasing within these divisions and subdivisions, one sees that the line provides the basic rhythmic unit, and keeps the sense of definite shape, but there is just enough run-over phrasing to provide satisfactory variation. It is within this well-composed structure that the characteristically refined and even slightly teasing phonetic texture provides its own kind of pleasure. Only two of the lines in the quatrains are rhymed, but other relationships operate ('flask-cask', 'held-hold', 'brush-break', 'tilt-drink') ...

'Still Life' obviously describes a picture by an unknown seventeenth-century artist, and says that the modern viewer can receive what the painter offers just as well as the first viewer did. But in doing this the poem does much more. It shows us the objects in the picture, arrested in stillness, as if out of time. The movement of the poem serves not only to articulate the painter's composition but also to register the movement of the beholder's mind, as it explores the work of art and reacts to it, and then goes on to sense the mystery of the hospitality and the communion (the latent sacramental analogy is surely discreetly intended) that the dead unknown painter still provides under the species of the bread and wine that he painted three centuries ago.

The poem recreates, in its own way, part of the problem Keats tried to grasp in 'Ode on a Grecian Urn'. Art defeats time by arresting things within its still duration. But the triumph of art is at a price: what it rescues — and gives back to us as an image of beauty or truth or fulfilment — has been taken out of life; though we have it, we have it only in the mode of art, not in actuality. The bread feeds the spirit, but it cannot be grasped and broken and eaten; the wine cannot be poured and drunk. The way the poem reminds us of this distinction is paradoxically by seeming to ignore it, as if one could reach into the picture-space and break the loaf and pour the wine. Rosemary Dobson's poem confines itself to thus setting up the mysterious mind-bemusing relation between the beholder's space and time and that within the picture. It has nothing of the tragic quality of Keats's anguished oscillation between an actuality of warm, breathing, unfulfilled desire and an image of beauty and joy that is silent and cold. The tone of 'Still Life' is one of gratitude and courtesy, expressed in the slightly mannered idiom pleasantly used in the last three lines.

James McAuley, 'The Poetry of Rosemary Dobson', *Australian Literary Studies*, vol. 6, no. 1, 1973, pp. 3-6

POEMS

Still Life

Tall glass, round loaf and tumbled cloth
And leaning flask of smoky brown,
The guttered candle and the cask;
And Time and Silence flowing down,

Welling against the canvas, held
By stroke and feather-touch of paint
As one might build a weir to hold
Some spreading pool in sweet restraint.

Whose was the hand that held the brush?
And who the guest who came to break
The loaf which I, three hundred years
Belated, still reach out to take?

I, who now pour the wine and tilt
The glass, would wish that well you fare,
Good sir, who set out food and drink
That all who see might take and share.

The Martyrdom of Saint Sebastian

My scarlet coat lies on the ground,
You note the texture of the fur,
What miracles of art, you say,
Those Flemish painters could command,
Each brush-stroke like a single hair.

How the eye focuses upon
The archer stiffly draped in black
Cutting the foreground to the right —
Masterly, that foreshortened arm,
Skilful, the modelling of the neck.

How colour, line, and form combine
To give the painting depth and space!
Beyond the stream, beyond the hill,
The village — each receding plane
Leads to the sky the travelling glance.

And in the sky the angels throng
Like glittering birds upon a tree —
Marvellous, you say, the mind that takes
A fantasy upon the wing
And out of prose makes poetry.

I am Sebastian. While you praise
I suffer and my lips are dumb,
The arrows pierce me through and through,
Yet you admire with abstract phrase
The torment of my martyrdom.

Country Press

Under the dusty print of hobnailed boot,
Strewn on the floor the papers still assert
In ornamental gothic, swash italics
And bands of printer's flowers (traditional)
Mixed in a riot of typographic fancy,
This is the *Western Star*, the Farmer's Guide,
The Voice of Progress for the Nyngle District.
Page-proofs of double-spread with running headlines
Paper the walls, and sets of cigarette-cards
Where pouter-bosomed showgirls still display
The charms that dazzled in the nineteen hundreds.

Through gaping slats
Latticed with sun the ivy tendrils fall
Twining the disused platen thrust away
Under a pall of dust in nineteen-twenty.
Draw up a chair, sit down. Just shift the galleys.
You say you have a notice? There's no one dies
But what we know about it. Births, deaths and marriages,
Council reports, wool prices, river-heights,
The itinerant poem and the classified ads —
They all come homewards to the *Western Star*.
Joe's our type-setter. Meet Joe Burrell. Joe's
A promising lad — and Joe, near forty-seven,
Peers from a tennis-shade and, smiling vaguely,
Completes the headline for the Baptist Social.
The dance, the smoke-oh, and the children's picnic
Down by the river-flats beneath the willows —
They all come homewards and Joe sets them all,
Between the morning and the mid-day schooner.
Oh, *Western Star* that bringest all to fold,
The yarding sales, the champion shorthorn bull,
And Williams' pain-relieving liniment,
When I shall die
Set me up close against my fellow-men,
Cheer that cold column headed 'Deaths' with flowers,
Or mix me up with Births and Marriages;
Surround the tragic statement of my death
With euchre-drives and good-times-had-by-all
That, with these warm concomitants of life
Jostled and cheered, in lower-case italics
I shall go homewards in the *Western Star*.

Country Morning

I heard the cock at morning crow
Among the bright-bunched parsley-leaves
And with my curious, wilful eye
Saw the bird of paradise,
Marvellous creature that can yet
In fury and in flame beget
Itself upon its own decay.

I heard in darkness as I lay
The horses' hoofbeats on the hill
And saw the coursers of the sun
Trampling into beaten gold
The patient labours of the frost.
Then wheeled, that fiery, fuming host,
And leapt the world from height to height.

The farmer's wife began her day
With yawns and sighs and sleepy cries
And though I knew she went to milk
My inward eye saw otherwise.
Oh strange — the rattle of the pail
Was Phoebus shaking out his mail
Who puts such glittering armour on.

The Birth

A wreath of flowers as cold as snow
Breaks out in bloom upon the night:
That tree is rooted in the dark,
It draws from dew its breath of life,
It feeds on frost, it hangs in air
And like a glittering branch of stars
Receives, gives forth, its breathing light.

Eight times it flowered in the dark,
Eight times my hand reached out to break
That icy wreath to bear away
Its pointed flowers beneath my heart.
Sharp are the pains and long the way
Down, down into the depths of night
Where one goes for another's sake.

Once more it flowers, once more I go
In dream at midnight to that tree,
I stretch my hand and break the branch
And hold it to my human heart.
Now, as the petals of a rose
Those flowers unfold and grow to me —
I speak as of a mystery.

Cock Crow

Wanting to be myself, alone,
Between the lit house and the town
I took the road, and at the bridge
Turned back and walked the way I'd come.

Three times I took that lonely stretch,
Three times the dark trees closed me round,
The night absolved me of my bonds;
Only my footsteps held the ground.

My mother and my daughter slept,
One life behind and one before,
And I that stood between denied
Their needs in shutting-to the door.

And walking up and down the road
Knew myself, separate and alone,
Cut off from human cries, from pain,
And love that grows about the bone.

Too brief illusion! Thrice for me
I heard the cock crow on the hill
And turned the handle of the door
Thinking I knew his meaning well.

SELECT BIBLIOGRAPHY

In a Convex Mirror, Dymock's, Sydney, 1944.
The Ship of Ice, Angus & Robertson, Sydney, 1948.
Child with a Cockatoo, Angus & Robertson, Sydney, 1955.
Selected Poems (Australian Poets series), Augus & Robertson, Sydney, 1963.
Rosemary Dobson Reads from her own Work, Poets on Record series, University of Queensland Press, Brisbane, 1970.
Selected Poems, Angus & Robertson, Sydney, 1973.

'Poetry in Australia: Rosemary Dobson', interviewed by John Thompson, *Southerly*, vol. 28, no. 3, 1968.
'A World of Difference', *Southerly*, vol. 33, no. 4, 1973 (text of the Blaiklock Lecture for 1973).

Burrows, J. F., 'Rosemary Dobson's Sense of the Past', *Southerly*, vol. 30, no. 3, 1970 (a list of reviews 1955-70 is given on p. 165).

Campbell, David, review of *Child with a Cockatoo*, in *Southerly*, vol. 17, no. 1, 1956.

Hope, A. D., 'Rosemary Dobson: a Portrait in a Mirror', *Quadrant*, vol. 16, no. 4, 1972.

Lee, Stuart, 'Rosemary Dobson', *Quadrant*, vol. 9, no. 4, 1965.

McAuley, James, 'The Poetry of Rosemary Dobson', *Australian Literary Studies*, vol. 6, no. 1, 1973.

NOTES

1 *The Landscape of Australian Poetry*, 1967, p. 306. The use of material drawn from cultural tradition, from reading and from works of art, is conspicuous to varying degrees in some other poets: Slessor, Hope, FitzGerald, Douglas Stewart, Harold Stewart, Francis Webb. It is prominent in my earlier work but not in recent work.

2 Rosemary Dobson recalls in her 1973 Blaiklock Lecture 'A World of Difference' (reprinted in *Southerly*, vol. 33, no. 4, 1973), that she studied design with Thea Proctor: 'I had no doubt as to which art — poetry or painting — I wished principally to pursue, but I believe one throws light on the other, and both engage my interest'. Her interest in typography was expressed in an essay she offered as an unmatriculated student in English at Sydney University, 'Typographical Design in the Twentieth Century'.

13

Continuity and Change in the Fifties

INTRODUCTION

The poets who emerged in the 1940s continued writing in the fifties and sixties, in some cases producing their best work. In Sydney Lex Banning and Ray Mathew produced their first volumes in 1951. So did Nancy Keesing. Her *Imminent Summer* (1951) followed by *Three Men and Sydney* (1955) and *Showground Sketchbook* (1968) established her as a cheerful and compassionate observer of urban and suburban life, as in the poem 'We Told You So' (p. 282). Elizabeth Riddell had produced a volume of verse, *The Untrammelled*, in 1940; in 1948 she gained more attention with *Poems*, but the later volume *Forebears* (1961) was perhaps the strongest. Armidale-born J. R. Rowland began writing out of his experience in different countries as a diplomat. Francis Webb had already published *A Drum for Ben Boyd* in 1948, but it was the poetry he wrote in the fifties that made him, with Vincent Buckley, the strongest new talent, with an influence extending to younger poets in the sixties. Charles Higham arrived from England and pursued a literary career in Sydney which has included the production of several books of verse; and T. H. Jones, a Welsh poet, became a university teacher in Newcastle until his death by drowning in 1965. These last two poets swelled the small list of immigrants who have written poetry in Australia. Among these Clive Sansom should be mentioned: he has continued to publish verse and verse plays in England, with an entirely English and European orientation, while residing in Tasmania — in a curious way he has never been a figure in the Australian literary scene, though recently he has surprisingly enough emerged as poetry reviewer for *Nation Review*.

In Queensland David Rowbotham was the first new voice to emerge. John Blight had published a first volume, *The Old Pianist*, in 1945; he published *The Two Suns Meet* in 1954, but he became better known in the sixties with the publication of *A Beachcomber's Diary* (1963) and *My Beachcombing Days* (1968). Martin Haley is an older Queensland poet whose outlook is Catholic in both senses of the word; he has published both original poems and translations, but the language is merely traditional rather than traditional-made-new, as is needed. Other poets of Queensland origin such as David Malouf and Thomas W. Shapcott can be considered among the developments of the next decade. In South Australia Geoffrey Dutton, who had produced an early volume in 1944, published *Antipodes in Shoes* in 1958; Max Harris had already in 1955 published a collection, *The Coorong*, in which he showed he had found a vein of racy verse with a local basis, in such poems as 'The Tantanoola Tiger'; Nancy Cato published *The Darkened Window* (1950) and *The Dancing Bough* (1957); and Robert Clark began to publish poems, though his first collection did not appear until 1962. In Hobart Vivian Smith published his first collection, *The Other Meaning* (1956), but his work belongs more to the next decade, as does that of Gwen Harwood. The West Australian novelist Randolph Stow produced a first volume of verse, *Act One* (1957), which, like the volume published by the Victorian-born novelist Hal Porter, *The Hexagon* (1956), demonstrated that the powers of a novelist do not often produce poetry of equal value. Porter published a second volume, *Elijah's Ravens*, in 1968 and a third, *In An Australian Country Graveyard,* in 1974. Stow continued with *Outrider* (1962) and *A Counterfeit Silence* (1969), but his rather facile and self-indulgent romantic vein has not developed strength, in spite of the friendly expectations of some of his critics.[1]

The most important development in the decade was the emergence of a group of poets in Melbourne, whose work one principally thinks of as the *new* poetry of the fifties. Sydney's hegemony was being challenged. The central figure in the group was Vincent Buckley, whose critical activity, even more than his poetry, became very influential; other poets were Evan Jones, Chris Wallace-Crabbe, R. A. Simpson, Alexander Craig, Noel Macainsh. Early in the next decade, four of these poets joined with four other Melbourne poets to produce *Eight by Eight* (1963) a collection containing eight poems by each of the contributors. This publication did not, however, define a like-minded group: the Hungarian immigrant, David Martin (who came to

S

Australia in 1949) was not concerned with the same problems of poetic method as those already mentioned; neither was Laurence Collinson; nor the older poet Max Dunn, a philosophic poet who became a Buddhist priest in 1956. It is chiefly with Buckley, Evan Jones, Wallace-Crabbe, and Simpson that something like a Melbourne school can be found in the fifties.

Before considering the work of this group, certain features of the situation in the early and middle fifties should be noted. A general literary history of the period would have to give considerable attention to the political factors involved, but this is much less important in regard to poetry. Political ideology and engagement with political issues have of course been present from the beginning. They are a notable feature of the work of Lawson and Gilmore and Brennan; yet in a selection of their best poems the political tends to disappear from view: one loses Lawson's radical vision of 'freedom on the wallaby', of blood staining the wattle, of a future in which 'there ain't no fore-'n'-aft', and Gilmore's utopianism and social indignation, and Brennan's anti-war and pro-war pontifications. In the forties there was an upsurge of left-wing partisanship among intellectuals and this affected the literary scene.

By 1950 *Meanjin*[2] in its editorial stance was clearly committed on the left side of the Cold War. But there was no change in the editor's established policy of being receptive to all material of literary merit; and in practice this meant that political poetry of a sentimental, rhetorical or propagandist kind was but a minor feature. Two other journals with an evident political orientation began publication during the decade. *Overland* in 1954, edited by Stephen Murray-Smith, started as a Communist-sponsored organ devoted to 'social realist' (or 'socialist realist') writing, but in 1956 the editor broke from this commitment and took the magazine on an independent left path. *Quadrant,* beginning at the turn of the year 1956-57, edited by myself, was sponsored by the Australian Association for Cultural Freedom and was clearly anti-Communist in outlook, but it too was receptive to work of literary merit without prejudice.

When Vincent Buckley surveyed left-wing poetry in a chapter of his *Essays in Poetry* (1957), he found only three poets to discuss: John Manifold, John Thompson, Laurence Collinson; though he also mentioned Victor Williams, Muir Holburn, Bartlett Adamson. He had no difficulty in showing that Manifold, Collinson and Thompson generally performed much better when they dropped their 'social realism' (that is, poetry enlisted in the Party cause) and wrote from their personal and private experience.[3] One of Manifold's most lively poems, written with the clean energetic strokes that characterize his best work, is 'The Sirens' in which personal experience and political commitment are held in balance:

> Odysseus heard the sirens; they were singing
> Music by Wolf and Weinberger and Morley
> About a region where the swans go winging,
> Vines are in colour, girls are growing surely
>
> Into nubility, and pylons bringing
> Leisure and power to farms that live securely
> Without a landlord. Still, his eyes were stinging
> With salt and sea-blink, and the ropes hurt sorely.
>
> Odysseus saw the sirens; they were charming,
> Blonde, with snub breasts and little neat posteriors,
> But could not take his mind off the alarming
>
> Weather report, his mutineers in irons,
> The radio failing: it was bloody serious.
> In twenty minutes he forgot the sirens.

In Australia such political poetry as exists has fared better when it has been generated by critical rejection of utopian and revolutionary myths and demands. One of John Thompson's most striking poems, 'Attis', is a very bitter protest against the self-mutilation of the poet in the interest of a doctrine and organization; it marks the end of his activist phase. Douglas Stewart's 'Terra Australis' is his critique of fanatical utopian idealism. My 'Incarnation of Sirius' and 'Philoctetes' and 'The Hero and the Hydra' express a rejection of the myth of revolution while my *Captain Quiros* agrees with Douglas Stewart in rejecting all utopianism, religious or secular, though it does so from a different point of view. Vincent Buckley's 'Eleven Political Poems' represents his critique of modern political activism — 'No New Thing' (p. 283) is the most forceful of this series. Chris Wallace-Crabbe, Evan Jones, Bruce Dawe and R. A. Simpson have attempted poems exploring the political violence of our times. More generally, it can be said that a political concern in a very broad sense — a care for the health of the *polis* — enters contemporary writing in many ways, explicitly and implicitly.

Although A. D. Hope's first mature work is properly placed in the 1940s, the impact of his first volume of verse, *The Wandering Islands* (1955) and his article 'The Discursive Mode: Reflections on the Ecology of Poetry' in the first issue of *Quadrant* was very important in the decade. That article drew attention to the disappearance from the literary landscape of the traditional forms and spoke disparagingly of the degenerate growths that have succeeded them:

> Just as a certain nobility of mind was lost with the passing of epic from the living forms, just as real magnanimity was lost with tragedy, so one by one the attitudes of mind and heart, which made the use and being of the other great forms, died out as they ceased to be practised. A loss and a limitation of consciousness followed, so that men, whether readers or poets, were unable any longer to understand what they had lost, or indeed what was meant by a 'form' at all. That the power and range of each kind of poetry was intimately related to the structure, the appropriate metres, the formal character of epic, of satire, of ode, or drama, exactly as the character and nature of each kind of plant or animal is the product of its 'form', it was no longer possible to recognize. Men could see nothing but arbitrary or chance types of construction, and they came to the perverse conclusion that these forms, having perished, had nothing to do with the essential nature of poetry. Poetry in its purest form they decided was to be found in the lyric. Edgar Allan Poe propounded the new heresy in an essay which became one of the bases of symbolist doctrine. Narrative, drama, excogitation, argument, description were rejected as having nothing to do with the pure essence of poetry. Poetry was music. Poetry was not the thing said, but continual evocation of delicious suggestions of meaning. Poetry was an unconscious crystallization of glittering images upon the bare twig of metre. Poetry, at the nadir of this search for its essence, became the formless babble and vomit of the poet's subconscious mind (pp. 29-30).[4]

(The argument could more plausibly be turned round the other way, to suggest that it was the dying out of certain attitudes of mind and heart that caused the passing away of related literary forms; this would tend to moderate one's expectation of what can be achieved simply by reinstating the genres.) Part of the suggested regimen was the cultivation of 'the middle form' of poetry, the discursive mode, for the purposes of 'narration, the essay, the letter, conversation, meditation, argument, exposition, description, satire or cheerful fun'. Another essential part of Hope's neo-formalism was a destructive analysis of the notion of free verse and a defence of the inexhaustible nature of the traditional resources of metre.[5] At the same time I was pursuing an analysis of poetic modernity through a critique of Romanticism and Symbolism;[6] and in another *Quadrant* article I made suggestions about the possible recuperative value of working again with some of the old poetic kinds: 'eclogue, elegy, epistle, epigram, epithalamium, epyllion — to name only a few', and also maintained that 'subtlety, complexity and balance are all on the side of the traditional verse'.[7] The closely similar critical positions expounded at that time by Hope and myself were partly an expression of fundamental principle, partly a tentative suggestion about a poetic regimen or strategy related to what we were trying to do at the time. The articles were called forth by the existence of *Quadrant* as a vehicle for discussion of this sort; they extended and consolidated a tendency which had already become evident in our work and in some degree influential.

One reaction to this was to see it as an unwelcome intrusion of intellectuals into the field of Australian poetry. This was expressed, oddly enough, by an academic, R. G. Howarth, in the Introduction he wrote to the first *Penguin Book of Australian Verse* (1958), which he edited with Slessor and John Thompson:

> Since the war a cluster of intellectuals, led by A. D. Hope and James McAuley, have become prominent. Formal, traditionalist, and rightist, leaning to satire, these have gained through certain critical assumptions an ascendancy that tends to restrain individualism and verbal experiment (p. 19).[8]

Opposition to intellectuals was frequently interchangeable at this time with complaints about invasion by academics. Certainly in the fifties an increasing number of poets were not only university graduates but also university teachers, and criticism of Australian literature was increasingly carried on by academics. The influence of the university environment on poetry and criticism has been discussed a good deal in recent years.[9] Some of the comment has been like the jostling and grumbling in the public service in the same period when graduates began to challenge 'sound practical men'.

Another reaction was embodied in an article, free-ranging and polemical in tone, by Geoffrey Dutton in the first issue of *Australian Letters* in which attention was concentrated on the question of diction and style.[10] The thesis is that a 'mixed' poetic idiom suited to Australia had been found already by Gordon and Paterson, and recovered by several poets following Slessor's lead (Douglas Stewart, Judith Wright, David Campbell, Ray Mathew, and others); whereas Hope and McAuley and Harold Stewart had been retrograde in reviving an inappropriate poetical diction:

> Hope, McAuley and Stewart are trying to bluff us, or themselves, that certain combinations of words will light up with fresh meaning and magic as if all a poet has to do was to connect the plug and turn on the switch. Alas! he has to generate the electricity as well

. . . At least our poetic diction used to be abreast of the generation, or a comfortable fifty years behind, but with Hope, McAuley and Stewart it turns tail for two or three hundred years.

All three poets catch some swingeing blows, but the attacks falls most heavily on Hope:

Hope's language is as wooden as his sexual bravado which sticks up like a painted Priapus in a suburban garden.

Though Dutton's critique was loaded and captious, he was right in making the question of language a crucial issue, and in seeing unresolved problems in the poetic practice, at that time, of the poets he was attacking.

Necessarily some prominence has had to be given to the impact of Hope and myself on the fifties; yet it did not seem to me at the time that an 'ascendancy' had been established or a 'counter-revolution' successfully conducted; and in fact the main effect on others was to set in motion what one might call the 'revisionism' developed by some younger poets, who, though in some cases initially influenced by aspects of our views and practice, soon looked further for answers to their needs.

Vincent Buckley's *Essays in Poetry, Mainly Australian* (1957) and other essays he wrote in the fifties give, as Brian Kiernan has said, 'the impression of one who is setting out to re-draw the literary map of Australia afresh by ignoring old boundaries and landmarks in favour of his own observations, well aware that this independence will be resented by many'.[11] We have already seen how he disposed of programmatic leftism. He regarded the question of programmatic nationalism, and the opposition between 'European culture and Australian fact' (p. 23) as one that has been left behind, and suggested that now:

The issue is one of spiritual development, of the social and cultural manners which will express that development, and of the poetic forms in which to contain and advance it (p. 26).

One of the main restraints in earlier decades on the growth to maturity of Australian poetry Buckley saw as vitalism. In praising Slessor and FitzGerald he said:

Yet there was a serpent in the garden of these men's literary beginnings; it was the serpent of vitalism as that creed was preached by the Lindsay group . . . Vitalism may be defined, very crudely, as the view which considers the primitive forces of life, amoral and irresistible, more important than the pattern of moral and aesthetic discriminations by which the adult human being lives. More than that; vitalism is anti-tragic, anti-spiritual, and ultimately anti-human (pp. 14-15).

It is probably because of the taint of vitalism that Buckley was rather severe upon 'the new Bulletin school'. This is the least satisfactory and coherent chapter in his survey. While he acknowledged that Douglas Stewart is a good poet, he showed no disposition to get inside his work. He was polite to David Campbell and Roland Robinson but did not seem really interested; Rosemary Dobson, briefly but courteously mentioned in another essay, was ignored entirely in this chapter;[12] Nan McDonald and Ronald McCuaig were also ignored. Nancy Keesing, Nancy Cato, Ray Mathew, William Hart-Smith, Brian Vrepont were severely criticized. The poetic line of those practising a genuine Australian idiom on which Dutton placed his hopes in his *Australian Letters* article was here seen as dwindling down to a 'flight from the poetic reality of Australia'! (p. 73).

When he turned to confront the 'classicism' of Hope and myself Buckley was also temperamentally at a distance. He generously praised aspects of our work but expressed and implied reservations, more strongly in regard to me; and finally concluded that:

> Whether they will have much influence on our poetry is irrelevant; whether they can, is doubtful. They are both classicists, but they have different, and in a sense complementary qualities. And they are part of a new and necessary tradition in Australian poetry, a tradition in which the most important questions about man's fate are coming to be asked, in which a choice is presented to its readers, and in which poetic forms are being chosen to aid in the posing of those questions (p. 194).

The search for such poetic forms and an appropriate idiom took the new poets on new paths.

One of the new tendencies in the late fifties and early sixties was a desire for greater concreteness and immediacy. Instead of generalizing the poem tends to particularize. Accidental circumstances and random details are not elided but caught up in an endeavour to give the reader the sense of experiences as they actually occur; and at the same time these details are made poetically functional because they help to establish mood and tone, to create ironies, and provide symbolic hints. Along this line we get the 'situation poem', which introduces us into a particular event or state of affairs: in its strict form everything the poem says has to be within that situation and expressed in terms of it. Evan Jones's laconically poignant poems about the relation between divorced father and son ('At the Airport' and 'Generations') (p. 290) are outstanding examples. The 'situation poem' is normally an 'ordinary-language' poem; the idiom is informal; the temperature usually cool; the diction is meant to co-operate with the theme by intensifying the sense of physical immediacy — the words are to 'enact' their meaning. One can see a number of twentieth-century tendencies converging here, not least perhaps some critical views of the English critic F. R. Leavis (a major influence on the English Department of Melbourne University) with his notion that literature should be the product of moral empiricism, a critical sensitivity encountering and evaluating each instant, and his insistence on a language of poetry that somehow (the notion is an indistinct one) 'enacts' what it says. While this kind of poem is perhaps the most typical development of the Melbourne revisionists seeking a way out of the past, it is not the only one. Indeed, one has a general impression of restless tentative movements in several directions, without many fully convincing results.

Buckley's own poetry shares in this restless exploration, though not as a standard case. His poem 'Stroke', written on the death of his father, is an expanded situation-poem with effective use of casual detail. It shows also an influence of Robert Lowell's poems of intimate personal experience. In Buckley's work a number of tendencies meet and mingle: there is a lyrical impulse, and a rhetorical one; there is the desire for a large statement, and the careful notation of concrete particulars; there is an extreme self-consciousness, the adoption of a *stance* or *attitude* (an important Melbourne occupation) and with it an awareness of how the stance or attitude adopted might look when viewed through different eyes; there is an uneasy balance between a private and a public mode of expression. The range and ambition of the poetry is very great. It is dense with the matter of life: personal experience, scenes and events and people, modern history; a recent work is a sequence called 'Golden Builders' consisting of free-form texts as well as more regularly formed poems, based on Melbourne University and the suburb of Carlton adjoining.[13] To the three-dimensional common world Buckley has continually sought to add a fourth dimension, not merely or chiefly by writing on religious themes: rather the poem itself must embody or be a manifestation of the sacred, become a word in which the Word can speak, be an utterance of, or on behalf of, humanity—and the world—as incorporated mystically in Christ, and provide 'an image of man' not merely in Australia but in a world *sub specie Deitatis*. So at least I understand the burden that the poet lays on his poetry by terms such as 'incarnational',[14] 'resurrectional',[15] and 'hierophany';[16] and by passages such as this, addressed to Francis Webb, where he says what he believes about the poet's words:

Our task is this: To keep them swept and sure,
An open courtyard where the poor may find,
Always, the walking Love, Who does not rest
In hearts which fear and hatred have defined.

They are more than refuge for our cowardice;
For hints of an action are established there
In image and in gesture, whence we may
Call out that Love upon the tideless air.

Each poem, too, is solar to this world
Of man and time, and will be raging soon.
Even if the heart die, some few will see it
At midnight flaring like the pitch of noon:

Target of light — to which our faith accords!

                         ('Impromptu for Francis Webb')

While this implies a theology of poetry, Buckley combines it
with a poetic humanism, which he has expressed as follows:

> . . . poetry can approach very closely, very closely indeed, to the
> actual texture of one's life. It can present it in an enhanced fashion,
> and can enhance *it*. I think it's the highest humanist act. That is,
> it's the act which can most show people what it means to be human.
> Now, by what means it does this . . . well, that's a long story, and
> it differs from poet to poet, anyway. But whether you deal with it
> in terms of rhythm, or in terms of metaphor, or in whatever terms
> you deal with it, it's a humanity-making act; more so than the novel,
> because the novel is in part some kind of mirror. I don't think poetry
> is anything like a mirror.
>
> Men just learn through poetry, if they approach it in a sustained
> and loving way. They learn what it's like to be a fully alive,
> rhythmically breathing being, who is conscious in ways that no other
> being is conscious. It seems to me that all this is just built into
> poetry, and the very shape of the poem is a kind of guarantee, or
> witness to this. If you began from scratch and asked what one kind
> of thing a man could do which would in its own inner structures
> show the meaning of being a man, you might well come up with
> the notion of poetry.[17]

Buckley's critical and poetical work has been important to the
Melbourne group and influential beyond it. Obviously, however,
because of its special preoccupations it is not typical, even while
it participates in an evolution of form and style and method which
is found more simply in other poets. Chris Wallace-Crabbe's essay,
'The Habit of Irony? Australian Poets of the Fifties' gives us a
representative view.[18] Wallace-Crabbe tried to summarize 'a new
direction among the young writers', and concluded that 'a habit

of irony' was indicating its distinctive feature. He related it to contemporary English and American tendencies, and also connected it with

> the fact that our society presents its spiritual, political and moral values in a state of extreme confusion; that nobody can speak of the future in simple terms of optimism (nor simply of pessimism); that no man, unless he claps his blind eye to the telescope, can say, 'I see the way for us all. Follow me. All will be clear'. And if man's vision of the world is confused, it seems proper — though sad — that the best poetry should reflect this confusion, even while seeking to transcend it (p. 170).

Elsewhere he saw the period as one of 'honest indecision and self-protective irony'. The kind of work he commended as true to the spirit of the period uses irony as a means of registering the complexity of experience, and as a means of control, of self-distancing, of refusal of commitment to any single response. The poetry prefers 'a neutral tone' (in Donald Davie's phrase); there is a concern for craftsmanship, for the well-made poem, and for wit and elegance, 'a plain urban style' — urbanity was a favourite word of the period — as well as a liking for paradox, surprise, anti-climax. Wallace-Crabbe recognizes that there is a danger that such poetry might become 'evasive, academic, or self-deprecating', a danger of 'withdrawal' and 'a drift towards triviality'. Yet he firmly made it clear that poets should get into line if they wished to be counted in:

> If poetry is to represent our age and our condition in any positive sense, it must, in some measure at least, be ironic (p. 170).

This begs a number of questions about the poet's duty to 'represent our age'. What 'the age demanded' has not always been what its poets wanted to give. In any case, generalizations about 'our age and condition' are perilous. Wallace-Crabbe drew too easy a contrast with the older poets:

> The optimism of Douglas Stewart and FitzGerald, the assertive clarity of McAuley and Roland Robinson, the political gusto of Manifold: all these qualities are recognizably those of older men. The younger poets are too involved in the contradictory post-war years to emulate them (p. 174).

This is a rather odd list, which omits some obvious names and fails to allow for doubt, division and disquiet in the work of the poets listed.

Wallace-Crabbe also had difficulty in fitting his younger poets into the framework he had constructed. He mentioned Evan Jones, J. R. Rowland, Ray Mathew, Bruce Dawe, Lex Banning, R. A. Simpson, Vincent Buckley, Francis Webb. Though Buckley uses irony he hardly conforms to the requirement of 'a habit of irony',[19] and Webb cannot possibly be made to fit. Of Evan Jones, Wallace-Crabbe himself says that he 'could seldom be described as an ironist at all', though there are ironic moments in his work. Mathew, Dawe and Banning do not really belong in the same group as the others. We are left with R. A. Simpson and J. R. Rowland, with whom Wallace-Crabbe himself must be joined. Irony, on this showing, is not the common distinguishing feature of the newer poets of the period, though it may be part of their equipment. Other aspects of Wallace-Crabbe's description are more persuasive: one did get the impression in the late fifties that much of the newer poetry aspired to be an 'extremely civilised poetry — idiomatic, unemphatic, and precise' — in the words Wallace-Crabbe has applied to J. R. Rowland's accomplished poem 'Cairo Hotel' (p. 288). The same poet's 'Canberra in April' provides another example:

> This clean suburbia, house-proud but servantless
> Is host to a multitude of children
> Nightly conceived, born daily, riding bikes,
> Requiring play-centres, schools and Progress
> Associations: in cardigans and slacks.
>
> Their mothers polish kitchens, or in silk
> White gloves and tight hats pour each other tea
> In their best china, canvassing the merits
> Of rival plumbers, grocers, Bega milk
> And the cost of oil-fired heating or briquettes.

The poem not only moves alertly among these mundanities, it reaches out to a hope for something to redeem 'purblind provincial comfort':

> A cure for habit, some beneficent
> Simplicity or steadiness of heart.

Some critics would give much more emphasis to the work of Francis Webb than I have done. Webb's first book appeared in 1948: his narrative sequence 'A Drum for Ben Boyd' seemed to place him in the *Bulletin*'s camp. That his basic concerns and modes of expression were radically different from the *Bulletin*'s normal range became evident in his later work. This is as intent as Buckley's work is upon the task of seeing the world in the light of Christ, and it uses a strenuously dense expressionist mode of composition, presenting a brilliant kaleidoscopic obscurity. That the powers of a remarkable poet were present in Webb one cannot doubt: that they were used effectively is open to considerable doubt. The case is complicated by the fact that he was a psychotic who spent most of his productive years in mental hospitals. Though this is obviously a fact of great importance, it decides nothing for us about the quality of the work. The poet, Craig Powell, who is a psychiatrist and knew Webb well in his later years, has quoted him as saying 'All my life has been chaos and horror. But I have tried to put order and beauty in my poems'.[20] This does not resolve the question how far he succeeded. H. P. Heseltine in an acute study[21] has examined Webb's concern with 'the fascist personality' — meaning irrational will and megalomania — projected into figures such as Leichhardt and Hitler, but also explored 'as it exists in his own self':

> At what cost to himself this exploration has proceeded we cannot begin to guess . . . What we can say is that the resulting poems offer us a psychic history unique in Australian literature . . . Webb's poetic aim is nothing less than the clinical utilization of those elements in our being which our modern tradition teaches us to find either trivial or intolerable . . . The most intensely characteristic pieces in *Birthday* [1953] quite nakedly use the materials of the real world to construct a map of a mind in which self-hate, arrogance, pride, memory, and an aching nostalgia for normalcy struggle for mastery . . . [*Socrates* (1961)] will, I believe, come to be regarded as the first in which Webb fully displayed the peculiarly daunting and compelling art which has imposed a new dimension on Australian Literature . . . I do not think that Webb is yet a great poet. I am not sure that he ever will be; he lacks that plentitude and ease of creation which the greatest writers possess. Yet out of his psychic predicament he can from time to time forge individual poems whose stature is unarguable.

The two poems I have selected are among the most accessible, and by common consent are representative of his best poetic achievement, though they do not exhibit the full range of his work and the problems he presents. 'A Death at Winson Green' is based on a mental institution in a suburb in Birmingham; in 'Five Days Old', which Webb is known to have thought his best poem, the Christian vision is particularly evident. If not sufficient to show his range, they are the best poems to induce the reader to explore further.

COMMENTARY

On Vincent Buckley

If Australian poetry has its critical establishment, Vincent Buckley is largely responsible for it. He is our most attentive critic, and it is not surprising that his own poetry lacks the attention it deserves; for while his critics are quick to point to characteristic faults of obscurity and strained rhetoric, they do not relate these either to the problems facing him or to his mastery of them. Only two judgments of his recent book *Masters in Israel* seem to me to open up a full discussion of his work: Gustav Cross's remark that 'perhaps the fault lies in the very intensity of Mr Buckley's vision, which demands a larger rhetoric than he allows himself here',* and Evan Jones's that Buckley offers 'a more full-scale vision of life than most Australian poets have yet offered' ... † Buckley's achievement is particularly important in the context of Australian poetry. Australian poets regularly show a promise and originality lacking in many of their English counterparts, and, failing as regularly to fulfil their promise, end defeated by their originality. The lack of adequate poetic tradition here first stimulates poets and then discourages them. Buckley looks like being the first Australian poet to create a poetic stance and language which will neither curtail his own development nor isolate him from the European tradition.

> Penelope Curtis, 'Vincent Buckley as Poet',
> *Quadrant,* vol. 6, no. 4, pp. 55 and 64-5

Generally one would feel little impulse to call his work ironic: concerned largely with personal and spiritual introspection, it achieves in its manner a curious blend of lyrical and rhetorical qualities. An air of grave formality informs a personal diction characterized by a song-like, slightly archaic quality. There is a great deal of overt personal statement — if statement is not too flat a word to describe it. In short I would want to call Buckley's poetry Romantic in temper.

But if I say Romantic it is with careful qualifications. Buckley is certainly not one of those poets whose Romanticism involves knowing too little about life. It is a Romanticism that has a rich and ambiguous pattern of response (the Tasmanian, Gwen Harwood, is another poet whom I would call Romantic in this way, and many of the remarks I make about Buckley's poetry

---

* Cross's remark occurs in his review of *Masters in Israel,* in the *Sydney Morning Herald,* 16 September 1961.
† Evan Jones's comment occurs in his review article 'Poets Galore', in *Prospect,* vol. 4, no. 4, 1961, p. 27.

would apply to her poems of psychological exploration). However there are recurrent strains in Buckley's poetry — not only in his first book, *The World's Flesh,* but in his subsequent writing during the past eight years — which serve to hold the Romantic impulse in check: to give it, at least, another dimension. And those strains can be said to represent two kinds of irony.

The first and less important of these strains has about it a strong flavour of habit. Some of the poems in *The World's Flesh* are marked by a mild, equivocal diction which has strong affinities with American poets like Ransom and Tate, and which seems alien to the characteristic tenor of Buckley's verse... a manner rather than an organic necessity... In the best poems this kind of verbal irony shades into an irony that is deeper and more characteristic of Buckley's response to life. A complex attitude is forced on the poet by the sheer complexity of his material: the Romantic explorer must take account of the contradictory nature of his discoveries; the voice of personal assertion is forced to come to terms with human failure and inadequacy. This is a poetry, at best, where Romanticism is not at odds with poetic irony, but is rounded out and completed by it. It is a mode where the poet recognizes the ambiguities of his situation, seeing himself as in several mirrors at once.

Chris Wallace-Crabbe, 'The Habit of Irony?—
Australian Poets of the Fifties', *Meanjin Quarterly,*
vol. 20, no. 2, 1961, pp. 170-1

On Francis Webb

His tendency to use the single image-laden line as the unit of composition has more affinities with modern European practice than Australian. The advantage of an image-language of this kind is that the reins of syntax can be loosened, with a gain in immediacy of effect. Its chief danger is an ambiguity that demands too much of the reader ... Buckley has been compared to Webb, but it is obvious that these two writers are radically different. Webb abounds in metaphor, is painstakingly sensitive to environmental nuance, and devalues, perhaps excessively, the personal ego. With Buckley's work this is largely reversed. Whereas Webb has drawn inward and humble from the sharp impress of the world, Buckley presses outward, and, in place of Webb's concrete and exorcising imagery, abounds in rhetorical generalizations.

Noel Macainsh, review of Webb's *Socrates* (1961)
and Buckley's *Masters in Israel* (1961), in
Overland, no. 22, 1961, pp. 52-3

Francis Webb is perhaps Australia's best poet, and it may be as well to enter his claim at the start. I realize that not many Australian reviewers have been eager to say so, even after Sir Herbert Read put the matter even more portentously than I have done: 'I cannot, after long meditation on his verse, place his achievement on a level lower than that suggested by [the] names' of Rilke, Eliot, Pasternak and Lowell. No such claim has ever before, to my knowledge, been made for an Australian poet.*

The nature of the achievement may be in question: the quantity and energy are not. This volume [*Collected Poems:* Angus and Robertson, Sydney] offers us more than 250 packed pages representing five collections made over a period of 22 years, between the 18th and 40th years of their author. The stamina alone, the sense of a dedication maintained and renewed, fought for and again renewed in the face of pressures that would have overwhelmed a lesser man, is most impressive.

Indeed, it is daunting. When Webb's poetry appears in any bulk, it seems to frighten the inattentive reader, and exhaust the attentive one. It is very hard to criticize, almost impossible to paraphrase. Its elaborately dense surface, and its often almost vehement reliance on metaphor, are too much for the prose mind. This is probably the reason why most critics still accept the view which was current several years ago, that Webb's achievement is chiefly in his long poems . . . There is good reason, then, to think that his power is shown best in short poems, and that the lyric scope presents his dramatic force most cleanly. All the poems

---

* Read's remark occurs in the Introduction (p. ix) he wrote for Webb's *Collected Poems* (1969). Such claims for an Australian poet are rare only from non-Australian critics: Australian criticism is littered with them. For three examples, Randolph Hughes on Brennan: 'It is not in the least extravagant to say that nothing greater than this poetry has yet been written in English in the course of the present century. . .' (*C. J. Brennan: An Essay in Values*, 1934, pp. 164-5); R. D. FitzGerald on McCrae: 'In the regrettable state of poetry in the world today, that McCrae must be assigned a high, perhaps the highest, place among living English-speaking poets is not flattery; were he considerably less than he is it would still be only too distressingly obvious' (in *The Australian Quarterly*, vol. 11, no. 4, 1939, p. 59); A. R. Chisholm on Bertram Higgins: 'in the poetic quality of "The Confrontation" and the metaphysical range of the "Mordecaius" Higgins surpasses T. S. Eliot' (letter to H. M. Green, 21 January 1930, quoted by Green in his *A History of Australian Literature*, vol. 2, p. 921n.). In regard to Webb, it may be noted that the anonymous reviewer of *Leichhardt in Theatre* (1952) in the *Times Literary Supplement,* 23 January 1953, said: 'Mr. Webb, if comparisons are at all helpful, has the descriptive force of Mr. Roy Campbell, the intellectual astringency of Mr. Robert Lowell. He is nearly, if not quite, their equal.'

which I think his best are short ones; and although a few of
these were first published, and are reprinted, as members of
groupings which to a superficial glance look like sequences, in
fact they contribute nothing to a dramatic or narrative unity in
the whole of the grouping. Effectively, they are separate short
poems, and ought to be treated as such.

When we really look at his short poems, we find that his chief
qualities have lasted with amazing persistence from first to last:

(a) The hour's a graven depth; all images gather
    To a giant balance, a level climax and height.
    You speak of colour — here's where all colour sleeps
    Misted by the breathing of wedded dimness and light.
    Each poised oar trails its phosphorescent feather,
    The curving brilliance leaps
    And shivers back to the dark lungs of the water.

                              ('Middle Harbour': 1942-48)

(b) It is an illusion, a dream then, that these are still
    And always yours, the sculptured shadows of the coves
    Crocketed with weathered houses
    And wharves askew; that the falling glass arouses
    Your voice, dazing the clouds; that your antique will
    Whitens into sail and is ever outward bound,
    While over lifting waves
    Come skipping like thin stones the spinet voices of the
        drowned.

                              ('Melville at Woods Hole': 1952)

(c) Past six o'clock. I have prayed. No one is sleeping.
    I have wandered past the old maternity home's
    Red stone fermented by centuries; and there comes
    New light, new light; and the cries of the rooks
        sweeping
    To their great nests are guerrilla light in a fusion
    — Murmurs, echoes, plainsong; and the night
    Will be all an abyss and depth of light between
    Two shorelines in labour: birth and death. O Passion
    (One light in the hospital window) of quickening light,
    O foetus quaking towards light, sound the gaunt green,
    Trawl Norfolk, and make shiver the window-blind,
    Harass nebulae for Bjorling. Find him, find.

                              ('Nessun Dorma': 1964)

Of these three extracts, the first comes from his 'juvenilia' and may have been written as early as 1942, and the third (dated 22 years later) is given last place in his *Collected Poems*. Naturally the three are not equal in quality, are not of a precisely equivalent fineness or subtlety or force; in fact, the first is slightly banal if one compares it with the occasional quaintness of phrasing and lovely remote singing quality of the second, or with the more insistent, rhetorical and impassioned quality of the third, written as it was on the death of the great tenor Jussi Bjorling. But a slightly more sweeping gaze would see a startling similarity between them. The chief features of this I may summarize as follows: A dense physicality, by no means constant, and very difficult to describe, but very striking; a very strong and rapidly changing reliance on metaphor; a tone of wryness likely at any moment to intrude into the deeper tonalities of a stanza; the cadencing of passages or sentences in a way which has surely been learned from music, and which tends to dominate the syntax; and the special effects, plangent and grand at once, which can be got by his vigorous and recurrent use of feminine rhymes. It is the last three of these that establish the unique music of his highly individual voice; the first two, which gave his voice such weight and resonance, also give rise to his obscurity, for the use of metaphor sets up a centrifugal activity which leads at times to disorganization.

Vincent Buckley, 'The Poetry of Francis Webb',
Quadrant, vol. 14, no. 2, 1970, pp. 11-13

Webb's poetry in 'Ward Two' is quite unlike that of Lowell, Plath and Sexton and what has been called the 'confessional' manner in contemporary writing. Webb's respect for the formal properties of stanzaic and rhyme structure remains as the distance in his sense of the character of himself as poet and as person; the Americans in eroding this distinction have produced sharper and more dramatic poems than Webb on the subject of mental illness, but there is a loss elsewhere in their work when they have less sympathy to commit to their subjects. In the 250 pages of his *Collected Poems* there is virtually no autobiographical element to Webb's writing even though there are few more personal documents in literature.

James Tulip, 'The Poetry of Francis Webb',
Southerly, vol. 29, no. 3, 1969, p. 190

T

On Charles Higham

Charles Higham is a poet of considerable resources. He knows what he is doing. Each mode is taken up and developed consistently. His verse is ruled by will and skill, so that different rhythms, textures and tunes emerge in an accomplished range ... There is in Higham an attraction towards the purely virtuoso performance ... But he has also written poems which require the subject — grief, love, dread, despair — to make its full human impact.

Yet here one finds a limitation. At times the situation is not clearly enough stated and individuated just when this is necessary ... And however animated the verse, however much the images are meant to touch the bared nerves, somehow all the violence of action and feeling is as if seen under glass.

James McAuley, review of *The Earthbound* (1959),
in *Quadrant*, vol. 4, no. 2, 1960, pp. 90-1

On Evan Jones

His strikingly individual poetry bears little suggestion of any recognizable period or manner, despite its strongly traditional values. In an emphatically clear and formal way, it is largely concerned with the presentation of emotional states: with sounding the full notes of celebration, elegy, etc., especially in terms of personal relationships. However there is a recurrent vein of asperity and wit which runs through it and which is sometimes turned obliquely on himself in epigrams or lyrics with a tart, ironic flavour. In a sense these are demanded of him, for at the same time he wants to assert the value of a stoical response to life and to criticize acutely the limits of stoicism.

Chris Wallace-Crabbe, 'The Habit of Irony?
Australian Poets in the Fifties', *Meanjin Quarterly*,
vol. 20, no. 2, 1961, p. 173

On Chris Wallace-Crabbe

The first section [of *The Music of Division*] bears a quote from John Manifold,

> Perhaps I have to emphasize for you
> First, that it scans, and second, that it's true

which fits the case well, though how much of the truth is represented is a matter for the reader ... In the excellent poem 'The Great Romantics', we gather that Chris Wallace-Crabbe's standpoint is not with 'the men who sing apart' but is spiritually near the centre of modern society. He is the alert observer, a member of, say, the professional classes who have no particular interest in extremities of any kind, and by nature and training are inclined to view all things from a critical, professional remove ... It [*The Music of Division*] holds a faithful mirror to a prevailing attitude. It is anti-romantic while confessing a certain attraction to romantic attitudes ... It is the depiction of man stripped of the traditional sources of spiritual sustenance and asked to continue with courageous humility in a cold and complex world. It is also a pleasure to read, not least for some of the obiter dicta to its main judgment.

Noel Macainsh, review of *The Music of Division*
(1959), in *Prospect,* vol. 3, no. 1, 1960, p. 26

Chris Wallace-Crabbe's *Where the Wind Came* shows the author constantly aware of and mildly amused by himself. Knowing that his own — and everyone's — grasp on reality is tenuous, he is concerned, but not very energetically, with a struggle to understand the world. His tolerant, amused, puzzled, calm outlook occupies itself largely with the sources of power and with the possibilities of action to impose local order on the chaos of events.

K. L. Goodwin, review of *Where the Wind Came*
(1971), in *Meanjin Quarterly,* vol. 31, no. 4, 1972, p. 505

NANCY KEESING

We Told You So

Suburbs are known only to dogs and children,
They sniff, circle, explore, trespass, uncover
Unguessed, circuitous byways and acquire
Bizarre acquaintances. Children and dogs discover
All of a suburb. Cats have some knowledge, but they
Too often take to trees or balance on fences —
Habits they share with their owners, traits which preclude
An intimate penetration of private defences.

But dogs and children range far, accepting titbits
Of neighbour food; unguarded talk; of scolding;
Love bought and sought or careless and indiscriminate;
To their own four walls they return always, withholding
Little of their adventures — yet the whole.
The dog cannot tell who patted, who kicked, who fed,
And the children's limpid accounts are so appalling
All commonsense adults reject whatever they said.

Each suburb is its own volcano, muttering beforehand
Delicate, unheeded warnings as its crust weakens
Of manner and custom. Dogs grow prick-eared, uneasy;
And children quiet or distracted for no good reasons
Until the explosion — the spewing of lava: the divorce,
The noose in the garage, the meek embezzler, the lies . . .
We discuss these eruptions in whispers — to shield our
    children?
Or ourselves from their dreadful candour, their unsurprise?

VINCENT BUCKLEY

Puritan Poet Reel

Mother at her novenas
Until her knees are brown
And father non-conforming
All around the town:

What images have brought
(Ah delicate and dry)
The tear of ambiguity
To stand within my eye?

Have built my world around me
Where, private as a mole,
I guard the fiercer virtues
And mentally control

Wind squeezing the houses,
Knocking the hedges down,
And father non-conforming
All around the town?

Mother it was that promised me
Position in the town
And father raised his fist and swore
We'd lie on beds of down:

But who will keep the promises
They made me as a boy?
Writing my twenty lines a day,
And simulating joy,

I make my life a model
And keep my bowels clear,
But, muse blow hot or muse blow cold,
Over the fence I hear

Mother at her rosary
Until her knees are brown
And father non-conforming
All around the town.

No New Thing

No new thing under the sun:
The virtuous who prefer the dark;
Fools knighted; the brave undone;
The athletes at their killing work;
The tender-hearts who step in blood;
The sensitive paralysed in a mood;
The clerks who rubber-stamp our deaths,
Executors of death's estate;
Poets who count their dying breaths;
Lovers who pledge undying hate;
The self-made and self-ruined men;
The envious with the strength of ten.

They crowd in nightmares to my side,
Enlisting even private pain
In some world-plan of suicide:
Man, gutted and obedient man,
Who turns his coat when he is told,
Faithless to our shining world.
And hard-faced men, who beat the drum
To call me to this Cause or that,
Those heirs of someone else's tomb,
Can't see the sweeter work I'm at,
The building of the honeycomb.

from *Stroke*

I

In the faint blue light
We are both strangers; so I'm forced to note
His stare that comes moulded from deep bone,
The full mouth pinched in too far, one hand
Climbing an aluminium bar.
Put, as though for the first time,
In a cot from which only a hand escapes,
He grasps at opposites, knowing
This room's a caricature of childhood.
'I'm done for.'

'They're treating you all right?'
We talk from the corners of our mouths
Like old lags, while his body strains
To notice me, before he goes on watching
At the bed's foot
His flickering familiars,
Skehan, Wilson, Ellis, dead men, faces,
Bodies, paused in the aluminium light,
Submits his answer to his memories,
'Yes, I'm all right. But still it's terrible.'

Words like a fever bring
The pillar of cloud, pillar of fire
Travelling the desert of the mind and face.
The deep-set, momentarily cunning eyes
Keep trying for a way to come
Through the bed's bars to his first home.
And almost find it. Going out I hear

Voices calling requiem, where the cars
Search out the fog and gritty snow,
Hushing its breathing under steady wheels.
Night shakes the seasonable ground.

VI

The roofs are lit with rain.
Winter. In that dark glow,
Now, as three months ago,
I pray that he'll die sane.

On tiles or concrete path
The old wheeling the old,
For whom, in this last world,
Hope is an aftermath,

And the damp trees extend
Branch and thorn. We live
As much as we believe.
All things covet an end.

Once, on the Kerrie road,
I drove with him through fire.
Now, in the burnt cold year,
He drains off piss and blood,

His wounded face tube-fed,
His arm strapped to a bed.

VII

At the merest handshake I feel his blood
Move with ebb-tide chill. Who can revive
A body settled in its final mood?
To whom, on what tide, can we move, and live?

Later I wheel him out to see the trees:
Willows and oaks, the small plants he mistakes
For rose bushes; and there
In the front, looming, light green, cypresses.
His pulse no stronger than the pulse of air.

Dying, he grows more tender, learns to teach
Himself the mysteries I am left to trace.
As I bend to say 'Till next time', I search
For signs of resurrection in his face.

FRANCIS WEBB

Five Days Old
(For Christopher John)

Christmas is in the air.
You are given into my hands
Out of quietest, loneliest lands.
My trembling is all my prayer.
To blown straw was given
All the fullness of Heaven.

The tiny, not the immense,
Will teach our groping eyes.
So the absorbed skies
Bleed stars of innocence.
So cloud-voice in war and trouble
Is at last Christ in the stable.

Now wonderingly engrossed
In your fearless delicacies,
I am launched upon sacred seas,
Humbly and utterly lost
In the mystery of creation,
Bells, bells of ocean.

Too pure for my tongue to praise,
That sober, exquisite yawn
Or the gradual, generous dawn
At an eyelid, maker of days:
To shrive my thought for perfection
I must breathe old tempests of action

For the snowflake and face of love,
Windfall and word of truth,
Honour close to death.
O eternal truthfulness, Dove,
Tell me what I hold —
Myrrh? Frankincense? Gold?

If this is man, then the danger
And fear are as lights of the inn,
Faint and remote as sin
Out here by the manger.
In the sleeping, weeping weather
We shall all kneel down together.

A Death at Winson Green

There is a green spell stolen from Birmingham;
Your peering omnibus overlooks the fence,
Or the grey, bobbing lifelines of a tram.
Here, through the small hours, sings our innocence.
Joists, apathetic pillars plot this ward,
Tired timbers wheeze and settle into dust,
We labour, labour: for the treacherous lord
Of time, the dazed historic sunlight, must
Be wheeled in a seizure towards one gaping bed,
Quake like foam on the lip, or lie still as the dead.

Visitors' Day: the graven perpetual smile,
String-bags agape, and pity's laundered glove.
The last of the heathens shuffles down the aisle,
Dark glass to a beauty which we hate and love.
Our empires rouse against this ancient fear,
Longsufferings, anecdotes, levelled at our doom;
Mine-tracks of old allegiance, prying here,
Perplex the sick man raving in his room.
Outside, a shunting engine hales from bed
The reminiscent feast-day, long since dead.

Noon reddens, trader birds deal cannily
With Winson Green, and the slouch-hatted sun
Gapes at windows netted in wire, and we
Like early kings with book and word cast down
Realities from our squared electric shore.
Two orderlies are whistling-in the spring;
Door slams; and a man is dying at the core
Of triumph won. As a tattered, powerful wing
The screen bears out his face against the bed,
Silver, derelict, rapt, and almost dead.

Evening gropes out of colour; yet we work
To cleanse our shore from limpet histories;

Traffic and factory-whistle turn beserk;
Inviolate, faithful as a saint he lies.
Twilight itself breaks up, the venal ship,
Upon the silver integrity of his face.
No bread shall tempt that fine, tormented lip.
Let shadow switch to light — he holds his place.
Unmarked, unmoving, from the gaping bed
Towards birth he labours, honour, almost dead.

The wiry cricket moiling at his loom
Debates a themeless project with dour night,
The sick man raves beside me in his room;
I sleep as a child, rouse up as a child might.
I cannot pray; that fine lip prays for me
With every gasp at breath; his burden grows
Heavier as all earth lightens, and all sea.
Time crouches, watching, near his face of snows.
He is all life, thrown on the gaping bed,
Blind, silent, in a trance, and shortly, dead.

J. R. ROWLAND

Cairo Hotel

A room the size of a warehouse
With chairs like stick-insects sheltering in corners
And a wide rhetorical bed.

Like a fruit display from the ceiling
The chandelier gleamed; four candelabra
Trophies, stags' heads, stared from the crimson walls.

An airless odour of camphor and fine dust
In the blank wardrobe; and in the topmost drawer
A flimsy envelope addressed in French.

The light-switch fell to pieces under my hand
There were three bells, for Waiter, Maid and Valet
And the traffic trembled all night under the bed

To which, unfortunately, no sequined countess
Mysteriously came, having perhaps mistaken
The door, or by an impulse. The great room

Smelling of dryness and impermanence
Withheld its opportunities: yet I felt
That, given time there, something would have happened.

CHARLES HIGHAM

The Kelly Show

The bouquet has mimosas, orchids, roses.
She smiles and gathers handfuls of applause;
Propped on the gallows-steps poor Ned composes
A final plea to make his killers pause;
Her womanhood is offered to the people,
His manhood's buckled under by the laws.
One iron bell bangs from the crooked steeple.

She simpers. He, thin, graceless, penitent,
Stares at the hood, the buckle, the cold drop;
His eyelids flutter still a weak dissent;
She starts to thinks the show may be a flop,
And hooks her skirts up to attentive smiles,
Thinks of the serpent, starts to whisper slop;
He gazes on the sparkling summer tiles.

It is her brother, bowing at her side,
It's he who shares her calm eclectic grace.
Because he stole the harness for the ride
She lets him steal the thunder from her face,
And, shadowed, watches cheers break over Jim.
But she can hear the manacles' disgrace
Clacking as Kelly retches to the hymn.

For it, she knew, had been a huge mistake:
Glenrowan was his sacrifice and splendour.
He could have vanished in a thorny brake,
And left his kin to make a grey surrender;
But chose to cling there to the exeunt,
Let fall the iron helmet like a fender,
Lift up an eye unquarrelling and blunt.

The curtain falls; she waves a final hand.
He quotes his jot of evidence; he treads
Into the proper place; his smile is bland.
Applause demands her curtsey into beds,
And so she lewdly nods her short assent.
He drops and twists: the watchers nod their heads
And write his name upon the continent.

EVAN JONES

Generations

I go to see my parents,
we chew the rag a bit;
I turn the telly on
and sit and look at it.

Not much gets said:
there doesn't seem much point.
But still they like to have
me hanging round the joint.

I go to see my son,
I'm like a Santa Claus:
he couldn't like me more;
mad about him, of course.

Still years before he learns
to judge, condemn, dismiss.
I stand against the light
and bleed for both of us.

At the Airport

Waving good-bye to mum,
Sometimes we go for walks;
More often, though, we come
Out here: planes are the thing
That sets him chattering —
Just three, he scarcely talks.

Gambolling on the lawn,
He watches for my grin
And grins and answers back.
The great planes, finely drawn,
Come shrieking down the track;
People walk out and in.

Nowadays I can tell
Kinds of air liner apart —
Wing-structure, fuselage:
It is details that compel —
Hardly my heritage,
An odd thing to learn by heart.

CHRIS WALLACE-CRABBE

Terra Australis

Here, and here only in an age of iron,
   The dreamers are proved right;
No armies underlie these rolling fields,
   No lost loves haunt the night,
Nor can the farmer, turning with his spade,
   Bring shard or helm to light.

Innocence clad in brown and faded gold
   Walks up and down these hills
Where unobtrusive flickering flowers rebuke
   The show of daffodils:
With sombre colours and with sparse designs
   Acre on acre fills.

Paradise lingers like a tapestry;
   The web has not been torn,
Luther and Cromwell, Socrates and Marx
   Have never yet been born,
Nor did a glowing Florence rise to shape
   The European dawn.

We are the final children of the earth
   Whom knowledge has not scarred,
Delighting still in sunlight and green grass
   Back in our own backyard:
Gaping, we hear the tales of adulthood
   Where life is dour and hard,
Far, far away, beyond some wicked wood.

The Apparition

After the entertainments of the night,
   Somewhere in limbo he had lost his way,
A dark empty suit in a dark street
   Swinging toward another nameless day.

Discarded leaves ran murmuring from his feet
   And agonies of perfume round his head
Drifted from shrubs he could no longer name:
   From petal, stem and calyx of the dead.

A Norfolk pine sprang skyward as he came.
    He knew it well — had climbed it as a child —
So when he saw a pale shape quit its port
    Of shade, he was already reconciled

To the small bent figure with collar caught
    Beneath her chin by a massive cameo;
To fragile glasses crooked on their bridge;
    To the known voice, its unperturbed hello.

'Robert,' she said. Light as a hovering midge
    She moved beside him now through vacant air.
'Those cannas which you planted are in bloom.
    The daisies too. But weeds are everywhere.

'For seven months I wilted in a room;
    It was your name that rose upon my breath
And yet my favourite grandson never came
    Into the narrow chamber of my death.'

As early-woken starlings cried for shame
    And a dry twig snapped where his footstep fell,
Robert addressed the hostile universe:
    'I was only a child. How could I tell?'

Her ghost had faded. Deep grey like a hearse,
    The sky bore downward with its close-webbed net
And every shaken leaf was echoing,
    'You always found it easy to forget.'

SELECT BIBLIOGRAPHY

NANCY KEESING

   Imminent Summer, Lyre Bird Writers, Sydney, 1951.
   Three Men and Sydney, Angus & Robertson, Sydney, 1955.
   Showground Sketchbook, Angus & Robertson, Sydney, 1968

VINCENT BUCKLEY

   The World's Flesh, Cheshire, Melbourne, 1954.
   Masters in Israel, Angus & Robertson, Sydney, 1961.
   Eight by Eight (with other authors), Jacaranda, Brisbane, 1963.
   Arcady and Other Places, Melbourne University Press, Melbourne, 1966.

Essays in Poetry, Mainly Australian, Melbourne University Press, Melbourne, 1957.
Poetry and Morality, Chatto and Windus, London, 1959.
Poetry and the Sacred, Chatto and Windus, London, 1968.
'An Interview with Vincent Buckley', by Henry Rosenbloom, *Meanjin Quarterly,* vol. 28, no. 3, 1969.

Andrews, W. T., review of *Arcady and Other Places,* in *Westerly,* no. 3, 1967.
Brady, Veronica, 'Return to the Centre: Vincent Buckley's Golden Builders', *Westerly,* no. 2, June 1973.
Curtis, Penelope, 'Vincent Buckley as Poet', *Quadrant,* vol. 6, no. 4, 1962.
Jones, Evan, review of *Masters in Israel,* in *Prospect,* vol. 4, 1961.
—— 'Australian Poetry Since 1920', in *The Literature of Australia,* ed. Geoffrey Dutton, Penguin Books, Melbourne, 1964, pp. 127-31.
Thomson, A. K., 'The Poetry of Vincent Buckley: An Essay in Interpretation', *Meanjin Quarterly,* vol. 28, no. 3, 1969.
Wallace-Crabbe, Chris, 'The Habit of Irony? Australian Poets of the Fifties', *Meanjin Quarterly,* vol. 20, no. 2, 1961; reprinted in *Twentieth Century Australian Criticism,* ed. Clement Semmler, Oxford University Press, Melbourne, 1967.
Wright, John M., 'Vincent Buckley's Golden Builders', *Westerly,* no. 3, 1973.

FRANCIS WEBB

A Drum for Ben Boyd, Angus & Robertson, Sydney, 1948.
Leichhardt in Theatre, Angus & Robertson, Sydney, 1952.
Birthday, (privately printed), 1953.
Socrates and Other Poems, Angus & Robertson, Sydney, 1961.
Collected Poems, Angus & Robertson, Sydney, 1969.

Ashcroft, W. D., 'The Storming of the Bastille: the Technique of Francis Webb's Poetry', *Southerly,* vol. 34, no. 4, 1974.
Buckley, Vincent, 'The Poetry of Francis Webb', *Meanjin,* vol. 12, no. 1, 1953.
—— 'The Poetry of Francis Webb', *Quadrant,* vol. 14, no. 2, 1970.
Cross, Gustav, 'Australian Poetry in the '60's', *Poetry Australia,* no. 5, 1965.
Feltham, Elizabeth, 'Francis Webb and Robert Lowell: Self-Exploration and Poetic Control', *Quadrant,* vol. 6, no. 2, 1962.
Heseltine, H. P., 'The Very Gimbals of Unease: the Poetry of Francis Webb', *Meanjin,* vol. 26, no. 3, 1967.
Tulip, James, 'The Poetry of Francis Webb', *Southerly,* vol. 29, no. 3, 1969.
Wallace-Crabbe, Chris, 'Order and Turbulence: the Poetry of Francis Webb' (C.L.F. Lecture, Australian National University), 1961.

J. R. ROWLAND

The Feast of Ancestors, Angus & Robertson, Sydney, 1965.
Snow and Other Poems, Angus & Robertson, Sydney, 1971.

CHARLES HIGHAM

A Distant Star, London, 1951.
Spring and Death, London, 1953.
The Earthbound, Angus & Robertson, Sydney, 1959.
Noonday Country, Angus & Robertson, Sydney, 1966.
The Voyage to Brindisi, Angus & Robertson, Sydney, 1970.

EVAN JONES

Inside the Whale, Cheshire, Melbourne, 1960.
Understandings, Melbourne University Press, Melbourne, 1967.

Steele, Peter, review of *Understandings,* in *Twentieth Century,* vol. 22, no. 4, 1968.

CHRIS WALLACE-CRABBE

The Music of Division, Angus & Robertson, Sydney, 1959.
In Light and Darkness, Angus & Robertson, Sydney, 1963.
Eight by Eight (with other authors), Jacaranda, Brisbane, 1963.
The Rebel General, Angus & Robertson, Sydney, 1967.
Where the Wind Came, Angus & Robertson, Sydney, 1971.
Selected Poems, Angus & Robertson, Sydney, 1973.
Chris Wallace-Crabbe Reads from his own Work, Poets on Record series, University of Queensland Press, Brisbane, 1974.
Melbourne or the Bush, Angus & Robertson, Sydney, 1974.

Colman, E. A. M., 'A Modest Radiance: the Poetry of Chris Wallace-Crabbe', *Westerly,* no. 1, 1969.
King, Alec, 'The Look of Australian Poetry in 1967', *Meanjin Quarterly,* vol. 27, no. 2, 1968.
Macainsh, Noel, review of *The Music of Division,* in *Prospect,* vol. 3, no. 1, 1960.
Steele, Peter, ' "To Move in the Light": The Poetry of Chris Wallace-Crabbe', *Meanjin Quarterly,* vol. 29, no. 2, 1970.

NOTES

[1] A quite different view of the value and importance of Stow's poetry is given by Alexander Craig in his Introduction to *Twelve Poets 1950-1970* (1971): 'There was a period lasting almost half the '60's, when Randolph Stow seemed to be the *only* truly modern, midcentury Australian poet' (p. 10). Craig sees him as 'disregarding the lesson supposed to have been taught once and for all by "Ern Malley" ', and also as reviving in his own way the poetic principle of another once-discredited group, the Jindyworobaks. Craig says of Stow's work: 'It's this connexion with the inner life, with a

subjectivism which we share as much as we do the outward, objective world, that gives Stow's poems so often their incantatory, profound power. In addition, Stow has helped to free the imagination for all poets in this country' (p. 11). Critics disappointed by Stow's development offer comment like John Thompson's in his review of *Outrider* (1962) in *Southerly*, vol. 23, no. 2, 1963: 'His new poetry often seems to be calculatedly unconscious. The imagery is apt to be startling, but it does not always stand up to a second look. It is never so far-fetched that it does not give a kind of perfume of reality, but in many instances the reality which it reflects is tenuous and slight. What Stow has to say is rather insubstantial and hazy' (p. 141).

2 For an interesting general review of this important magazine, see A. M. Gibbs, 'Meanjin and The Australian Literary Scene', *Journal of Commonwealth Literature*, no. 4, 1967.

3 I do not mean to imply that politics is not a proper subject for poetry or that political commitment necessarily militates against artistic success. Many examples in literature demonstrate otherwise. But there has been an incompatibility in this century between modern political ideologies and poetry, and even more clearly between writing in aid of a political organization and writing in accordance with poetic integrity. A. D. Hope has some comments on this in his essay 'The Activists', originally published in *Prospect*, vol. 3, no. 4, 1960 and reprinted in *The Cave and the Spring* (1965).

4 *Quadrant* vol. 1, no. 1, 1956-57; reprinted in *The Cave and the Spring* (1965).

5 'Free Verse: a Post-Mortem', *Quadrant*, vol. 4, no. 2, 1960; reprinted in *The Cave and the Spring.*

6 'The Magian Heresy', *Quadrant*, vol. 1, no. 4, 1957; reprinted in *The End of Modernity* (1959); the thesis is recapitulated in an essay, 'Journey into Egypt' in my second book of essays, *The Grammar of the Real* (1975).

7 'From a Poet's Notebook', *Quadrant*, vol. 2, no. 4, 1958; reprinted in *The End of Modernity*. I have pursued the analysis of verse further in *A Primer of English Versification* (1966) and in a short essay, 'The Dynamics of Verse', in *The Grammar of the Real.*

8 Charles Higham, quoting this in a review (*Quadrant*, vol. 3, no. 1, 1959) characterized it as an 'anti-intellectual sneer', and commented with lively asperity: 'We know what he means by assumptions, presumptions; by cluster, flea-swarm. And what he means all through, and his fellow-editors have discreetly let him mean, is that this book, this little book at least, would not be marred by "classicism" or "academicism"— those bogies of the popularist of poetry; that he would rather see in it, and has put in it, poems inspired by the touching belief that a sparkling thought or two, a knowledge of prosody and a degree of stylistic know-how are enough to fix a poem in eternity' (p. 100).

9 See for example Max Harris, 'Conflicts in Australian Intellectual Life 1940-1964', in *Literary Australia*, ed. Clement Semmler and Derek Whitelock (1966). A. D. Hope's misgivings are expressed in 'Literature versus the Universities', in *The Cave and the Spring* (1965 — not reprinted in the 1974 edition) and in his satire *Dunciad Minor* (1970) where he sees as a result of Eng. Lit. in universities:

> Now Arnold's nightmare children walk the land;
> *Culture* and *Anarchy* go hand in hand.
>
> (III.171-2)

U

My comments, 'Literature and the Academics' in *An Introduction to Australian Literature* (1964), were made at the request of the editor of that symposium, Professor C. D. Narasimhaiah of Mysore University.

10 'Australian Poetic Diction', *Australian Letters*, vol. 1, no. 1, 1957; reprinted in *Twentieth Century Australian Literary Criticism*, ed. Clement Semmler, 1967. A later article by Ray Mathew, 'Noble Candid Speech', *Australian Letters*, vol. 2, no. 2, 1959, is pointed in the same direction but to no clear effect. Criticism directed at myself was renewed in vol. 2, no. 3, 1959 by Geoffrey Dutton, 'The Classic Pose'.

11 Brian Kiernan, *Criticism* (Australian Writers and their Work series), 1974, p. 44.

12 In a letter in *Southerly*, vol. 19, no. 2, 1958, replying to S. E. Lee's review of *Essays in Poetry*, Buckley said, 'I see no reason for giving special attention to the work of Rosemary Dobson' (p. 118).

13 Published in *Poetry Australia*, no. 42, 1972, but not with all the divisions of the text shown.

14 See for a fleeting example *Essays in Poetry*, p. 189; the term is a key-word in his thinking.

15 The term is used in a paper, 'Reflections on the Future' which he delivered at a Pax Romana conference at Lyons, 1966.

16 The notion that anything at all may become a hierophany, that is, something by which the sacred is manifest to a particular person or community was developed by Buckley from the writings of Mircéa Eliade. The idea is related to poetry in Buckley's third critical book *Poetry and the Sacred* (1968). I am not myself sure that poetry can bear this burden, or even the burden of being 'the highest humanist act' imposed on it in the interview quoted in the next paragraph.

17 Henry Rosenbloom, 'An Interview with Vincent Buckley', *Meanjin Quarterly*, vol. 28, no. 3, 1969, p. 323.

18 *Meanjin Quarterly*, vol. 20, no. 2, 1961; reprinted in *Twentieth Century Australian Literary Criticism*, ed. Clement Semmler, 1967.

19 As Wallace-Crabbe admits: 'Generally one would feel little impulse to call his work ironic: concerned largely with personal and spiritual introspection, it achieves, in its manner, a curious blend of lyrical and rhetorical qualities'. Buckley separated himself from some younger contemporaries in another way, in a comment in *Essays in Poetry* (1957): 'I see a good deal of the verse of young men, the men who are between five and ten years younger than myself; and I know that they place great stress — I would add, a humble stress — on the necessity for technical resources. They have learnt that poetry is not mere self-expression, that it is a personal task, and that it has something quite intimate to do with their responsibility as men towards their fellow-men. *I feel that they are probably wrong in their preoccupation with technique. I do not share the desire which they apparently feel to bring other lives, the lives of obscure and average men, directly into their poetry*' (p. 50, my italics). He added, prophetically: 'Insofar as their researches *are* technical, I feel that they will learn more from contemporary American poetry than from British' (p. 51). Buckley's distrust of 'preoccupation with technique' is related to his belief that 'technical developments are valuable only if they are first spiritual ones, interior and personal and profound' (p. 50).

20 'Baudelaire's *Fleurs du Mal* — an Incomplete Oresteia', *Quadrant*, vol. 17, no. 3, 1973, p. 23.

21 'The Very Gimbals of Unease: the Poetry of Francis Webb', *Meanjin Quarterly*, vol. 26, no. 3, 1967.

14

The Sixties and After

INTRODUCTION

The nearer one comes to the present the harder it is to draw a map with confidence. The poets represented in the selection are ones whose reputation was more or less established before new stirrings began among younger poets about 1967-68: stirrings which will be briefly discussed later in this section. Some of the poets here represented were beginning to be known in the previous decade. Vivian Smith published his first volume, *The Other Meaning*, in 1956. Gwen Harwood was publishing poems in the late fifties under her own and other names ('Francis Geyer', 'Walter Lehmann', 'Miriam Stone').[1] Bruce Dawe's work was also gaining attention. These writers can be seen as making their individual contributions within a continuity of development from the fifties; the characteristic line of their work was already recognizable.

Gwen Harwood's *Poems* (1963) established her at once as an original talent. Her originality is won from the absorption of many influences — which include Australian contemporaries and some American poets; it shows itself in an unmistakable personal tone, a sharp nervous brilliance, feelings touched to the quick — and an eye hungry both for detail and for general atmospheric effects:

> Wind crosshatches shallow water.
> Paddocks rest in the sea's arm.
> Swamphens race through spiky grass.
> A wire fence leans, a crazy stare
> with sticks for barlines, wind for song.
> Over us, interweaving light
> with air and substance, ride the gulls.

('Estuary')

The next volume, *Poems: Volume Two* (1968) — from which the above quotation is taken — showed these qualities exercised with more disciplined sureness, a corresponding gain in intensity and less danger of lapsing into obscurity or forcing the note. The crown of her work so far is in some more recent poems — such as 'Barn Owl' and the superbly managed 'David's Harp', both in the selection. Gwen Harwood's range includes not only the bared nerve of poignancy but also the sardonic and savage. There are also the two notable groups of poems which essay a complex kind of intellectual and sentimental vaudeville: the earlier group is centred on Professor Eisenbart, a dry ageing scholar, and the later group presents Professor Kröte, a musician in exile given to drunkenness and near to despair. While these constructions are no doubt a means of working out personal concerns, Gwen Harwood's best work is that which draws, or seems to draw, more directly upon private experience. She has lived in Hobart since 1945, and the Tasmanian landscape and seascape are present in many poems. Several of her best poems, however, go back to her native Brisbane, and gather energy from memories of childhood and youth:

> I dream I stand once more
> in Ann Street by the old
> fire station. The palms
> like feather dusters move
> idly in stifling air.
> The sky's dusted with gold.
> A footfall; someone comes;
> I cannot speak for love.

> ('Dust to Dust')

Tasmania is in the background of the poems in Vivian Smith's first volume, *The Other Meaning* (1956), and for many of the poems in *An Island South* (1967). He has been settled in Sydney since 1967. Most of his work is meditative: the eye searching the landscape is at the same time deeply introspective. A close study of Rilke seems implied in some of the poems. The poet seeks but refuses to impose a meaning, an order; he knows the discomfort of such searchings; he stresses the need for patience, tentativeness, acceptance of unresolved states, an inner truthfulness that does not try to make the words enact solutions that have not been won in experience:

> Discordant season: moments of despair:
> We glimpse the cracks that run all through our lives;
> The heart we lightly thought rich and austere;
> The mind's disordered drawer of borrowed knives.

Don't run with words. Don't seek them. Words aren't wise.
The mind's eclipses move to prove its suns.
And nudity of all is best disguise:
stay bare in stillness . . . Vanity runs.

There is a characteristic quietness of tone, a discretion and
delicacy, which stops short of preciosity and should not obscure
from the reader the unusual tough underlying strength. Because
of this prevailing quietness one is all the more startled by
occasional poems which do something unexpected, like the
languid ironic comedy to be found in 'Quiet Evening', the
different comedy of 'Bus Ride', the disconcerting surrealist vision
of 'The Man Fern near the Bus Stop'[2] and the scarifying satire
of 'Deathbed Sketch' which transfixes a literary type:

His first book made him known to a small band;
it passed in the Antipodes for Art,
with verses full of God and sex and wars.
It proved he had no ear and far less heart.

In time our poet found his public role;
opinion-making offers sure returns
as those who trade in reputations find —
theirs is the first the careless goddess spurns.

Appeared as poet-critic on TV:
'Poets are good at stirring others up.'
Increasing dangers of complacency
followed by *Comments on the Melbourne Cup*.

He stood amazed to see his small part growing,
an invitation here, addresses there;
'When all I want is to be with the Muse
my social conscience leads me to despair' —

He always found the crowd that needed him
to tell them what to think, to set their fashion
in art and comment: 'The whole country needs
my kind of person's tragic sense of mission.'

'I'll never write again,' he used to smile,
'This country's done my talent too much harm';
and saw within the mirror how the leaks
were slowly spreading through his schoolboy charm.

And yet from time to time a verse appeared
saying how big men are compared with birds;

and these were one day gathered in a second
book that was merely ideas set to words.

Of course we all agreed we would be kind,
haunted by our own sense of deeper failure.
It's human not to keep your standards high.
We need his type of person in Australia.

Bruce Dawe is one of the most accessible of recent poets.
His poetry inhabits the man-made environment — urban, suburban, or rural; it is not austere or egocentric or peculiarly private; it performs its public role with a sense of mission as well as
a gift for entertainment. His best poems are social rather than
political in their concern. 'Life-Cycle' (p. 326) shows his gift
for comedy, and 'Drifters' (p. 326) his compassion and pathos.
As professed satirist and moralist his touch is more uncertain.
Much of Dawe's poetry may be said to represent a revival
of the recitation-poem: it does not want just to lie on the
page, it needs to live in the voice and be shared with an
audience. Dawe's independently dissenting political attitudes —
especially his protest against war — and his tendency to an
openwork informality make him congenial to recent younger
poets, though his work seems unaffected by the American
and English influences which interest them strongly. Geoffrey
Lehmann's notice of his work, from which I have quoted in the
critical section, seems to me to provide a useful summary.

Les Murray is the most ambitious of these poets in range
and variety. The heartland of his work is the dairy-farming
country at Bunyah on the North Coast of New South Wales,
where he grew up. This is the core of reality for him; and, more
widely, it is in the 'weatherboard cathedrals' and 'sanctuaries of
dry grass' of rural Australia that his spirit makes its primary
devotions, with a Virgilian *pietas* towards parents and ancestors
and the earth itself, *justissima tellus*. The realism passes over into
a mythic vision or acquires a suggestion of sacred meaning or
ritual. The implication of the phrase 'weatherboard cathedrals' is
paralleled, for example, in the surprising vision of the secular as
somehow exhibiting the sacred which emerges in the poem
'Blood' (p. 325), of which Murray has said that it is 'one of several
poems written in Canberra and Wales on aspects of the Eucharist
in everyday life'.[3] From his rural base, Murray's thought and
experience reach out into the city, into other countries, into
history and politics and anthropology; but everything is tested
against the local reality, as in the poem 'Shorelines', where the
poet and his friend walk by an inland lake and ponder human
destiny:

From upriver, two fishermen in a country boat
With chicken-wire nets and fruit tins, drift and row.
We walk on the wet shore. Horses, feeding, raise
Their heads from the rushy grass to watch us go

Thoughtfully through their dreaming vision, while
In talk and silence, we tap and probe the future
And the great past for legends, patterns, tales
In which to see, and move, and know our nature

And be complete, a world of balanced kingdoms
In each of us, and each in such a world.
As evening comes, horizons slowly harden.
Shallows are deepened. Farm buildings shrink with cold.

And, as the rising east wind dulls the water
And bends brusque reeds for the passage of the sky,
We, growing weary, trudge miles out to high ground
And strike the world-road, firm and fast and dry.

Murray is a versatile poet using both formal and irregular verse, with moods ranging from sheer exhilaration to solemnity. He has himself recognized the need 'to restrain a natural garrulity'.[4] His more relaxed style is shown in poems like 'Evening Alone at Bunyah', where the poet, back for a visit, stays at home while his widower father goes out dancing:

My father will be there now, at a hall
In the dark of the country, shining at the waltz,
Spry and stately, twirling the foursome reels
On a roaring waxed-plank floor.
    The petrol lamps
Sizzle and glare now the clapping has died down.
They announce some modern dance. He steps outside
To where cigarettes glow sparsely in the dark,
Joins some old friends and yarns about his son.

With Geoffrey Lehmann we are back, most of the time, in Sydney. His first publication was shared with Les Murray as a joint collection, *The Ilex Tree* (1965). Lehmann's poetic mind is not solitary, as is that of many poets: it is companionable, concerned with people, family, friends, those whom he loves, likes, finds interesting. He has a keen sense of place, period, style: his poems are a means of storing memorable things, such as his recollections of visiting Murray's home country with him, in 'The Trip to Bunyah', where he shows us the poet

> Reading the fine-grained lines of your country's hand,
> Explaining to us how hawks patrol the hill-tops,
> Nesting among the high and windy places,
> How cows are man-shy, foxes cough at night,
> And land requires three generations to tame it.
> Your words made a general blur jump into focus,
> Showed trees and ridges with sharp glittering edges,
> Turned landscape into manscape, soil to cherish,
> And on this sleeping breast of hills and grasslands,
> Darkening and brightening with the moods of clouds,
> Rosellas dropped like fruit before your rifle.

The danger is of being too facile, of assuming that the copious recording of things with a loving exactness and elegance is enough. An additive syntax is always a danger sign. But the pleasure offered, the civilized grace and humane feeling, are very persuasive.

Although Bruce Beaver is the second oldest of the poets represented, I have placed him last because his work exhibits a transition towards the new methods and styles of younger recent poets. The poem selected is from *Letters to Live Poets* (1969), perhaps his most successful volume, where the poems, though they read a little too much like wordy improvisations, impromptus, nevertheless have force and truth in them. These are intensely personal poems, partly 'confessional' in character — dealing with his poetic vocation, his spiritual search, his childhood, and his spells of manic-depressive psychosis: 'cyclothymic, non-certifiable', he says elsewhere. (The fellow-poet immured in Callan Park asylum in 'Letter XII' is Francis Webb.) Of this volume, James Tulip wrote: 'But it is *Letters to Live Poets* . . . which is at the centre of the change in recent Australian poetry'.[5] In his next book, *Lauds and Plaints* (1974), the poet uses typographical spacing to articulate his lines; the poems reach out and gather miscellaneous and partly fortuitous detail into a meditation — but the speaker has moved out of the close range of *Letters;* he is attempting something further and is less easily understood. The phrases are spaced instead of being punctuated:

> but at times the word-maker is alone
> with his silence and as empty of obvious
> meanings as a sandscape of immediate
> contours   something like the programme of the
> dedicated sweeping priests at Ryoanji
> takes place then   one becomes conscious
> again of the taken-for-granted rocks the clusters
> and separate presences of stone

surrounded by a visually bland tactilely
abrasive sea of sand   the engrossed
sweeper priest accentuates some innate pattern
of currents swirls and vortices of grains
around about the island rocks

Some other poets stand with Beaver as responsive to recent
influences and in sympathy with new trends among younger
poets. Thomas W. Shapcott and Rodney Hall have not only
anthologized the work of younger poets but also moved in an
'experimental' direction in their own work. Grace Perry,[6] a
Sydney medical practitioner, and presiding spirit of the magazine
Poetry Australia and of South Head Press, has published five
volumes of her own work and also volumes by Bruce Beaver,
Craig Powell, Norman Talbot, and John Millett. Craig Powell, a
Sydney psychiatrist, has moved away from the formal structures
of his earlier poems; much of his work, like some of Grace Perry's,
is based upon his professional experience. David Malouf, a
Queenslander by origin, after returning from Europe produced a
small volume, *Bicycle*, (1970), which is contemporary and informal in a moderate style and won critical esteem. A second
volume, *Neighbours in a Thicket* (1974), shows growing strength.
Norman Talbot has a wilder romantic subjective poetry in *Poems
for a Female Universe* (1968) and *Son of a Female Universe* (1971),
two volumes of a three-part series.

Australia lost a conspicuous talent when Peter Porter emigrated
from Brisbane to England in 1951 at the age of twenty-one. His
entire poetic career belongs to the English scene. When consulted
he gave it as his opinion that it would not be appropriate to
represent him in this volume. It is a case similar to that of
W. J. Turner, whose career as poet and music critic belongs
entirely to England, though he grew up in Victoria.

Since about 1967 a new mood has been manifest in Australian
poetry, though it is not clear how far this will prevail. The
movement has been towards neo-romanticism and a revival of
free-form and 'experimental' writing, with stress upon spontaneity, often with acceptance in varying degrees of irrationality
as part of a poetic method. The models are American (William
Carlos Williams, the Black Mountain poets, and 'beat' poetry)
and English (the 'underground' poets[7]) and some recent European
poetry, usually in translation, such as that of Paul Celan. A sign
of the changing mood was an article written by Chris Wallace-
Crabbe after a visit to America, in which he contrasted 'open' and
'closed' poetry.[8] By 'closed' poetry he meant poetry as it has
nearly always been written, which develops a theme in an orderly

way and brings it to a resolution and final balance, a process matched by the form. By 'open' poetry he meant chiefly some recent American poetry by Creeley, Bly and others, which 'seizes an instant or an upsurge of feeling out of the flux and tries to hold it there quivering'. Wallace-Crabbe uses a poem by the American poet James Wright to indicate typical features:

> quest for the private, the local, the spontaneous . . . the idiom has an unbuttoned ease . . . The verse is extremely free, the syntax is commonplace . . . Moreover, the verse follows no rational logic but that of the concurrence of observed images, images which are set down with a distinct immediate vividness . . . We have a conscious opposition between schools of recent American poetry, then: the 'Fifties' men too cool, easy, knowledgeable, almost too much in control of their forming and shaping; the later sub-generation . . . hunting for freedom, harshness, vivid flatness, and laying themselves open to the daemons of private disorder and aggressively Americanized romanticism (pp. 74-5).

Wallace-Crabbe, outstandingly in the late fifties and early sixties a practitioner of the well-ordered 'closed' poem, has in recent work moved — like Louis Simpson in the United States — 'to court open or organic forms'.

A later discussion of the American experience, with a more advanced prescription for Australian practice, is given in an article by another poet, Andrew Taylor, written on return from a period in the United States: 'Irrationality Individuality Drug Poetry Romanticism — Where We Are Today'.[9] The title gives the prescription. The basic assumption is stated late in the article, that the essential self is irrational and that contemporary poetry's proper business is to render in words the movements of this essential self:

> The poetry I've pointed to is *honest to* the innermost psychic activities of the individual that are accessible to language. To demand that these be rational would be irrational, dishonest to our own experience. And the honesty with which these poets approach the irrationality — yet logic — of innermost experience, and the strange, restless relationship of *that* with the outer, social world results in an accuracy which carries their poetry out of the realms of case history into that of art (p. 384).

The issues raised in this passage are important and require serious debate of a kind which does not occur frequently enough in Australia.[10] Andrew Taylor's Australian representatives of this trend include Michael Dransfield[11] and J. S. Harry. He also (but more contestably) cites Vincent Buckley's large composition 'Golden Builders'.[12] Other relevant names might include Robert Adamson and John E. Tranter. The modestly urbane well-made poem approved by Chris Wallace-Crabbe for the early sixties, which was also Andrew Taylor's original mode, is now firmly rejected:

> Much English and Australian poetry of the fifties and sixties seems to diminish, rather than enhance the stature of the persons involved: scrupulously mean and small, it picks away at what's wrong, rather than living out what's right (p. 383).

John E. Tranter, in an article in *New Poetry*,[13] has given a commentary on the revolution or attempted revolution begun by younger poets in 1967-68. He surveys the rapid proliferation of little magazines and small publishing presses, and he gives a critical view of several poets, including Graham Rowlands, Alan Wearne, Richard Packer, Peter Annand, Antigone Kefala, Rae Desmond Jones. His concluding summary of the state of Australian poetry as a whole is as follows:

> In the comparisons that must now be made our traditional attitudes are seen wanting, our big fish are seen as minnows in the ocean of poetry, and one is finally forced to realize that not one Australian poet has influenced the development of modern poetry in English. Our parochialism has been so total that we are unaware of it (p. 61).

The charge is not, however, well framed. There are reasons of cultural communications that work against the likelihood of Australian poetry influencing developments in England and America; the worth of the best Australian writing has in any case to be judged independently of such traffic considerations. Furthermore, Tranter in his article is interested only in an 'ability to forge useful links with the best of *contemporary experimental poetry*' (p. 60, my italics). This limited kind of up-to-dateness has only a limited value, and the question of parochialism should not be decided by it: the neo-anarchist dreamboat is not the only craft in contemporary waters. It is nevertheless true that a great deal of Australian writing has been and is parochial, incurious, impervious to the challenge of outside influences. But this has not been true of some of the best poets, notably and obviously including poets whose work appears here in the selections for the fifties and sixties.

A wider survey of recent poetry has been made by K. L. Goodwin,[14] relying partly on Thomas W. Shapcott's anthology *Australian Poetry Now* (1970), which represents the work, among others, of Rhyll McMaster, Peter Skrzynecki, Tim Thorne, Garrie Hutchinson, B. A. Breen, Charles Buckmaster.[15] A later anthology of interest is *The First Paperback Poets Anthology* (ed. Roger McDonald, 1974) giving work by poets who have published in the Paperback Poets series of the University of Queensland Press.

This tentative survey can be concluded by two observations. The long hegemony of Sydney in poetry has been broken over the past two decades, with activity spread more widely, though mainly in the eastern states. And the most recent new voices are too varied to be brought under the banner of any single poetic, radical or otherwise. There has been no occasion to mention poets as diverse as Anne Elder, Leon Slade, Miles Little, Graeme Hetherington, for example, in the framework of this discussion of trends and trendiness, and from the standpoint of a few years hence other names will doubtless be seen to have deserved more consideration. Some comments relating to recent poetry have been included in the critical extracts, because they raise questions of general importance. This is particularly true of the passage from that generously keen critic, the late Alec King, in which, by way of a comment on two poems by Rodney Hall, he brings us back to the problem of poetic language, and its relation to an implied audience.

COMMENTARY

On Gwen Harwood

Gwen Harwood's poems [*Poems,* 1963] are densely evocative of a world of place, particularly of a sea-coast and a small city, and of a world of the mind which is distinctively that of European music, art and ideas. If they move freely and naturally in both, taking each on a level with the other, it is because they have their origin altogether from another, inner and wholly personal world... The major and most rewarding struggle is with pain, whether arbitrary physical pain, or the inevitable pain of love and work frustrated by the nature of things or by time. In either case the only victory possible is acceptance of the intolerable, or, rather, to incorporate the intolerable within the accepted order of things... These poems are sometimes joyful, more often tragic, and usually true. The hesitation is partly a wondering *how* true; partly the unfamiliarity, the genuine originality of the sensibility they express. The degree of truthfulness is a matter of how accurately 'the protean inscape of self' is caught. At this reviewing level it seems to me that a rough discrimination might be made in this way. The less interesting poems are that for one or both of two reasons: either they are of that order of polished perceptive nearly anonymous verse, more characteristic of international poetry magazines than of individual talents; and/or they fail to transform personal revulsions into experiences of common relevance. The latter is particularly the danger in Mrs Harwood's satire; a judgment in one could be applied to itself — it has the awkwardness of 'heart's blood on a public page' ('Dichterliebe').

At the same time there may be an essential connection between the element of savagery in such poems, and the impressively strong and challenging originality of her best work. That includes about half the poems in this volume — poems distinctively her own, such as no-one else could have written, and of general relevance. I am inclined to guess that what so distinguishes them is that they are wholly feminine — it might be as true to say: unalloyed with egotism. The unguarded revulsions of the satiric poems are in fact instinctive rejections of egotism and its stifling pretences and pedantries. And what awakens an equally instinctive acceptance are those experiences, whether of pain or joy, which liberate the spirit into creative activity.

David Moody, 'The Poems of Gwen Harwood',
Meanjin Quarterly, vol. 22, no. 4, 1963, pp. 418-21

One of the first things to strike a reader of Gwen Harwood's poetry must surely be her brilliance. This is not, as it looks, a simple uncritical gasp, a spontaneous cry of admiration: in her second book, as in first, Mrs Harwood's weaknesses as well as her greatest virtues can be associated with brilliance of texture and effect. At best, her poetry convinces us of the truth of its intensities, its cries of pain, keen pangs of longing, its catching of intense moments when the heart cries 'Remember me', or 'I cannot hear what you say', or 'Look. Remember this'. At worst, she tends to keep experience high-pitched in the interests of art, so that language is overcharged with words like 'blaze', 'glitter', 'torment', 'beatitude', and the dullest academic party becomes a jazzy, floodlit battlefield of innuendo and bitchery. (Or are Hobart parties ferocious in ways unknown on the mainland?)

Poems/Volume Two is a distinguished and moving collection. Its concerns are very similar to those in Mrs Harwood's first volume, which made such an impact when it came out five years ago. Again the poems are predominantly charged with loss and hurt, lacerated by the pastness of the past, its taunting inaccessibility ('The substance of that world is gone'), and the intensity with which it burns through present rhythms of habit and encroaching mortality:

My ghost, my self, most intimate stranger
standing beneath these lyric trees
with your one wineglassful of morning
snatched from the rushing galaxies,

bright-haired and satin-lipped you offer
the youth I shall not taste again.
I know, I bear to know, your future
unlooked-for love, undreamed-of pain.

('In Brisbane')

Chris Wallace-Crabbe, 'My Ghost, My Self: the
Poetry of Gwen Harwood', *Meanjin Quarterly*,
vol. 28, no. 2, 1969, p. 264

On Vivian Smith

With the help of Vivian Smith's poetry (his second volume was
published last year) I want to make a final point on the relationship between a writer and his readers which the unashamedly
touching language of poetry so intimately wants to establish. If
our taste for life is too far from that of a poet — a taste that is
peculiarly a matter of language, its idiom, rhythm, articulation
— we turn away from him. If the rough-edged vulgar-tasting
common speech is one through which we want to grope for a
sustaining image of our contemporary self, impatient of inherited
formulas of belief, of any inherited ritual of feeling and valuing,
then the poetry of Vivian Smith may seem tasteless, too smooth,
too neat, too sheltered. But our taste-buds may mislead us here
(mine did on my first reading of these poems). In its clarity,
lightness, its clean musical speech defining a soft-spoken imagination touched with fancifulness, Vivian Smith's is a genuine kind
of 'pastoral' poetry, a poetry which says there is order, symmetry,
composure, into which we can move by almost deliberately
simplifying ourselves. It is a poetry that clears a space in the mad
world by a self-contained delicacy. Its danger, of course, is life-
lessness, a danger not always avoided. But most of it is authentic-
ally alive; for all its quietness the flexible, supple, nervous,
rhythms are there to convince us that the pastoral retreat is real
and not made-up.

Alec King, 'The Look of Australian Poetry in 1967',
Meanjin Quarterly, vol. 27, no. 2, 1968, p. 183

An Island South places itself in the central tradition of closed,
formal verse where the mind of the poet enacts, as it were, the
mind of the things it contemplates. Here, the objectifying of
insight and response is achieved in the hard disciplines of making

the verse right in terms of the intrinsic demands of line and stanzaic structure. In this regard, Vivian Smith deserves high praise. Some lines from 'At an Exhibition of Historical Paintings, Hobart' illustrate this skill, at the same time they point in another direction:

[stanzas 2-4]

Lines such as these do carry an air of impersonality about them, and yet there are some very real personal presuppositions underlying them. The right to observe, analyse, discriminate; the right to judge one's world, in fact: these human acts are all there, and the quatrain is the right and necessary means through which the objects rendered are realized and the subject rendering them placed finitely as a common, if fine, intelligence. Vivian Smith's interplay of subject and object, at this point, is the distinctive achievement of his book.

One begins to wonder, however, whether the objects he has chosen to render for himself are adequate even for his own concerns and interests. The sense in the above lines of the most active response going to the qualities and disparities and effects of the paintings suggests a certain leaning towards another role of experiencing in Smith other than that of the judge. A certain impatience is there at the necessary condescension demanded to feel and enjoy this particular world. It does not surprise, therefore, to find this acute observer putting his finger on the problem in his own way.

> Is this the self I thought I knew, within
> this narrow world of helpless self-concern,
> where in fatigue huge images begin
> to grope at knowledge, thinking to discern
>
> recognitions, motives slyly caught,
> suspicions looming in a hostile sky.
> Hell is other people, Sartre thought.
> The threat of others, ill-will; all my I . . .

Even the finely poised resolution of this probing:

> to walk with images that change and chill
> the contours of reality's design
> along the failing tightrope of the will

suggests no answer since all things, self included, in this world are mere objects in dichotomy with the subject. An endless circle of deepening ironies is the only possible outcome. And the point from this for criticism is that the quality of the poetry is affected; a self-depressive intonation is felt in poem after poem of *An Island South*.

I found myself instinctively liking those poems where Vivian Smith commits himself to a longer rhythmic unit than the four-line stanza; it was as though the poet was sinking into a situation larger than himself.

James Tulip, review of *An Island South* (1967),
in *Southerly*, vol. 28, no. 1, 1968, pp. 73-4

On Bruce Dawe

Bruce Dawe is that rare phenomenon, a natural poet with a superlative feeling for language. He is an inventor, a conjurer, the words twinkling from his hands seemingly without effort. As well as having an exact feel for dialogue and social detail, which is unmatched by any Australian novelist now writing (with the possible exception of Hal Porter), Bruce Dawe also has great concern and responsibility. Some of his more outrageously funny pieces may be seen as savagely satirical, but in fact they are generally motivated by affection and love. Dawe, unlike a lot of other poets who are grouped as belonging to the left, has worked for much of his life as a laborer and mostly hated it. Dawe's social concern is a very real thing, not just a willed poetic pose.

This [*Beyond the Subdivisions*] is his fourth published book of poetry. It is uneven. Dawe has such facility with words that he sometimes parodies himself. The satire runs away with the poem and the original intention gets lost in a nasty joke. Dawe has on occasions criticised the cruelty of some of his own poems.

Occasionally, I also feel that there is too much compassion and not enough toughness and rejoicing. 'Miss Mac' is delicately and imaginatively written, but the pathos is excessive as Miss Mac meanders off into a maudlin Sargasso Sea for old-age pensioners:

> In order to be forgotten
> it's not necessary to do much
> except watch the wrinkles gather
> and the old friends depart
> for distant suburbs where excavators aren't forever lowering
> in at the windows and the wrecker's iron ball
> slogging like a hammer at the heart.

This passage from 'Miss Mac' illustrates Dawe's weaknesses and strengths. The opening is much too sentimental, but the last three lines are extraordinarily strong. The image of the wrecker's iron ball is quite devastating. Dawe continually rescues a slight or trivial poem with a brilliant line or image. In addition the poems link up to create a world, the sum of which is greater than the parts. It is a world of the suburbs, the pensioner, migrants, the TAB, a raped girl.

Perhaps the best poems in this book relate to the war in Vietnam. 'Home-coming' is the best poem I have read anywhere about the war. In its sheer power it is comparable with the poems of Wilfred Owen written in World War I. Dawe, in his poem, does not accuse or blame, it is simply an awe-inspiring statement of anguish. There is a tolerance point where excruciating pain becomes angelic singing, and this poem exists at that point. 'Phantasms of Evening' is another very haunting poem:

> Light fails. From here
> it's hard to see
> whether those young men ghost-dancing into their graves
> are Viet Cong or Sioux . . .
> Say, are those plumed shadows
>
> Flying Horseman of the First Air Cavalry Division,
> or Hittites bringing the gospel of iron
> to confound the Egyptians?
> What war are we up to now?
> Whose mourning is it?

'The Fate of Armies' is another remarkably haunting poem (perhaps reminiscent of Kenneth Slessor's 'Beach Burial'?). It is a poem which achieves eloquent inevitability within a tight structure:

> Now I know to what cool earth the armies
> return, return, in absolute silence
> under the hurt gaze of the moon.

Another aspect of Bruce Dawe's work is his Catholicism. He is a convert. Religion does not often appear in his poetry, however. Religion has been so often misused by poets in the past as an extension of their rhetoric that one can understand Dawe's caution about this. It probably informs his concern and humanity at a deeper level. 'At Mass' is a poem for a friend resigning from the priesthood and it movingly portrays the dilemma of contemporary Catholicism:

> Your stand a cry
> from the southern Church of Silence where to speak
> what's in the heart is some dishonour . . .
> Snap-frozen in some seminary,
> the Word, secured against the ubiquitous shock
> of honest air or breath, rots as it thaws.

> Geoffrey Lehmann, review of *Beyond the Subdivisions*,
> in the *Bulletin*, 2 May 1970, p. 56

V

In a Commonwealth Literary Fund lecture which he gave in 1964, Dawe spoke of

> a painful lack of social awareness in our poetry . . . So few genuine poems reflect directly or indirectly an awareness of the social problems of our country . . . those which concern people everywhere in one way or another . . . All are relevant to us because we are men. I mean such issues as graft and corruption in government, business and industry, spiritual wickedness in high places. I mean the never-ending tussle of State versus the individual, no matter how good the State or civic-minded the individual . . . There are the lost people in our midst for whom no one speaks and who cannot speak for themselves — the old and lonely; the middle-aged whose sin is that they're not young any more . . . It's not good enough to retreat to up-country pubs or to creek-beds where we can hope to play alone . . . We seem either too smug or too shy to have a good hard look at the world we live in . . . the suffering, poignant and necessary world which men (and poets *as* men) must walk in . . .

These admirable remarks give a better idea of Dawe's vision and aims than do some of his recent poems. Public poetry is probably the hardest to write, for reasons already suggested. 'Poets as men', Dawe rightly insists; and the public poet has to convince us that it's a *man* speaking, and a full man, one who has, besides convictions, a complex awareness of complex questions. The directness of Dawe's approach to these, which understandably appeals to so many people (for, as he says, such awareness is rare in our poetry), can result in language which is not rich enough to elicit a whole response from the reader, or even to suggest the scope of the poet's own awareness and sympathy, so apparent in the lecture.

Philip Martin, 'Public Yet Personal: Bruce Dawe's Poetry', *Meanjin Quarterly*, vol. 25, no. 3, 1966, p. 291

On Les A. Murray

The conditions put forward by Rex Ingamells in 1936 in *Conditional Culture* could as easily have been advanced by Les Murray in 1970: 'a clear recognition of environmental values; the debunking of much nonsense; an understanding of Australia's history and traditions, primaeval, Colonial, and modern'. The Jindyworobak movement declined because the restrictions subsequently imposed on subject-matter and vocabulary produced 'Australian' verse that was unacceptable to most Australians no matter what their literary taste (or political convictions). Les

Murray doesn't appear as yet to have limited himself to certain 'suitable' or 'typical' kinds of subject or language. His most overtly 'Australian' pieces are glorious gallimaufries of narrative, idiomatic direct-speech interjections and authorial comment. The whole effect is of a chaotic gleefulness that has been ... the essence of Murray's Australia.

Dianne Ailwood, 'The Poetry of Les Murray',
Southerly, vol. 31, no. 3, 1971, p. 198

On Bruce Beaver

Lowell was the first of a wave of American poets to write in a confessional style. Australian poets have been slow to follow, and *Letters to Live Poets* is the first fully confessional book of verse to be produced here. One can see the beginnings of this in previous books of Beaver. He has never been a poet to dress his subject up. One of his methods has always been to mix incongruities. He has always preferred a vigorous untidiness to smoothly articulated surfaces.

Letters to Live Poets continues and intensifies this direction. It is in fact a long poem cycle written on a day-to-day basis. The parts loosely link up, sometimes refer to each other, but there is no overall schemata. The coherence of the sequence derives from the poet's own personality, appreciating, responding, joking, pestered by sinusitis, praising his wife or condemning involvement in Vietnam.

Some of the sections revolve around incidents of the day — weather, scenery and people. Others take up general themes or recollections. Beaver presents himself with candor and lack of pretension, living unglamorously at Manly, involved in the dull round of shopping, wandering along the beach among washed-up socks, but always concerned with the life of the imagination. These are poems haunted by the ordinariness of our lives. He writes:

> You know ugliness isn't so bad —
> an honest ugliness, I mean.
> It makes a statement from and to
> concerning appearances about now and then.
> Like beauty it appears to be, it *is*
> a silent volubility.
> It's the ordinariness of faces and figures
> that overwhelms and blinds the seeing
> eye — the way some tall, thin men
> walk with backsides lacking in loose
> trousers . . .

This is Beaver at his best and his own involvement is obvious in such passages. On occasions, however, when describing his own sinusitis or his wife's rheumatism, one feels the poetry becoming trivial and losing perspective... Beaver avoids the brilliant (but perhaps simplifying) insight, the startling *mot juste*. This is poetry which hurts and abrades with its rawness. With considerable skill he adjusts his poetic voice to the voice of normal speech.

Geoffrey Lehmann, review of *Letters to Live Poets* (1969),
in the *Bulletin*, 30 May 1970, pp. 50-1

On Recent Poetry

Here are comments on Rodney Hall's *Eyewitness*: 'A series of impressionistic and oddly disturbing images', 'a welcome truculence and strength of observation', 'incisiveness of tone and image', 'perceptive freshness of observation particularly of social reflexes and hypocrisies', 'a man with his eye on the world', 'fresh, vigorous, sinewy', 'his spiritual exploration of life's meanings for our war-torn, revolution-rife, hate-filled generation, is strangely sombre and moving...' These are all quotations from brother critics to be found in the blurb of the new volume. I quote them not in derision but in agreement. To say things like this about Rodney Hall's poetry is, as we add up the comments, to say that he has a poet's natural gift, an interested eye, a fresh inventive imagination, a feeling-love of words, a serious but not solemn mind. What I want to say about his poetry is something else which seems to be characteristic of our time, and has to do not only with the poet and his craft, but with his audience.

A very recent poem by Hall, printed in *The Australian* of 23 December last year, is a useful starting point:

Mrs Macintosh

Mrs Macintosh reduced
the world's dilemma to a single
fixed obsession — birdcage buying.
So now the cages fill her rooms:
Some are miniature pagodas,
and one a jail of cells.
The smallest, made from a lost
girl's hand, is bones enmeshed
in silver wire. The largest
looks an anarchy of cleverness

the total snub of cage-convention,
a cloud so frail and knobbled
it dangles crazily askew, high
against the inconvenience of a wall.

These, her eccentricities,
are cherished, catalogued,
paraded for the delectation
of any visiting evangelist,
salesman, or charity collector.
Her cages, Mrs Macintosh
is careful to point out, are empty.
Birds revolt her — frighten
her wrinkled eye with theirs
and mock her ways with harsh high
female voices; or sing so sweetly
they could almost lure her back
to join the world. Unbearable.
No, she likes her symbolism:
cages free of birds, pure captivity
that's innocent of pain.

She's quite the favourite topic
of the neighbourhood, brisk
around her massive house,
singing while she polishes the windows.
She flutters in and out at whim
(as brilliant as a parrot), crawls
on knees and elbows, chattering to God
inside her cage of cast-iron balconies.

This is good, surely; not only the original invention of its total image, but the wit, the mixture of crazy-gay outward feeling and compassionate inner feeling. The poem mixes us up with its ambivalent insight, anything but solemn, altogether serious. It seems to me, too, to be structured right; the details of the general metaphoric image fall into place naturally with a deliberate lack of eloquent rhythm which suits the crazy house of life Mrs Macintosh lives in; and the rather brittle diction and sound reinforce this. I have one point of critical trouble to make. Let me put it as a question: is it the audience for poetry in Australia that made Rodney Hall introduce his metaphoric invention with three lines of explanatory prose? And made him come out of his invention (at the end of the second section) to explain to us that Mrs Macintosh *likes* her *symbolism*?

I chose a poem printed in a newspaper because the problem of contemporary poetry everywhere is bound up with the disintegration of an informed and substantial body of readers. A poet's language is not his own; he cannot wave it around like a walking stick; he is writing with the common language of his fellows, and therefore their 'mind' enters into his poem from the start. But a poet's fellows today are in chaos, and their 'mind' is, in fact, a spectrum of minds, ranging (so far as poetic language is concerned) from bored and ignorant unbelievers to highly sophisticated experts in all possible ranges and kinds of imaginative speech. Douglas Stewart's implicit audience is a layer of unsophisticated minds, rather childlike (why not?) with a liking for poetry as one likes hymns sung in childhood. Dorothy Auchterlonie's implicit audience is a layer of highly trained experts, in a sense outsiders or fringe-dwellers.* As I have made clear, this does not mean that either is inept as a poet. It means that their poetry has to get on without that kind of vitality which a poet, open to the living speech of our time, its idiom and rhythm, gets from it in the working house of his own mind — even if that living speech is ridiculously muddled, fortuitous, even absurd. Rodney Hall seems to me to open the door to this living speech, in a way neither of the other two do; but the result is that it often reflects the fortuitous uncertainties of the speech that enters his inward door of imagination. Almost any poem in the new volume will show what I mean. Take 'I'm a Killer, I Am'.:

Catapults in hand and pocket,
children scramble past me, pinning
my ears with their excited screams
*We hit him. Did you see that shot —
the aim, and Piinnggg! I'm a killer, I am.*
At the stoning-point of jubilance
a lorikeet rolls its nape in the gutter,
one foot pinching the leap of air
(two toes forward, two toes back)
green as feathered sap of woodland,
nimble as life with sky in its bones.
But the dainty stove-in breast is heavy.
And its eye, that one surviving weapon,
holds-off crouching spellbound huntsmen.

Somewhere, huge within me,
dark wings unfold.

* The reference is to Dorothy Auchterlonie's second book of verse, *The Dolphin* (1967).

The sixth line in this poem, 'At the stoning-point of jubilance' — what let this dollop of academic complexity through into the middle of a visually structured poem which in idiom is anyone's language, even if haunted by a genuine poet's flair for words (even 'nimble as life with sky in its bones' is accidentally possible in a pop-song). And the last two lines — where did this portentous remnant of romantic innuendo come from? From — I suggest — the reservoir in the common mind today of poesy-tastes and flavours. I would bet that if you got hold of the right layer in the strata of possible readers, you would find dozens who thought them the most poetic and the best lines in the poem. I would want to say they are the worst. And don't tell me that poets are not aware of this tug-of-war in the place where words begin to form into poems. I am not belittling Rodney Hall; I enjoy his poetry perhaps more than that of any of the younger poets writing; and part of my enjoyment — even if it is perverse — is to watch a poet with real talent struggling with the confusing invitations he receives from our age to write for you — or you — or you — or me — never for 'us'; for 'we' the audience is a mob not a society; and perhaps so far as poetry is concerned, the Australian 'we' is more a mob than almost anywhere else.

Alec King, 'The Look of Australian Poetry in 1967', *Meanjin Quarterly*, vol. 27, no. 2, 1968, pp. 174-6

In this process the accepted masters are not Eliot or Pound or Yeats. Many young writers would find a dictum such as 'Poetry must be at least as well written as prose' an intolerable constraint. Australian poetry has, indeed, never assimilated much of the modernist tradition in verse represented by Eliot and Pound. The best poets have for the most part worked in other (generally earlier) traditions; the mediocre have, over the past couple of decades, progressed from neo-Georgianism to the slackness of contemporary free-field verse, bypassing the exacting apprenticeship required by the craft of Eliot or Pound. The accepted masters are now William Carlos Williams ('no ideas but in things') and Charles Olson ('one perception must immediately and directly lead to a further perception'). There is a touching belief now among young Australian poets in the inherent poetic quality of things or objects, as if the reality of the materials used guaranteed the reality of the result produced.

In constructing poems from 'objective' elements, these young poets usually prefer to set down their feelings towards the objects they describe rather than any feelings arising from contemplation of the objects. Intelligent ratiocination seems suspect. Poets are content to express commonly held attitudes that are subject to becoming quickly dated and 'irrelevant'. There is much verse seemingly designed only for here and, as Shapcott would have it, 'now'. It tends to dwell on data drawn from suburbia, fast cars, hitch-hiking, land development, skyscrapers, and Vietnam.

K. L. Goodwin, review of *Australian Poetry Now*
(ed. Thomas W. Shapcott, 1970), *Meanjin Quarterly*,
vol. 30, no. 3, 1971, p. 363

GWEN HARWOOD

In the Park

She sits in the park. Her clothes are out of date.
Two children whine and bicker, tug her skirt.
A third draws aimless patterns in the dirt.
Someone she loved once passes by — too late

to feign indifference to that casual nod.
'How nice,' etcetera. 'Time holds great surprises.'
From his neat head unquestionably rises
a small balloon ... 'but for the grace of God ...'

They stand awhile in flickering light, rehearsing
the children's names and birthdays. 'It's so sweet
to hear their chatter, watch them grow and thrive,'
she says to his departing smile. Then, nursing
the youngest child, sits staring at her feet.
To the wind she says, 'They have eaten me alive.'

Barn Owl

Daybreak: the household slept.
I rose before the sun.
A horny fiend, I crept
out with my father's gun.
Let him dream of a child
obedient, angel-mild —

old No-sayer, robbed of power
by sleep. I knew my prize
who swooped home at this hour
with daylight-riddled eyes
to his place on a high beam
in our old stables, to dream

light's useless time away.
I stood, holding my breath,
in urine-scented hay,
master of life and death,
a wisp-haired judge whose law
would punish beak and claw.

My first shot struck. He swayed,
ruined, beating his only
wing as I watched, afraid
by the fallen gun, a lonely
child who believed death clean
and final, not the obscene

bundle of stuff that dropped,
and dribbled through loose straw
tangling its bowels, and hopped
blindly closer. I saw
those eyes that did not see
mirror my cruelty

while the wrecked thing that could
not bear the light nor hide
hobbled in its own blood.
My father reached my side,
gave me the fallen gun.
'End what you have begun.'

I fired. The blank eyes shone
once into mine, and slept.
I leaned my head upon
my father's arm, and wept
owl-blind in morning sun
for what I had begun.

David's Harp

Saturday morning. I rehearse
the Sunday hymns, fortissimo,
in the cool twilight of the church,
adding new stops at every verse.
Someone creaks the west door. I know
I am the object of his search,
gazed at, as though from far away;
he must be thirty if a day.

I turn my seventeen-year-old
profile a trifle heavenwards,
and hastily reduce the sound,
accommodating to his bold
descant on *David's Harp*. The Lord's
house might as well be Circe's ground.
  'With thee all night I mean to stay
  and wrestle till the break of day.'

—'With thee all night.' So Wesley wrote,
though not with secular intent.
What flourishes that tune will bear!
My tenor wreathes it note by note
in rich Handelian ornament.
Faint burnt-out incense on the air
offends his Presbyterian nose.
He sneezes, stares across the rows

of empty pews between us; still
singing, walks to the organ; stands
beside me; puts his arms around
my waist and squeezes me until
I gasp, then gently lifts my hands
in his, and kisses me. He's sound
of wind. His kiss is long. We share
at last a common need for air.

'Give me one kiss, my bonnie lass!'
Vain as a cat, I frown and toss
my head. He watches Brisbane's hot
sunshine, strained through Victorian glass,
lacquer a Station of the Cross.

He scowls and thunders: 'Thou shalt not
make any graven images.'
But as he bends his head to kiss

the image of his hope, the door
moves with its useful warning creak.
He steps aside. I start to play.
He fills his lungs, and sings once more:
    'Speak to me now, in mercy speak.'
A death-pale curate come to pray
kneels and is forced to find his Lord
through a loud F sharp major chord.

Where's that bright man who loved me when
there was not much to love? He died
soon after. The undying flow
of music bears him close again,
handsome and young, while I am tried
in time's harsh fires. Dear man, I know
your worth, being now less ignorant of
the nature and the names of love.

GEOFFREY LEHMANN

Saving the Harvest

The darkened farmhouse is asleep
And we the sleepers burrow deep
With warm breath into the body's night,
Dumb in our soft quilts with no dreams,
Safe in the smell of timber beams,
Of cattle dung and milk and hay.

Stars burn cold fields with arctic light,
And hour by hour the mercury falls;
Night is a slowly tightening vice
Gripping the apple-trees with frost,
Menacing fragile blossoms with ice
So a whole harvest may be lost.
Numb in the night no animal calls
And tussocks shrivel in cold clay,
The blossoms will begin to die
Stiffened stars in the frozen night.

Wakened from far countries of sleep,
Groaning at three o'clock we creep
From bed, pull on our boots and light
Our hurricane lamps and tramp outside
Into the glacier of the air.
Through orchards of ice our ghost-breaths glide.
The cold has set off our warning bell,
Rattling beneath the frozen sky
So windows light up in the dark,
Dogs shake their chains and start to bark,
Rattling of death in sleepy ears,
The death of half a million flowers,
Blotched sour and withering in the freeze,
A year's work gone in a few hours.

Quickly we each light up a flare,
Run down the lines of apple-trees
And light the burners with a roar.
A hundred burners blast and pour
Heat at the sky, boiling with oil,
And apple-trees dance in their glare.
Ice cracks and thaws deep in the soil.

Slouching back to our rumpled beds
Gone cold, we scratch at listless dreams
And in our singed and frozen heads,
Tingling with hot and cold extremes,
See snow petals flicker with wild light,
And oil burners roaring in the night.

For J.A.R. McKellar

Gods, men in straw hats, girls in calico
Wave from the buntinged ferry of your rhyme,
And the festoons of forty years ago
Fade, dwindling down the hurrying tide of time.

The hours, the sea, Rome and a scattered rose,
And Newton in a cosmos that made sense,
A cricket field . . . all through your verse there blows
A gracious, clean, colonial innocence.

What pleasure to browse through your sweet, rare yield,
And quicken at the name of Jove or Mars,
And hear balls crack across a fading field
As flannelled ghosts bowl under the first stars.

LES A. MURRAY

The Princes' Land
for Valerie, on her birthday

Leaves from the ancient forest gleam
In the meadow brook, and dip, and pass.
Six maidens dance on the level green,
A seventh toys with an hourglass,

Letting fine hours sink away,
Turning to sift them back again.
An idle prince, with a cembalo,
Sings to the golden afternoon.

Two silver knights, met in a wood,
Tilt at each other, clash and bow.
Upon a field semé of birds
Tom Bread-and-Cheese sleeps by his plough.

But now a deadly stillness comes
Upon the brook, upon the green,
Upon the seven dancing maids,
The dented knights are dulled to stone.

The hours in the hourglass
Are stilled to fine fear, and the wood
To empty burning. Tom the hind
Walks in his sleep in pools of blood . . .

The page we've reached is grey with pain.
Some will not hear, some run away,
Some go to write books of their own,
Some few, as the tale grows cruel, are gay.

But we who have no other book
Spell out the gloomy, blazing text,
Page by slow page, wild year by year,
Our hope refined to what comes next,

And yet attentive to each child
Who says he's looked ahead and seen
How the tale will go, or spied
A silver page two pages on,

For, as the themes knit and unfold,
Somewhere far on, where all is changed,
Beyond all twists of grief and fear,
We look to glimpse that land again:

The brook descends in music through
The meadows of that figured land,
Nine maidens from the ageless wood
Move in their circles, hand in hand.

Two noble figures, counterchanged,
Fence with swift passion, pause and bow.
All in a field impaled with sun
The Prince of Cheese snores by his plough.

Watching bright hours file away,
Turning to sift them back again,
The Prince of Bread, with a cembalo
Hums to the golden afternoon.

Blood

Pig-crowds in successive, screaming pens
We still to greedy drinking, trough by trough,
Tusk-heavy boars, fat mud-beslabbered sows:
Gahn, let him drink, you slut, you've had enough!

Laughing and grave by turns, in milky boots,
We stand and yarn, and whet our butcher's knife,
Sling cobs of corn — hey, careful of his nuts!
It's made you cruel, all that smart city life.

In paper spills, we roll coarse, sweet tobacco.
That's him down there, the one we'll have to catch,
That little Berkshire with the pointy ears.
I call him Georgie. Here, you got a match?

The shadow of a cloud moves down the ridge,
On summer hills, a patch of autumn light.
My cousin sheaths in dirt his priestly knife.
They say pigs see the wind. You think that's right?

I couldn't say. It sounds like a good motto.
There are some poets — Yah! get back, you sods.
Let him drink his fill: it's his last feed.
He'll get some peaches after. Hell, what odds?

I'm sentimental — not like these damn flies.
Beyond the circle of my jabbing stick
Excited, mobbing pigs roll puzzled eyes,
Peer at our favourite munching, and the thick

Peach-drool adrip from his froth-whiskered snout.
Grunting, reek of sties. He's finished now.
Melon-sized and muscular, with shrieks
The pig is seized and bundled anyhow

His twisting strength permits, then sternly held.
My cousin tests his knife, sights for the heart
and sinks the blade with one long, even push.
A wild scream bursts as knife and victim part

And hits the showering heavens as our beast
Flees straight downfield, choked in his pumping gush
That feeds the earth, and drags him to his knees —
Bleed, Georgie, pump! And with a long-legged rush

My cousin is beside the thing he killed
And pommels it, and lifts it to the sun:
I should have knocked him out, poor little bloke.
It gets the blood out if you let them run.

We hold the dangling meat. Wet on its chest
The narrow cut, the tulip of slow blood.
We better go. We've got to scald him next.
Looking at me, my cousin shakes his head:

What's up, old son? You butchered things before . . .
It's made you squeamish, all that city life.
Sly gentleness regards me, and I smile:
You're wrong, you know. I'll go and fetch the knife.

I walk back up the trail of crowding flies,
Back to the knife which pours deep blood, and frees
Sun, fence and hill, each to its holy place.
Strong in my valleys, I may walk at ease.

A world I thought sky-lost by leaning ships
In the depth of our life — I'm in that world once more.
Looking down, we praise for its firm flesh
The creature killed according to the Law.

BRUCE DAWE

Drifters

One day soon he'll tell her it's time to start packing,
and the kids will yell 'Truly?' and get wildly excited for no
   reason,
and the brown kelpie pup will start dashing about, tripping
   everyone up,
and she'll go out to the vegetable-patch and pick all the green
   tomatoes from the vines,
and notice how the oldest girl is close to tears because she was
   happy here,
and how the youngest girl is beaming because she wasn't.
And the first thing she'll put on the trailer will be the bottling-
   set she never unpacked from Grovedale,
and when the loaded ute bumps down the drive past the
   blackberry-canes with their last shrivelled fruit,
she won't even ask why they're leaving this time, or where they're
   heading for
—she'll only remember how, when they came here,
she held out her hands bright with berries,
the first of the season, and said:
'Make a wish, Tom, make a wish.'

Life-Cycle

for Big Jim Phelan

When children are born in Victoria
they are wrapped in the club-colours, laid in beribboned cots,
having already begun a lifetime's barracking.

Carn, they cry, Carn . . . feebly at first
while parents playfully tussle with them
for possession of a rusk: Ah, he's a little Tiger! (And they are . . .)

Hoisted shoulder-high at their first League game
they are like innocent monsters who have been years swimming
towards the daylight's roaring empyrean

Until, now, hearts shrapnelled with rapture,
they break surface and are forever lost,
their minds rippling out like streamers

In the pure flood of sound, they are scarfed with light, a voice
like the voice of God booms from the stands
Ooohh you bludger and the covenant is sealed.

Hot pies and potato-crisps they will eat,
they will forswear the Demons, cling to the Saints
and behold their team going up the ladder into Heaven,

And the tides of life will be the tides of the home-team's fortunes
—the reckless proposal after the one-point win,
the wedding and honeymoon after the grand final . . .

They will not grow old as those from more northern States grow
        old,
for them it will always be three-quarter-time
with the scores level and the wind advantage in the final term,

That passion persisting, like a race-memory, through the welter
        of seasons,
enabling old-timers by boundary-fences to dream of resurgent
        lions
and centaur-figures from the past to replenish continually the
        present,

So that mythology may be perpetually renewed
and Chicken Smallhorn return like the maize-god
in a thousand shapes, the dancers changing

But the dance forever the same—the elderly still
loyally crying Carn'. . . Carn . . . (if feebly) unto the very end,
having seen in the six-foot recruit from Eaglehawk their hope
        of salvation.

VIVIAN SMITH

At an Exhibition of Historical Paintings, Hobart

The sadness in the human visage stares
out of these frames, out of these distant eyes;
the static bodies painted without love
that only lack of talent could disguise.

W

Those bland receding hills are too remote
where the quaint natives squat with awkward calm.
One carries a kangaroo like a worn toy,
his axe alert with emphasized alarm.

Those nearer woollen hills are now all streets;
even the water in the harbour's changed.
Much is alike and yet a slight precise
disparity seems intended and arranged—

as in that late pink terrace's façade.
How neat the houses look. How clean each brick.
One cannot say they look much older now,
but somehow more themselves, less accurate.

And see the pride in this expansive view:
churches, houses, farms, a prison tower;
a grand gesture like wide-open arms
showing the artist's trust, his clumsy power.

And this much later vision, grander still:
the main street sedate carriages unroll
towards the inappropriate, tentative mountain:
a flow of lines the artist can't control—

the foreground nearly breaks out of its frame
the streets end so abruptly in the water . . .
But how some themes return. A whaling ship.
The last natives. Here that silent slaughter

is really not prefigured or avoided.
One merely sees a profile, a full face,
a body sitting stiffly in a chair:
the soon-forgotten absence of a race . . .

Album pieces: bowls of brown glazed fruit . . .
I'm drawn back yet again to those few studies
of native women whose long floral dresses
made them first aware of their own bodies.

History has made artists of all these
painters who lack energy and feature.
But how some gazes cling. Around the hall
the pathos of the past, the human creature.

An Effect of Light

Swans in their grey and silver park
hiss from the reeds their indignation
where looking back to what was wake
the pool suggests a moment's agitation . . .

After work in solitary rooms
I've sought this hour in the tranquil park
where things assume their proper shapes again,
as trees and steeples for the waiting dark.

Work I say. It's self-work that I mean.
Days and hours full of disarray
when life is a discarded scratched-out note
one cannot read . . . And how can words convey

this sense without an image for the mind?
Life's promised tapestry grows more undone;
or does one merely see the underside,
where to observers burns a modest sun?

I would ask this as clearly if I could
as that white dove that's tumbling in the sky:
how can a sense of meaning still persist
so interwined with sense of no reply?

I turn towards the sight of paddling swans.
What is confusion but no attitude;
or is tranquillity a touch of light
that merely lingers till the mind's subdued?

I watch the fussing wings across the pool
and wonder what it means, regeneration;
and see within the circles ruffling out,
the water-lily's simple revelation.

BRUCE BEAVER

from *Letters to Live Poets*
Letter XII

Three anti-depressants and one diuretic a day
seven and five times a week respectively
save me from the pit.
I pray while I'm taking them and in between doses
because, as Dylan Thomas says, *I have seen the gates of hell.*
Once I drew back in distaste from the metho drinker
and his bleary lady friend — you've seen them
weaving a way through non-existent traffic.
He, swollen faced, with a backside kicked in
by what the tougher call life. She,
the terrible veteran doll of Pantagruel's nursery.
Let them pass into the peaceful holocaust.
In Rushcutter's park they congregated over bottles.
Walking, we avoided them as mined ground,
fearful of their implosions bloodying the day.
Later I fell so far into self-sickness
I envied them. My thoughts
haunted their submerged wreckage like a squid.
At their groaning subsidence I retreated
into a pall of ink.
                    Whatever I tell you,
you have heard before.
                    I remembered Swift's
fascination with the insane. I whistled
Childe Roland to the Dark Tower Came
outside the grimy walls of Callan Park.
Inside — *il miglior fabbro* — the best of us all
chewing bloody knuckles, wet dry,
daft as a headless chicken circling in the dust.
Where are prayers said for him and the parkside horrors?
Some prayed for us, I know. I'm still here
partially, trying to live detachedly.
Is it only the exceptional ones, the broken battlers,
shred me into uselessness? Does it mean
I'd pick and choose in hell? Discriminative?
Like a dog in rut — no,
self-abasement's out. So is complacency.
I'm never likely to forget
the day I walked on hands and knees
like Blake's Nebuchadnezzar, scenting the pit.

So it's one day at a time spent checking
the menagerie of self; seeing
the two-headed man has half as much
of twice of everything; curbing the tiger;
sunning the snake; taking stock of
Monkey, Piggsy, Sandy's belt of skulls.

SELECT BIBLIOGRAPHY

GWEN HARWOOD

Poems, Angus & Robertson, Sydney, 1963.
Poems, Volume Two, Angus & Robertson, Sydney, 1968.

Douglas, Dennis, 'Gwen Harwood — the Ghost as Doppelganger', *Quadrant*, vol. 13 (misnumbered 14), no. 2, 1969. (See a reply by A. D. Hope, 'Gwen Harwood and the Professors', *Australian Literary Studies*, vol. 5, no. 3, 1972, and Dennis Douglas's rejoinder, 'A Prodigious Dilemma: Gwen Harwood's Professor Eisenbart and the Vices of the Intellect', *Australian Literary Studies*, vol. 6, no. 1, 1973.

VIVIAN SMITH

The Other Meaning, Lyre Bird Writers, Sydney, 1956.
An Island South, Angus & Robertson, Sydney, 1967.

Campbell, David, review of *The Other Meaning*, in *Southerly*, vol. 17, no. 4, 1956, followed in the same issue by a review by Ray Mathew.
King, Alec, 'The Look of Australian Poetry in 1967', *Meanjin Quarterly*, vol. 27, no. 2, 1968.
Tulip, James, review of *An Island South*, in *Southerly*, vol. 28, no. 1, 1968.

BRUCE DAWE

No Fixed Address, Cheshire, Melbourne, 1962.
A Need of Similar Name, Cheshire, Melbourne, 1965.
An Eye for a Tooth, Cheshire, Melbourne, 1968.
Beyond the Subdivisions, Cheshire, Melbourne, 1969.
Condolences of the Season, Cheshire, Melbourne, 1971 (selection with new poems).
Bruce Dawe Reads from his own Work, Poets on Record series, University of Queensland Press, Brisbane, 1971.

'Recent Trends in Australian Poetry', *Twentieth Century*, vol. 19, no. 1, 1964 (text of a C.L.F. lecture given at the Adelaide Arts Festival).

Curtis, Graeme, 'Some Aspects of Bruce Dawe's Poetry', *Makar*, vol. 6, no. 4, 1970.
Lehmann, Geoffrey, review of *Beyond the Subdivisions*, in the *Bulletin*, 30 May 1970.

McAuley, James, review of *An Eye for a Tooth,* in *Twentieth Century,* vol. 23, no. 1, 1968.

Martin, Philip, 'Public yet Personal: Bruce Dawe's Poetry', *Meanjin Quarterly,* vol. 25, no. 3, 1966.

Wright, John M., 'Bruce Dawe's Poetry', *Westerly,* no. 1, 1974.

LES A. MURRAY

The Ilex Tree (with Geoffrey Lehmann), Australian National University Press, Canberra, 1965.

The Weatherboard Cathedral, Angus & Robertson, Sydney, 1969.

Poems against Economics, Angus & Robertson, Sydney, 1972.

Lunch and Counter Lunch, Angus & Robertson, Sydney, 1974.

Lehmann, Geoffrey, review of *The Weatherboard Cathedral,* in the *Bulletin,* 7 February 1970.

Tulip, James, review of *The Weatherboard Cathedral,* in *Southerly,* vol. 30, no. 2, 1970.

GEOFFREY LEHMANN

The Ilex Tree (with Les A. Murray), Australian National University Press, Canberra, 1965.

A Voyage of Lions, Angus & Robertson, Sydney, 1968.

Conversation with a Rider, Angus & Robertson, Sydney, 1972.

BRUCE BEAVER

Under the Bridge, Beaujon Press, Sydney, 1961.

Seawall and Shoreline, South Head Press, Sydney, 1964.

Open at Random, South Head Press, Sydney, 1967.

Letters to Live Poets, South Head Press, Sydney, 1969.

Lauds and Plaints, South Head Press, Sydney, 1974.

Fitzgerald, Robert D., 'Bruce Beaver's Poetry', *Meanjin Quarterly,* vol. 28, no. 3, 1969.

Lehmann, Geoffrey, review of *Letters to Live Poets,* in the *Bulletin,* 30 May 1970.

Powell, Craig, 'Gift-Bearing Hands: the Poetry of Bruce Beaver', *Quadrant,* vol. 12, no. 5, 1968.

Tulip, James, review of *Letters to Live Poets,* in *Southerly,* vol. 30, no. 2, 1970.

RECENT TRENDS

Blight, John, 'An Elder Practising Poet's Point of View — Some Australian Contemporary Poetry', *Southerly,* vol. 34, no. 2, 1974.

Craig, Alexander, ed., *Twelve Poets,* 1971.

FitzGerald, Robert D., 'Verse and Worse', *Southerly,* vol. 33, no. 2, 1973.

Goodwin, K. L., 'Recent Australian Poetry', *World Literature Written in English,* vol. 2, no. 2, 1972.

———— 'Poetry Chronicle 1971', *Meanjin Quarterly,* vol. 31, no. 4, 1972.

Hall, Rodney and Shapcott, Thomas, *New Impulses in Australian Poetry,* University of Queensland Press, Brisbane, 1968.

Hemensley, Kris, 'First Look at "The New Australian Poetry" ', *Meanjin Quarterly*, vol. 29, no. 1, 1970 (commented on in the same issue by Max Richards, 'A Poetry which Matters: Notes from Above Ground', and by Carl Harrison-Ford in the next issue, 'Poetics before Politics: a Note on Kris Hemensley's "New Australian Poetry" ').

Macainsh, Noel, 'Australian Poetry — the Tradition of the New', *Quadrant*, vol. 19, no. 2, 1975.

Packer, Richard, 'Against the Epigones', *Quadrant*, vol. 19, no. 3, 1975.

Taylor, Andrew, 'Irrationality Individuality Drug Poetry Romanticism — Where we are Today', *Meanjin Quarterly*, vol. 31, no. 4, 1972.

Tulip, James, 'Contemporary Australian Poetry: I The Context', *Southerly*, vol. 31, no. 2, 1972, 'II Transition and Advance', *Southerly*, vol. 31, no. 3, 1972.

NOTES

[1] Gwen Harwood's first published poem, 'Rite of Spring', appeared in *Meanjin*, vol. 3, no. 3, 1944 under her maiden name, Gwendoline Foster. The poet does not deny that there may be other poems under yet other names to be found by the diligent searcher. A more recent use by Gwen Harwood of a pseudonym is in *Australian Poetry Now* (ed. Thomas W. Shapcott, 1970), where poems by 'Timothy Kline' appear.

[2] Published in the *Australian*, 9 May 1973, and in a revised version in *Outposts*, no. 100, Spring 1974.

[3] Afterword to the selection in *Twelve Poets* (ed. Alexander Craig, 1971) p. 219.

[4] *ibid.*

[5] *Southerly*, vol. 32, no. 2, 1972, p. 89.

[6] 'For the past five years she has been racing around in Sydney's poetry circles as though the second coming was at hand. Her energy is prodigious. At a time when Australian poetry is booming, and indeed seems on the point of exploding, she is leading the field not merely in production herself but in producing other poets as well . . . when the time comes for a history of poetry in the 1960's to be written, her place in the changing climate of opinion and taste will be a key one.' (James Tulip, reviewing *Frozen Section*, 1967, in *Southerly*, vol. 28, no. 1, 1968, p. 69).

[7] See for example the influential Penguin anthology *Children of Albion: Poetry of the Underground in Britain*, ed. Michael Horovitz, 1969.

[8] 'Poetry, Open and Closed', *Quadrant*, vol. 11, no. 3, 1967.

[9] *Meanjin Quarterly*, vol. 31, no. 4, 1972.

[10] See, however, some pertinent remarks in Vincent Buckley's 'Poetry in a Pop Culture World', *Quadrant*, vol. 15, no. 4, 1971.

[11] Died in 1973 at the age of 24.

[12] First published in *Poetry Australia*, no. 42, 1972.

[13] 'Notes on Some Recent Australian Poetry', *New Poetry*, vol. 22, no. 1, 1974.

[14] 'Recent Australian Poetry', *World Literature Written in English*, vol. 2, no. 2, 1972. See also James Tulip, 'Contemporary Australian Poetry — II', *Southerly*, vol. 32, no. 3, 1972. Max Harris, who has been there before, has a characteristic general comment: 'This necessary young movement is not

without talent. Young poets are emerging at a moment when we are all coming to realize that the established names in Australian Poetry have become boring, insistent, repetitive and irrelevant. . . For all these positives, there remains the hard-core fact that young poets are rushing like Gadarene swine towards their great, muddy, emotional wallow. And there is no critical apparatus, no ideology, no set of views about the properties of words, to keep the mass of meandering, formless, post-pubescent meditations out of print. What's worse, we all have to pretend that it's beaut or that it has its place. Otherwise, we are Philistine hangovers from the birdies-and-beasties era of formal, modern Australian verse' (*The Angry Eye*, 1973, p. 236).

15 Died in 1973.

Acknowledgements

We are grateful to the following poets, critics and publishers for permission to include copyright material:

L. H. ALLEN   Miss Joan Allen and Angus & Robertson
BRUCE BEAVER   Bruce Beaver and South Head Press
C. J. BRENNAN   Angus & Robertson
VINCENT BUCKLEY   Vincent Buckley
J. F. BURROWS   J. F. Burrows
DAVID CAMPBELL   Angus & Robertson
A. R. CHISHOLM   A. R. Chisholm
BRUCE DAWE   Longman Cheshire Pty Ltd
ROSEMARY DOBSON   Angus & Robertson
R. D. FITZGERALD   Angus & Robertson
MARY GILMORE   Angus & Robertson
H. M. GREEN   Mrs Dorothy Green
GWEN HARWOOD   Gwen Harwood and Angus & Robertson
BERTRAM HIGGINS   Mrs B. Higgins
CHARLES HIGHAM   Angus & Robertson and *Quadrant*
A. D. HOPE   Angus & Robertson and Curtis Brown (Aust.) Pty Ltd
EVAN JONES   Melbourne University Press
NANCY KEESING   Angus & Robertson
LEONIE KRAMER   Leonie Kramer
GEOFFREY LEHMANN   Angus & Robertson
JAMES MCAULEY   Curtis Brown (Aust.) Pty Ltd
DOROTHEA MACKELLAR   Curtis Brown (Aust.) Pty Ltd
J. A. R. MCKELLAR   Angus & Robertson
KENNETH MACKENZIE   Angus & Robertson
HUGH MCCRAE   Angus & Robertson
RONALD MCCUAIG   Angus & Robertson
NAN MACDONALD   Angus & Robertson
J. S. MANIFOLD   J. S. Manifold
F. H. MARES   F. H. Mares
A. C. W. MITCHELL   A. C. W. Mitchell
ERNEST G. MOLL   Ernest G. Moll
LES MURRAY   Angus & Robertson
JOHN SHAW NEILSON   Angus & Robertson
ROLAND ROBINSON   Roland Robinson and Edwards & Shaw
J. R. ROWLAND   J. R. Rowland
KENNETH SLESSOR   Angus & Robertson

VIVIAN SMITH   Vivian Smith, Angus & Robertson, and the *Bulletin*
DOUGLAS STEWART   Angus & Robertson
HAROLD STEWART   Harold Stewart
JOHN THOMPSON   Australian Broadcasting Commission and *Southerly*
CHRIS WALLACE-CRABBE   Angus & Robertson
FRANCIS WEBB   Angus & Robertson
G. A. WILKES   G. A. Wilkes
JUDITH WRIGHT   Angus & Robertson and *Meanjin*

COVER   The outline map reproduced on the cover has been made available by courtesy of the Director, Division of National Mapping, Department of Minerals and Energy, Canberra.

Index

337